WileyPLUS

W9-BSW-667

WileyPLUS is a research-based, online environment for effective teaching and learning.

The market-leading homework experience in *WileyPLUS* offers:

A Blank Sheet of Paper Effect

The *WileyPLUS* homework experience, which includes type-ahead for account title entry, imitates a blank sheet of paper format so that students use recall memory when doing homework and will do better in class, on exams, and in their professions.

A Professional Worksheet Style

The professional, worksheet-style problem layouts help students master accounting skills while doing homework that directly applies to the classroom and the real world.

The Opportunity to Catch Mistakes Earlier

Multi-part problems further help students focus by providing feedback at the part-level. Students can catch their mistakes earlier and access content-specific resources at the point of learning.

WileyPLUS includes a **full ebook, interactive tutorials, assessment capabilities, and Blackboard integration.**

STARR COMPANY Trial Balance June 30, 2014		
	Debit	**Credit**
cal	$	

Cash
Owner's Capital

Type-ahead feature for account title entry replaces drop-down menus.

www.wileyplus.com

WileyPLUS

ALL THE HELP, **RESOURCES,** AND PERSONAL SUPPORT YOU AND YOUR STUDENTS NEED!

www.wileyplus.com/resources

1st DAY OF CLASS ...AND BEYOND!

2-Minute Tutorials and all of the resources you and your students need to get started

WileyPLUS
Student Partner Program

Student support from an experienced student user

Wiley Faculty Network

Collaborate with your colleagues, find a mentor, attend virtual and live events, and view resources
www.WhereFacultyConnect.com

WileyPLUS
Quick Start

Pre-loaded, ready-to-use assignments and presentations created by subject matter experts

Technical Support 24/7 FAQs, online chat, and phone support
www.wileyplus.com/support

Your *WileyPLUS* Account Manager, providing personal training and support

ACCOUNTING PRINCIPLES

SIXTH CANADIAN EDITION

→ Jerry J. Weygandt *Ph.D., CPA*
University of Wisconsin—Madison

→ Donald E. Kieso *Ph.D., CPA*
Northern Illinois University

→ Paul D. Kimmel *Ph.D., CPA*
University of Wisconsin—Milwaukee

→ Barbara Trenholm *MBA, FCA*
University of New Brunswick—Fredericton

→ Valerie A. Kinnear *M.Sc. (Bus. Admin.), CA*
Mount Royal University

→ Joan E. Barlow *B.Comm., CA*
Mount Royal University

WILEY

To our students—past, present, and future

Copyright © 2013 John Wiley & Sons Canada, Ltd.

Copyright © 2012 John Wiley & Sons Inc.

All rights reserved. No part of this work covered by the copyrights herein may be reproduced or used in any form or by any means—graphic, electronic, or mechanical—without the prior written permission of the publisher.

Any request for photocopying, recording, taping, or inclusion in information storage and retrieval systems of any part of this book shall be directed in writing to The Canadian Copyright Licensing Agency (Access Copyright). For an Access Copyright Licence, visit www.accesscopyright.ca or call toll-free, 1-800-893-5777.

Care has been taken to trace ownership of copyright material contained in this text. The publishers will gladly receive any information that will enable them to rectify any erroneous reference or credit line in subsequent editions.

Library and Archives Canada Cataloguing in Publication
Accounting principles / Jerry Weygandt ... [et al.]. — 6th Canadian ed.

Includes indexes.
Issued also in a 2 vol. set.
ISBN 978-1-118-30678-9 (pt. 1).—ISBN 978-1-118-30679-6 (pt. 2).--
ISBN 978-1-118-30680-2 (pt. 3)

1. Accounting--Textbooks.   I. Weygandt, Jerry J

HF5636.A33 2012   657ʹ.044   C2012-906476-9

Production Credits

Acquisitions Editor: Zoë Craig
Vice President and Publisher: Veronica Visentin
Vice President, Market Development: Carolyn Wells
Marketing Manager: Anita Osborne
Editorial Manager: Karen Staudinger
Production Manager: Tegan Wallace
Developmental Editor: Daleara Jamasji Hirjikaka
Media Editor: Channade Fenandoe
Editorial Assistant: Luisa Begani
Design: Interrobang Graphic Design, Inc.
Typesetting: Aptara
Cover Design: Sean Goodchild
Cover Photo: © ooyoo/Vetta/Getty
Printing and Binding: Friesens Corporation

Printed and bound in Canada
1 2 3 4 5 FP 17 16 15 14 13

John Wiley & Sons Canada, Ltd.
6045 Freemont Blvd.
Mississauga, Ontario L5R 4J3
Visit our website at: www.wiley.ca

BRIEF CONTENTS

CONTENTS – PART TWO

CHAPTER EIGHT

ACCOUNTING FOR RECEIVABLES

THE NAVIGATOR

CONCEPTS FOR REVIEW

Before studying this chapter, you should understand or, if necessary, review:

a. How to record revenue. (ch. 3, pp. 123–124 and ch. 5, pp. 244–248)

b. Why adjusting entries are made. (ch. 3, pp. 115–116)

c. How to calculate interest. (ch.3, pp. 125–126)

d. What is the difference between permanent and temporary accounts. (ch. 4, p. 174)

e. What is a subsidiary ledger. (ch. 5, pp. 240–241)

f. How to record to bank credit card transactions. (ch. 7, pp. 366–368)

TRYING TO COLLECT FROM INCOMMUNICADO CLIENTS

SAINT JOHN, N.B.—Bell Aliant is the product of the 1999 merger of four Atlantic telephone service providers: New Brunswick Telephone, Maritime Tel, Island Tel, and Newfoundland Tel. The history of these four companies goes back 100 years in providing telephone service to Atlantic Canadians. In 2006, the company expanded westward with the purchase of Bell Canada's rural telephone lines in Ontario and Quebec; at the same time, it sold Bell its wireless business. In 2009, Bell Aliant became the first company in Canada to offer fibre-to-the-home technology to an entire city. Today, Bell Aliant is one of North America's largest regional communications providers, offering voice, data, Internet, and television services to customers across six provinces. With a staff of approximately 7,000, the company earns $2.8 billion a year under the brands Bell Aliant in Atlantic Canada and Bell in Ontario and Quebec, as well as Télébec, Northern Tel, and Kenora Municipal Telephone Services.

Bell Aliant's main sources of revenue are fees for local and long-distance phone services, high-speed Internet services, and television. In most areas, the company's services are bundled with wireless services from Bell Mobility. It also receives revenue from equipment rentals and value-added technology business solutions for large enterprises.

"Our total receivables balance is typically around $370 million at any one month end," says Eleanor Marshall, Vice-President and Treasurer at Bell Aliant. On the balance sheet, under IFRS, this amount includes accounts receivable the company has sold as part of its securitization program. The proceeds from the securitized receivables are reflected as short-term borrowing.

Certain of Bell Aliant's billing terms are regulated by the Canadian Radio-television and Telecommunications Commission (CRTC). The company bills monthly for services in arrears, and payments are due within 21 days of the billing date. This results in receivables being about 31 to 35 days outstanding, Ms. Marshall explains.

"The vast majority of our consumer customers pay on or slightly before the due date," she says. "We have very few accounts outstanding beyond 30 days." In contrast, businesses take longer to pay, usually 35 to 50 days.

Even though the bills are due within 21 days of the billing date, late payment charges begin to accrue at 30 days from the billing date. "Late payment charges are intended to be punitive. Since we primarily bill monthly recurring charges, we really want customers to pay on time, so they do not get behind," Ms. Marshall explains. "As such, these charges are currently set at 3% per month."

Bell Aliant classifies customers as low risk, high risk, or unknown, and this classification will determine how large and how far in arrears the company will allow the bill to get before taking action. It may also require a deposit if a customer has no or poor credit history.

If the bill does not get paid on time, Bell Aliant will start making calls, sending reminder notices and perhaps negotiating new payment terms. If there is still no payment, the company will suspend the account for 21 days, then reconnect for one day, and contact the client again. If the bill still isn't paid, it will permanently disconnect the customer. The company then sends two notices to the client, and finally the bill goes to a collection agency.

"We establish provisions for bad debts long before it gets to this point," Ms. Marshall adds. Receivables are assigned aging categories and certain percentages, which are based on experience, apply to each to estimate the amount of bad debt. The company recognizes bad debt expense, which is typically just under 1% of revenue, each month.

THE NAVIGATOR

>> STUDY **OBJECTIVES**

After studying this chapter, you should be able to:

1. Record accounts receivable transactions.

2. Calculate the net realizable value of accounts receivable and account for bad debts.

3. Account for notes receivable.

4. Demonstrate the presentation, analysis, and management of receivables.

THE NAVIGATOR

As indicated in our feature story, management of receivables is important for any company that sells on credit, as Bell Aliant does. In this chapter, we will first review the journal entries that companies make when goods and services are sold on account and when cash is collected from those sales. Next, we will learn how companies estimate, record, and then, in some cases, collect their uncollectible accounts. We will also learn about notes receivable, the statement presentation of receivables, and management of receivables.

The chapter is organized as follows:

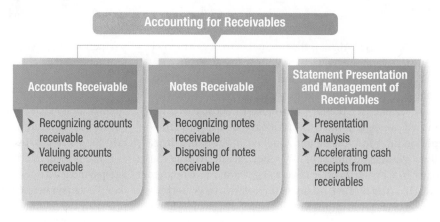

Accounts Receivable

The term "receivables" refers to amounts due to a company from individuals and other companies. They are claims that are expected to be collected in cash. The two most common types of receivables are accounts receivable and notes receivable.

Accounts receivable are amounts owed by customers on account. They result from the sale of goods and services. These receivables are generally expected to be collected within 30 days or so, and are classified as current assets. **Notes receivable** are claims for which formal instruments of credit (a written note) are issued as proof of the debt. A note normally requires the debtor to pay interest and extends for longer than the company's normal credit terms. Accounts and notes receivable that result from sale transactions are often called **trade receivables**. In this section, we will learn about accounts receivable. Notes receivable will be covered later in the chapter.

Accounts receivable are usually the most significant type of claim held by a company. Two important accounting issues—recognizing accounts receivable and valuing accounts receivable—will be discussed in this section. A third issue—accelerating cash receipts from receivables—is discussed later in the chapter.

RECOGNIZING ACCOUNTS RECEIVABLE

» **STUDY OBJECTIVE 1**

Record accounts receivable transactions.

Recognizing accounts receivable is relatively straightforward. Normally, for a service company, an asset, accounts receivable, is recorded when the service is provided on account and the revenue is recognized. The company has an asset because the company is going to receive cash from its customer in the future. For a merchandising company, a receivable is recorded at the point of sale of merchandise on account. Recall that in Chapter 5 we also saw how accounts receivable are reduced by sales returns and allowances and sales discounts. The asset is reduced because the returns and discounts will result in less cash being received from the customer.

To review, assume that Adorable Junior Garment sells merchandise on account to The Bay on July 1 for $1,000 with payment terms of 2/10, n/30. On July 4, The Bay returns merchandise worth $100 to Adorable Junior Garment. On July 10, Adorable Junior Garment receives payment from The Bay for the balance due. The journal entries to record these transactions on the books of Adorable Junior Garment are as follows:

July 1	Accounts Receivable—The Bay		1,000	
	Sales			1,000
	To record sale of merchandise on account.			
4	Sales Returns and Allowances		100	
	Accounts Receivable—The Bay			100
	To record merchandise returned.			
10	Cash [($1,000 − $100) × 98%]		882	
	Sales Discounts [($1,000 − $100) × 2%]		18	
	Accounts Receivable—The Bay ($1,000 − $100)			900
	To record collection of accounts receivable.			

A = L + OE
+1,000   +1,000
Cash flows: no effect

A = L + OE
−100   −100
Cash flows: no effect

A = L + OE
+882   −18
−900
↑Cash flows: +882

If Adorable Junior Garment uses a perpetual inventory system, a second journal entry to record the cost of the goods sold (and the cost of the goods returned) would be required for the July 1 and July 4 transactions.

Subsidiary Accounts Receivable Ledger

Adorable Junior Garment does not have only The Bay as a customer. It has hundreds of customers. If it recorded the accounts receivable for each of these customers in only one general ledger account, as we did above in Accounts Receivable, it would be hard to determine the balance owed by a specific customer, such as The Bay, at a specific point in time. It is critical that a company knows what each customer owes so that it can collect the cash owed to it by its customers.

Most companies that sell on account use a subsidiary ledger to keep track of individual customer accounts. As we learned in Chapter 5, a subsidiary ledger gives supporting detail to the general ledger. The company's Accounts Receivable account in the general ledger is the control account that provides the balance in accounts receivable reported on the balance sheet. Illustration 8-1 shows the information

▶ **ILLUSTRATION 8-1**
Accounts receivable general ledger control account and subsidiary ledger

GENERAL LEDGER

Accounts Receivable is a control account.

Accounts Receivable   No. 112

Date	Explanation	Ref.	Debit	Credit	Balance
2014					
July 4				100	(100)
31			10,000		9,900
31				5,900	4,000 ◀

ACCOUNTS RECEIVABLE SUBSIDIARY LEDGER

The subsidiary ledger is separate from the general ledger.

Kids Online   No. 112-203

Date	Explanation	Ref.	Debit	Credit	Balance
2014					
July 11	Invoice 1310		6,000		6,000
19	Payment			4,000	2,000 ◀

Snazzy Kids Co.   No. 112-413

Date	Explanation	Ref.	Debit	Credit	Balance
2014					
July 12	Invoice 1318		3,000		3,000
21	Payment			1,000	2,000 ◀

The Bay   No. 112-581

Date	Explanation	Ref.	Debit	Credit	Balance
2014					
July 1	Invoice 1215		1,000		1,000
4	Credit Memo 1222			100	900
10	Payment			900	0 ◀

included in an accounts receivable subsidiary ledger and the general ledger for a simple manual accounting system, using assumed data.

Each entry that affects accounts receivable is basically posted twice: once to the subsidiary ledger and once to the general ledger. Normally, in a manual system, entries to the subsidiary ledger are posted daily, while entries to the general ledger are summarized and posted monthly. For example, the $1,000 sale to The Bay was posted to The Bay's account in the subsidiary ledger on July 1. It was also summarized with other sales entries (Kids Online $6,000 + Snazzy Kids $3,000 + The Bay $1,000 = $10,000) in a special sales journal and posted to the accounts receivable control account in the general ledger at the end of the month, on July 31.

Collections on account (Kids Online $4,000 + Snazzy Kids $1,000 + The Bay $900 = $5,900) were also posted individually to the subsidiary ledger accounts and summarized and posted in total to the general ledger account. Non-recurring entries, such as the sales return of $100, are posted to both the subsidiary and general ledgers individually.

Note that the balance of $4,000 in the control account in the general ledger agrees with the total of the balances in the individual accounts receivable accounts in the subsidiary ledger (Kids Online $2,000 + Snazzy Kids $2,000 + The Bay $0). There is more information about how subsidiary ledgers work in Appendix C at the end of this textbook.

Today, most businesses use computerized accounting systems that automatically update the subsidiary ledger and general ledger when a journal entry is recorded. Regardless of whether the accounting system is computerized or manual, the accounting records must provide accurate, up-to-date information for each customer account and the total of the customer account balances must equal the total in the general ledger control account.

Interest Revenue

At the end of each month, the company can use the subsidiary ledger to easily determine the transactions that occurred in each customer's account during the month and then send the customer a statement of transactions for the month. If the customer does not pay in full within a specified period (usually 30 days), most retailers add an interest (financing) charge to the balance due.

When financing charges are added, the seller increases the accounts receivable and recognizes interest revenue. If Kids Online still owes $2,000 at the end of the next month, August 31, and Adorable Junior Garment charges 18% on the balance due, the entry that Adorable Junior Garment will make to record interest revenue of $30 ($2,000 × 18% × $\frac{1}{12}$) is as follows:

A	=	L	+	OE
+30				+30

Cash flows: no effect

Aug. 31	Accounts Receivable—Kids Online	30	
	Interest Revenue		30
	To record interest on amount due.		

Bell Aliant in our feature story starts to accrue interest if payment is not received from the customer within 30 days of the billing date. The interest charges are meant to be punitive and the customer charges are 3% per month. As discussed in Chapter 5, interest revenue is included in other revenues in the non-operating section of the income statement.

Nonbank Credit Card Sales

In Chapter 7, we learned that debit and bank credit card sales are typically treated as cash sales. Sales on credit cards that are not directly associated with a bank are reported as credit sales, not cash sales. Nonbank credit card sales result in an account receivable until the credit card company pays the amount owing to the seller.

To illustrate, assume that Kerr Music accepts a nonbank credit card on October 24 for a $500 bill. An asset, accounts receivable, is recorded for the amount of cash that will be received, an expense is recorded for the service fee charged by the credit card company, and revenue is recorded for the amount of the sale. The entry for the sale by Kerr Music (assuming a 4% service fee) is:

A	=	L	+	OE
+480				−20
				+500

Cash flows: no effect

Oct. 24	Accounts Receivable—Credit Card Company	480	
	Credit Card Expense ($500 × 4%)	20	
	Sales		500
	To record nonbank credit card sale.		

When Cash is received from the credit card company, the asset cash is increased and accounts receivable is reduced for the amount collected. The entry that Kerr Music will record is as follows:

Nov. 7	Cash	480	
	Accounts Receivable—Credit Card Company		480
	To record nonbank credit card sale.		

A = L + OE
+480
−480

↑ Cash flows: +480

Advances in technology have created a rapidly changing credit card industry. Transactions and payments can be processed much more quickly, and often electronically, which reduces the time to collect cash from the credit card company. As collection time becomes shorter, credit card transactions are becoming more like cash transactions to the business.

How does a business know if it should debit Cash or Accounts Receivable when it processes a credit card transaction? Basically, it should consider how long it takes to collect the cash. If it takes longer than a few days to process the transaction and collect the cash, it should be treated as a credit sale, as shown above.

Companies that issue their own credit cards, such as Canadian Tire, always record sales paid by their cards as credit sales. When the credit card transaction results in an account receivable from the customer—as opposed to from the credit card company, as shown above—there is no service fee and the accounting treatment is the same as we have previously seen for accounts receivable.

As discussed in Chapter 7, credit card expenses, along with debit card expenses, are reported as operating expenses in the income statement.

ACCOUNTING IN ACTION
ALL ABOUT YOU INSIGHT

Interest rates on bank credit cards can vary depending on the card's various features; recently, the interest rates on Canadian bank credit cards ranged from 5.99% to 20.5%. Credit cards with lower interest rates usually have annual fees and may only be available to those with an excellent credit rating. Nonbank cards can charge significantly higher interest rates, such as retailer HBC's interest rate of 29.9%. At the same time, the Canadian banks' prime lending rate was 3.0%. The prime lending rate, the rate banks charge their best customers, changes depending on the supply and demand for money. Credit card interest rates, on the other hand, hardly budge at all. Why are credit card rates so much higher than other interest rates?

The higher rate is due to the risk involved. A bank loan, such as a mortgage, is a secured loan because the loan is backed by a tangible asset: a house. Using a credit card is essentially taking out an unsecured loan because nothing physical is used as security for the lender. In addition, credit cards are much more susceptible to fraud, and thus require a consistently high interest rate.

Sources: Credit Cards Canada website at http://www.creditcardscanada.ca; Garry Marr, "Borrowers Will Suffer After Interest Rate Hike," *National Post*, April 17, 2012; "HBC Account Agreement," available at http://financial.hbc.com/en/credit/terms.shtml.

Should you use credit cards or not?

⟳ BEFORE YOU GO ON...

Do It

Information for Kinholm Company follows for its first month of operations:

	Credit Sales			Cash Collections	
Jan. 5	Sych Co.	$12,000	Jan. 16	Sych Co.	$9,000
9	Downey Inc.	5,000	22	Downey Inc.	3,500
13	Pawlak Co.	6,000	28	Pawlak Co.	6,000

Action Plan

- Use T accounts as a simple method of calculating account balances.
- Create separate accounts for each customer and post their transactions to their accounts.
- Create one account for the Accounts Receivable general ledger (control) account.
- Post the total credit sales and the total cash collections to the general ledger.

⊘ BEFORE YOU GO ON continued...

Calculate (a) the balances that appear in the accounts receivable subsidiary ledger for each customer, and (b) the accounts receivable balance that appears in the general ledger at the end of January.

Solution

ACCOUNTS RECEIVABLE SUBSIDIARY LEDGER

Sych Co.

Jan. 5	12,000	Jan. 16	9,000
Bal.	3,000		

Downey Inc.

Jan. 9	5,000	Jan. 22	3,500
Bal.	1,500		

Pawlak Co.

Jan. 13	6,000	Jan. 28	6,000
Bal.	0		

GENERAL LEDGER

Accounts Receivable

Jan. 31	23,000ᵃ	Jan. 31	18,500ᵇ
Bal.	4,500		

ᵃ $12,000 + $5,000 + $6,000 = $23,000
ᵇ $9,000 + $3,500 + $6,000 = $18,500

Related exercise material: BE8–1, BE8–2, BE8–3, BE8–4, E8–1, and E8–2.

THE NAVIGATOR

VALUING ACCOUNTS RECEIVABLE

» STUDY OBJECTIVE 2

Calculate the net realizable value of accounts receivable and account for bad debts.

After receivables are recorded in the accounts, the next question is how these receivables should be reported on the balance sheet. Receivables are assets, but determining the amount to report as an asset is sometimes difficult because some receivables will become uncollectible. A receivable can only be reported as an asset if it will give a future benefit. This means that only collectible receivables can be reported as assets in the financial statements. This collectible amount is called the receivables' **net realizable value.** Reporting accounts receivable at net realizable value provides information to investors and creditors on the company's ability to generate cash.

In order to minimize the risk of uncollectible accounts, companies consider the creditworthiness of potential credit customers. But even if a customer satisfies the company's credit requirements before the credit sale was approved, inevitably, some accounts receivable still become uncollectible. For example, a usually reliable customer may suddenly not be able to pay because of an unexpected decrease in its revenues or because it is faced with unexpected bills.

Why do companies still decide to sell goods or services on credit if there is always a risk of not collecting the receivable? It is because they are expecting that the increase in revenues and profit from selling on credit will be greater than any uncollectible accounts or credit losses. Such losses are considered a normal and necessary risk of doing business on a credit basis.

When receivables are written down to their net realizable value because of expected credit losses, owner's equity must also be reduced so that assets remain equal to liabilities plus owner's equity. As we learned in Chapter 1, a decrease in an asset that results in a decrease in owner's equity (excluding withdrawals by owners) is an expense. The expense for credit losses is called **bad debt expense.**

Alternative terminology Bad debt expense is also sometimes called *uncollectible account expense.*

The key issue in valuing accounts receivable is to estimate the amount of accounts receivable that will not be collected. If the company waits until it knows for sure that a specific account will not be collected, it could end up overstating the asset accounts receivable on the balance sheet and understating expenses.

Consider the following example. Assume that in 2014, Quick Buck Computer Company decides it could increase its revenues by offering computers to students without requiring any money down and with no credit approval process. On campuses across the country, it sells 100,000 computers with a selling price of $400 each. This increases Quick Buck's receivables and revenues by $40 million. The promotion is a huge success! The 2014 balance sheet and income statement look great. Unfortunately, in 2015, nearly 40% of the student customers **default** on (do not pay) their accounts. This makes the 2015 balance sheet and income statement look terrible. Illustration 8-2 shows that the promotion in 2014 was not such a great success after all.

Year 2014

Huge sales promotion. Accounts receivable increase dramatically. Profit increases dramatically.

Year 2015

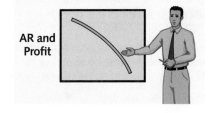

Customers default on amounts owed. Accounts receivable drop dramatically. Bad debt expense increases and profit decreases dramatically.

If credit losses are not recorded until they occur, the accounts receivable in the balance sheet are not reported at the amount that is actually expected to be collected. Quick Buck Computer's receivables were overstated at the end of 2014, which misrepresented the amount that should have been reported as an asset.

In addition, bad debt expense will not be matched to sales revenues in the income statement. Recall from Chapter 3 that expenses that are directly related to revenue must be recorded in the same period as the sales they helped generate. Consequently, Quick Buck Computer Company's profit was overstated in 2014 and understated in 2015 because the revenues were recorded in 2014 and the expenses directly related to the revenue were recorded in 2015.

To avoid overstating assets and profit, we cannot wait until we know exactly which receivables are uncollectible. Because we do not know which specific accounts receivable will need to be written off, we use what is known as the **allowance method** in which we estimate uncollectible accounts at the end of each accounting period. In this method, the estimated uncollectible accounts are recorded as a credit balance in a contra asset account, **Allowance for Doubtful Accounts**. The allowance is deducted from Accounts Receivable on the balance sheet to report the net realizable value of the receivables.

The allowance method also gives better matching of expenses with revenues on the income statement because credit losses that are expected to happen from sales or service revenue in that accounting period are recorded in the same accounting period as when the revenue was earned. The allowance method is required for financial reporting purposes and has three essential features:

1. **Recording estimated uncollectibles:** The amount of uncollectible accounts receivable is estimated at the end of the accounting period. An adjusting journal entry is recorded to adjust the allowance for doubtful accounts to the estimated uncollectible amount and to record bad debt expense.
2. **Writing off uncollectible accounts:** Actual uncollectibles are written off when the specific account is determined to be uncollectible.
3. **Collection of a previously written-off account:** If an account that was previously written off is later collected, the original write off is reversed and the collection is recorded.

We explain these features of the allowance method in the following sections.

1. Recording Estimated Uncollectibles

Estimating the Allowance for Doubtful Accounts. To illustrate the allowance method, assume that Adorable Junior Garment has accounts receivable of $200,000 at December 31, 2014. Not all of these receivables will be collected. As it is not known at December 31, 2014, which specific accounts are uncollectible, the amount of uncollectibles must be estimated. How is this amount estimated? The most common method used by companies is the percentage of receivables approach.

Under the **percentage of receivables approach**, management uses experience to estimate the percentage of receivables that will become uncollectible accounts. The easiest way to do this is to multiply the total amount of accounts receivable by a percentage based on an overall estimate of the total uncollectible accounts. The problem with this simple approach is that it doesn't take into consideration that the longer a receivable is past due or outstanding, the less likely it is to be collected.

Alternative terminology The percentage of receivables approach is sometimes referred to as the *balance sheet approach*.

Therefore, the more common practice is to use different percentages depending on how long the accounts receivable have been outstanding. This is more sensitive to the actual status of the accounts receivable. Bell Aliant in our feature story uses this approach.

A schedule must be prepared, called an **aging schedule**, which shows the age of each account receivable. After the age of each account receivable is determined, the loss from uncollectible accounts is estimated. This is done by applying percentages, based on experience, to the totals in each category. The estimated percentage of uncollectible accounts increases as the number of days outstanding increases. An aging schedule for Adorable Junior Garment is shown in Illustration 8-3.

▶ **ILLUSTRATION 8-3**
Aging schedule

Customer	Total	Number of Days Outstanding				
		0–30	31–60	61–90	91–120	Over 120
Bansal Garments	$ 6,000		$ 3,000	$ 3,000		
Bortz Clothing	3,000	$ 3,000				
Kids Online	4,500				$ 2,000	$ 2,500
Snazzy Kids Co.	17,000	2,000	5,000	5,000	5,000	
Tykes n' Tots	26,500	10,000	10,000	6,000	500	
The Bay	42,000	32,000	10,000			
Walmart	61,000	48,000	12,000	1,000		
Others	40,000	5,000	10,000	10,000	5,000	10,000
	$200,000	$100,000	$50,000	$25,000	$12,500	$12,500
Estimated percentage uncollectible		5%	10%	20%	30%	50%
Estimated uncollectible accounts	$25,000	$ 5,000	$ 5,000	$ 5,000	$ 3,750	$ 6,250

The $25,000 total for estimated uncollectible accounts is the amount of existing receivables that are expected to become uncollectible in the future. This also means that Adorable Junior Garments expects to collect the remaining accounts receivable of $175,000 ($200,000 of accounts receivable in total less the estimated uncollectible accounts of $25,000). As Adorable Junior Garment expects to collect only $175,000, this is the amount that should be shown in the balance sheet as an asset, not $200,000.

As previously explained, since Adorable Junior Garment doesn't know specifically which accounts receivable it will not collect, we do not know which specific accounts to credit in the subsidiary ledger. We cannot simply credit the Accounts Receivable control account to reduce it from $200,000 to $175,000 because the subsidiary ledger accounts must balance with Accounts Receivable, the control account.

The problem is solved by using the contra asset account, Allowance for Doubtful Accounts, instead of crediting Accounts Receivable. Remember that the balance of a contra asset account (a credit) is deducted from the related asset on the balance sheet (a debit). The difference between Adorable Junior Garment's **gross accounts receivable** and its allowance for doubtful accounts is the net realizable value (the collectible amount) of its accounts receivable. This can be represented by the formula shown in Illustration 8-4.

▶ **ILLUSTRATION 8-4**
Formula for calculating net realizable value

Gross Accounts Receivable	−	Allowance for Doubtful Accounts	=	Net Realizable Value
$200,000	−	$25,000	=	$175,000

In the current assets section of the balance sheet, Accounts Receivable, the Allowance for Doubtful Accounts, and the net realizable value are reported as follows (using assumed data for the other current asset accounts):

ADORABLE JUNIOR GARMENT		
Balance Sheet (partial)		
December 31, 2014		
Current assets		
Cash		$ 14,800
Accounts receivable	$200,000	
Less: Allowance for doubtful accounts	25,000	175,000
Merchandise inventory		310,000
Prepaid expenses		25,000
Total current assets		$524,800

Notice that the net realizable value of the accounts receivable—$175,000—is the amount added to cash, merchandise inventory, and prepaid expenses to calculate total current assets, not the total accounts receivable ($14,800 + 175,000 + 310,000 + 25,000).

Determining Bad Debt Expense. Although the balance in the Allowance for Doubtful Accounts is $25,000, it is important to understand that this is not necessarily equal to the bad debt expense in the income statement. Why? Recall that a contra asset account is a permanent account. That means the balance in a contra asset account is carried forward to the next accounting period. We need to know the unadjusted balance in the Allowance for Doubtful Accounts in order to adjust the account to its required balance of $25,000. This adjusting entry also records the bad debt expense. Since bad debt expense is a temporary account, it starts each accounting period with a zero balance. Thus the amount in the adjusting entry will be equal to the bad debt expense reported in the income statement.

To illustrate, let us assume that Adorable Junior Garment has an unadjusted credit balance of $1,000 in its Allowance for Doubtful Accounts. Because the account already has a credit balance, it needs to be adjusted by only the difference between the required balance of $25,000 and the existing balance of $1,000. Thus the amount of the adjusting entry, which is equal to the bad debt expense, is $24,000, as shown in Illustration 8-5.

Required Balance in the Allowance for Doubtful Accounts (estimated uncollectible accounts)	–	Unadjusted **credit** balance in the Allowance for Doubtful Accounts	=	Bad debt expense
$25,000	–	$1,000	=	$24,000

▶ **ILLUSTRATION 8-5**
Calculation of bad debt expense—unadjusted credit balance in allowance

The adjusting entry for $24,000 is as follows:

Dec. 31	Bad Debt Expense	24,000	
	Allowance for Doubtful Accounts		24,000
	To record estimate of uncollectible accounts.		

A	=	L	+	OE
−24,000				−24,000

Cash flows: no effect

After the adjusting entry is posted, the balance in the Allowance for Doubtful Accounts will be equal to the estimated uncollectible accounts calculated in Illustration 8-3. This is shown in Adorable Junior Garment's accounts:

Bad Debt Expense		Allowance for Doubtful Accounts		
Dec. 31 Adj. 24,000			Dec. 31 Unadj. Bal.	1,000
			31 Adj.	24,000
			Dec. 31 Bal.	25,000

Bad debt expense of $24,000 is reported in the income statement in the period when the sales are recognized. Notice this is less than the balance in the Allowance for Doubtful Accounts. This will always be the case when there is a credit amount in the unadjusted balance of the allowance account.

Occasionally, the allowance account will have a debit balance before recording the adjusting entry. This happens when write offs in the year are higher than the previous estimates for bad debts (we will discuss write offs in the next section). If there is a debit balance prior to recording the adjusting entry, the debit balance is added to the required balance when the adjusting entry is made. For example, if there had been a $500 debit balance in the Adorable Junior Garment allowance account before adjustment, the adjusting entry would have been for $25,500, to arrive at a credit balance in the allowance account of $25,000. The calculation of the adjusting entry is shown in Illustration 8-6.

▶ **ILLUSTRATION 8-6**
Calculation of bad debt expense—unadjusted debit balance in the allowance

Required Balance in the Allowance for Doubtful Accounts (estimated uncollectible accounts)	+	Unadjusted **debit** balance in the Allowance for Doubtful Accounts	=	Bad debt expense
$25,000	+	$500	=	$25,500

In this case, the adjusting entry is for $25,500 as follows:

A = L + OE
−25,500   −25,500

Cash flows: no effect

Dec. 31	Bad Debt Expense	25,500	
	Allowance for Doubtful Accounts		25,500
	To record estimate of uncollectible accounts.		

After the adjusting entry is posted, the balance in the Allowance for Doubtful Accounts is equal to the estimated uncollectible accounts calculated in Illustration 8-3. This is shown in Adorable Junior Garment's accounts:

Bad Debt Expense		Allowance for Doubtful Accounts	
Dec. 31 Adj. 25,500			Dec. 31 Unadj. Bal. 500
			31 Adj. 25,500
			Dec. 31 Bal. **25,000**

Notice that, although the adjusted balance in the Allowance for Doubtful Accounts is the same amount in the two examples shown, the Bad Debt Expense is different. In this case, it is higher than the balance in the allowance in order to compensate for the fact that Adorable Junior Garment underestimated its allowance and bad debts last year.

When preparing annual financial statements, all companies must report accounts receivable at their net realizable value, so companies must estimate the required allowance. However, when preparing monthly financial statements, some companies use a simplified approach in which bad debt expense is calculated by estimating the percent of sales that will not be collected. This approach, called the percentage of sales approach, is covered in intermediate textbooks.

2. Writing Off Uncollectible Accounts

Companies use various methods for collecting past-due accounts, including letters, calls, and legal actions. Bell Aliant, in our feature story, classifies customers by risk levels, which it uses to determine how large and how far in arrears it will allow the bill to get before taking action. Bell Aliant follows up on late accounts with letters and calls, and will cut back or suspend service if the customer does not negotiate new payment terms. If there is still no payment from the customer, service is permanently cut off. The final step involves sending the account to a collection agency.

When all the ways of collecting a past-due account have been tried and collection appears impossible, the account should be written off. To prevent premature write offs, each write off should be approved in writing by management. To keep good internal control, the authorization to write off accounts should not be given to someone who also has responsibilities related to cash or receivables.

To illustrate a receivables write off, assume that the vice-president of finance of Adorable Junior Garment authorizes the write off of a $4,500 balance owed by a delinquent customer, Kids Online, on March 1, 2015. The entry to record the write off is as follows:

Mar. 1	Allowance for Doubtful Accounts	4,500	
	Accounts Receivable—Kids Online		4,500
	Write off of uncollectible account.		

A = L + OE
+4,500
−4,500

Cash flows: no effect

Bad Debt Expense is not increased (debited) when the write off occurs. Under the allowance method, every account write off is debited to the allowance account rather than to Bad Debt Expense. A debit to Bad Debt Expense would be incorrect because the expense was already recognized when the adjusting entry was made for estimated bad debts last year.

Instead, the entry to record the write off of an uncollectible account reduces both Accounts Receivable and Allowance for Doubtful Accounts. After posting, using an assumed balance of $230,000 in Accounts Receivable on February 28, 2015, the general ledger accounts will appear as follows:

Accounts Receivable				Allowance for Doubtful Accounts			
Feb. 28 Bal.	230,000	Mar. 1	4,500	Mar. 1	4,500	Jan. 1 Bal.	25,000
Mar. 1 Bal.	225,500					Mar. 1 Bal.	20,500

A write off affects only balance sheet accounts. The write off of the account reduces both Accounts Receivable and Allowance for Doubtful Accounts. Net realizable value in the balance sheet remains the same, as shown below:

	Before Write Off	After Write Off
Accounts receivable	$230,000	$225,500
Less: Allowance for doubtful accounts	25,000	20,500
Net realizable value	$205,000	$205,000

As mentioned earlier, the allowance account can sometimes end up in a debit balance position after the write off of an uncollectible account. This can happen if the writeoffs in the period are more than the opening balance of the allowance. It means the actual credit losses were greater than the estimated credit losses. The balance in Allowance for Doubtful Accounts will be corrected when the adjusting entry for estimated uncollectible accounts is made at the end of the period.

3. Collection of a Previously Written-Off Uncollectible Account

Occasionally, a company collects cash from a customer after its account has been written off. Two entries are required to record the collection of a previously written-off account: (1) the entry previously made when the account was written off is reversed to restore the customer's account; and (2) the collection is recorded in the usual way.

To illustrate, assume that on July 1, 2015, Kids Online pays the $4,500 amount that had been written off on March 1. The entries are as follows:

	(1)		
July 1	Accounts Receivable—Kids Online	4,500	
	Allowance for Doubtful Accounts		4,500
	To reverse write off of Kids Online account.		

A = L + OE
+4,500
−4,500

Cash flows: no effect

	(2)		
July 1	Cash	4,500	
	Accounts Receivable—Kids Online		4,500
	To record collection from Kids Online.		

A = L + OE
+4,500
−4,500

↑ Cash flows: +4,500

Note that the collection of a previously written-off account, like the write off of a bad debt, affects only balance sheet accounts. The net effect of the two entries is a debit to Cash and a credit to Allowance for Doubtful Accounts for $4,500. Accounts Receivable is debited and later credited for two reasons. First, the company must reverse the write off. Second, Kids Online did pay, so the Accounts Receivable account in the general ledger and Kids Online's account in the subsidiary ledger, if a subsidiary ledger is used, should show this payment as it will need to be considered in deciding what credit to give to Kids Online in the future.

Summary of Allowance Method

In summary, there are three types of transactions that you may need to record when valuing accounts receivable using the allowance method:

1. The estimated uncollectible accounts is determined by using the percentage of receivables approach. The estimated uncollectible accounts is the required balance in the Allowance for Doubtful Accounts, which is deducted from Accounts Receivable on the balance sheet to show the net realizable value of the receivables. The estimated uncollectible accounts receivable is recorded by using an adjusting entry at the end of the period in which Bad Debt Expense is debited and the Allowance for Doubtful Accounts is credited. The amount in the adjustment—the bad debt expense—is the difference between the required balance and the unadjusted balance in the allowance account.
2. Write offs of actual uncollectible accounts are recorded in the next accounting period by debiting Allowance for Doubtful Accounts and crediting Accounts Receivable.
3. Later collections of previously written-off accounts, if any, are recorded in two separate entries. The first reverses the write off by debiting Accounts Receivable and crediting Allowance for Doubtful Accounts. The second records the normal collection of the account by debiting Cash and crediting Accounts Receivable.

These entries are summarized in the following T accounts:

Accounts Receivable		Allowance for Doubtful Accounts	
Beginning balance	Cash collections	Write offs	Beginning balance
Credit sales	Write offs		Reverse write-off
Later recoveries			Bad debt adjusting entry
Ending balance			Ending balance

Action Plan
- Apply percentages to the receivables in each age category to determine total estimated uncollectible accounts. This is the ending balance required in the allowance account.
- Net realizable value is equal to the balance in Accounts Receivable minus the required balance in Allowance for Doubtful Accounts.
- Use the unadjusted balance in the allowance account to determine the adjusting entry. If the unadjusted balance in the allowance account is a credit, the amount of the adjustment is equal to the required balance minus the unadjusted credit balance. If the unadjusted balance is a debit, the amount of the adjustment is equal to the required balance plus the unadjusted debit balance.

BEFORE YOU GO ON...

Do It

The following information for Woo Wholesalers Co. accounts receivable is available at December 31:

Number of Days Outstanding	Accounts Receivable	Estimated Percentage Uncollectible
0–30 days	$ 85,000	5%
31–60 days	25,000	15%
Over 61 days	10,000	25%
Total	$120,000	

(a) Calculate the estimated uncollectible accounts and the net realizable value of Woo's accounts receivable at December 31.
(b) Prepare the adjusting journal entry to record bad debt expense for each of the following independent situations:
　1. The Allowance for Doubtful Accounts has an unadjusted $2,000 credit balance.
　2. The Allowance for Doubtful Accounts has an unadjusted $1,200 debit balance.
(c) Prepare the required journal entry if Woo learns that its $1,500 receivable from Kruger Retailers is not collectible.
(d) Prepare the required journal entries if Woo subsequently collects the $1,500 receivable from Kruger Retailers that was previously written off.

Solution

(a) Estimated uncollectible accounts = ($85,000 × 5%) + ($25,000 × 15%) + ($10,000 × 25%)

= $10,500

Net Realizable Value = $120,000 − $10,500

= $109,500

(b) 1. Bad Debt Expense ($10,500 − $2,000)	8,500	
Allowance for Doubtful Accounts		8,500
To record estimate of uncollectible accounts.		
2. Bad Debt Expense ($10,500 + $1,200)	11,700	
Allowance for Doubtful Accounts		11,700
To record estimate of uncollectible accounts.		
(c) Allowance for Doubtful Accounts	1,500	
Accounts Receivable—Kruger Retailers		1,500
To record write off of account receivable.		
(d) Accounts Receivable—Kruger Retailers	1,500	
Allowance for Doubtful Accounts		1,500
To reverse write off of Kruger Retailers' account receivable.		
Cash	1,500	
Accounts Receivable		1,500
To record collection from Kruger Retailers.		

Related exercise material: BE8–5, BE8–6, BE8–7, BE8–8, BE8–9, BE8–10, E8–4, E8–5, E8–6, and E8–7.

- Record the write offs of accounts and subsequent collection of accounts written off only in the balance sheet accounts, Accounts Receivable and Allowance for Doubtful Accounts.

THE **NAVIGATOR**

Notes Receivable

Credit may also be granted in exchange for a formal credit instrument known as a promissory note. A **promissory note** is a written promise to pay a specified amount of money on demand or at a definite time. Promissory notes may be used (1) when individuals and companies lend or borrow money, (2) when the amount of the transaction and the credit period are longer than normal limits, or (3) in the settlement of accounts receivable.

In a promissory note, the party making the promise to pay is called the **maker**. The party to whom payment is to be made is called the **payee**. In the note shown in Illustration 8-7, Higly Inc. is the maker and Wolder Company is the payee. To Wolder Company, the promissory note is a note receivable. To Higly Inc., it is a note payable.

>> STUDY OBJECTIVE 3

Account for notes receivable.

▶ **ILLUSTRATION 8-7**
Promissory note

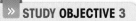

A promissory note might also contain other details such as whether any security is pledged as collateral for the loan and what happens if the maker defaults.

A note receivable is a formal promise to pay an amount that bears interest from the time it is issued until it is due. An account receivable is an informal promise to pay that bears interest only after its due date. Because it is less formal, it does not have as strong a legal claim as a note receivable. Most accounts receivable are due within a short period of time, usually 30 days, while a note can extend over longer periods of time.

There are also similarities between notes and accounts receivable. Both are credit instruments. Both can be sold to another party. Both are valued at their net realizable values. The basic issues in accounting for notes receivable are the same as those for accounts receivable, as follows:

1. Recognizing notes receivable
2. Disposing of notes receivable

RECOGNIZING NOTES RECEIVABLE

Like accounts receivable, a note receivable is an asset, as the company will collect cash in the future. To illustrate the basic entries for notes receivable, we will use the $10,000, four-month, 6% promissory note shown in Illustration 8-7. Assuming that Higly Inc. wrote the note in settlement of an account receivable, Wolder Company makes the following entry for the receipt of the note:

```
A      =   L   +   OE
+10,000
−10,000
```
Cash flows: no effect

May 31	Notes Receivable—Higly	10,000	
	Accounts Receivable—Higly		10,000
	To record acceptance of Higly note.		

If a note is exchanged for cash instead of an account receivable, the entry is a debit to Notes Receivable and a credit to Cash for the amount of the loan.

The note receivable is recorded at its principal amount (the value shown on the face of the note). No interest revenue is reported when the note is accepted because, according to the revenue recognition principle, revenue is not recognized until it is earned. Interest is earned (accrued) as time passes.

Recording Interest

As we learned in Chapter 3, the basic formula for calculating interest on an interest-bearing note is the following:

▶ **ILLUSTRATION 8-8**
Formula for calculating interest

Principal Amount of Note	x	Annual Interest Rate	x	Time in Terms of One Year	=	Interest
$10,000	x	6%	x	$4/12$	=	$200

Recall from Chapter 3 that the principal amount is the amount borrowed, or the amount still outstanding on a loan, separate from interest. This is also the balance in Wolder's Notes Receivable account or Higly's Note Payable account.

The interest rate specified in a note is an annual rate of interest. There are many factors that affect the interest rate. You will learn more about that in a finance course. Interest rates may also be fixed for the term of the note or may change over the term. In this textbook, we will always assume that the rate remains fixed for the term.

The time factor in the above formula gives the fraction of the year that the note has been outstanding. As we did in past chapters, to keep it simple we will assume that interest is calculated in months rather than days. Illustration 8-8 shows the calculation of interest revenue for Wolder Company and interest expense for Higly Inc. for the term of the note.

If Wolder Company's year end was June 30, the following adjusting journal entry would be required to accrue interest for the month of June:

```
A    =   L   +   OE
+50            +50
```
Cash flows: no effect

June 30	Interest Receivable	50	
	Interest Revenue ($10,000 × 6% × $1/12$)		50
	To accrue interest on Higly note receivable.		

Notice that interest on a note receivable is not debited to the Notes Receivable account. Instead, a separate asset account for the interest receivable is used. The Note Receivable account balance must be equal to the amount still outstanding on the note, in order to correctly calculate interest.

Valuing Notes Receivable

Like accounts receivable, notes receivable are reported at their net realizable value. Each note must be analyzed to determine how likely it is to be collected. If eventual collection is doubtful, bad debt expense and an allowance for doubtful notes must be recorded in the same way as for accounts receivable. Some companies use only one allowance account for both accounts and notes, and call it Allowance for Doubtful Accounts.

DISPOSING OF NOTES RECEIVABLE

Notes are normally held to their maturity date, at which time the principal plus any unpaid interest is collected. This is known as honouring (paying) the note. Sometimes, the maker of the note defaults and an adjustment to the accounts must be made. This is known as dishonouring (not paying) the note.

Honouring of Notes Receivable

A note is honoured when it is paid in full at its maturity date. The amount due at maturity is the principal of the note plus interest for the length of time the note is outstanding (assuming interest is due at maturity rather than monthly). If Higly Inc. honours the note when it is due on September 30—the maturity date—the entry by Wolder Company to record the collection is:

Sept. 30	Cash	10,200	
	Notes Receivable—Higly		10,000
	Interest Revenue		150
	Interest Receivable		50
	To record collection of Higly note.		

A	=	L	+	OE
+10,200				+150
−10,000				
−50				

↑ Cash flows: +10,200

Recall that one month of interest revenue, $50 ($10,000 \times 6\% \times {}^{1}/_{12}$), was accrued on June 30, Wolder's year end. Consequently, only three months of interest revenue, $150 ($10,000 \times 6\% \times {}^{3}/_{12}$), is recorded in this period.

Dishonouring of Notes Receivable

A **dishonoured note** is a note that is not paid in full at maturity. Since a dishonoured note receivable is no longer negotiable, the Notes Receivable account must be reduced by the principal of the note. The payee still has a claim against the maker of the note for both the principal and any unpaid interest and will transfer the amount owing to an Accounts Receivable account if there is hope that the amount will eventually be collected.

To illustrate, assume that on September 30, Higly Inc. says that it cannot pay at the present time but Wolder Company expects eventual collection. Wolder would make the following entry at the time the note is dishonoured:

Sept. 30	Accounts Receivable—Higly	10,200	
	Notes Receivable—Higly		10,000
	Interest Revenue		150
	Interest Receivable		50
	To record dishonouring of Higly note where collection is expected.		

A	=	L	+	OE
+10,200				+150
−10,000				
−50				

Cash flows: no effect

Note that the amount recorded in the accounts receivable is the total amount owed (interest and principal) by Higly.

Wolder will continue to follow up with Higly. If the amount owing is eventually collected, Wolder will simply debit Cash and credit Accounts Receivable. If Wolder decides at a later date that it will never collect this amount from Higly, Wolder will write off the account receivable in the same way we learned earlier in the chapter—debit Allowance for Doubtful Accounts, and credit Accounts Receivable.

On the other hand, Wolder could directly write the note off on September 30 if it decided there was no hope of collection. Assuming Wolder uses one allowance account for both accounts and notes, it would record the following:

A   =   L   +   OE
+10,050
−10,000
−50
Cash flows: no effect

Sept. 30	Allowance for Doubtful Accounts	10,050	
	Notes Receivable—Higly		10,000
	Interest Receivable		50
	To record dishonouring of Higly note where collection is not expected.		

No interest revenue is recorded, because collection will not occur. The interest receivable that previously had been accrued is also written off and the Allowance for Doubtful Accounts is debited for both the principal amount owed and the interest receivable.

BEFORE YOU GO ON...

Do It

Action Plan

- Calculate the accrued interest. The formula is: Principal × annual interest rate × time in terms of one year.
- Record the interest accrued on June 30 to follow revenue recognition criteria. Use Interest Receivable, not Notes Receivable, for accrued interest.
- If the note is honoured, calculate the interest accrued after June 30 and the total interest on the note. Record the interest accrued and the collection of the note and the total interest.
- If the note is dishonoured, record the transfer of the note and any interest earned to an accounts receivable account if eventual collection is expected or to an allowance account if collection is not expected.

On May 1, Gambit Stores accepts from J. Nyznyk a $3,400, three-month, 5% note in settlement of Nyznyk's overdue account. Interest is due at maturity. Gambit has a June 30 year end.

(a) Prepare the required journal entry to record the issue of the note on May 1, the adjusting journal entry on June 30, and the settlement of the note on August 1 assuming Nyznyk honours the note.

(b) Prepare the required journal entry on August 1 if Nyznyk does not pay the note and collection is not expected in the future.

Solution

(a)	May 1	Notes Receivable—J. Nyznyk	3,400	
		Accounts Receivable—J. Nyznyk		3,400
		To replace account receivable with 5% note receivable, due August 1.		
	June 30	Interest Receivable	28	
		Interest Revenue ($3,400 × 5% × 2/12)		28
		To record interest earned to June 30.		
	Aug. 1	Cash	3,442	
		Interest Receivable		28
		Notes Receivable—J. Nyznyk		3,400
		Interest Revenue ($3,400 × 5% × 1/12)		14
		To record collection of Nyznyk note plus interest.		
(b)	Aug. 1	Allowance for Doubtful Accounts	3,428	
		Interest Receivable		28
		Notes Receivable—J. Nyznyk		3,400
		To record dishonouring of Nyznyk note as collection is not expected.		

Related exercise material: BE8–11, BE8–12, BE8–13, E8–8, E8–9, and E8–10.

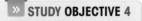

THE NAVIGATOR

Statement Presentation and Management of Receivables

» STUDY OBJECTIVE 4

Demonstrate the presentation, analysis, and management of receivables.

The way receivables are presented in the financial statements is important because receivables are directly affected by how a company recognizes its revenue and bad debt expense. In addition, these reported numbers are critical for analyzing a company's liquidity and how well it manages its receivables. In the next sections, we will discuss the presentation, analysis, and management of receivables.

PRESENTATION

Each of the major types of receivables should be identified in the balance sheet or in the notes to the financial statements. Other receivables include interest receivable, loans or advances to employees, and recoverable sales and income taxes. These receivables are generally classified and reported as separate items in the current or noncurrent sections of the balance sheet, according to their due dates. Notes receivable may also be either current assets or long-term assets, depending on their due dates.

In addition to the net realizable value of the receivables shown on the balance sheet, both the gross amount of receivables and the allowance for doubtful accounts must be disclosed in either the balance sheet or the notes to the financial statements.

Bad debt expense is reported in the operating expenses section of the income statement. At the time this textbook was being written, standard setters were proposing that bad debt expense be reported in the revenue section of the income statement as a contra revenue account—a deduction from revenues. If this change is approved, it will decrease both net sales and total operating expenses, but total profit will not change.

Illustration 8-9 shows the presentation of receivables for Shaw Communications Inc., which provides television, Internet, and other media services.

▶ ILLUSTRATION 8-9
Presentation of receivables

SHAW COMMUNICATIONS INC. Notes to the Financial Statements (partial) August 31, 2011 (in thousands)		
Note 3: Accounts Receivable	2011	2010
Subscriber and trade receivables	$424,451	$209,817
Due from officers and employees	159	148
Due from related parties	1,236	1,689
Miscellaneous receivables	45,768	3,730
	471,614	215,384
Less: Allowance for doubtful accounts	(28,797)	(18,969)
	$442,817	$196,415
Included in operating, general and administrative expenses is a provision for doubtful accounts of $33,686 (2010 − $33,746; 2009 − $19,298).		

In Note 3, Shaw discloses the components of its receivables. The net realizable value of the accounts receivable of $442 million in 2011 and $196 million in 2010 was reported in the current assets section of Shaw's balance sheet. Note that subscriber and trade receivables increased from $209 million in 2010 to $424 million in 2011. This is because in October 2010, Shaw acquired $296.6 million of receivables when it purchased Canwest Global Communications Corp.

Shaw also reports in its note to the financial statements that its allowance for doubtful accounts is determined by considering the number of days the account is past due, whether or not the customer continues to receive service, the company's collection history, and changes in business circumstances.

ANALYSIS

Management of accounts receivable is critical to a business's success. Accounts receivable are generally the most important source of cash for business. If sales increase, then accounts receivable are also expected to increase. On the other hand, an increase in accounts receivable might signal trouble. Perhaps the company increased its sales by loosening its credit policy, and these receivables may be difficult or impossible to collect. The company could also end up with higher costs because of the increase in sales since it may need more cash to pay for inventory and salaries.

Recall that the ability to pay obligations as they come due is measured by a company's liquidity. How can we tell if a company's management of its receivables is helping or hurting the company's liquidity? One way of doing this is to calculate a ratio called the **receivables turnover ratio**. This ratio measures the number of times, on average, that receivables are collected during the period. It is calculated by dividing net credit sales by average gross receivables during the year.

Unfortunately, companies rarely report the amount of net sales made on credit in their financial statements. As a result, net sales (including both cash and credit sales) is used as a substitute. As long as net sales are used to calculate the ratio for all companies being compared, the comparison is fair.

In Illustration 8-10, the substitute figures of total sales and trade and other receivables were used to calculate Reitmans' 2012 accounts receivable turnover.

▶**ILLUSTRATION 8-10**
Receivables turnover

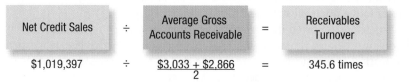

The result indicates an accounts receivable turnover ratio of 345.6 times per year for Reitmans. The higher the turnover ratio, the more liquid the company's receivables are.

A popular variation of the receivables turnover ratio is to convert it into the number of days it takes the company to collect its receivables. This ratio, called the **collection period**, is calculated by dividing 365 days by the receivables turnover, as shown for Reitmans in Illustration 8-11.

▶**ILLUSTRATION 8-11**
Collection period

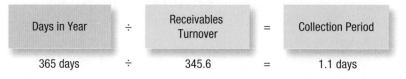

This means that in fiscal 2012, Reitmans collected its receivables, on average, in approximately 1.1 days. Reitmans does not have its own credit card. Its accounts receivable are from customers using credit cards such as MasterCard or Visa where the sales haven't been collected in cash from the credit card company prior to the year end. Reitmans' high turnover ratio and low collection period indicate that the company's receivables are highly liquid and that the company is receiving payment from the credit card companies quickly.

Bell Aliant, in our feature story, states that the vast majority of its consumer customers pay within 30 days but that it takes from 35 to 50 days to collect from businesses. The result is an overall average of between 31 and 35 days.

The collection period is often used to judge how effective a company's credit and collection policies are. The general rule is that the collection period should not be much longer than the credit term period (that is, the time allowed for payment). Accounts receivable are basically an interest-free loan to the customer, so the faster they are collected, the better.

Both the receivables turnover and the collection period are useful for judging how efficiently a company converts its credit sales to cash. Remember that these measures should also be compared with industry averages, and with previous years.

In addition, these measures should be analyzed along with other information about a company's liquidity, including the current ratio and inventory turnover. For example, low receivables may result in a low current ratio, which might make the company look like it has poor liquidity. But the receivables may be low because they are turning over quickly. In general, the faster the turnover, the more reliable the current ratio is for assessing liquidity.

The collection period can also be used to assess the length of a company's operating cycle. Recall from Chapter 4 that the operating cycle is the time it takes to go from cash to cash in producing revenues. In a merchandising company, the operating cycle may be measured by determining the average time that it takes to purchase inventory, sell it on account, and then collect cash from customers. In Chapter 6, we learned how to calculate days sales in inventory, which is the average age of the inventory on hand. The combination of the collection period and days sales in inventory is a useful way to measure the length of a company's operating cycle. Using the number of days sales in inventory calculated in Chapter 6, this calculation is shown in Illustration 8-12 for Reitmans.

This means that in fiscal 2012, it took 77.1 days on average from the time Reitmans purchased its inventory until it collected cash.

ACCELERATING CASH RECEIPTS FROM RECEIVABLES

If a company sells on credit, it has to wait until the customer pays the receivable before it has cash available to pay for such items as inventory and operating expenses. As credit sales and receivables increase in size and significance, waiting for receivables to be collected increases costs because the company cannot use the revenue from the sale until cash is collected. If a company can collect cash more quickly from its receivables, it can shorten the cash-to-cash operating cycle discussed in the previous section. One benefit of decreasing the operating cycle is that a company can invest in additional inventory and increase sales and profit.

There are two typical ways to collect cash more quickly from receivables: using the receivables to secure a loan and selling the receivables.

Loans Secured by Receivables

One of the most common ways to speed up cash flow from accounts receivable is to go to a bank and borrow money using accounts receivable as collateral. While this does have a cost (interest has to be paid to the bank on the loan), the cash is available for the company to use earlier. The loan can then be repaid as the receivables are collected. Generally, banks are willing to give financing of up to 75% of receivables that are less than 90 days old. Quite often, these arrangements occur through an operating line of credit, which is discussed in Chapter 10.

Sale of Receivables

Companies also frequently sell their receivables to another company because it provides an immediate source of cash. There are two other reasons for the sale of receivables. The first is their size. To be competitive, sellers often give financing to purchasers of their goods to encourage the sale of the product. But the companies may not want to hold large amounts of receivables. As a result, many major companies in the automobile, truck, equipment, computer, and appliance industries have created wholly owned finance companies that accept responsibility for accounts receivable financing. An example is Ford Credit Canada, owned by the Ford Motor Company of Canada.

Another reason for selling receivables is to reduce the costs of monitoring and collecting receivables. For example, it is often more cost-effective for a retailer to sell its receivables to credit card companies, such as Visa and MasterCard, which specialize in billing and collecting accounts receivable.

Factoring. One way to accelerate receivables collection is by sale to a factor. A **factor** is a finance company or bank that buys receivables from businesses and then collects the cash directly from the customer. If the customer does not pay, the business is usually responsible for reimbursing the factor for the uncollected amounts. This is known as selling receivables on a recourse basis.

Securitization of Receivables. Another way to accelerate cash received from receivables is through a process called **securitization**. Receivables are moved to an independent trust that holds them as an investment. This converts the receivables into securities of the trust, which is why the term "securitization of receivables" is used. In some cases, the transfer is treated as a sale of receivables; in other cases, it is treated as a secured loan. For such companies as Bell Aliant, securitization of receivables is one method of using their receivables to obtain cash.

The differences between factoring and securitization are that securitization involves many investors and the cost is lower, the receivables are of higher quality, and the seller usually continues to be involved with collecting the receivables. In factoring, the sale is usually to only one company, the cost is higher, the receivables quality is lower, and the seller does not normally have any involvement with collecting the receivables.

ACCOUNTING IN ACTION
ACROSS THE ORGANIZATION

U.S. discount department store chain **Target Corp.** announced in early 2011 that it was going to get out of the credit card business and sell its credit card receivables. The retailer said it wanted to use the money from the sale to buy more inventory, pay down debt, and help pay for its planned expansion into Canada by taking over some Zellers stores from the **Hudson's Bay Company.** It also wanted to focus on merchandising instead of financial services. A year later, Target said it had not received an acceptable offer for the receivables and would hold off on selling them until late 2012 or early 2013. Some analysts thought that waiting was likely a smart move, because as the economy improves and the number of shoppers defaulting on their credit card payments declines, the value of Target's credit card receivables would increase. Others thought that the delay of the sale meant that the company was overvaluing its receivables. In the third quarter of 2011, Target's bad debts declined by 64% to $40 million, while its profit from its credit card business increased by 10%. In that period, the company's gross credit card receivables totalled $6.1 billion.

Sources: Thomas Lee, "Target Does Things Its Way—For Better or Worse," *Minneapolis StarTribune*, January 25, 2012; James Callan and Matt Townsend, "Target Suspends Efforts to Sell Credit Card Receivables," Bloomberg, January 18, 2012; Karen Talley, "Target Is Entering Canada, Selling Card Receivables," Dow Jones Newswires, January 13, 2011.

Question: What might be the advantages to Target of having its own credit card? What might be the disadvantages?

BEFORE YOU GO ON...

Do It

The following information is available for Jupiter Company.

	2015	2014	2013
Net credit sales	$1,500,000	$1,300,000	$1,350,000
Gross accounts receivable	127,000	124,000	118,000
Days sales in inventory	44.5 days	43 days	

Calculate the accounts receivable turnover ratio, collection period, and operating cycle in days and comment on any trends.

Action Plan
- Calculate the average gross accounts receivable using the accounts receivable balance at the beginning and ending of the year.
- Divide net credit sales by the average accounts receivable for that year to calculate receivables turnover.
- Divide 365 by the receivables turnover to calculate collection period.
- Add the collection period to days sales in inventory to calculate operating cycle in days.

Solution

	2015	2014
Receivables turnover	$11.95 \text{ times} = \dfrac{\$1,500,000}{[(127,000 + 124,000) \div 2]}$	$10.74 \text{ times} = \dfrac{\$1,300,000}{[(124,000 + 118,000) \div 2]}$
Collection period	$30.54 \text{ days} = \dfrac{365 \text{ days}}{11.95 \text{ times}}$	$34 \text{ days} = \dfrac{365 \text{ days}}{10.74 \text{ times}}$
Operating cycle in days	75 days = 30.54 + 44.5	77 days = 34 + 43

The accounts receivable turnover has increased and the collection period decreased. In general, it is better to have a higher accounts receivable turnover and a lower collection period. Even though the days sales in inventory had increased, the operating cycle has decreased, which generally is better for the company.

THE **NAVIGATOR**

Related exercise material: BE8–14, BE8–15, BE8–16, E8–3, E8–11, E8–12, and E8–13.

■Comparing IFRS and ASPE ■

Key Differences	International Financial Reporting Standards (IFRS)	Accounting Standards for Private Enterprises (ASPE)	
No significant differences			

THE NAVIGATOR

Demonstration Problem

On February 28, Dylan Co. had the following balances in select accounts:

Accounts Receivable	$200,000
Allowance for Doubtful Accounts (credit)	12,500

Selected transactions for Dylan Co. follow. Dylan's year end is June 30.

Mar.	1	Sold $20,000 of merchandise to Potter Company, terms n/30.
	1	Accepted Juno Company's $16,500, six-month, 6% note for the balance due on account.
	11	Potter Company returned $600 worth of goods.
	13	Made Dylan Co. credit card sales for $13,200.
	30	Received payment in full from Potter Company.
Apr.	13	Received collections of $8,200 on Dylan Co. credit card sales. Added interest charges of 18% to the remaining balance.
May	10	Wrote off as uncollectible $15,000 of accounts receivable.
June	30	Estimated uncollectible accounts are determined to be $20,000 at June 30.
	30	Recorded the interest accrued on the Juno Company note.
July	16	Received payment in full, $4,000, on an account that was previously written off in May.
Sept.	1	Collected cash from Juno Company in payment of the March 1 note receivable.

Instructions

(a) Prepare the journal entries for the transactions. Ignore cost of goods sold entries for purposes of this question.

(b) Open T accounts for Accounts Receivable and the Allowance for Doubtful Accounts, and post the relevant journal entries to these accounts. Calculate the balance in these accounts at June 30 and at September 1.

(c) Calculate the net realizable value of the accounts receivable at June 30 and September 1.

ACTION PLAN

- Record receivables at the invoice price.
- Recognize that sales returns and allowances reduce the amount received on accounts receivable.
- Calculate interest by multiplying the principal by the interest rate by the part of the year that has passed.
- Record write offs of accounts and collection of previously written-off accounts only in balance sheet accounts.
- Consider any existing balance in the allowance account when making the adjustment for uncollectible accounts.
- Recognize any remaining interest on notes receivable when recording the collection of a note.

Solution to Demonstration Problem

(a)

Mar.	1	Accounts Receivable—Potter	20,000	
		Sales		20,000
		To record sale on account.		
	1	Notes Receivable—Juno	16,500	
		Accounts Receivable—Juno		16,500
		To record acceptance of Juno Company note.		
	11	Sales Returns and Allowances	600	
		Accounts Receivable—Potter		600
		To record return of goods.		
	13	Accounts Receivable	13,200	
		Sales		13,200
		To record company credit card sales.		
	30	Cash ($20,000 − $600)	19,400	
		Accounts Receivable—Potter		19,400
		To record collection of account receivable.		

Apr. 13	Cash	8,200	
	Accounts Receivable		8,200
	To record collection of credit card accounts receivable.		
13	Accounts Receivable [($13,200 − $8,200) × 18% × $^1/_{12}$]	75	
	Interest Revenue		75
	To record interest on amount due.		
May 10	Allowance for Doubtful Accounts	15,000	
	Accounts Receivable		15,000
	To Record write off of accounts receivable.		
June 30	Bad Debt Expense ($20,000 + $2,500)	22,500	
	Allowance for Doubtful Accounts		22,500
	To record estimate of uncollectible accounts.		
30	Interest Receivable ($16,500 × 6% × $^4/_{12}$)	330	
	Interest Revenue		330
	To record interest earned.		
July 16	Accounts Receivable	4,000	
	Allowance for Doubtful Accounts		4,000
	To reverse write off of account receivable.		
16	Cash	4,000	
	Accounts Receivable		4,000
	To record collection of account receivable.		
Sept. 1	Cash [$16,500 + ($16,500 × 6% × $^6/_{12}$)]	16,995	
	Interest Revenue ($16,500 × 6% × $^2/_{12}$)		165
	Interest Receivable		330
	Note Receivable		16,500
	To record collection of note receivable plus interest.		

(b)

Accounts Receivable

Feb. 28	Bal.	200,000		16,500
		20,000		600
		13,200		19,400
		75		8,200
				15,000
June 30	Bal.	173,575		
		4,000		4,000
Sept. 1	Bal.	173,575		

Allowance for Doubtful Accounts

		15,000	Feb. 28	Bal.	12,500
June 30	Bal.	2,500			
			June 30	Adj.	22,500
			June 30	Bal.	20,000
					4,000
			Sept. 1	Bal.	24,000

(c)

	June 30	Sept. 1
Accounts receivable	$173,575	$173,575
Less: Allowance for doubtful accounts	20,000	24,000
Net realizable value	$153,575	$149,575

THE **NAVIGATOR**

▶ Summary of Study Objectives

1. **Record accounts receivable transactions.** Accounts receivable are recorded at the invoice price. They are reduced by sales returns and allowances, and sales discounts. Accounts receivable subsidiary ledgers are used to keep track of individual account balances. When interest is charged on a past-due receivable, this interest is added to the accounts receivable balance and is recognized as interest revenue. Sales using nonbank credit cards result in a receivable, net of the credit card charges, from the credit card company; sales using company credit cards result in a receivable from the customer.

2. **Calculate the net realizable value of accounts receivable and account for bad debts.** Accounts receivable must be reported at their net realizable value on the balance sheet. The allowance method is used to record the estimated uncollectible accounts in the Allowance for Doubtful Accounts. The net realizable value of the receivables is equal to the gross accounts receivable minus the allowance. A percentage of total receivables, or an aging schedule applying different percentages to different categories of receivables, is used to estimate the allowance for doubtful accounts. The allowance method also matches bad debt expense against revenue in the period when the revenue is recognized. Bad debt expense is equal to the difference between the required balance and the unadjusted balance in the allowance for doubtful accounts.

   When a specific account receivable is determined to be uncollectible, the account is written off and the allowance is reduced. When a previously written-off account is collected, the entry previously made to write off the account is reversed and the collection is recorded.

3. **Account for notes receivable.** Notes receivable are recorded at their principal amount. Interest is earned from the date the note is issued until it matures and must be recorded in the correct accounting period. Interest receivable is recorded in a separate account from the note. Like accounts receivable, notes receivable are reported at their net realizable value.

   Notes are normally held to maturity. At that time, the principal plus any unpaid interest is due and the note is removed from the accounts. If a note is not paid at maturity, it is said to be dishonoured. If eventual collection is still expected, an account receivable replaces the note receivable and any unpaid interest. Otherwise, the note must be written off.

4. **Demonstrate the presentation, analysis, and management of receivables.** Each major type of receivable should be identified in the balance sheet or in the notes to the financial statements. Both the gross amount of receivables and the allowance for doubtful accounts/notes is required to be reported in the balance sheet or the notes to the financial statements. Bad debt expense is reported in the income statement as an operating expense.

   The liquidity of receivables can be evaluated by calculating the receivables turnover and collection period ratios. The receivables turnover is calculated by dividing net credit sales by average gross accounts receivable. This ratio measures how efficiently the company is converting its receivables into sales. The collection period converts the receivables turnover into days, dividing 365 days by the receivables turnover ratio. It shows the number of days, on average, it takes a company to collect its accounts receivable. The combination of the collection period and days sales in inventory is a useful way to measure the length of a company's operating cycle.

   Companies may accelerate the collection of cash by using the receivables to secure a loan, by selling the receivables to a factor, or by securitizing them.

Flash cards

▶ Glossary

Accounts receivable Amounts owed by customers on account. (p. 416)

Aging schedule A list of accounts receivable organized by the length of time they have been unpaid. (p. 422)

Allowance for Doubtful Accounts A contra asset account that is deducted from gross account receivables to report receivables at their net realizable value. (p. 421)

Allowance method The method of accounting for bad debts that involves estimating uncollectible accounts at the end of each period. (p. 421)

Bad debt expense An expense account to record uncollectible receivables. (p. 420)

Collection period The average number of days that receivables are outstanding. It is calculated by dividing 365 days by the receivables turnover. (p. 432)

Default What happens when the maker of the note does not pay the note in full. Also referred to as dishonouring the note. (p. 420)

Dishonoured note A note that is not paid in full at maturity. (p. 429)

Factor A finance company or bank that buys receivables from businesses and then collects the payments directly from the customers. (p. 433)

Gross accounts receivable The total accounts receivable in the control account in the general ledger; includes both collectible and uncollectible accounts. (p. 422)

Maker The party making the promise to pay a promissory note. (p. 427)

Net realizable value The net amount of receivables expected to be collected. (p. 420)

Notes receivable Claims for which formal instruments (written instruments) of credit are issued as evidence of the debt. (p. 416)

Payee The party to whom payment is to be made. (p. 427)

Percentage of receivables approach The approach used to estimate uncollectible accounts where the allowance for

doubtful accounts is calculated as a percentage of receivables. (p. 421)

Promissory note A written promise to pay a specified amount of money on demand or at a definite time. (p. 427)

Receivables turnover ratio A measure of the liquidity of receivables, calculated by dividing net credit sales by average gross accounts receivable. (p. 431)

Securitization The transfer of receivables to a trust that holds them as an investment. This converts the receivables into securities. (p. 433)

Trade receivables Accounts and notes receivable that result from sales transactions. (p. 416)

▶ Self-Study Questions

Answers are at the end of the chapter.

(SO 1) AP 1. On August 10, Pi Company sells merchandise on account to Murray Co. for $2,000, terms 2/10, n/30. On August 15, Murray returns merchandise worth $400 to Pi. On August 20, payment is received from Murray for the balance due. What is the amount of cash received?
  (a) $1,560   (c) $1,568
  (b) $1,600   (d) $1,960

(SO 1) AP 2. Manery Company accepts a nonbank credit card on September 5 in payment of a $2,000 purchase. The credit card company charges a 2% fee. What is the amount recorded in accounts receivable on September 5?
  (a) $2,000   (c) $2,040
  (b) $1,960   (d) $0

(SO 2) AP 3. Kartik Company's accounts receivable are $200,000 at the end of the year. The allowance for doubtful accounts has a credit balance of $4,000 before any adjustments have been made. The company estimates that 5% of accounts receivable will not be collected. What is the net realizable value of the accounts receivable at the end of the year?
  (a) $196,000   (c) $186,000
  (b) $200,000   (d) $190,000

(SO 2) AP 4. Sanderson Company has a credit balance of $6,000 in Allowance for Doubtful Accounts before any adjustments are made. Based on an aging of its accounts receivable at the end of the period, the company estimates that $80,000 of its receivables are uncollectible. What is the amount of bad debt expense that should be reported for this accounting period?
  (a) $74,000   (c) $86,000
  (b) $6,000   (d) $80,000

(SO 2) AP 5. Use the same information as in question 4, except that Sanderson Company has a debit balance of

$6,000 in Allowance for Doubtful Accounts before any adjustments are made. In this situation, what is the amount of bad debt expense that should be reported for this accounting period?
  (a) $74,000   (c) $86,000
  (b) $6,000   (d) $80,000

(SO 2) AP 6. On January 1, 2014, the Allowance for Doubtful Accounts has a credit balance of $18,000. During 2014, $30,000 of uncollectible accounts receivable were written off. An aging schedule indicates that uncollectible accounts are $20,000 at the end of 2014. What is the required adjustment to the allowance for doubtful accounts at December 31, 2014?
  (a) $2,000   (c) $20,000
  (b) $8,000   (d) $32,000

(SO 2) AP 7. On January 1, 2014, Allowance for Doubtful Accounts had a credit balance of $40,000. In 2014, $30,000 of uncollectible accounts receivable were written off. On December 31, 2014, the company had accounts receivable of $900,000. Experience indicates that 4% of total receivables will become uncollectible. The adjusting journal entry that would be recorded on December 31, 2014, would be:

(a) Allowance for Doubtful Accounts	26,000	
Accounts Receivable		26,000
(b) Bad Debt Expense	36,000	
Accounts Receivable		36,000
(c) Bad Debt Expense	26,000	
Allowance for Doubtful Accounts		26,000
(d) Bad Debt Expense	36,000	
Allowance for Doubtful Accounts		36,000

(SO 3) AP 8. On June 1, Sorenson Co. accepts a $2,000, four-month, 6% promissory note in settlement of an account with Parton Co. Sorenson has a July 31 fiscal year end. The adjusting entry to record interest on July 31 is:

(a) Interest Receivable	20	
Interest Revenue		20
(b) Interest Receivable	120	
Interest Revenue		120
(c) Notes Receivable	120	
Unearned Interest Revenue		120
(d) Interest Receivable	40	
Interest Revenue		40

(SO 3) AP 9. Schlicht Co. holds Osgrove Inc.'s $10,000, four-month, 9% note. If no interest has been accrued, when the note is collected, the entry made by Schlicht Co. is:

(a) Cash	10,300	
Notes Receivable		10,300
(b) Cash	10,900	
Interest Revenue		900
Notes Receivable		10,000
(c) Accounts Receivable	10,300	
Notes Receivable		10,000
Interest Revenue		300
(d) Cash	10,300	
Notes Receivable		10,000
Interest Revenue		300

(SO 3) AP 10. When a note is dishonoured, an entry is made to:
(a) Reverse the interest revenue previously recognized.
(b) Record bad debt expense.
(c) Record an account receivable for the principal amount of the note and the accrued interest if the company expects to collect the amount owing.
(d) Write off the note whether or not the company expects to collect the amount owing.

(SO 4) C 11. The allowance for doubtful accounts is presented in the financial statements as:
(a) a current liability in the balance sheet.
(b) a deduction from accounts receivable in the balance sheet.
(c) a contra revenue account in the income statement.
(d) an operating expense in the income statement.

(SO 4) AP 12. Moore Company had net credit sales of $800,000 in the year and a cost of goods sold of $500,000. The balance in Accounts Receivable at the beginning of the year was $100,000 and at the end of the year it was $150,000. What were the receivables turnover and collection period ratios, respectively?
(a) 4.0 and 91 days
(b) 5.3 and 69 days
(c) 6.4 and 57 days
(d) 8.0 and 46 days

▶ Questions

(SO 1) C 1. When should a receivable be recorded for a service company? For a merchandising company?

(SO 1) K 2. Why are accounts receivable and notes receivable sometimes called trade receivables?

(SO 1) C 3. (a) What information does a company need to manage its accounts receivable? (b) How is this information tracked in an accounting system?

(SO 1) K 4. Under what circumstances is interest normally recorded for an account receivable?

(SO 1) C 5. Ernie Andrews thinks that a sale on a nonbank credit card should be recorded as a debit to cash, as cash will be received from the credit card company. Is Ernie correct? Explain.

(SO 2) C 6. Why can't a company know with certainty whether or not a customer will pay its account receivable?

(SO 2) C 7. ACCT Company has had significant bad debts in previous years. To eliminate the risk of bad debts, the accounting manager of ACCT Company has recommended to the sales manager to make only cash sales. The sales manager does not think this is the best business decision. Do you agree or disagree with the sales manager? What do you recommend the company do to reduce the risk of bad debts?

(SO 2) C 8. What is the net realizable value of accounts receivable? Why is it important that accounts receivable be reported at net realizable value?

(SO 2) K 9. Explain the allowance method of accounting for bad debts. How does this method result in (a) assets not being overstated, and (b) the matching of expenses with revenues?

(SO 2) C 10. (a) What is the purpose of the account Allowance for Doubtful Accounts? (b) Although the normal balance of this account is a credit balance, it sometimes has a debit balance. Explain how this can happen.

(SO 2) C 11. Dimitri doesn't understand why the bad debt expense reported in the income statement is usually not equal to the allowance for doubtful accounts reported in the balance sheet. Explain why this happens.

(SO 2) C 12. Zahra doesn't understand why bad debt expense is not increased when a specific customer account is determined to be uncollectible and written off. Explain.

(SO 2) C 13. What is an aging schedule? How is the aging schedule used to estimate the amount of uncollectibles?

(SO 2) C 14. When an account receivable that was written off is later collected, two journal entries are usually made. Explain why.

(SO 3) K 15. Explain how notes receivable and accounts receivable are the same and how they are different.

(SO 3) C 16. Why will a company take a note receivable from a customer in settlement of a late account receivable?

(SO 3) C 17. Danielle does not understand why a note receivable is not immediately recorded at its maturity value (principal plus interest). After all, you know you are going to collect both the principal amount and the interest and you know how much each will be. Explain to Danielle why notes are not recorded at their maturity value.

(SO 3) C 18. What does it mean if a note is dishonoured?

(SO 3) C 19. How would the entries differ if a note receivable is dishonoured and eventual collection is expected versus a note receivable where collection is not expected?

(SO 4) C 20. Mac Leonard is preparing the financial statements and has reported the Allowance for Doubtful Accounts in the current liabilities section of the balance sheet because the normal balance of the allowance is a credit. Do you agree with this treatment? Explain.

(SO 4) C 21. Saucier Company has accounts receivable, notes receivable due in three months, notes receivable due in two years, an allowance for doubtful accounts, sales taxes recoverable, and income tax receivable. How should the receivables be reported on the balance sheet?

(SO 4) C 22. The president of Unlimited Enterprises proudly announces that her company's liquidity has improved. Its current ratio increased substantially this year. Does an increase in the current ratio always indicate improved liquidity? What other ratio(s) might you review to determine whether or not the increase in the current ratio represents an improvement in the company's financial health?

(SO 4) C 23. Canadian Worldwide Communications Co.'s receivables turnover was 6.5 times in 2013 and 5.9 times in 2014. Has the company's receivables management improved or worsened?

(SO 4) C 24. Why might a company not want to have a receivables turnover that is significantly higher than that of its competitors?

(SO 4) K 25. Why do companies sometimes sell their receivables?

▶ Brief Exercises

Identify impact of transaction on receivables, total assets, liabilities, and owner's equity. (SO 1) K

BE8–1 Seven transactions follow. For each transaction, indicate if the transaction increases, decreases, or has no effect on (a) accounts receivable, (b) notes receivable, (c) total assets, (d) total liabilities, and (e) owner's equity. Use the following format, in which the first transaction is given as an example:

Transaction:	(a) Accounts Receivable	(b) Notes Receivable	(c) Total Assets	(d) Total Liabilities	(e) Owner's Equity
1. Performed services on account for a customer.	Increase	No effect	Increase	No effect	Increase
2. A customer paid cash for services to be provided next month.					
3. Performed services for a customer in exchange for a note.					
4. Collected cash from the customer in transaction 1. above.					
5. Performed services for a customer for cash.					
6. Extended a customer's account for three months by accepting a note in exchange for it.					
7. Performed services for a customer who had paid in advance.					

Record accounts receivable transactions. (SO 1) AP

BE8–2 Record the following transactions on the books of Marsh Co:

(a) On September 1, Marsh Co. sold merchandise on account to Pellerin Inc. for $20,000, terms 2/10, n/30. The cost of the merchandise sold was $12,000. Marsh Co. uses a perpetual inventory system.
(b) On September 4, Pellerin Inc. returned merchandise worth $4,000 to Marsh Co. The original cost of the merchandise was $2,400. The merchandise was returned to inventory.
(c) On September 10, Pellerin Inc. paid for the merchandise.

Record accounts receivable transactions. (SO 1) AP

BE8–3 Record the following transactions on the books of Fowler Co.:

(a) On May 1, Fowler Co. sold merchandise on account to Kaneva Inc. for $30,000, terms 2/10, n/30. Ignore any entries that affect inventory and cost of goods sold for purposes of this question.
(b) On May 6, Kaneva Inc. returned merchandise worth $6,000 to Fowler Co.

(c) On June 30, Fowler Co. charged Kaneva Inc. one month's interest for the overdue account. Fowler charges 10% on overdue accounts. (Round calculation to the nearest dollar.)

(d) On July 5, Kaneva paid the amount owing to Fowler Co.

BE8-4   Imports to You Co. accepted a credit card in payment of a $600 purchase of merchandise on August 7. For each of the following assumptions, prepare the journal entry to record the sale.

Record credit card transactions. (SO 1) AP

(a) The customer used a nonbank card and the company charges a 3% fee.

(b) The customer used a Visa card and Visa charges a 3% fee.

(c) The customer used an Imports to You Co. credit card.

BE8-5   Gourdeau Co. uses an aging schedule to determine its estimated uncollectible accounts at December 31. Complete the following schedule and determine the required balance in the allowance for doubtful accounts and the net realizable value of the accounts receivable.

Complete aging schedule and determine the allowance and net realizable value. (SO 2) AP

Number of Days Outstanding	Accounts Receivable	Estimated % Uncollectible	Estimated Uncollectible Accounts
0–30 days	$265,000	1%	
31–60 days	70,000	4%	
61–90 days	45,000	10%	
Over 90 days	20,000	20%	
Total	$400,000		

BE8-6   Refer to the data in BE8-5 for Gourdeau Co.

Determine bad debt expense. (SO 2) AP

(a) Assuming the allowance for doubtful accounts has an unadjusted credit balance of $4,500 at December 31, what is the bad debt expense for the year?

(b) Assume instead that the allowance for doubtful accounts had a debit balance of $2,500. What is the bad debt expense for the year?

BE8-7   Qinshan estimates that 4% of total accounts receivable will become uncollectible. Accounts receivable at December 31, 2014, are $250,000.

Determine the allowance and net realizable value and record bad debts. (SO 2) AP

(a) Determine the required balance in the allowance for doubtful accounts and the net realizable value of the accounts receivable.

(b) The allowance for doubtful accounts has an unadjusted debit balance of $1,500 at December 31, 2014. Prepare the adjusting entry to record bad debt expense in 2014.

(c) Assume instead that the allowance has an unadjusted credit balance of $500 at December 31, 2014. Prepare the adjusting entry to record bad debt expense.

BE8-8   Stilton Company reported the following in its general ledger. Using your knowledge of receivable transactions, match each of the transactions (a) to (f) with the best description of the economic event.

Analyze accounts receivable transactions. (SO 2) AP

Accounts Receivable			
Jan. 1	20,000	(b)	80,000
(a)	120,000	(c)	500
Dec. 31	59,500		
(e)	500	(f)	500

Service Revenue		
	120,000	(a)

Allowance for Doubtful Accounts			
		Jan. 1.	2,000
(c)	500	(d)	900
		Dec. 31	2,400
		(e)	500

Bad Debt Expense		
(d)	900	

1. Collect previously written-off account _____
2. Provide service on account _____
3. Write off uncollectible account _____
4. Collect accounts receivable _____
5. Record bad debt expense _____
6. Reverse previously written-off account _____

Record write off and compare net realizable value. (SO 2) AP

BE8–9   At the end of 2014, Perry Co. has an allowance for doubtful accounts of $28,000. On January 31, 2015, when it has accounts receivable of $575,000, Perry Co. learns that its $5,500 receivable from Young Inc. is not collectible. Management authorizes a write off.

(a) Record the write off.

(b) What is the net realizable value of the accounts receivable (1) before the write off, and (2) after the write off?

Record collection of account previously written off. (SO 2) AP

Calculate interest on notes receivable. (SO 3) AP

BE8–10   Assume the same information as in BE8–9. Young Inc.'s financial difficulties are over. On June 4, 2014, Perry Co. receives a payment in full of $5,500 from Young Inc. Record this transaction.

BE8–11   Hochelaga Co. has three outstanding notes receivable at its December 31, 2014, fiscal year end. For each note, calculate (a) total interest revenue, (b) interest revenue to be recorded in 2014, and (c) interest revenue to be recorded in 2015.

Issue Date	Term	Principal	Interest Rate
1. August 31, 2014	9 months	$15,000	6%
2. November 1, 2014	6 months	44,000	8%
3. October 1, 2014	15 months	30,000	7%

Record notes receivable transactions. (SO 3) AP

BE8–12   Alikhan Co. sold merchandise on account to Emerald Co. for $42,000, terms n/30, on April 1, 2014. Alikhan uses a perpetual inventory system and the merchandise had a cost of $25,200. On June 1, 2014, Emerald gave Alikhan a six-month, 6% promissory note in settlement of the account. Interest is to be paid at maturity. On December 1, Emerald paid the note and accrued interest. Record the above transactions for Alikhan Co. Alikhan Co. has a July 31 fiscal year end and adjusts its accounts annually.

Record notes receivable transactions. (SO 3) AP

BE8–13   Lee Company accepts a $27,000, four-month, 6% note receivable in settlement of an account receivable on June 1, 2014. Interest is to be paid at maturity. Lee Company has a December 31 year end and adjusts its accounts annually.

(a) Record (1) the issue of the note on June 1 and (2) the settlement of the note on October 1, assuming the note is honoured.

(b) Assume instead that the note is dishonoured but eventual collection is expected. Record the October 1 journal entry.

(c) Assume instead that the note is dishonoured and eventual collection is not expected. Record the October 1 journal entry.

Record notes receivable transactions and indicate statement presentation. (SO 3, 4) AP

BE8–14   Chanticlerc Co. lent Sharp Inc. $100,000 cash in exchange for a five-year, 4% note on July 1, 2014. Interest is payable quarterly on January 1, April 1, July 1, and October 1 each year. Chanticlerc Co. has a December 31 year end.

(a) Record Chanticlerc's entries related to the note to January 1, 2015.

(b) Indicate what amounts will be reported in Chanticlerc's December 31, 2014, balance sheet and where the amounts will be classified.

Prepare current assets section. (SO 4) AP

BE8–15   WAF Company's general ledger included the following accounts at November 30, 2014:

Accounts payable	$145,500
Accounts receivable	109,000
Allowance for doubtful accounts	6,950
Bad debt expense	35,970
Cash	74,000
GST recoverable	21,850
Interest receivable	2,500
Interest revenue	10,000
Merchandise inventory	110,800
Note receivable—due April 23, 2015	50,000
Note receivable—due May 21, 2018	150,000
Prepaid expenses	15,300
Short-term investments	80,500

Prepare the current assets section of the balance sheet.

Prepare current assets section. (SO 4) AN

BE8–16   The financial statements of **Maple Leaf Foods Inc.** reported the following for the years ended December 31, 2011, 2010, and 2009.

Financial Statement Data (in thousands of dollars)			
	2011	2010	2009
Sales	$4,893,624	$4,968,119	$5,221,602
Accounts receivable	133,504	108,379	372,330

(a) Calculate Maple Leaf's receivables turnover and collection period for 2011 and 2010.

(b) Has the company's liquidity improved or weakened?

▶ Exercises

E8–1 Selected transactions for Theatre Productions follow. Theatre Productions uses a perpetual inventory system.

Identify impact and record accounts receivable transactions. (SO 1) AP

May	8	Sold merchandise costing $5,980 to Grande Theatre for $13,000, terms 2/10, n/30.
	10	Grande returned $1,000 of the merchandise. This merchandise had originally cost Theatre $460 and was returned to inventory.
	18	Grande paid Theatre the amount owing.
	19	Sold merchandise costing $3,600 to Summer Productions for $6,000, terms 1/10, n/30.
	20	Summer Productions returned $500 of the merchandise because it was damaged. The merchandise had originally cost Theatre Productions $300. Theatre Productions scrapped the merchandise.
July	19	Added interest charges for one month to the amount owing by Summer Productions. Theatre charges 15% on outstanding receivables.
	22	Summer Productions paid the amount owing.

Instructions

(a) For each of these transactions, indicate if the transaction has increased (+) or decreased (−) cash, accounts receivable, inventory, and owner's equity and by how much. If the item is not changed, write NE to indicate there is no effect. Use the following format, in which the first one has been done for you as an example.

Transaction Date	Cash	Accounts Receivable	Inventory	Owner's Equity
May 8	NE	+$13,000	−$5,980	+$7,020

(b) Prepare journal entries to record the above transactions.

E8–2 Transactions follow for the Extreme Sports Ltd. store and three of its customers in the company's first month of business:

Record accounts receivable transactions. Post to subsidiary and general ledgers. (SO 1) AP

June	3	Ben Kidd used his Extreme Sports credit card to purchase $1,050 of merchandise.
	6	Biljana Pavic used her Extreme Sports credit card to purchase $840 of merchandise.
	8	Biljana Pavic returned $210 of merchandise on credit.
	9	Nicole Montpetit purchased $421 of merchandise and paid for it with Visa. Visa charges a 2% service fee.
	18	Ben Kidd used his Extreme Sports credit card to purchase an additional $348 of merchandise.
	19	Bonnie Cutcliffe used her debit card to purchase $230 of merchandise. There is a $0.50 service charge on all debit card transactions.
	20	Biljana Pavic made a $315 payment on her credit card account.
	23	Nicole Montpetit used her Extreme Sports credit card to purchase $498 of merchandise.
	25	Ben Kidd paid the amount owing on his June 3 purchase.
	30	Biljana Pavic used her Extreme Sports credit card to purchase $420 of merchandise.

Instructions

(a) Record the above transactions. Ignore any inventory or cost of goods sold entries for purposes of this question.
(b) Set up T accounts for the Accounts Receivable general ledger (control) account and for the Accounts Receivable subsidiary ledger accounts. Post the journal entries to these accounts.
(c) Prepare a list of customers and the balances of their accounts from the subsidiary ledger. Prove that the total of the subsidiary ledger is equal to the control account balance.

E8–3 Krazy Hair Salon accepts its own credit card, as well as debit cards and bank and nonbank credit cards. Krazy is charged 3.5% for all bank credit card transactions, 4.25% for all nonbank credit card transactions, and $0.50 per transaction for all debit card transactions. In October and November 2014, the following summary transactions occurred:

Record credit card transactions and indicate statement presentation. (SO 1, 4) AP

Oct.	15	Performed services totalling $15,000 for customers who used Krazy credit cards.
	20	Performed services totalling $7,500 for customers who used Visa credit cards.
	30	Performed services totalling $2,000 for customers who used nonbank credit cards.
	31	Performed services totalling $5,000 for customers who used debit cards (100 transactions).
Nov.	15	Collected $9,000 on Krazy credit cards.
	18	Collected the amount owing from the nonbank credit card companies for the October 30 transactions.
	30	Added interest charges of 24% to outstanding Krazy credit card balances. Interest is charged after 30 days from date of purchase.

Instructions

(a) Record the above transactions for Krazy Hair Salon.

(b) In addition to these transactions, Krazy Hair Salon had rent expense of $4,000, supplies expense of $500, and salary expense of $5,000 for the months of October and November. Prepare a multi-step income statement for Krazy Hair Salon for the two months ended November 30.

Calculate net realizable value and record bad debts.
(SO 2) AP

E8-4 Assen Company's general ledger at December 31, 2014, the end of the current year, shows Accounts Receivable $210,000 and Allowance for Doubtful Accounts $1,300 (credit). Uncollectible accounts are estimated to be 10% of accounts receivable.

Instructions

(a) Calculate the net realizable value of the accounts receivable.
(b) Record the adjusting journal entry at December 31, 2014.
(c) Assume instead that the Allowance for Doubtful Accounts had a debit balance of $2,800 at December 31, 2014. What is the net realizable value of the accounts receivable at December 31, 2014, and what is bad debt expense for 2014?

Prepare aging schedule and record bad debts. (SO 2) AP

E8-5 Rowen Company has accounts receivable of $241,000 at September 30, 2015. An analysis of the accounts shows the following:

Month of Sale	Balance
September	$170,000
August	35,700
July	20,000
April, May, and June	15,300
	$241,000

Credit terms are 2/10, n/30. On October 1, 2014, the Allowance for Doubtful Accounts had a credit balance of $17,600. During the year, the company wrote off accounts receivable of $19,000 as uncollectible. The company uses an aging schedule to estimate uncollectible accounts. The company's percentage estimates of bad debts are as follows:

Number of Days Outstanding	Estimated % Uncollectible
0–30	1%
31–60	10%
61–90	25%
Over 90	60%

Instructions

(a) Prepare an aging schedule to determine the total estimated uncollectible accounts at September 30, 2015.
(b) What is the net realizable value of the accounts receivable at September 30, 2015?
(c) Prepare the adjusting entry at September 30 to record bad debt expense.

Determine missing amounts and describe the accounts receivable transactions.
(SO 1, 2) AP

E8-6 Chelsea Corporation reported the following information in its general ledger at December 31.

Accounts Receivable			
Beg. bal.	15,000	35,200	
	(1)	(2)	
End. bal.	(3)		

Sale	
	45,000

Allowance for Doubtful Accounts			
		Beg. bal.	1,200
	800		(4)
		End. bal.	(5)

Bad Debt Expense	
(4)	

All sales were on account. At the end of the year, uncollectible accounts were estimated to be 10% of accounts receivable.

Instructions

(a) Using your knowledge of receivables transactions, determine the missing amounts. (*Hint:* You may find it helpful to reconstruct the journal entries.)
(b) Describe each transaction that has been recorded.
(c) What is the amount of cash collected?

Record bad debts, write off, and collection of previously written-off account; calculate net realizable value.
(SO 2) AP

E8-7 Accounts receivable transactions are provided below for J Looney Co.

Dec. 31, 2014   The company estimated that 5% of its accounts receivable would become uncollectible. The balances in the accounts receivable account and allowance for doubtful accounts were $650,000 and $2,300 (debit), respectively.

Mar. 5, 2015	The company determined that R. Black's $3,700 account and D. Wight's $6,900 account were uncollectible. The company's accounts receivable were $685,000 before the accounts were written off.
June 6, 2015	Wight paid his account that had been written off on March 5. The company's accounts receivable were $641,000 prior to recording the cash receipt for Wight.

Instructions

(a) Prepare the journal entries on December 31, 2014, March 5, 2015, and June 6, 2015.

(b) Post the journal entries to Allowance for Doubtful Accounts and calculate the new balance after each entry.

(c) Calculate the net realizable value of accounts receivable both before and after writing off the two accounts on March 5, 2015.

(d) Calculate the net realizable value of the accounts receivable both before and after recording the cash receipt from Wight on June 6, 2015.

E8–8 Data on three promissory notes accepted by Levin Ltd. during 2014 follow.

Calculate interest. (SO 3) AP

Date of Note	Term in Months	Principal	Interest Rate	Total Interest	Interest Revenue to Record for Year Ended December 31
Oct. 1	3	$180,000	10%	(c)	(d)
Aug. 1	6	120,000	(b)	$4,800	(e)
Nov. 1	24	(a)	6%	12,000	(f)

Instructions

Determine the missing amounts.

E8–9 Passera Supply Co. has the following transactions:

Record notes receivable transactions. (SO 3) AP

Nov.	1	Loaned $60,000 cash to A. Morgan on a one-year, 8% note.
	15	Sold goods to H. Giorgi on account for $12,000, terms n/30. The goods cost Passera $7,500. Passera uses the perpetual inventory system.
Dec.	1	Sold goods to Wrightman, Inc., receiving a $21,000, three-month, 6% note. The goods cost Passera $14,000.
	15	H. Giorgi was unable to pay her account. Giorgi gave Passera a six-month, 7% note in settlement of her account.
	31	Accrued interest revenue on all notes receivable. Interest is due at maturity.
Mar.	1	Collected the amount owing on the Wrightman note.
June	15	H. Giorgi defaults on the note. Future payment is expected.

Instructions

Record the transactions for Passera Supply Co. (Round calculations to the nearest dollar.)

E8–10 The following are notes receivable transactions for Rather Co.:

Record notes receivable transactions. (SO 3) AP

May	1	Received a $15,000, six-month, 6% note from Jioux Company in settlement of an account receivable. Interest is due at maturity.
June	30	Accrued interest on the Jioux note, at Rather's year end. Adjustments are recorded annually.
July	31	Lent $2,000 cash to an employee, Noreen Irvine, receiving a three-month, 5% note. Interest is due at the end of each month.
Aug.	31	Received the interest due from Ms. Irvine.
Sept.	30	Received the interest due from Ms. Irvine.
Oct.	31	Received payment in full for the employee note from Ms. Irvine.
Nov.	1	Jioux Company defaults on its note. Rather does not expect to collect on the note.

Instructions

Record the transactions for Rather Co. (Round calculations to the nearest dollar.)

E8–11 Ni Co. has the following notes receivable outstanding at December 31, 2014:

Record notes receivable transactions and indicate statement presentation. (SO 3, 4) AP

Issue Date	Term	Principal	Interest Rate
1. August 31, 2013	2 years	$15,000	4%
2. October 1, 2013	18 months	46,000	5%
3. February 1, 2014	1 year	32,000	4%
4. May 31, 2014	5 years	22,000	6%
5. October 31, 2014	7 months	9,000	5%

For notes with terms of one year or longer, interest is payable on the first day of each month, for interest earned the previous month. For notes with terms less than one year, interest is payable at maturity.

Instructions

(a) Calculate the interest revenue that Ni Co. will report on its income statement for the year ended December 31, 2014. Indicate where this will be presented on the income statement. (Round calculations to the nearest dollar.)

(b) Calculate the amounts related to these notes that will be reported on Ni Co.'s balance sheet at December 31, 2014. Indicate where they will be presented. Assume all required interest payments have been received on time. (Round calculations to the nearest dollar.)

Record bad debts, prepare partial balance sheet, and calculate ratios. (SO 2, 4) AP

E8-12 In its first year of operations, AJS Company had sales of $4 million (all on credit) and cost of goods sold of $1,750,000. Sales allowances of $100,000 were given on substandard merchandise. During the year, the company collected $3.2 million cash on account. At year end, December 31, 2014, the credit manager estimates that 4% of the accounts receivable will become uncollectible.

At December 31, 2014, the balances in selected other accounts were:

Accounts payable	$350,000
Cash	40,000
Interest receivable	1,125
Interest revenue	2,250
Merchandise inventory	325,000
Notes receivable, due April 10, 2017	45,000
Prepaid insurance	8,000
Short-term investments	50,000
Unearned sales revenue	25,000

Instructions

(a) Prepare the journal entry to record the bad debt expense.

(b) Prepare the current assets section of the balance sheet for AJS Company at December 31, 2014.

(c) Calculate the receivables turnover and collection period. (Remember that this is the end of the first year of business.)

Calculate ratios and comment. (SO 4) AN

E8-13 The following information (in millions) was taken from the December 31 financial statements of **Canadian National Railway Company**:

	2011	2010	2009
Accounts receivable, gross	$ 836	$ 796	$ 831
Allowance for doubtful accounts	16	21	34
Accounts receivable, net	820	775	797
Revenues	9,028	8,297	7,367
Total current assets	1,848	1,590	1,490
Total current liabilities	1,715	1,906	1,237

Instructions

(a) Calculate the 2011 and 2010 current ratios.

(b) Calculate the receivables turnover and average collection period for 2011 and 2010.

(c) Comment on any improvement or weakening in CN's liquidity and its management of accounts receivable.

▶ Problems: Set A

Record accounts receivable transactions. Post to subsidiary and general ledgers and prepare adjusting entry. (SO 1, 2) AP

P8-1A At December 31, 2014, the general ledger and subsidiary ledger for Albert's, a small auto parts store, showed the following:

General Ledger		Accounts Receivable Subsidiary Ledger	
Accounts receivable	$75,000	Best Auto Repair	$ 3,800
Allowance for doubtful accounts	3,750	Brown's Repair	23,000
		Custom Repair	0
		Jen's Auto Body	35,000
		Luxury Autos	13,200
		Total	$75,000

Jan. 3   Brown's Repair paid $18,000 on its account.
     4   Custom Repair paid $1,400 on its account that had previously been written off.
     8   Jen's Auto Body purchased $3,800 of merchandise on account.
     9   Antique Auto Repair paid cash for $1,500 of merchandise.
    18   Jen's Auto Body returned $800 of merchandise.
    19   Luxury Autos paid $13,200 on its account.
    20   Jen's Auto Body paid $25,000 on its account.
    23   Brown's Repair purchased $5,600 on account.
    25   Custom Repair purchased $10,000 of merchandise on Visa.
    26   Luxury Autos purchased $18,000 of merchandise on account.
    31   Albert's determined that the Best Auto Repair account receivable was not collectible.

Instructions

(a) Record the above transactions. Ignore credit card fees and any entries to inventory or cost of goods sold for purposes of this question.
(b) Set up T accounts for the Accounts Receivable general ledger (control) account, the Allowance for Doubtful Accounts general ledger account, and the Accounts Receivable subsidiary ledger accounts. Post the journal entries to these accounts.
(c) Albert's estimated that 10% of accounts receivable is not collectible. Record the required adjustment to the allowance for doubtful accounts.
(d) Prepare a list of customers and the balances of their accounts from the subsidiary ledger. Prove that the total of the subsidiary ledger is equal to the control account balance.

TAKING IT FURTHER   What types of errors could result in the total of the account balances in the subsidiary ledger not agreeing with the general ledger control account?

P8–2A   Silk Co. reported the following information on its December 31, 2014, balance sheet:

Accounts receivable	$760,000
Less: Allowance for doubtful accounts	76,000

Record accounts receivable and bad debt transactions; show balance sheet presentation. (SO 1, 2, 4) AP

During 2015, the company had the following transactions related to receivables:

1. Sales on account, $2,800,000
2. Sales returns and allowances, $325,000
3. Collections of accounts receivable, $2,410,000
4. Interest added to overdue accounts, $72,000
5. Write offs of accounts considered uncollectible, $58,400
6. Collection of accounts previously written off as uncollectible, $5,200

Instructions

(a) Prepare the summary journal entries to record each of these six transactions.
(b) Enter the December 31, 2014, balances in the Accounts Receivable and Allowance for Doubtful Accounts general ledger accounts, post the entries to the two accounts, and determine the balances.
(c) Calculate the net realizable value of accounts receivable at December 31, 2015. Uncollectible accounts are estimated at 10% of accounts receivable.
(d) Prepare the journal entry to record bad debt expense for 2015.
(e) Show the balance sheet presentation of the receivables as at December 31, 2015.

TAKING IT FURTHER   For several years, Silk Co. has estimated uncollectible accounts at 10% of accounts receivable. Discuss whether or not the company should continue to do this at December 31, 2015.

P8–3A   At the beginning of the current period, Huang Co. had a balance of $100,000 in Accounts Receivable and a $7,000 credit balance in Allowance for Doubtful Accounts. In the period, it had net credit sales of $400,000 and collections of $361,500. It wrote off accounts receivable of $10,500 as uncollectible. After a $1,750 account was written off as uncollectible, it was subsequently collected. This is in addition to the other cash collections. Based on an aging schedule, uncollectible accounts are estimated to be $8,000 at the end of the period.

Record accounts receivable and bad debt transactions; show financial statement presentation. (SO 1, 2, 4) AP

Instructions

(a) Record sales and collections in the period.
(b) Record the write off of uncollectible accounts in the period.
(c) Record the collection of the account previously written off as uncollectible.
(d) Record the bad debt expense adjusting entry for the period.
(e) Show the balance sheet presentation of the receivables at the end of the period.
(f) What is the amount of bad debt expense on the income statement for the period?

TAKING IT FURTHER   Why is bad debt expense not increased when an account receivable is written off because it is determined to be uncollectible?

Calculate bad debt amounts and answer questions. (SO 2) AP

P8–4A Information on Hohenberger Company for 2014 follows:

Total credit sales	$1,000,000
Accounts receivable at December 31	400,000
Uncollectible accounts written off	17,500
Amount collected on accounts previously written off (after write off but before year end)	2,500

Instructions

(a) Assume that Hohenberger Company decides to estimate its uncollectible accounts using the allowance method and an aging schedule. Uncollectible accounts are estimated to be $24,000. What amount of bad debt expense will Hohenberger Company record if Allowance for Doubtful Accounts had an opening balance of $20,000 on January 1, 2014?

(b) Assume the same facts as in (a) except that the Allowance for Doubtful Accounts had a $12,000 balance on January 1, 2014. What amount of bad debt expense will Hohenberger record on December 31, 2014?

(c) How does the amount of accounts written off during the period affect the amount of bad debt expense recorded at the end of the period?

(d) How does the collection of an account that had previously been written off affect the net realizable value of accounts receivable?

TAKING IT FURTHER Why doesn't a company sell to only those customers it knows for sure it can collect from?

Prepare aging schedule and record bad debts and explain method. (SO 2) AP

P8–5A Pearson Company uses the allowance method to estimate uncollectible accounts receivable. The company produced the following information from aging its accounts receivable at year end:

		Number of Days Outstanding			
	Total	0–30	31–60	61–90	91–120
Accounts receivable	$640,000	$360,000	$140,000	$100,000	$40,000
Estimated % uncollectible		2%	5%	10%	30%
Estimated uncollectible accounts					

The unadjusted balance in Allowance for Doubtful Accounts is a debit of $3,000.

Instructions

(a) Complete the aging schedule and calculate the total estimated uncollectible accounts.

(b) Record the bad debt adjusting entry using the information determined in (a).

(c) In the following year, $18,000 of the outstanding accounts receivable is determined to be uncollectible. Record the write off of the uncollectible accounts.

(d) The company collects $4,500 of the $18,000 of accounts that was determined to be uncollectible in (c). The company also expects to collect an additional $1,000. Record the journal entry (or entries) to restore the accounts receivable and the cash collected. Collection of the $1,000 is expected in the near future.

(e) Explain how using the allowance method matches expenses with revenues.

(f) Explain how using the allowance method values Accounts Receivable at net realizable value on the balance sheet.

TAKING IT FURTHER What are the advantages and disadvantages to the company of using an aging schedule to estimate uncollectible accounts, as compared with estimating uncollectible accounts as 10% of total accounts receivable?

Prepare aging schedule and record bad debts. (SO 2) AP

P8–6A An aging analysis of Hagiwara Company's accounts receivable at December 31, 2014 and 2015, showed the following:

Number of Days Outstanding	Estimated % Uncollectible	Accounts Receivable	
		2015	2014
0–30 days	3%	$115,000	$145,000
31–60 days	6%	35,000	63,000
61–90 days	12%	45,000	38,000
Over 90 days	25%	80,000	24,000
Total		$275,000	$270,000

Additional information:

1. At December 31, 2014, the unadjusted balance in Allowance for Doubtful Accounts was a credit of $6,600.

2. In 2015, $23,500 of accounts was written off as uncollectible and $2,200 of accounts previously written off was collected.

Instructions

(a) Prepare an aging schedule to calculate the estimated uncollectible accounts at December 31, 2014, and at December 31, 2015.
(b) Calculate the net realizable value of Hagiwara's accounts receivable at December 31, 2014, and December 31, 2015.
(c) Record the following:
   1. The adjusting entry on December 31, 2014
   2. The write off of uncollectible accounts in 2015
   3. The collection in 2015 of accounts previously written off
   4. The adjusting entry on December 31, 2015

TAKING IT FURTHER   What are the implications of the changes in the age of the receivables from 2014 to 2015?

P8–7A   The following information was reported in Nenshi Company's general ledger at September 30:

Determine missing amounts.
(SO 2) AN

Accounts Receivable				Sales		
Beg.	bal.	845,000	(b)			5,370,000
		(a)	(c)			
		4,200	(f)			
End.	bal.	(d)				

Allowance for Doubtful Accounts				Bad Debt Expense	
			Beg. bal. 76,050	(e)	
	50,400		(e)		
			(b)		
		End. bal. 83,475			

All sales were made on account. Uncollectible accounts are estimated to be 9% of accounts receivable.

Instructions

Determine the missing amounts in Nenshi Company's accounts. State what each of these amounts represents. You will not be able to determine the missing items in alphabetical order. (To solve this problem, it might help if you reconstruct the journal entries.)

TAKING IT FURTHER   Explain the differences between bad debt expense and the allowance for doubtful accounts.

P8–8A   Bassano Company prepares monthly financial statements and estimates its uncollectible accounts at the end of each month. Bassano Company has an October 31 fiscal year end, closes temporary accounts annually, and uses a perpetual inventory system.

Identify impact of accounts receivable and bad debt transactions; determine statement presentation.
(SO 1, 2, 4) AP

On August 31, 2014, after completing its month-end adjustments, it had accounts receivable of $74,500, a credit balance of $1,480 in Allowance for Doubtful Accounts, and bad debt expense of $9,860. In September and October, the following occurred:

September
1. Sold $56,300 of merchandise on account; the cost of the merchandise was $25,335.
2. A total of $900 of the merchandise sold on account was returned. These customers were issued credit memos. The cost of the merchandise was $400 and it was returned to inventory.
3. Collected $59,200 cash on account from customers.
4. Interest charges of $800 were charged to outstanding accounts receivable.
5. Recorded the monthly adjustment for bad debts. Uncollectible accounts were estimated to be 4% of accounts receivable.

October
1. Credit sales in the month were $66,300; the cost of the merchandise was $28,700.
2. Received $350 cash from a customer whose account had been written off in July.
3. Collected $58,500 cash, in addition to the cash collected in (2) above, from customers on account.
4. Wrote off $7,500 of accounts receivable as uncollectible.
5. Interest charges of $700 were charged to outstanding accounts receivable.
6. Recorded the year-end adjustment for bad debts. Uncollectible accounts were estimated to be 4% of accounts receivable.

Instructions

(a) For each of these transactions, indicate if the transaction has increased (+) or decreased (−) Cash, Accounts Receivable, Allowance for Doubtful Accounts, Inventory, Total Assets, and Owner's Equity and by how much. If the item is not changed, write NE to indicate there is no effect. Use the following format, in which the first one has been done for you as an example.

Transaction	Cash	Accounts Receivable	Allowance for Doubtful Accounts	Inventory	Total Assets	Owner's Equity
September:						
1.	NE	+$56,300	NE	−$25,335	+$30,965	+$30,965

(b) Show how accounts receivable will appear on the October 31, 2014, balance sheet.
(c) What amount will be reported as bad debt expense on the income statement for the year ended October 31, 2014?

TAKING IT FURTHER If Bassano's credit manager increases the amount of credit checking the company does before granting credit on all of its customers, will that eliminate the bad debts? Explain.

Record receivables transactions. (SO 1, 3) AP

P8–9A Ku Company has an April 30 fiscal year end and adjusts accounts annually. Selected transactions in the year included the following:

Jan.	2	Sold $24,000 of merchandise to Richards Company, terms n/30. The cost of the goods sold was $14,400. Ku uses the perpetual inventory system.
Feb.	1	Accepted a $24,000, four-month, 5% promissory note from Richards Company for the balance due. (See January 2 transaction.) Interest is payable at maturity.
	15	Sold $15,000 of merchandise costing $9,000 to Garrison Company and accepted Garrison's three-month, 5% note in payment. Interest is payable at maturity.
Mar.	15	Sold $12,000 of merchandise to Mantha Co., terms n/30. The cost of the merchandise sold was $7,200.
Apr.	30	Accepted a $12,000, two-month, 7% note from Mantha Co. for its balance due. Interest is payable at maturity. (See March 15 transaction.)
	30	Accrued interest at year end.
May	15	Collected the Garrison note in full. (See February 15 transaction.)
June	1	Collected the Richards Company note in full. (See February 1 transaction.)
June	30	Mantha Co. dishonours its note of April 30. Mantha Co. is bankrupt and there is no hope of future settlement.
July	13	Sold $6,000 merchandise costing $3,600 to Zorilla Inc. and accepted Zorilla's $6,000, three-month, 7% note for the amount due, with interest payable at maturity.
Oct.	13	The Zorilla Inc. note was dishonoured. (See July 13 transaction.) It is expected that Zorilla will eventually pay the amount owed.

Instructions

Record the above transactions. (Round calculations to the nearest dollar.)

TAKING IT FURTHER What are the advantages and disadvantages of Ku Company accepting notes receivable from its customers?

Record note receivable transactions; show balance sheet presentation. (SO 3, 4) AP

P8–10A Tardif Company adjusts its books monthly. On September 30, 2014, notes receivable include the following:

Issue Date	Maker	Principal	Interest	Term
Aug. 1, 2013	RJF Inc.	$19,000	4.5%	2.5 years
Mar. 31, 2014	Resolute Co.	17,000	5.0%	7 months
May 31, 2014	Imaging Ltd.	17,500	5.5%	18 months
Aug. 31, 2014	Dragon Co.	6,000	8.5%	2 months
Sept. 30, 2014	MGH Corp.	20,500	6.0%	16 months

Interest is payable on the first day of each month for notes with terms of one year or longer. Interest is payable at maturity for notes with terms less than one year. In October, the following transactions were completed:

Oct. 1   Received payment of the interest due from RJF Inc.
     1   Received payment of the interest due from Imaging Ltd.
     31   Received notice that the Dragon Co. note had been dishonoured. (Assume that Dragon is
          expected to pay in the future.)
     31   Collected the amount owing from Resolute Co.

Instructions

(a) Calculate the balance in the Interest Receivable and Notes Receivable accounts at September 30, 2014.
(b) Record the October transactions and the October 31 adjusting entry for accrued interest receivable.
(c) Enter the balances at October 1 in the receivables accounts, and post the entries to the receivables accounts.
(d) Show the balance sheet presentation of the interest and notes receivable accounts at October 31.
(e) How would the journal entry on October 31 be different if Dragon were not expected to pay in the future?

TAKING IT FURTHER   The interest rate for the Dragon note is higher than the other notes. Why might that have been the case?

P8–11A   Tocksfor Company's general ledger included the following selected accounts (in thousands) at September 30, 2014:

Prepare assets section of balance sheet; calculate and interpret ratios. (SO 4) AN

Accounts payable	$1,077.3
Accounts receivable	590.4
Accumulated depreciation—equipment	858.7
Allowance for doubtful accounts	35.4
Bad debt expense	91.3
Cash	395.6
Cost of goods sold	660.4
Equipment	1,732.8
Interest revenue	19.7
Merchandise inventory	630.9
Notes receivable—due May 15, 2015	96.0
Notes receivable—due in 2018	191.1
Prepaid expenses and deposits	20.1
Sales	4,565.5
Sales discounts	31.3
Short-term investments	194.9
Supplies	21.7
Unearned sales revenue	56.3

Additional information:

1. On September 30, 2013, Accounts Receivable was $611.1 thousand and the Allowance for Doubtful Accounts was $36.6 thousand.
2. The receivables turnover was 8.3 the previous year.

Instructions

(a) Prepare the assets section of the balance sheet.
(b) Calculate the receivables turnover and average collection period. Compare these results with the previous year's results and comment on any trends.

TAKING IT FURTHER   What other information should Tocksfor consider when analyzing its receivables turnover and average collection period?

P8–12A   Presented here is selected financial information (in millions) from the 2011 financial statements of Rogers Communications Inc. and Shaw Communications Inc.:

Calculate and interpret ratios. (SO 4) AN

	Rogers	Shaw
Sales	$12,428	$4,740.9
Allowance for doubtful accounts, beginning of year	138	19.0
Allowance for doubtful accounts, end of year	129	28.8
Accounts receivable balance (net), beginning of year	1,443	196.4
Accounts receivable balance (net), end of year	1,574	442.8

Instructions

(a) Calculate the receivables turnover and average collection period for both companies.

(b) Comment on the difference in their collection experiences.

TAKING IT FURTHER Shaw acquired Canwest Global Communications Corp. in October 2010. As part of the transaction, Shaw acquired $296.6 million of receivables. What impact might this acquisition have on its 2011 receivable turnover ratio? Note that Shaw's fiscal year end was August 31, 2011. Explain.

Evaluate liquidity. (SO 4) AN **P8–13A** The following ratios are available for Satellite Mechanical:

	2015	2014	2013
Current ratio	2.0 to 1	1.6 to 1	1.4 to 1
Acid-test ratio	1.1 to 1	0.8 to 1	0.7 to 1
Receivables turnover	7.3 times	10.1 times	10.3 times
Inventory turnover	6.3 times	6.1 times	6.4 times

Instructions

(a) Calculate the collection period, days sales in inventory, and operating cycle in days for each year.

(b) Has Satellite Mechanical's liquidity improved or weakened over the three-year period? Explain.

(c) Do changes in turnover ratios affect profitability? Explain.

(d) Do changes in turnover ratios affect cash flow? Explain.

TAKING IT FURTHER At the beginning of 2014, the owner of Satellite Mechanical decided to eliminate sales discounts because she thought it was costing the company too much money. The terms of credit sales were changed from 2/10, n/30 to n/30. Evaluate this decision.

▶ Problems: Set B

Record accounts receivable transactions. Post to subsidiary and general ledgers. (SO 1, 2) AP **P8–1B** At December 31, 2014, the general ledger and subsidiary ledger for Wow's, a small beauty supply company, showed the following:

General Ledger		Accounts Receivable Subsidiary Ledger	
Accounts receivable	$35,000	Hair Designs	$ 8,000
Allowance for doubtful accounts	3,500	Great Looks	11,000
		Ken's Salon	9,000
		Luxury Spa	7,000
		New Do	0
		Total	$35,000

Jan.	3	Hair Designs paid $8,000 on its account.
	4	New Do paid $900 on its account that had previously been written off.
	8	Great Looks purchased $3,000 of merchandise on account.
	9	Your Spa paid cash for $2,000 of merchandise.
	18	Great Looks returned $500 of merchandise.
	19	Luxury Spa paid $5,000 on its account.
	20	Great Looks paid $10,000 on is account.
	23	Hair Designs purchased $9,000 on account.
	24	Ken's Salon paid $3,000 on account.
	25	New Do purchased $5,000 of merchandise on Visa.
	26	Luxury Spa purchased $12,000 of merchandise on account.
	31	Wow determined that the Ken's Salon account receivable was not collectible.

Instructions

(a) Record the above transactions. Ignore credit card fees and inventory and cost of goods sold entries for purposes of this question.

(b) Set up T accounts for the Accounts Receivable general ledger (control) account, the Allowance for Doubtful Accounts general ledger account, and the Accounts Receivable subsidiary ledger accounts. Post the journal entries to these accounts.

(c) Wow estimated that 10% of accounts receivable is not collectible. Record the required adjustment to the allowance for doubtful accounts.

(d) Prepare a list of customers and the balances of their accounts from the subsidiary ledger. Prove that the total of the subsidiary ledger is equal to the control account balance.

TAKING IT FURTHER   What types of errors could result if the total of the account balances in the subsidiary ledger did not agree with the general ledger control account?

P8–2B   Textile Imports reported the following information on its December 31, 2014, balance sheet:

Accounts receivable	$1,580,000
Less: Allowance for doubtful accounts	94,800

Record accounts receivable and bad debt transactions; show balance sheet presentation.
(SO 1, 2) AP

During 2015, the company had the following transactions related to receivables:

1. Sales on account, $4,800,000
2. Sales returns and allowances, $120,000
3. Collections of accounts receivable, $4,700,000
4. Interest added to overdue accounts, $200,000
5. Write offs of accounts deemed uncollectible, $179,000
6. Collection of bad debts previously written off as uncollectible, $24,000

Instructions

(a) Prepare the summary journal entries to record each of these six transactions.
(b) Enter the January 1, 2015, balances in the Accounts Receivable and Allowance for Doubtful Accounts general ledger accounts, post the entries to the two accounts, and determine the balances.
(c) Record bad debt expense for 2015. Uncollectible accounts are estimated at 6% of accounts receivable.
(d) Calculate the net realizable value of accounts receivable at December 31, 2015.
(e) Show the balance sheet presentation of accounts receivable at December 31, 2015.

TAKING IT FURTHER   For several years, Textile Imports has estimated uncollectible accounts at 6% of accounts receivable. Discuss whether or not the company should continue to do this at December 31, 2015.

P8–3B   At the beginning of the current period, Fassi Co. had a balance of $800,000 in Accounts Receivable and a $44,000 credit balance in Allowance for Doubtful Accounts. In the period, it had net credit sales of $1,900,000 and collections of $2,042,000. It wrote off accounts receivable of $58,000. After a $4,000 account was written off as uncollectible, it was subsequently collected. This is in addition to the other cash collections. Based on an aging schedule, uncollectible accounts are estimated to be $36,000 at the end of the period.

Record accounts receivable and bad debt transactions; show financial statement presentation. (SO 1, 2, 4) AP

Instructions

(a) Record sales and collections in the period.
(b) Record the write off of uncollectible accounts in the period.
(c) Record the collection of the account previously written off.
(d) Record the bad debt expense adjusting entry for the period.
(e) Show the balance sheet presentation of the accounts receivable at the end of the period.
(f) What is the bad debt expense on the income statement for the period?

TAKING IT FURTHER   Why is bad debt expense not reduced when a previously written-off account is collected?

P8–4B   Information for Tisipai Company in 2014 follows:

Total net credit sales	$3,300,000
Accounts receivable at December 31	1,250,000
Accounts receivable written off	48,000
Amount collected on accounts previously written off (after write off but before year end)	8,000

Calculate bad debt amounts and answer questions.
(SO 2) AP

Instructions

(a) Assume that Tisipai Company decides to use the allowance method and estimates its uncollectible accounts to be $52,000 based on an aging schedule. What amount of bad debt expense will Tisipai record if Allowance for Doubtful Accounts had an opening balance of $30,000 on January 1, 2014?
(b) Assume the same facts as in (a), except that the Allowance for Doubtful Accounts had a $42,250 balance on January 1, 2014. What amount of bad debt expense will Tisipai record on December 31, 2014?
(c) How does the amount of accounts written off during the period affect the amount of bad debt expense recorded at the end of the period?
(d) How does the collection of an account that had previously been written off affect the net realizable value of accounts receivable?

TAKING IT FURTHER Why is a company not certain what accounts are not collectible?

Prepare aging schedule and record bad debts and comment. (SO 2) AP

P8-5B Creative Co. uses the allowance method to estimate uncollectible accounts receivable. The computer produced the following aging of the accounts receivable at year end:

		Number of Days Outstanding			
	Total	0–30	31–60	61–90	91–120
Accounts receivable	$210,000	$120,000	$55,000	$20,000	$15,000
Estimated % uncollectible		1%	7%	12%	25%
Estimated uncollectible accounts					

The unadjusted balance in Allowance for Doubtful Accounts is a credit of $5,000.

Instructions

(a) Complete the aging schedule and calculate the total estimated uncollectible accounts from the above information.
(b) Record the bad debt adjusting entry using the above information.
(c) In the following year, $12,200 of the outstanding accounts receivable is determined to be uncollectible. Record the write off of the uncollectible accounts.
(d) The company collects $3,400 of the $12,200 of accounts receivable that were determined to be uncollectible in (c). No further amounts are expected to be collected. Prepare the journal entry (or entries) to record the collection of this amount.
(e) Comment on how your answers to parts (a) to (d) would change if Creative Co. used a percentage of total accounts receivable of 8% instead of aging the accounts receivable.

TAKING IT FURTHER What are the advantages for the company of aging the accounts receivable rather than applying a percentage to total accounts receivable?

Prepare aging schedule and record bad debts. (SO 2) AP

P8-6B An aging analysis of Hake Company's accounts receivable at December 31, 2014 and 2015, showed the following:

Number of Days Outstanding	Estimated % Uncollectible	December 31 2015	December 31 2014
0–30 days	2.5%	$190,000	$220,000
31–60 days	6%	40,000	105,000
61–90 days	18%	65,000	40,000
Over 90 days	25%	75,000	25,000
Total		$370,000	$390,000

Additional information:

1. At December 31, 2014, the unadjusted balance in Allowance for Doubtful Accounts was a debit of $3,400.
2. In 2015, $22,300 of accounts was written off as uncollectible and $2,500 of accounts previously written off was collected.

Instructions

(a) Prepare an aging schedule to calculate the estimated uncollectible accounts at December 31, 2014, and at December 31, 2015.
(b) Calculate the net realizable value of Hake's accounts receivable at December 31, 2014, and December 31, 2015.
(c) Record the following:
   1. The adjusting entry on December 31, 2014
   2. The write off of uncollectible accounts in 2015
   3. The collection in 2015 of accounts previously written off
   4. The adjusting entry on December 31, 2015

TAKING IT FURTHER What are the implications of the changes in the age of accounts receivable from 2014 to 2015?

P8–7B The following information was reported in Beckford Company's general ledger at August 31:

Determine missing amounts.
(SO 2) AN

Accounts Receivable				Sales	
Beg. bal.	360,000	2,545,000			(a)
	(a)	(d)			
	(b)	5,520			
End. bal.	(c)				

Allowance for Doubtful Accounts				Bad Debt Expense	
		Beg. bal.	(e)	(f)	
	28,540		(b)		
			(f)		
		End. bal.	29,400		

All sales were made on account. At the beginning of the year, uncollectible accounts were estimated to be 6% of accounts receivable. At the end of the year, uncollectible accounts were estimated to be 7% of accounts receivable.

Instructions

Determine the missing amounts in Beckford Company's accounts. State what each of these amounts represents. You will not be able to determine the missing items in alphabetical order. (To solve this problem, it might help if you reconstruct the journal entries.)

TAKING IT FURTHER Explain the difference between bad debt expense and the allowance for doubtful accounts.

P8–8B Assiniboia Co. prepares monthly financial statements and estimates its uncollectible accounts at the end of each month. Assiniboia Co. has a May 31 fiscal year end, closes temporary accounts annually, and uses the perpetual inventory system.

Identify impact of accounts receivable and bad debt transactions; determine statement presentation.
(SO 1, 2, 4) AP

On March 31, 2014, after completing its month-end adjustments, it had accounts receivable of $89,200, a credit balance of $4,930 in Allowance for Doubtful Accounts, and a debit balance in Bad Debt Expense of $17,980. In April and May, the following occurred:

April

1. Sold $65,100 of merchandise on credit. The cost of the merchandise was $35,530.
2. Accepted $800 of returns on the merchandise sold on credit. These customers were issued credit memos. The merchandise had a cost of $440 and was discarded because it was damaged.
3. Collected $69,200 cash on account from customers.
4. Interest charges of $1,700 were charged to outstanding accounts receivable.
5. Recorded the monthly adjustment for bad debts. Uncollectible accounts were estimated to be 6% of accounts receivable.

May

1. Credit sales were $76,600. The cost of the merchandise was $42,130.
2. Received $450 cash from a customer whose account had been written off in March.
3. Collected $78,500 cash, in addition to the cash collected in (2) above, from customers on account.
4. Wrote off $9,580 of accounts receivable as uncollectible.
5. Interest charges of $1,480 were charged to outstanding accounts receivable.
6. Recorded the year-end adjustment for bad debts. Uncollectible accounts were estimated to be 6% of accounts receivable.

Instructions

(a) For each of these transactions, indicate if the transaction has increased (+) or decreased (−) Cash, Accounts Receivable, Allowance for Doubtful Accounts, Inventory, Total Assets, and Owner's Equity and by how much. If the item is not changed, write NE to indicate there is no effect. Use the following format, in which the first one has been done for you as an example.

Transaction	Cash	Accounts Receivable	Allowance for Doubtful Accounts	Inventory	Total Assets	Owner's Equity
April: 1.	NE	+$65,100	NE	−$35,530	+$29,570	+$29,570

(b) Show how accounts receivable will appear on the May 31, 2014, balance sheet.

(c) What amount will be reported as bad debt expense on the income statement for the year ended May 31, 2014?

TAKING IT FURTHER   To eliminate bad debt expense, should Assiniboia require all of its customers to pay cash? Explain.

Record receivables transactions. (SO 1, 2, 3) AP

P8–9B   On January 1, 2014, Alexi Co. had a $20,000, five-month, 6% note receivable from Figaro Company dated October 31, 2012. Interest receivable of $200 was accrued on the note on December 31, 2013. Alexi Co. has a December 31 fiscal year end and adjusts its accounts annually. In 2014, the following selected transactions occurred:

Jan.	2	Sold $25,000 of merchandise costing $13,750 to Braun Company, terms 2/10, n/30. Alexi Co. uses the perpetual inventory system.
Feb.	1	Accepted Braun Company's $25,000, three-month, 6% note for the balance due. (See January 2 transaction.) Interest is due at maturity.
Mar.	31	Received payment in full from Figaro Company for the amount due.
May	1	Collected Braun Company note in full. (See February 1 transaction.)
	25	Accepted Noah Inc.'s $12,000, two-month, 6% note in settlement of a past-due balance on account. Interest is payable monthly.
June	25	Received one month's interest from Noah Inc. on its note. (See May 25 transaction.)
July	25	The Noah Inc. note was dishonoured. (See May 25 transaction.) Noah Inc. is bankrupt and future payment is not expected.
Oct.	1	Loaned Martin Rowe, an employee, $4,000 on a four-month, 6% note. Interest is due at maturity.
Nov.	30	Gave UOA Corp. a $10,000 cash loan and accepted UOA's four-month, 4.5% note.
Dec.	1	Martin Rowe left for a job at another company. Alexi Co. asked him to immediately pay the note receivable. (See October 1 transaction.) Martin told the company that he does not have the money to do so.
	31	Accrued interest is recorded on any outstanding notes at year end.

Instructions

Record the above transactions.

TAKING IT FURTHER   Do you think the note receivable from Martin Rowe should be written off as at the year end? If not, do you think interest should be accrued on this note receivable at year end? What actions might the company have taken before Martin left the company to collect the note or part of it?

Record note receivable transactions; show balance sheet presentation. (SO 3, 4) AP

P8–10B   Ouellette Co. adjusts its books monthly. On June 30, 2014, notes receivable include the following:

Issue Date	Maker	Principal	Term	Interest
May 1, 2013	ALD Inc.	$ 6,000	3 years	4.0%
October 31, 2013	Kabam Ltd.	10,000	15 months	5.0%
January 31, 2014	Best Foot Forward Shoe Co.	15,000	6 months	5.5%
May 31, 2014	DNR Co.	4,800	2 months	8.75%
June 30, 2014	M&J Hardware Corp.	9,000	8 months	5.0%

Interest is payable on the first day of each month for notes with terms of one year or longer. Interest is payable at maturity for notes with terms less than one year. In July, the following transactions were completed:

July	1	Received payment of the interest due from ALD Inc.
	2	Received payment of the interest due from Kabam Ltd.
	31	Collected the full amount on the Best Foot Forward Shoe Co. note.
	31	Received notice that the DNR Co. note has been dishonoured. Assume that DNR Co. is expected to pay in the future.

Instructions

(a) Calculate the balance in the Interest Receivable and Notes Receivable accounts at June 30, 2014.

(b) Record the July transactions and the July 31 adjusting entry for accrued interest receivable.

(c) Enter the balances at July 1 in the receivables accounts. Post the entries to the receivables accounts.

(d) Show the balance sheet presentation of the receivables accounts at July 31, 2014.

(e) How would the journal entry on July 31 be different if DNR Co. were not expected to pay in the future?

TAKING IT FURTHER   The interest rate for the DNR note is higher than the other notes. Why might that be the case?

P8–11B   Norlandia Saga Company's general ledger included the following selected accounts (in thousands) at November 30, 2014:

Prepare assets section of balance sheet; calculate and interpret ratios. (SO 4) AN

Accounts payable	$ 546.2
Accounts receivable	311.4
Accumulated depreciation—equipment	471.7
Allowance for doubtful accounts	14.8
Bad debt expense	43.6
Cash	417.1
Cost of goods sold	353.0
Equipment	924.2
Interest revenue	10.7
Merchandise inventory	336.5
Notes receivable—due in 2015	51.2
Notes receivable—due in 2018	101.9
Prepaid expenses and deposits	19.3
Sales	2,823.8
Sales discounts	18.5
Short-term investments	224.6
Supplies	15.9
Unearned sales revenue	40.2

Additional information:

1. On November 30, 2013, Accounts Receivable was $271.7 thousand and the Allowance for Doubtful Accounts was $13.6 thousand.
2. The receivables turnover was 9.1 the previous year.

Instructions

(a) Prepare the assets section of the balance sheet.
(b) Calculate the receivables turnover and average collection period. Compare these results with the previous year's results and comment on any trends.

TAKING IT FURTHER   What other information should Norlandia Saga consider when analyzing its receivables turnover and average collection period?

P8–12B   Presented here is selected financial information from the 2011 financial statements of **Nike** (in U.S. millions) and **Adidas** (in euro millions):

Calculate and interpret ratios. (SO 4) AN

	Nike	Adidas
Sales	$20,862	€13,344
Allowance for doubtful accounts, Jan. 1	74	127
Allowance for doubtful accounts, Dec. 31	74	151
Accounts receivable balance (net), Jan. 1	2650	1,667
Accounts receivable balance (net), Dec. 31	3,138	1,707

Instructions

Calculate the receivables turnover and average collection period for both companies and compare the two companies. Comment on the difference in the two companies' collection experiences.

TAKING IT FURTHER   Adidas's financial statements are prepared using euros, while Nike uses U.S. dollars. How does this affect our ability to compare sales for the two companies? To compare the receivables turnover and collection period?

P8–13B   The following ratios are available for Western Roofing:

Evaluate liquidity. (SO 4) AN

	2015	2014	2013
Current ratio	1.6 to 1	2.0 to 1	1.9 to 1
Acid-test ratio	0.8 to 1	1.3 to 1	1.2 to 1
Receivables turnover	10.6 times	8.9 times	9.0 times
Inventory turnover	7.3 times	7.6 times	7.5 times

Instructions

(a) Calculate the collection period, days sales in inventory, and operating cycle for each year.

(b) Has Western Roofing's liquidity improved or weakened over the three-year period? Explain.

(c) Do changes in turnover ratios affect profitability? Explain.

(d) Do changes in turnover ratios affect cash flow? Explain.

TAKING IT FURTHER At the beginning of 2015, the owner of Western Roofing decided to start offering customers a sales discount for early payment. The terms of credit sales were changed from n/30 to 2/10, n/30. Evaluate this decision.

▶ Continuing Cookie Chronicle

(*Note:* This is a continuation of the Cookie Chronicle from Chapters 1 through 7.)

Natalie has been approached by one of her friends, Curtis Lesperance. Curtis runs a coffee shop where he sells specialty coffees and prepares and sells muffins and cookies. He is very anxious to buy one of Natalie's fine European mixers because he would then be able to prepare larger batches of muffins and cookies. Curtis, however, cannot afford to pay for the mixer for at least 30 days. He has asked Natalie if she would be willing to sell him the mixer on credit.

Natalie comes to you for advice and asks the following questions.

1. Curtis has given me a set of his most recent financial statements. What calculations should I do with the data from these statements? What questions should I ask him after I have analyzed the statements? How will this information help me decide if I should extend credit to Curtis?
2. Is there another alternative to extending credit to Curtis for 30 days?
3. If, instead of extending credit to Curtis for 30 days, I have Curtis sign a promissory note and he is unable to pay at the end of the agreement term, will having that signed promissory note really make any difference?
4. I am thinking seriously about being able to have my customers use credit cards. What are some of the advantages and disadvantages of letting my customers pay by credit card? Are there differences in the types of credit cards that my customers can use?

The following transactions occur in April and May 2014:

April	1	After much thought, Natalie sells a mixer to Curtis for $1,050 (the cost of the mixer was $553). Curtis signs a two-month, 7.5% promissory note. Curtis can repay the note at any time before the due date, with interest accruing to the date of payment.
	30	Curtis calls Natalie. He expects to pay the amount outstanding in the next week or so.
May	15	Natalie receives a cheque from Curtis in payment of his balance owing plus interest that has accrued.

Instructions

(a) Answer Natalie's questions.

(b) Prepare journal entries for the transactions that occurred in April and May.

CHAPTER 8 | BROADENING YOUR PERSPECTIVE

▶ Financial Reporting and Analysis

Financial Reporting Problem

BYP8–1 The receivables turnover, collection period, and operating cycle for **Reitmans (Canada) Limited** were calculated in this chapter, based on the company's financial statements for the 2012 fiscal year. These financial statements are presented in Appendix A.

Instructions

(a) Calculate Reitmans' receivables turnover, collection period, and operating cycle for the 2011 fiscal year.
(b) Comment on any significant differences you observe between the ratios for 2012 (as calculated in the chapter) and 2011 (as calculated by you above).
(c) As noted earlier in the chapter, Reitmans' accounts receivable are from customers using credit cards such as MasterCard or Visa where the sales haven't been collected in cash from the credit card company prior to the year end. Are Reitmans' receivables turnover and collection period for 2012 and 2011 consistent with this information? Explain.
(d) Given that Reitmans' accounts receivable are from customers using credit cards such as MasterCard or Visa, is Reitmans at risk of having significant uncollectible accounts receivable? Explain.

Interpreting Financial Statements

BYP8–2   Shaw Communications Inc. is a diversified Canadian communications company whose core operating business is providing broadband cable television services, Internet, telecommunications services, satellite services, and programming content. Shaw reported the following information (in millions) in its financial statements for the fiscal years 2009 through 2011:

	2011	2010	2009
Operating revenues (assume all credit)	$4,741	$3,718	$3,391
Cash and cash equivalents	443	217	254
Short-term securities	0	0	199
Accounts receivable (gross)	472	215	212
Allowance for doubtful accounts	29	19	17
Inventories	97	54	52
Other current assets	279	129	58
Total current liabilities	1,131	1,019	1,377

Additional detail about Shaw's receivables includes the following:

Bad debt expense (or provision for doubtful accounts as Shaw calls it) of $33.7 (2010 − $33.7; 2009 − $19.3) is included in operating, general, and administrative expenses. Shaw writes off uncollectible accounts receivable against the allowance account based on the age of the account and payment history.

Instructions

(a) Calculate the current ratios, acid-test ratios, receivables turnover ratios, and average collection periods for fiscal 2011 and 2010. Comment on Shaw's liquidity for each of the years.
(b) Based on the information provided, calculate the amount of accounts receivable that was written off in 2011.
(c) Shaw indicates in its notes to the financial statements that it reduces the risk of uncollectible accounts by billing in advance of providing service. How does billing in advance of providing service reduce the risk of uncollectible accounts?

▶ Critical Thinking

Collaborative Learning Activity

Note to instructor: Additional instructions and material for this group activity can be found on the Instructor Resource Site and in *WileyPLUS*.

BYP8–3   In this group activity, you will prepare the year-end adjustment for bad debt expense, and finalize the financial statements, using company information given to you by your instructor. You will be required to use professional judgment to determine the amount of the adjustment and explain your rationale. Your instructor will assume the role of the company's external auditor and will judge you on the appropriateness of the amount and your rationale.

Communication Activity

BYP8–4   Toys for Big Boys sells snowmobiles, personal watercraft, ATVs, and the like. Recently, the credit manager of Toys for Big Boys retired. The sales staff threw him a big retirement party—they were glad to see him go because they felt his credit policies restricted their selling ability. The sales staff convinced management that there was no need to replace the credit manager since they could handle this responsibility in addition to their sales positions.

Management was thrilled at year end when sales doubled. However, accounts receivable quadrupled and cash flow halved. The company's average collection period increased from 30 days to 120 days.

Instructions

In a memo to management, explain the financial impact of allowing the sales staff to manage the credit function. Has the business assumed any additional credit risk? What would you recommend the company do to better manage its increasing accounts receivable?

Ethics Case

BYP8–5   The controller of Proust Company has completed draft financial statements for the year just ended and is reviewing them with the president. As part of the review, he has summarized an aging schedule showing the basis of estimating uncollectible accounts using the following percentages: 0–30 days, 5%; 31–60 days, 10%; 61–90 days, 30%; 91–120 days, 50%; and over 120 days, 80%.

The president of the company, Suzanne Bros, is nervous because the bank expects the company to sustain a growth rate for profit of at least 5% each year over the next two years—the remaining term of its bank loan. The profit growth for the past year was much more than 5% because of certain special orders with high margins, but those orders will not be repeated next year, so it will be very hard to achieve even the same profit next year, and even more difficult to grow it another 5%. It would be easier to show an increase next year if the past year's reported profit had been a little lower. President Bros recalls from her college accounting course that bad debt expense is based on certain estimates subject to judgement. She suggests that the controller increase the estimate percentages, which will increase the amount of the required bad debt expense adjustment and therefore lower profit for last year so that it will be easier to show a better growth rate next year.

Instructions

(a) Who are the stakeholders in this case?
(b) Does the president's request create an ethical dilemma for the controller?
(c) Should the controller be concerned with Proust Company's reported profit growth rate in estimating the allowance? Explain your answer.

"All About You" Activity

BYP8–6   In the "All About You" feature, you learned about interest rates charged on credit cards and some of the advantages and disadvantages of credit cards. To get the most from your credit card and to save money, you need to understand the features of your credit card and how interest is charged on credit cards.

Instructions

Go to the Financial Consumer Agency of Canada, Credit Cards at **http://www.fcac-acfc.gc.ca/eng/consumers/ creditcard/index-eng.asp** and answer the following questions:

(a) Go to the related resource, "Be Smart with Your Credit Card: 10 Tips to Help You Use Your Card Wisely." What are the 10 tips?
(b) Go to "Credit Cards: Understanding Your Rights and Responsibilities" and then go to "Understanding Your Credit Card Payment Terms." Credit cards provide interest-free loans on the purchase of goods, as long as you pay your bill in full by the end of the grace period. What is the required minimum grace period? Assume you used a credit card to purchase your textbooks on September 15, and the last date covered by your statement is October 7 and the grace period is 21 days. How many days is the interest-free period?
(c) There is no interest-free period on cash advances or balance transfers on credit cards. What is a cash advance? What is a balance transfer?
(d) Suppose you have one month left in the semester and you take a $1,000 cash advance on your credit card on April 1 to cover your living expenses until you get your first paycheque from your summer job on May 15. The interest rate on your credit card is 19%. Assuming that is the only charge on your credit card, calculate the interest you will be charged assuming you pay your bill in full on May 15. (*Hint:* Go to "How Interest Charges Are Calculated" on the website under "Credit Cards: Understanding Your Rights and Responsibilities: Understanding Your Credit Card Payment Terms.")
(e) Go to the Financial Consumer Agency of Canada's interactive tool "Credit Card Payment Calculator." (*Hint:* To find the Credit Card Payment Calculator, go to **http://www.fcac-acfc.gc.ca/eng/consumers/creditcard/ index-eng.asp** and click on "Resources," then click on "Tools and Calculators," then click on the credit card icon, and then click on the credit card payment calculator.)
    1. For option A, assume you have a credit card balance of $1,000, the interest rate is 19%, and the minimum monthly payment is $10 or 3%, whichever is greater.

2. For option B, assume the same information as in part 1, but you make an additional monthly payment of $10.

3. For option C, assume the same information as in part 1, but you make a monthly payment of $100.

For each of the options A, B, and C, calculate how long it will take to pay off the credit card, assuming there are no additional purchases made, and calculate the total amount of interest paid.

ANSWERS TO CHAPTER QUESTIONS

ANSWERS TO ACCOUNTING IN ACTION INSIGHT QUESTIONS

All About You Insight, p. 419

Q: Should you use credit cards or not?

A: Credit cards can make your life easier, as long as they are used properly. They certainly have advantages: (1) they provide interest-free loans on the purchase of goods, as long as you pay your bill in full by the end of the grace period; (2) monthly credit card statements provide detailed records of all transactions, payments, and returned merchandise; and (3) many transactions, such as Internet purchases, are difficult or impossible to carry out without a credit card.

However, credit cards also have disadvantages: (1) if you do not pay your bill in full every month, expect to pay a very high interest rate on the unpaid balance; (2) they are so easy to use that you might start buying items without thinking about whether you really need them—and can afford them; and (3) credit cards can be stolen, which might damage your credit rating.

Across the Organization Insight, p. 434

Q: What might be the advantages to Target of having its own credit card? What might be the disadvantages?

A: If customers have a Target credit card, they might be more likely to shop at Target rather than at another department store. Target can also earn interest income on any late accounts. The disadvantages might include higher administration costs to operate the credit card division and also the risk of customers defaulting on their credit card payments.

ANSWERS TO SELF-STUDY QUESTIONS

1. c   2. b   3. d   4. a   5. c   6. d   7. c   8. a   9. d   10. c   11. b   12. c

> *Remember to go back to the beginning of the chapter to check off your completed work!*
> ←

 THE **NAVIGATOR**

- ☐ Understand *Concepts for Review*
- ☐ Read *Feature Story*
- ☐ Scan *Study Objectives*
- ☐ Read *Chapter Preview*
- ☐ Read text and answer *Before You Go On*
- ☐ Review *Comparing IFRS and ASPE*
- ☐ Work *Demonstration Problems*
- ☐ Review *Summary of Study Objectives*
- ☐ Answer *Self-Study Questions*
- ☐ Complete assignment
- ☐ Go to *WileyPLUS* for practice and tutorials

CONCEPTS FOR **REVIEW**

Before studying this chapter, you should understand or, if necessary, review:

a. Expense recognition criteria (Ch. 3, pp. 114–115).

b. What depreciation is, and how to make adjustments for it. (Ch. 3, pp. 119–120).

c. Non-current assets and the classified balance sheet (Ch. 4, p. 187).

BUILDING FOR LEARNING

TORONTO, Ont.—When George Brown College in Toronto, one of the oldest colleges in Ontario, was created in 1967, its land and buildings were provided by the provincial government at nominal value. The province launched community colleges to provide vocational training for its burgeoning industries like the automotive sector and forestry. Today, however, colleges have to be much more self-sufficient when adding classrooms, labs, and other facilities.

George Brown's most recent expansion is a brand new, 380,000-square-foot (35,000-square-metre) health sciences building, the first phase of its Waterfront campus overlooking Toronto's harbour, which opened in the fall of 2012. The construction costs were estimated at about $175 million. "Out of that, there's about $92 million roughly that is funding from both the provincial and federal governments," says Controller Ric Ho. "And then we had to put in about $25 million of our own money. And we also are expected to do fundraising, up to $35 million, as part of the capital campaign." The college also expected to receive a capital contribution from Waterfront Toronto, an intergovernmental agency to develop the harbour.

How does the college determine what is a capital versus an operating expenditure and how does it account for these costs? Anything that will be used up within a fiscal year, such as office supplies, is expensed in that year. Anything that has a useful life of more than a year and is worth $5,000 or more is capitalized and depreciated. "There needs to be a threshold because we cannot capitalize every little chair or something that comes around, otherwise your capital asset list is going to be huge and doesn't serve any purpose," says Dominic Noronha, the college's Manager of Financial Services.

The college depreciates the buildings it owns using the straight-line method (partly because it's the simplest) over 40 years. While most buildings last longer than 40 years, "That's the level that's been traditionally used by other colleges," Mr. Noronha says. For space it leases, such as one floor of a building on the nearby Ryerson University campus, George Brown amortizes the leasehold improvements—considered to be assets—over the term of the lease.

Like most colleges, buildings are George Brown's most valuable long-lived assets. Its equipment and buildings have a net book value (or carrying amount) of approximately $328 million. Among its equipment are workshop benches for its programs in the trades, kitchens for its hospitality school, computers for its school of design, and costumes for its animation program. The college depreciates most equipment over five years, although its computer equipment—which can quickly become technologically obsolete—is depreciated over three years. George Brown does not recognize any intangible assets on its books. "We don't have any goodwill or intellectual property, such as patents or copyrights," says Mr. Ho.

THE NAVIGATOR

>> STUDY **OBJECTIVES**

After studying this chapter, you should be able to:

1. Determine the cost of property, plant, and equipment.

2. Explain and calculate depreciation.

3. Explain the factors that cause changes in periodic depreciation and calculate revisions.

4. Account for the disposal of property, plant, and equipment.

5. Calculate and record depreciation of natural resources.

6. Identify the basic accounting issues for intangible assets and goodwill.

7. Illustrate the reporting and analysis of long-lived assets.

THE NAVIGATOR

For organizations such as George Brown College, making the right decisions about long-lived assets is critical because these assets represent huge investments. Organizations must make decisions about what assets to acquire, how to account for them, and when to dispose of them.

In this chapter, we address these and other issues surrounding long-lived assets. Our discussions will focus on three types of long-lived assets: (1) property, plant, and equipment; (2) natural resources; and (3) intangible assets.

The chapter is organized as follows:

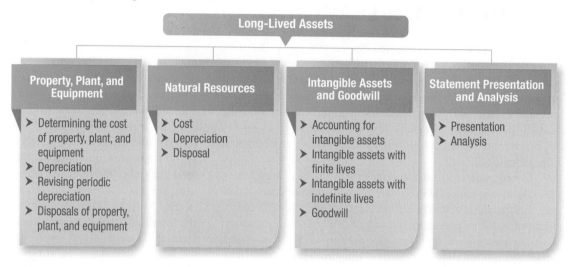

Property, Plant, and Equipment

Alternative terminology Property, plant, and equipment are also commonly known as *fixed assets*; *land, building, and equipment*; or *capital assets*.

Property, plant, and equipment are long-lived assets that the company owns and uses for the production and sale of goods or services to consumers. They have three characteristics. They (1) have a physical substance (a definite size and shape), (2) are used in the operations of the business, and (3) are not intended for sale to customers. Unlike current assets, these assets are expected to provide services to a company for a number of years.

In the following sections, we will learn more about property, plant, and equipment: determining their cost, their depreciation, and the accounting for their disposal.

DETERMINING THE COST OF PROPERTY, PLANT, AND EQUIPMENT

» STUDY OBJECTIVE 1

Determine the cost of property, plant, and equipment.

The cost of an item of property, plant, and equipment includes the following:

1. The purchase price, plus any non-refundable taxes, less any discounts or rebates
2. The expenditures necessary to bring the asset to the required location and make it ready for its intended use

If there are obligations to dismantle, remove, or restore the asset when it is retired, an initial estimate of these costs is also included in the cost of the long-lived asset. These are known as **asset retirement costs**. Accounting for these costs can be complex and we will leave that discussion to a future accounting course. But you should be aware that the cost of some property, plant, and equipment items includes the cost of retiring the asset. For simplicity, we will assume asset retirement costs are equal to zero in the examples in this text.

Alternative terminology Asset retirement costs are also called *decommissioning costs*.

These costs are **capitalized** (recorded as property, plant, and equipment), rather than expensed, if it is probable that the company will receive an economic benefit in the future from the asset. Determining which costs to include in a long-lived asset account and which costs not to include is very important. Costs that benefit only the current period are expensed. Such costs are called **operating expenditures**. Costs that benefit future periods are included in a long-lived asset account. These costs are called **capital expenditures**.

For example, the cost to purchase equipment is recorded as a capital expenditure, because the equipment will benefit future periods. In addition, the insurance paid on the equipment as it is shipped to the company should also be capitalized because the insurance during transit benefits more than just the current period. It is considered a necessary expenditure to get the equipment to its required location and ready for use.

However, it is also important to note that companies will expense, rather than capitalize, low-cost long-lived assets. For example, George Brown College, in the feature story, capitalizes anything that has a useful life of more than a year and is worth $5,000 or more. This is an application of a concept known as materiality, which you will learn more about in Chapter 11. It allows companies to immediately record immaterial expenditures as an expense.

Subsequent to acquisition, the same distinction exists between capital and operating expenditures. For example, once the asset is in use, having an insurance policy benefits only the current period and is treated as an expense. But major expenditures that are incurred once the asset is in use that increase the life of the asset or its productivity are capitalized. We will discuss expenditures subsequent to acquisition in more depth later in the chapter.

Property, plant, and equipment are often subdivided into four classes:

1. **Land**, such as a building site
2. **Land improvements**, such as driveways, parking lots, fences, and underground sprinkler systems
3. **Buildings**, such as stores, offices, factories, and warehouses
4. **Equipment**, such as store checkout counters, cash registers, office furniture, computer equipment, factory equipment, and delivery equipment

Determining the cost of each of the major classes of property, plant, and equipment is explained in the following sections.

Land

The cost of land includes (1) the purchase price, (2) closing costs such as surveying and legal fees, and (3) the costs of preparing the land for its intended use, such as the removal of old buildings, clearing, draining, filling, and grading. All of these costs (less any proceeds from salvaged materials) are debited to the Land account.

To illustrate, assume that the Budovitch Manufacturing Company purchases real estate for $100,000 cash. The property contained an old warehouse that is removed at a net cost of $6,000 ($7,500 to remove it less $1,500 received for materials from the warehouse that were salvaged and later sold). Additional expenditures include the legal fee of $3,000. The cost of the land is $109,000, calculated as follows:

Land	
Cash price of property	$100,000
Net cost of removing warehouse ($7,500 − $1,500)	6,000
Legal fees	3,000
Cost of land	$109,000

When recording the acquisition, Land is debited for $109,000 and Cash is credited for $109,000 (assuming the costs were paid in cash). Land is a unique long-lived asset. Its cost is not depreciated—allocated over its useful life—because land has an unlimited useful life.

Land Improvements

Land improvements are structural additions made to land, such as driveways, sidewalks, fences, and parking lots. Land improvements, unlike land, decline in service potential over time, and require maintenance and replacement. Because of this, land improvements are recorded separately from land and are depreciated over their useful lives.

Many students confuse the cost to get land ready for its intended use with land improvements. They think, for example, that removing an old building or grading the land is "improving" the land, and thus incorrectly reason that these costs should be considered land improvements. When classifying costs, it is important to remember that one-time costs required for getting the land ready to use are always charged to the Land account, not the Land Improvement account.

Buildings

All costs that are directly related to the purchase or construction of a building are debited to the Buildings account. When a building is purchased, these costs include the purchase price and closing costs (such as legal fees). The costs of making a building ready to be used as intended can include expenditures for remodelling, and for replacing or repairing the roof, floors, electrical wiring, and plumbing. These costs are also debited to Buildings.

When a new building is built, its cost includes the contract price plus payments for architects' fees, building permits, and excavation costs. The interest costs of financing the construction project are also included in the asset's cost when a significant amount of time is needed to get the building ready to be used. In these circumstances, interest costs are considered to be as necessary as materials and labour are. However, only interest costs that occur during the construction period are included. After construction is finished, the company records future interest payments on funds borrowed to finance the construction as debits (increases) to Interest Expense.

Equipment

The "equipment" classification is a broad one that can include delivery equipment, office equipment, computers, machinery, vehicles, furniture and fixtures, and other similar assets. The cost of these assets includes the purchase price; freight charges and insurance during transit paid by the purchaser; and the costs of assembling, installing, and testing the equipment. These costs are treated as capital expenditures because they benefit future periods.

Annual costs such as motor vehicle licences and insurance on company trucks and cars are treated as operating expenditures because they are recurring expenditures that do not benefit future periods.

To illustrate, assume that 1 Stop Florists purchases a used delivery truck on January 1, 2014, for $24,500 cash. Related expenditures include painting and lettering, $500; a motor vehicle licence, $80; and a one-year insurance policy, $2,600. The cost of the delivery truck is $25,000, calculated as follows:

Delivery Truck	
Cash price	$24,500
Painting and lettering	500
Cost of delivery truck	$25,000

The cost of the motor vehicle licence is recorded as an expense and the cost of the insurance policy is recorded as a prepaid asset. The entry to record the purchase of the truck and related expenditures, assuming they were all paid for in cash, is as follows:

```
A    =  L  +  OE
+25,000        −80
+2,600
−27,680

↓ Cash flows: −27,680
```

Jan. 1	Vehicles	25,000	
	Licence Expense	80	
	Prepaid Insurance	2,600	
	Cash		27,680
	To record purchase of delivery truck and related expenditures.		

Allocating Cost to Multiple Assets or Significant Components

Alternative terminology A basket purchase is also known as a *lump sum purchase.*

Multiple Assets. Property, plant, and equipment are often purchased together for a single price. This is known as a **basket purchase**. We need to know the cost of each individual asset in order to journalize the purchase, and later calculate the depreciation of each asset. When a basket purchase occurs, we determine individual costs by allocating the total price paid for the group of assets to each individual asset based on its relative fair value.

To illustrate, assume Sega Company purchased land, a building, and some equipment on July 31 for $400,000 cash. The land was appraised at $135,000, the building at $270,000, and the equipment at $45,000. The $400,000 cost should be allocated based on fair values (i.e., appraised values), as shown in Illustration 9-1.

Asset	Fair Value	Percent of Total Fair Value			Total Purchase Price		Cost of Each Asset
Land	$135,000	30%	($135,000 ÷ $450,000)	×	$400,000	=	$120,000
Building	270,000	60%	($270,000 ÷ $450,000)	×	$400,000	=	240,000
Equipment	45,000	10%	($ 45,000 ÷ $450,000)	×	$400,000	=	40,000
Totals	$450,000	100%					$400,000

▶ILLUSTRATION 9-1
Allocating cost in a basket purchase

The journal entry to record this purchase is as follows:

July 31	Land		120,000	
	Building		240,000	
	Equipment		40,000	
	Cash			400,000
	To record purchase of land, building, and equipment with costs allocated based on appraised values of $135,000, $270,000, and $45,000, respectively.			

```
A    =   L   +   OE
+120,000
+240,000
 +40,000
-400,000
```
↓ Cash flows: −400,000

Significant Components. When an item of property, plant, and equipment includes individual components that have different useful lives, the cost of the item should be allocated to each of its significant components. This allows each component to be depreciated separately over the different useful lives or possibly by using different depreciation methods. For example, an aircraft and its engine may need to be treated as separate depreciable assets if they have different useful lives.

Separating the cost of the entire asset into its significant components can be accomplished using the same process to allocate cost illustrated above for a basket purchase. The asset's total cost would be allocated to the significant components based on the components' relative fair values. The calculations would be similar to those in Illustration 9-1.

Further discussion of calculating depreciation for the different parts of an asset will be left to a later accounting course. For simplicity, we will assume in this text that all of the components of the depreciable asset have the same useful life, and we will depreciate assets as a whole.

BEFORE YOU GO ON...

Do It

Assume that factory equipment is purchased on November 6 for $10,000 cash and a $40,000 note payable. Related cash expenditures include insurance during shipping, $500; the annual insurance policy, $750; and installation and testing, $1,000. (a) What is the cost of the equipment? (b) Record these expenditures.

Solution

Factory Equipment

Purchase price	$50,000
Insurance during shipping	500
Installation and testing	1,000
Cost of equipment	$51,500

Action Plan
- Capitalize expenditures that are made to get the equipment ready for its intended use.
- Expense operating expenditures that benefit only the current period, or are recurring costs.

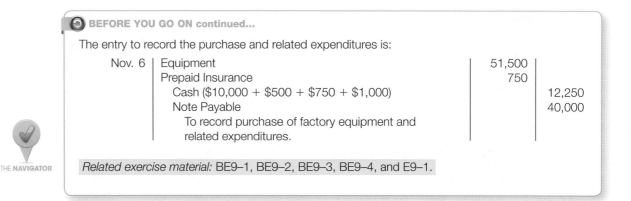

BEFORE YOU GO ON continued...

The entry to record the purchase and related expenditures is:

Nov. 6	Equipment	51,500	
	Prepaid Insurance	750	
	Cash ($10,000 + $500 + $750 + $1,000)		12,250
	Note Payable		40,000
	To record purchase of factory equipment and related expenditures.		

Related exercise material: BE9–1, BE9–2, BE9–3, BE9–4, and E9–1.

THE NAVIGATOR

DEPRECIATION

» **STUDY OBJECTIVE 2**

Explain and calculate depreciation.

Under International Financial Reporting Standards, companies have two models they can choose between to account for their property, plant, and equipment: the cost model or the revaluation model. The cost model is the more commonly used method, and is the only model allowed under ASPE. We will cover the cost model in the following sections of the chapter and refer briefly to the revaluation model in a later section.

The **cost model** records property, plant, and equipment at cost of acquisition. After acquisition, depreciation is recorded each period and the assets are carried at cost less accumulated depreciation.

As we learned in Chapter 3, depreciation is the systematic allocation of the cost of a long-lived asset, such as property, plant, and equipment, over the asset's useful life. The cost is allocated to expense over the asset's useful life so that expenses are properly matched with the expected use of the asset.

You will recall that depreciation is recorded through an adjusting journal entry that debits Depreciation Expense and credits Accumulated Depreciation. Depreciation Expense is an operating expense on the income statement. Accumulated Depreciation appears on the balance sheet as a contra account to the related long-lived asset account. The resulting balance, cost less accumulated depreciation, is the carrying amount of the depreciable asset, as defined in Chapter 4.

Alternative terminology An asset's *carrying amount* is also called its *carrying value, book value,* or *net book value.*

It is important to understand that **depreciation is a process of cost allocation, not a process of determining an asset's real value.** Illustration 9-2 shows this. Under the cost model, an increase in an asset's fair value is not relevant because property, plant, and equipment are not for resale. (Fair values are only relevant if an impairment loss has occurred, which we will discuss later in the chapter.) As a result, the carrying amount of property, plant, or equipment (cost less accumulated depreciation) may be very different from its fair value.

▶ **ILLUSTRATION 9-2**
Depreciation as an allocation concept

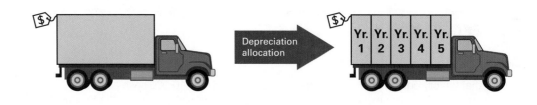

It is also important to understand that **depreciation neither uses up nor provides cash to replace the asset**. The balance in Accumulated Depreciation only represents the total amount of the asset's cost that has been allocated to expense so far. It is not a cash fund. Cash is neither increased nor decreased by the adjusting entry to record depreciation.

During a depreciable asset's useful life, its revenue-producing ability declines because of physical factors such as wear and tear, and economic factors such as obsolescence. For example, a company may replace a truck because it is physically worn out. On the other hand, companies replace computers long before they are physically worn out because improvements in hardware and software have made the old computers obsolete.

Factors in Calculating Depreciation

In Chapter 3, we learned that depreciation expense was calculated by dividing the cost of a depreciable asset by its useful life. At that time, we assumed the asset's residual value was zero. In this chapter, we will now include a residual value when calculating depreciation. Consequently, there are now three factors that affect the calculation of depreciation:

Cost. The factors that affect the cost of a depreciable asset were explained earlier in this chapter. Remember that the cost of property, plant, and equipment includes the purchase price plus all costs necessary to get the asset ready for use. Cost includes an initial estimate of the retirement costs, if there are any.

Useful Life. **Useful life** is (a) the period of time over which an asset is expected to be available for use or (b) the number of units of production (such as machine hours) or units of output that are expected to be obtained from an asset. Useful life is an estimate based on such factors as the asset's intended use, its expected need for repair and maintenance, and how vulnerable it is to wearing out or becoming obsolete. The company's past experience with similar assets often helps in estimating the expected useful life. George Brown College, in the feature story, uses a five-year useful life for most of its equipment, but only three years for computers because computer equipment can quickly become technologically obsolete.

Residual Value. **Residual value** is the estimated amount that a company would obtain from disposing of the asset at the end of its useful life. Residual value is not depreciated, since the amount is expected to be recovered at the end of the asset's useful life.

Alternative terminology Residual value is sometimes called *salvage value.*

Illustration 9-3 summarizes these three factors in calculating depreciation.

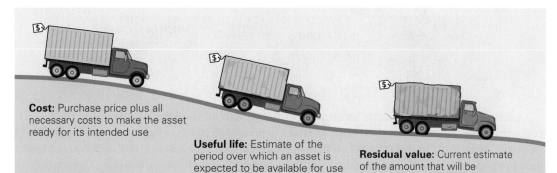

▶ **ILLUSTRATION 9-3**
Three factors in calculating depreciation

Cost: Purchase price plus all necessary costs to make the asset ready for its intended use

Useful life: Estimate of the period over which an asset is expected to be available for use

Residual value: Current estimate of the amount that will be received from the disposal of the asset

The difference between an asset's cost and its residual value is called the **depreciable amount**, which is the total amount to be depreciated over the useful life. As we learned in Chapter 3, companies reporting under ASPE may use the term "amortization" instead of "depreciation." Because of this, the depreciable amount is often called the amortizable cost.

Depreciation Methods

Depreciation is generally calculated using one of the following methods:

1. Straight-line
2. Diminishing-balance
3. Units-of-production

The straight-line method of depreciation is used by the majority of publicly traded companies. But how do companies decide which of the three depreciation methods to use? Management must choose the method that best matches the estimated pattern in which the asset's future economic benefits are expected to be consumed. The depreciation method must be reviewed at least once a year. If the expected pattern of consumption of the future economic benefits has changed, the depreciation method must be changed, and the change disclosed in the notes to the financial statements.

To learn how to calculate the three depreciation methods and to compare them, we will use the following data for the small delivery truck bought by 1 Stop Florists on January 1, 2014:

Cost (as shown earlier in the chapter)	$25,000
Estimated residual value	$2,000
Estimated useful life (in years)	5
Estimated useful life (in kilometres)	200,000

Straight-Line. The straight-line method was first defined in Chapter 3. We will define it again here, this time including the impact of a residual value on the calculation. The **straight-line method** of calculating depreciation has two steps. First, residual value is deducted from the asset's cost to determine an asset's depreciable amount. Second, the depreciable amount is divided by the asset's useful life to calculate the annual depreciation expense.

The depreciation expense will be the same for each year of the asset's useful life if the cost, the useful life, and the residual value do not change. The calculation of depreciation expense in the first year for 1 Stop Florists' delivery truck is shown in Illustration 9-4.

▶ **ILLUSTRATION** **9-4**
Formula for straight-line method

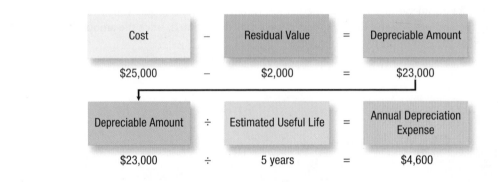

Alternatively, we can calculate an annual percentage rate to use when determining the delivery truck's straight-line depreciation expense. First, the depreciation rate is calculated by dividing 100% by the useful life in years. In this case, the straight-line depreciation rate is 20% (100% ÷ 5 years). Second, the depreciation expense is calculated by multiplying the asset's depreciable amount by the straight-line depreciation rate shown in the depreciation schedule in Illustration 9-5.

▶ **ILLUSTRATION** **9-5**
Straight-line depreciation schedule

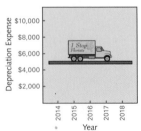

							End of Year	
Year	**Depreciable Amount**	**×**	**Depreciation Rate**	**=**	**Depreciation Expense**		**Accumulated Depreciation**	**Carrying Amount**
								$25,000
2014	$23,000		20%		$ 4,600		$ 4,600	20,400
2015	23,000		20%		4,600		9,200	15,800
2016	23,000		20%		4,600		13,800	11,200
2017	23,000		20%		4,600		18,400	6,600
2018	23,000		20%		4,600		23,000	2,000
					$23,000			

1 STOP FLORISTS
Straight-Line Depreciation Schedule

Note that the depreciation expense of $4,600 is the same each year. Also note that the column total for depreciation expense is equal to the asset's depreciable amount, and that the carrying amount at the end of the useful life is equal to the estimated $2,000 residual value.

What happens when an asset is purchased during the year, rather than on January 1 as in our example? In that case, it is necessary to **pro-rate the annual depreciation for the part of the year that the asset was used.** If 1 Stop Florists' delivery truck was ready to be used on April 1, 2014, the truck would be depreciated for nine months in 2014 (April through December). The depreciation for 2014 would be $3,450 ($23,000 × 20% × $^9/_{12}$). Note that depreciation is normally rounded to the nearest month. Since depreciation is an estimate, calculating it to the nearest day gives a false sense of accuracy.

To keep things simple, some companies establish a policy for partial-period depreciation rather than calculating depreciation monthly. Companies may choose to record a full year's depreciation in the year of acquisition and none in the year of disposal. Others may record a half year's depreciation in the year of acquisition and a half year's depreciation in the year of disposal. Whatever policy is chosen for partial-year depreciation, the impact is not significant in the long run if the policy is used consistently.

Recall that the depreciation method used must be consistent with the pattern in which the economic benefits from owning the asset are expected to be consumed. Therefore, it is appropriate to use the straight-line method when the asset is used quite uniformly throughout its useful life. Examples of assets that deliver their benefit primarily as a function of time include office furniture and fixtures, buildings, warehouses, and garages for motor vehicles. George Brown College, in the feature story, uses straight-line depreciation for its buildings.

Diminishing-Balance. The **diminishing-balance method** produces a decreasing annual depreciation expense over the asset's useful life. It is called the "diminishing-balance" method because the periodic depreciation is calculated based on the asset's carrying amount, which diminishes each year because accumulated depreciation increases. Annual depreciation expense is calculated by multiplying the carrying amount at the beginning of the year by the depreciation rate. **The depreciation rate remains constant from year to year, but the rate is applied to a carrying amount that declines each year.**

Alternative terminology The diminishing-balance method is also sometimes called the *declining-balance* method.

The carrying amount for the first year is the asset's cost, because the balance in Accumulated Depreciation at the beginning of the asset's useful life is zero. In the following years, the carrying amount is the difference between the cost and the accumulated depreciation at the beginning of the year. Unlike the other depreciation methods, the diminishing-balance method does not use a depreciable amount. **Residual value is not used in determining the amount that the diminishing-balance depreciation rate is applied to.** Residual value does, however, limit the total depreciation that can be taken. Depreciation stops when the asset's carrying amount equals its estimated residual value.

The diminishing-balance method can be applied using different rates, which results in varying speeds of depreciation. You will find rates such as one time (single), two times (double), and even three times (triple) the straight-line rate of depreciation. A depreciation rate that is often used is double the straight-line rate. This method is referred to as the **double diminishing-balance method**.

If 1 Stop Florists uses the double diminishing-balance method, the depreciation rate is 40% (2 × the straight-line rate of 20%). Illustration 9-6 shows the calculation of depreciation on the delivery truck for the first year.

Helpful hint The straight-line rate is determined by dividing 100% by the estimated useful life. In 1 Stop Florist's case, it is 100% ÷ 5 = 20%.

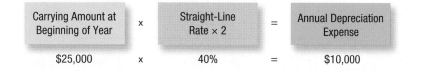

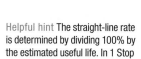

▶ **ILLUSTRATION** **9-6**
Formula for double diminishing-balance method

The depreciation schedule under this method is given in Illustration 9-7.

When an asset is purchased during the year, it is necessary to pro-rate the diminishing-balance depreciation in the first year, based on time. For example, if 1 Stop Florists had purchased the delivery truck on April 1, 2014, the depreciation for 2014 would be $7,500 ($25,000 × 40% × $^9/_{12}$) if depreciation is calculated monthly. The carrying amount for calculating depreciation in 2015 would then become $17,500 ($25,000 − $7,500). The depreciation for 2015 would be $7,000 ($17,500 × 40%). Future calculations would follow from these amounts until the carrying amount equalled the residual value.

▶**ILLUSTRATION** **9-7**
Double diminishing-
balance depreciation schedule

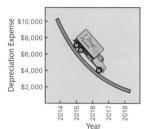

1 STOP FLORISTS
Double Diminishing-Balance Depreciation Schedule

Year	Carrying Amount Beginning Year	×	Depreciation Rate	=	Depreciation Expense	End of Year Accumulated Depreciation	End of Year Carrying Amount
							$25,000
2014	$25,000		40%		$10,000	$10,000	15,000
2015	15,000		40%		6,000	16,000	9,000
2016	9,000		40%		3,600	19,600	5,400
2017	5,400		40%		2,160	21,760	3,240
2018	3,240		40%		1,240*	23,000	2,000
					$23,000		

*The calculation of $1,296 ($3,240 × 40%) is adjusted to $1,240 so that the carrying amount will equal the residual value.

Returning to Illustration 9-7, which assumes the asset was bought at the start of the year, you can see that the delivery truck is 70% depreciated ($16,000 ÷ $23,000) at the end of the second year. Under the straight-line method, it would be 40% depreciated ($9,200 ÷ $23,000) at that time. Because the diminishing-balance method produces higher depreciation expense in the early years than in the later years, it is considered an *accelerated* depreciation method. In later years its depreciation expense will be less than the straight-line depreciation expense. Regardless of the method that is used, the total amount of depreciation over the life of the delivery truck is $23,000—the depreciable amount.

Managers must choose the diminishing-balance, or another accelerated method, if the company receives more economic benefit in the early years of the asset's useful life than in the later years. That is, this method is used if the asset, for example, has higher revenue-producing ability in its early years, or if the asset is expected to become less useful over time.

Alternative terminology The units-of-production method is often called the *units-of-activity method.*

Units-of-Production. Useful life can be expressed in ways other than time. In the **units-of-production method**, useful life is either the estimated total units of production or total expected use from the asset, not the number of years that the asset is expected to be used. The units-of-production method is ideal for equipment whose activity can be measured in units of output, such as kilometres driven or hours in use. The units-of-production method is generally not suitable for buildings or furniture, because depreciation of these assets is more a result of time than of use.

In this method, the total units of production for the entire useful life are estimated. This amount is divided into the depreciable amount (cost − residual value) to determine the depreciable amount per unit. The depreciable amount per unit is then multiplied by the actual units of production during the year to calculate the annual depreciation expense.

To illustrate, assume that the 1 Stop Florists' delivery truck is driven 30,000 kilometres in the first year of a total estimated life of 200,000 kilometres. Illustration 9-8 shows the calculation of depreciation expense in the first year.

▶**ILLUSTRATION** **9-8**
Formula for units-of-
production method

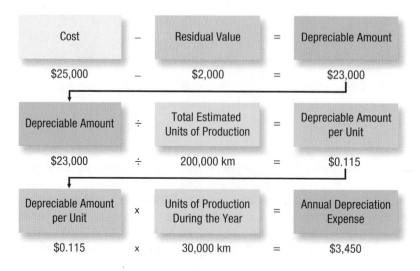

Illustration 9-9 shows the units-of-production depreciation schedule, using assumed units of production (kilometres driven) for the later years.

	1 STOP FLORISTS					
	Units-of-Production Depreciation Schedule					
					End of Year	
Year	Units of Production	×	Depreciable Cost/Unit	=	Depreciation Expense	Accumulated Depreciation	Carrying Amount
							$25,000
2014	30,000		$0.115		$ 3,450	$ 3,450	21,550
2015	60,000		$0.115		6,900	10,350	14,650
2016	40,000		$0.115		4,600	14,950	10,050
2017	50,000		$0.115		5,750	20,700	4,300
2018	20,000		$0.115		2,300	23,000	2,000
	200,000				$23,000		

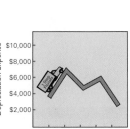

In the example in Illustration 9-9, the total actual units of production equal the original estimated total units of production of 200,000 kilometres. But in most real-life situations, the total actual units of production do not exactly equal the total estimated units of production. This means that the final year's depreciation will have to be adjusted—as we saw in the double diminishing-balance method in Illustration 9-7—so that the ending carrying amount is equal to the estimated residual value.

This method is easy to apply when assets are purchased during the year. The actual units of production already show how much the asset was used during the year. Therefore, the depreciation calculations do not need to be adjusted for partial periods as is done in the straight-line and diminishing-balance methods.

The units-of-production method is used for assets whose activity can be measured in units of output. But it can only be used if it is possible to make a reasonable estimate of total activity. Later in this chapter, we will see that this method is widely used to depreciate natural resources. The units-of-production method results in the best matching of expenses with revenues when the asset's productivity varies significantly from one period to another.

Comparison of Depreciation Methods

Illustration 9-10 presents a comparison of annual and total depreciation expense for 1 Stop Florists under each of the three depreciation methods. In addition, if we assume for simplicity that profit before deducting depreciation expense is $50,000 for each of the five years, we can clearly see the impact that the choice of method has on profit.

| | Straight-Line | | Double Diminishing-Balance | | Units-of-Production | |
Year	Depreciation Expense	Profit	Depreciation Expense	Profit	Depreciation Expense	Profit
2014	$ 4,600	$ 45,400	$10,000	$ 40,000	$ 3,450	$ 46,550
2015	4,600	45,400	6,000	44,000	6,900	43,100
2016	4,600	45,400	3,600	46,400	4,600	45,400
2017	4,600	45,400	2,160	47,840	5,750	44,250
2018	4,600	45,400	1,240	48,760	2,300	47,700
	$23,000	$227,000	$23,000	$227,000	$23,000	$227,000

Recall that straight-line depreciation results in the same amount of depreciation expense and therefore profit each year. Diminishing-balance depreciation results in a higher depreciation expense in early years, and therefore lower profit, and a lower depreciation expense and higher profit in later years. Results with the units-of-production method vary, depending on how much the asset is used each year. While the depreciation expense and profit will be different each year for each method, *total* depreciation expense and *total* profit after the five-year period are the same for all three methods.

The balance sheet is also affected by the choice of depreciation method because accumulated depreciation is increased by depreciation expense and owner's equity is increased by profit. There is no impact on cash flow because depreciation does not involve cash.

As explained earlier, management should choose the method that best matches the estimated pattern in which the asset's economic benefits are expected to be consumed. If the economic benefit of owning an asset is fairly consistent over time, the straight-line method is appropriate. The diminishing-balance method is appropriate if the company receives more economic benefit in the early years of the asset's useful life than in the later years. The units-of-production method is appropriate for assets whose usage varies over time. Because companies have more than one type of asset, they often use more than one depreciation method.

ACCOUNTING IN ACTION
BUSINESS INSIGHT

Why does **Morris Formal Wear** use the units-of-production method for its tuxedos? The reason is that the Ottawa-based family business wants to track wear and tear on each of its 5,200 tuxedos individually. Each tuxedo has its own bar code. When a tux is rented, a clerk runs its code across an electronic scanner. At year end, the computer adds up the total rentals for each of the tuxedos, then divides this number by expected total use to calculate the rate. For instance, on a two-button black tux, Morris expects a life of 30 rentals. In one year, the tux was rented 13 times. The depreciation rate for that period was 43% (13 ÷ 30) of the depreciable cost.

Is the units-of-production method the best depreciation method for Morris Formal Wear to use for its tuxedos or would you recommend another method?

Depreciation and Income Tax

The Canada Revenue Agency (CRA) allows companies to deduct a specified amount of depreciation expense when they calculate their taxable income. As we have just learned, for accounting purposes, a company must choose the depreciation method that best reflects the pattern in which the asset's future economic benefits are consumed. The CRA does not permit a choice among the three depreciation methods. Instead, it requires taxpayers to use the single diminishing-balance method on the tax return, regardless of what method is used in the financial statements.

> **Helpful hint** Depreciation for accounting purposes is usually different from depreciation for income tax purposes.

In addition, the CRA does not allow taxpayers to estimate the useful lives of assets or depreciation rates. Assets are grouped into various classes and maximum depreciation rates for each class are specified. Depreciation allowed for income tax purposes is calculated on a class (group) basis and is called **capital cost allowance (CCA)**. Capital cost allowance is an optional deduction from taxable income, but depreciation expense is not optional in calculating profit. Consequently, you may see a company deduct depreciation on its income statement, which is required by generally accepted accounting principles, but not deduct CCA for income tax purposes.

BEFORE YOU GO ON...

Action Plan
- Under straight-line depreciation, annual depreciation expense is equal to the depreciable amount (cost less residual value) divided by the estimated useful life.

Do It

On October 1, 2014, Iron Mountain Ski Company purchases a new snow grooming machine for $52,000. The machine is estimated to have a five-year useful life and a $4,000 residual value. It is also estimated to have a total useful life of 6,000 hours. It is used 1,000 hours in the year ended December 31, 2014, and 1,300 hours in the year ended December 31, 2015. How much depreciation expense should Iron Mountain Ski record in each of 2014 and 2015 under each depreciation method: (a) straight-line, (b) double diminishing-balance, and (c) units-of-production?

Solution

	2014	2015
Straight-line	$2,400	$ 9,600
Double diminishing-balance	5,200	18,720
Units-of-production	8,000	10,400

(a) Straight-line: ($52,000 − $4,000) ÷ 5 years = $9,600 per year
2014: $9,600 × $3/_{12}$ = $2,400

(b) Double diminishing-balance: 100% ÷ 5 years = 20% straight-line rate
20% × 2 = 40% double diminishing-balance rate
2014: $52,000 × 40% × $3/_{12}$ = $5,200
2015: ($52,000 − $5,200) × 40% = $18,720

(c) Units-of-production: ($52,000 − $4,000) ÷ 6,000 hours = $8.00 per hour
2014: 1,000 × $8.00 = $8,000
2015: 1,300 × $8.00 = $10,400

Related exercise material: BE9–5, BE9–6, BE9–7, BE9–8, BE9–9, E9–2, E9–3, E9–4, and E9–5.

THE **NAVIGATOR**

- Under double diminishing-balance depreciation, annual depreciation expense is equal to double the straight-line rate of depreciation times the asset's carrying amount at the beginning of the year. Residual values are ignored in this method.
- Under the straight-line and diminishing-balance methods, the annual depreciation expense must be pro-rated if the asset is purchased during the year.
- Under units-of-production depreciation, the depreciable amount per unit is equal to the total depreciable amount divided by the total estimated units of production. The annual depreciation expense is equal to the depreciable amount per unit times the actual usage in each year.

REVISING PERIODIC DEPRECIATION

During the useful life of a long-lived asset, the annual depreciation expense needs to be revised if there are changes to the three factors that affect the calculation of depreciation: the asset's cost, useful life, or residual value. Thus, depreciation needs to be revised if there are (1) capital expenditures during the asset's useful life, (2) impairments in the value of an asset, (3) changes in the asset's fair value when using the revaluation model, and/or (4) changes in the appropriate depreciation method, or in the asset's estimated useful life or residual value. In the following sections, we discuss each of these items and then show how to revise depreciation calculations.

» **STUDY OBJECTIVE 3**

Explain the factors that cause changes in periodic depreciation and calculate revisions.

Capital Expenditures During Useful Life

Earlier in the chapter, we learned that companies can have both operating and capital expenditures when a long-lived asset is purchased. Similarly, during the useful life of a long-lived asset, a company may incur costs for ordinary repairs, or for additions or improvements.

Ordinary repairs are costs to *maintain* the asset's operating efficiency and expected productive life. Motor tune-ups and oil changes, repainting a building, or replacing worn-out gears on equipment are examples of ordinary repairs. These costs are frequently fairly small amounts that occur regularly. They may also be larger, infrequent amounts, but if they simply restore an asset to its prior condition, they are considered an ordinary repair. Such repairs are debited to Repair (or Maintenance) Expense as they occur. Ordinary repairs are operating expenditures.

Additions and improvements are costs that are incurred to *increase* the asset's operating efficiency, productive capacity, or expected useful life. These costs are usually large and happen less often. Additions and improvements that add to the future cash flows associated with that asset are not expensed as they occur—they are capitalized. As capital expenditures, they are generally debited to the appropriate property, plant, or equipment account, or to the specific component of that asset. The capital expenditure will be depreciated over the remaining life of the original structure or the useful life of the addition. Additions and improvements can also increase the useful life of the original structure. The depreciation calculations need to be revised when a company makes an addition or improvement.

Impairments

As noted earlier in the chapter, under the cost model, the carrying amount of property, plant, and equipment is cost less any accumulated depreciation since its acquisition. And, as already discussed, the carrying amount of property, plant, and equipment is rarely the same as its fair value. Remember that the fair value is normally not relevant since property, plant, and equipment are not purchased for resale, but rather for use in operations over the long term.

While it is accepted that long-lived assets such as property, plant, and equipment may be under-valued on the balance sheet, it is not appropriate if property, plant, and equipment are overvalued. Property, plant, and equipment are considered impaired if the asset's carrying amount exceeds its **recoverable amount**. The recoverable amount is the greater of the asset's fair value less costs to sell, or the value in use, which is based on its future cash flows. When an asset is impaired, an **impairment loss** is recorded that is the amount by which the asset's carrying amount exceeds its recoverable amount. The rules for determining if an asset is impaired are somewhat different under ASPE and IFRS. While the details of these differences are left to an intermediate accounting course, it should be noted that under ASPE, impairments are recorded less often.

Companies are required to determine on a regular basis if there is any indication of impairment. If there is no such indication, it is not necessary to test the asset for impairment. If there is an indication of possible impairment, then an impairment test must be done. For example, if a machine has become obsolete, or if the market for a product made by a machine has dried up or has become very competitive, there is a strong possibility that an impairment loss exists. Management is then required to do an impairment test, which involves estimating the machine's recoverable amount.

To illustrate an impairment loss on a long-lived asset, assume that on December 31, Piniwa Company reviews its equipment for possible impairment. The equipment has a cost of $800,000 and accumulated depreciation of $200,000. The equipment's recoverable amount is currently $500,000. The amount of the impairment loss is determined by comparing the asset's carrying amount with its recoverable amount as follows:

Carrying amount ($800,000 − $200,000)	$600,000
Recoverable amount	500,000
Impairment loss	$100,000

The journal entry to record the impairment is:

A	=	L	+	OE
−100,000				−100,000

Cash flows: no effect

Dec. 31	Impairment Loss	100,000	
	Accumulated Depreciation—Equipment		100,000
	To record impairment loss on equipment.		

Assuming that the asset will continue to be used in operations, the impairment loss is reported on the income statement as part of operating profit rather than as "other expense." Often the loss is combined with depreciation expense on the income statement. The Accumulated Depreciation account, not the asset account, is credited for the impairment loss. Recording the loss this way keeps a record of the asset's original cost.

We had previously defined an asset's carrying amount as its cost less accumulated depreciation. This is still the case, but the Accumulated Depreciation account can now include more than just the depreciation recorded on the asset to date. It will also include impairment losses, if there have been any. Future depreciation calculations will need to be revised because of the reduction in the asset's carrying amount.

IFRS allow the reversal of a previously recorded impairment loss. Under IFRS, at each year end, the company must determine whether or not an impairment loss still exists by measuring the asset's recoverable amount. If this recoverable amount exceeds the current carrying amount, then a reversal is recorded. The reversal for an asset is limited to the amount required to increase the asset's carrying amount to what it would have been if the impairment loss had not been recorded. When an impairment loss is reversed, we simply credit the impairment loss account and debit the accumulated depreciation account. The reversal will result in additional revisions to depreciation calculations. As previously discussed, although impairment losses are recorded less often under ASPE, once an impairment has been recorded, it cannot be reversed later.

Cost Model Versus Revaluation Model

As previously mentioned, under IFRS, companies can choose to account for their property, plant, and equipment under either the cost model or the revaluation model. We have used the cost model in this chapter because it is used by almost all companies. Only about 3% of companies reporting under IFRS use the revaluation model. The revaluation model is allowed under IFRS mainly because it is particularly useful in countries that experience high rates of inflation or for companies in certain industries, such as investment or real estate companies, where fair values are more relevant than cost. It is not allowed under ASPE.

Under the **revaluation model**, the carrying amount of property, plant, and equipment is its fair value less any accumulated depreciation less any subsequent impairment losses. This model can be applied only to assets whose fair value can be reliably measured, and revaluations must be carried out often enough that the carrying amount is not materially different from the asset's fair value at the balance sheet date. The accounting in the revaluation model is relatively complex and will not be covered in this textbook.

Changes in Depreciation Method, Estimated Useful Life, or Residual Value

As previously explained, the depreciation method used should be consistent with the pattern in which the asset's future economic benefits are expected to be consumed by the company. The appropriateness of the depreciation method should be reviewed at least annually in case there has been a change in the expected pattern. Management must also review its estimates of the useful life and residual value of the company's depreciable assets at least at each year end. If wear and tear or obsolescence indicates that the estimates are too low or too high, estimates should be changed. If the depreciation method, estimated useful life, or residual values are changed, this will cause a revision to the depreciation calculations.

Revised Depreciation Calculations

All of the above discussed factors will result in a revision to the depreciation calculation. In each case, the revision is made for current and future years only. The revision is not made retroactively for past periods. Thus, when a change in depreciation is made, (1) there is no correction of previously recorded depreciation expense, and (2) depreciation expense for current and future years is revised. The rationale for this treatment is that the original calculation made in the past was based on the best information available at that time. The revision is based on new information that should affect only current and future periods. In addition, if past periods were often restated, users would feel less confident about financial statements.

To calculate the new annual depreciation expense, we must first calculate the asset's carrying amount at the time of the change. This is equal to the asset's original cost minus the accumulated depreciation to date, plus any capital expenditures, minus any impairment in value. We must also determine if the original depreciation method, residual value, and useful life are still appropriate. If not, we must determine which method is now appropriate, and the revised residual value and useful life.

To illustrate how to revise depreciation, assume that 1 Stop Florists decides on December 31, 2017—before recording its depreciation for 2017—to extend the estimated useful life of its truck by one more year (to December 31, 2019) because of its good condition. As a result of using the truck an extra year, the estimated residual value is expected to decline from its original estimate of $2,000 to $700. Assume that the company has been using straight-line depreciation and determines this is still the appropriate method. Recall that the truck was purchased on January 1, 2014, for $25,000 and originally had an estimated useful life of five years, with annual depreciation expense of $4,600.

The carrying amount at December 31, 2017—before recording depreciation for 2017—is $11,200 [$25,000 − (3 × $4,600)]. This is also the amount shown in Illustration 9-5 as the carrying amount at December 31, 2016. The remaining useful life of three years is calculated by taking the original useful life of five years, subtracting the three years where depreciation has already been recorded, and adding the additional estimated years of useful life—in this case one year. The new annual depreciation is $3,500, calculated as in Illustration 9-11.

Helpful hint Carrying amount = Cost − Accumulated Depreciation.

▶**ILLUSTRATION 9-11**
Formula for revised straight-line depreciation

Carrying Amount at Time of Change in Estimate	−	Revised Residual Value	=	Remaining Depreciable Amount at Time of Change in Estimate
$11,200	−	$700	=	$10,500

Remaining Depreciable Amount at Time of Change in Estimate	÷	Remaining Estimated Useful Life	=	Revised Annual Depreciation Expense
$10,500	÷	3 years	=	$3,500

As a result of the revision to the truck's estimated useful life and residual value, 1 Stop Florists will record depreciation expense of $3,500 on December 31 of 2017, 2018, and 2019. The company will not go back and change the depreciation for 2014, 2015, and 2016. Accumulated depreciation will now equal $24,300 [($4,600 × 3) + ($3,500 × 3)] at the end of the six-year useful life instead of the $23,000 that was originally calculated. The $1,300 increase in accumulated depreciation is because the estimated residual value was revised and decreased by $1,300 ($2,000 − $700).

If the units-of-production depreciation method is used, the calculation is the same as we just saw except that the remaining useful life is expressed as units rather than years. If the diminishing-balance method is used, the revised rate would be applied to the carrying amount at the time of the change in estimate. The rate must be revised because the useful life has changed.

BEFORE YOU GO ON...

Do It

Action Plan
- Understand the difference between an operating expenditure (benefits only the current period) and a capital expenditure (benefits future periods).
- To revise annual depreciation, calculate the carrying amount (cost less accumulated depreciation) at the revision date. Note that the cost of any capital expenditure will increase the carrying amount of the asset to be depreciated.

On August 1, 1999, just after its year end, Fine Furniture Company purchased a building for $500,000. The company used straight-line depreciation to allocate the cost of this building, estimating a residual value of $50,000 and a useful life of 30 years. After 15 years of use, on August 1, 2014, the company was forced to replace the entire roof at a cost of $25,000 cash. The residual value was expected to remain at $50,000 but the total useful life was now expected to increase to 40 years. Prepare journal entries to record (a) depreciation for the year ended July 31, 2014; (b) the cost of the addition on August 1, 2014; and (c) depreciation for the year ended July 31, 2015.

Solution

(a)

July 31, 2014	Depreciation Expense [($500,000 − $50,000) ÷ 30]	15,000	
	Accumulated Depreciation—Building		15,000
	To record annual depreciation expense.		

(b)

Aug. 1, 2014	Building	25,000	
	Cash		25,000
	To record replacement of roof.		

(c) Cost:		$500,000
Less: Accumulated depreciation $15,000 per year × 15 years		225,000
Carrying amount before replacement of roof, August 1, 2014		275,000
Add: Capital expenditure (roof)		25,000
Carrying amount after replacement of roof, August 1, 2014		300,000
Less: Revised residual value		50,000
Remaining depreciable amount		250,000
Divide by: Remaining useful life (40 − 15)		÷ 25 years
Revised annual depreciation		$ 10,000

July 31, 2015	Depreciation Expense	10,000	
	Accumulated Depreciation—Building		10,000
	To record revised annual depreciation expense.		

• Subtract any revised residual value from the carrying amount at the time of the change in estimate (plus the capital expenditure in this case) to determine the remaining depreciable amount.
• Allocate the revised depreciable amount over the remaining (not total) useful life.

THE NAVIGATOR

Related exercise material: BE9–10, BE9–11, E9–6, E9–7, and E9–8.

DISPOSALS OF PROPERTY, PLANT, AND EQUIPMENT

Companies dispose of property, plant, or equipment that is no longer useful to them. Illustration 9-12 shows three methods of disposal.

» STUDY **OBJECTIVE 4**

Account for the disposal of property, plant, and equipment.

Retirement
Equipment is scrapped or discarded.

Sale
Equipment is sold.

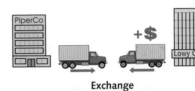

Exchange
Existing equipment is traded for new equipment.

▶ **ILLUSTRATION 9-12**
Methods of property, plant, and equipment disposal

Steps in Recording Disposals of Property, Plant, and Equipment

Whatever the disposal method, a company must take the following four steps to record the retirement, sale, or exchange of the property, plant, or equipment:

Alternative terminology *Derecognition* is a term used under IFRS to describe the removal of a long-lived asset from the accounts when it is disposed of or no longer provides any future benefit.

Step 1: Update Depreciation.

Depreciation must be recorded over the entire period of time an asset is available for use. Therefore, if the disposal occurs in the middle of an accounting period, depreciation must be updated for the fraction of the year since the last time adjusting entries were recorded up to the date of disposal.

Step 2: Calculate the Carrying Amount.

Calculate the carrying amount at the date of disposal after updating the accumulated depreciation for any partial year depreciation calculated in Step 1 above:

Step 3: Calculate the Gain or Loss.

Determine the amount of the gain or loss on disposal, if any, by comparing the proceeds received from the disposal with the carrying amount at the date of disposal.

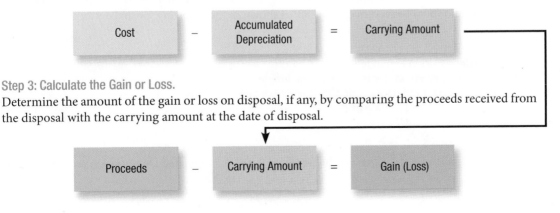

If the proceeds of the sale are more than the carrying amount of the property, plant, or equipment, there is a gain on disposal. If the proceeds of the sale are less than the carrying amount of the asset sold, there is a loss on disposal.

Step 4: Record the Disposal.

The journal entry to record the disposal always involves removing the asset's cost and the accumulated depreciation from the accounts. These are the same amounts used to calculate the carrying amount in Step 2 above. The journal entry may also include recording the proceeds and the gain or loss on disposal if there are any proceeds and if there is a gain or loss. Gains on disposal are recorded as credits because credits increase owner's equity; losses on disposal are recorded as debits because debits decrease owner's equity.

> Dr. Cash (or other account)
> Dr. Accumulated Depreciation
> Dr. Loss on Disposal OR Cr. Gain on Disposal
>   Cr. Property, plant, or equipment account

Gains and losses are reported in the operating section of a multiple-step income statement. Why? Recall that depreciation expense is an estimate. A loss results when the annual depreciation expense has not been high enough so that the carrying amount at the date of disposal is equal to the proceeds. Gains are caused because annual depreciation expense has been too high, so the carrying amount at the date of disposal is less than the proceeds. Thus gains and losses are basically just adjustments to depreciation expense and should be recorded in the same section of the income statement.

Retirement of Property, Plant, and Equipment

Instead of being sold or exchanged, some assets are simply retired at the end of their useful lives. For example, some productive assets used in manufacturing may have highly specialized uses and consequently have no market when the company no longer needs the asset. In this case, the asset is simply retired.

When an asset is retired, there are no proceeds on disposal. The Accumulated Depreciation account is decreased (debited) for the full amount of depreciation taken over the life of the asset. The asset account is reduced (credited) for the asset's original cost. Even if the carrying amount equals zero, a journal entry is still required to remove the asset and its related depreciation account from the books, as shown in the following example.

To illustrate the retirement of a piece of property, plant, and equipment, assume that on December 31, 2014, Baseyev Enterprises retires equipment, which cost $31,200. At the time of purchase, on January 1, 2011, the equipment was expected to have a four-year useful life and no residual value. Baseyev used straight-line depreciation and the annual depreciation expense was $7,800 per year ($31,200 ÷ 4). The balance in the Accumulated Depreciation account at Baseyev's year end, December 31, 2013, was $23,400 ($7,800 × 3). Before recording the disposal, Baseyev must first record depreciation from the last time it was recorded—December 31, 2013—to the date of disposal—December 31, 2014. As this is one year, the amount to be recorded is $7,800, as shown in the following journal entry:

A	=	L	+	OE				
−7,800				−7,800	2014	Depreciation Expense	7,800	
					Dec. 31	Accumulated Depreciation—Equipment		7,800
Cash flows: no effect						To record depreciation expense from last time it was recorded to date of disposal.		

After this journal entry is posted, the Equipment and Accumulated Depreciation accounts appear as follows:

Equipment	
Jan. 1, 2011 31,200	

Accumulated Depreciation—Equipment	
	Dec. 31, 2011 7,800
	Dec. 31, 2012 7,800
	Dec. 31, 2013 7,800
	Balance 23,400
	Dec. 31, 2014 7,800
	Balance 31,200

The equipment is now fully depreciated with a carrying amount of zero (cost of $31,200 − accumulated depreciation of $31,200). As the equipment is being retired, there are zero proceeds, and since the carrying amount is equal to the proceeds and there is no gain or loss on disposal. All that is required is an entry to remove the cost and accumulated depreciation of the equipment, as follows:

2014 Dec. 31	Accumulated Depreciation—Equipment	31,200	
	Equipment		31,200
	To record retirement of fully depreciated equipment.		

A   =   L   +   OE
+31,200
−31,200

Cash flows: no effect

After this entry is posted, the balance in the Equipment and Accumulated Depreciation—Equipment accounts will be zero.

What happens if a company is still using a fully depreciated asset? In this case, the asset and its accumulated depreciation continue to be reported on the balance sheet, without further depreciation, until the asset is retired. Reporting the asset and related depreciation on the balance sheet informs the reader of the financial statements that the asset is still being used by the company. Once an asset is fully depreciated, even if it is still being used, no additional depreciation should be taken. Accumulated depreciation on a piece of property, plant, and equipment can never be more than the asset's cost.

If a piece of property, plant, and equipment is retired before it is fully depreciated and no residual value is received, a loss on disposal occurs. Assume that Baseyev Enterprises retires its equipment on January 1, 2014. The loss on disposal is calculated by subtracting the asset's carrying amount from the proceeds that are received. In this case, there are no proceeds and the carrying amount is $7,800 (cost of $31,200 − accumulated depreciation of $23,400), resulting in a loss of $7,800:

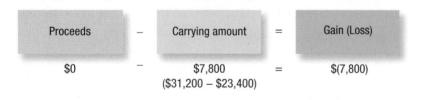

Proceeds	−	Carrying amount	=	Gain (Loss)
$0	−	$7,800 ($31,200 − $23,400)	=	$(7,800)

The entry to record the retirement of equipment is as follows:

Jan. 1	Accumulated Depreciation—Equipment	23,400	
	Loss on Disposal	7,800	
	Equipment		31,200
	To record retirement of equipment at a loss.		

A   =   L   +   OE
+23,400   −7,800
−31,200

Cash flows: no effect

You should also note that there will never be a gain when an asset is retired. The proceeds are always zero and therefore can never be greater than the carrying amount of the retired asset.

Sale of Property, Plant, and Equipment

In a disposal by sale, there are proceeds that must be recorded. Both gains and losses on disposal are common when an asset is sold. Only by coincidence will the asset's carrying amount and fair value (the proceeds) be the same when the asset is sold. We will illustrate the sale of furniture at both a gain and a loss in the following sections.

Gain on Disposal. To illustrate a gain, assume that on April 1, 2014, Baseyev Enterprises sells office furniture for $15,000 cash. The office furniture had originally been purchased on January 1, 2010, at a cost of $60,200. At that time, it was estimated that the furniture would have a residual value of $5,000 and a useful life of five years.

The first step is to update any unrecorded depreciation. Annual depreciation using the straight-line method is $11,040 [($60,200 − $5,000) ÷ 5]. The entry to record the depreciation expense and update accumulated depreciation for the first three months of 2014 is as follows:

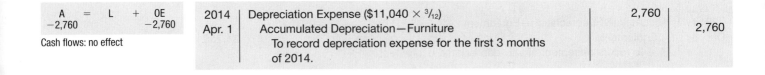

	A	=	L	+	OE
	−2,760				−2,760

Cash flows: no effect

2014 Apr. 1	Depreciation Expense ($11,040 × 3/12)	2,760	
	Accumulated Depreciation—Furniture		2,760
	To record depreciation expense for the first 3 months of 2014.		

After this journal entry is posted, the Furniture and Accumulated Depreciation accounts appear as follows:

Furniture	
Jan. 1, 2010 60,200	

Accumulated Depreciation—Furniture	
	Dec. 31, 2010 11,040
	Dec. 31, 2011 11,040
	Dec. 31, 2012 11,040
	Dec. 31, 2013 11,040
	Apr. 1, 2014 2,760
	Balance 46,920

The second step is to calculate the carrying amount on April 1, 2014. Note that the balance in Accumulated Depreciation of $46,920 is equal to four years (January 1, 2010, to December 31, 2013) at $11,040/year plus $2,760 for 2014.

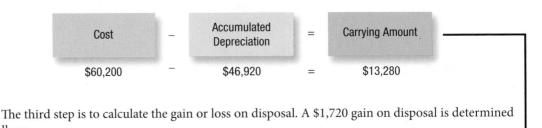

Cost	−	Accumulated Depreciation	=	Carrying Amount
$60,200	−	$46,920	=	$13,280

The third step is to calculate the gain or loss on disposal. A $1,720 gain on disposal is determined as follows:

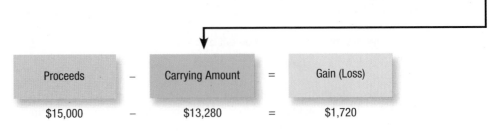

Proceeds	−	Carrying Amount	=	Gain (Loss)
$15,000	−	$13,280	=	$1,720

The fourth step is the entry to record the sale of the office furniture as follows:

Apr. 1	Cash	15,000	
	Accumulated Depreciation—Furniture	46,920	
	Gain on Disposal		1,720
	Furniture		60,200
	To record the sale of office furniture at a gain.		

A = L + OE
+15,000   +1,720
+46,920
−60,200

↑ Cash flows: +15,000

Notice that the carrying amount of $13,280 does not appear in the journal entry. Instead, the asset's cost ($60,200) and the total accumulated depreciation ($46,920) are used. **Remember the carrying amount is simply a number calculated to determine the gain or loss.** It is not an account and cannot be debited or credited.

Loss on Disposal. Assume that instead of selling the furniture for $15,000, Baseyev sells it for $9,000. In this case, a loss of $4,280 is calculated as follows:

| Proceeds | − | Carrying Amount | = | Gain (Loss) |
| $9,000 | − | $13,280 | = | $(4,280) |

The entry to record the sale of the office furniture is as follows:

Apr. 1	Cash	9,000	
	Accumulated Depreciation—Furniture	46,920	
	Loss on Disposal	4,280	
	Furniture		60,200
	To record the sale of office furniture at a loss.		

A = L + OE
+9,000   −4,280
+46,920
−60,200

↑ Cash flows: +9,000

As previously explained, the loss on disposal is the result of not recording enough depreciation expense prior to selling the asset.

Exchanges of Property, Plant, and Equipment

An exchange of assets is recorded as the purchase of a new asset and the sale of an old asset. Typically a **trade-in allowance** on the old asset is given toward the purchase price of the new asset. An additional cash payment is usually also required for the difference between the trade-in allowance and the stated purchase price (list price) of the new asset. The trade-in allowance amount, however, is often affected by price concessions for the new asset and therefore rarely reflects the fair value of the asset that is given up. Consequently, as fair value is what matters, trade-in allowances are ignored for accounting purposes.

Instead of using the stated purchase price, the new asset is recorded at the fair value of the asset given up plus any cash paid (or less any cash received). Instead of using the trade-in allowance, the fair value of the asset given up is used to calculate the gain or loss on the asset being given up. A loss results if the carrying amount of the asset being given up is more than its fair value. A gain results if the carrying amount is less than its fair value.

Thus, the procedure to account for exchanges of assets is as follows:

Step 1: Update any unrecorded depreciation expense on the asset being given up to the date of the exchange.

Step 2: Calculate the carrying amount of the asset being given up (cost − accumulated depreciation).

Step 3: Calculate any gain or loss on disposal [fair value − carrying amount = gain (loss)].

Step 4: Record the exchange as follows:

- Remove the cost and the accumulated depreciation of the asset that is given up.
- Record any gain or loss on disposal.
- Record the new asset at the fair value of the old asset plus any cash paid (or less any cash received).
- Record the cash paid or received.

To illustrate an exchange of long-lived assets, assume that Chilko Company exchanged an old vehicle for a new vehicle on October 1, 2014. The original cost of the old vehicle was $61,000 on January 1, 2009. Depreciation was calculated using the straight-line method, over a six-year useful life, with an estimated residual value of $1,000. The fair value of the old vehicle on October 1, 2014, is $3,000.

The list price of the new vehicle was $51,000. Chilko received an $8,000 trade-in allowance from the vehicle dealership for the old vehicle and paid $43,000 cash ($51,000 − $8,000) for the new vehicle. Chilko's year end is December 31.

The first step is to update the depreciation on the old vehicle for the nine months ended October 1, 2014. Annual depreciation expense is $10,000 [($61,000 − $1,000) ÷ 6], so depreciation for nine months is $7,500 ($10,000 × $^9/_{12}$).

A	=	L	+	OE				
−7,500				−7,500				

Cash flows: no effect

Oct. 1	Depreciation Expense			7,500		
	Accumulated Depreciation—Vehicles				7,500	
	To record depreciation expense for the first 9 months of 2014.					

After this journal entry is posted, the Vehicles and Accumulated Depreciation accounts appear as follows:

Vehicles	
Jan. 1, 2009 61,000	

Accumulated Depreciation—Vehicles	
	Dec. 31, 2009 10,000
	Dec. 31, 2010 10,000
	Dec. 31, 2011 10,000
	Dec. 31, 2012 10,000
	Dec. 31, 2013 10,000
	Oct. 1, 2014 7,500
	Balance 57,500

The next step is to calculate the carrying amount on October 1, 2014. Note that the balance in Accumulated Depreciation of $57,500 is equal to five years (January 1, 2009, to December 31, 2013) at $10,000/year plus $7,500 for 2014.

On October 1, 2014, the carrying amount is $3,500 (cost of $61,000 − accumulated depreciation of $57,500). The loss on disposal on the old vehicle is determined by comparing the carrying amount with the fair value, which represents the proceeds in this situation:

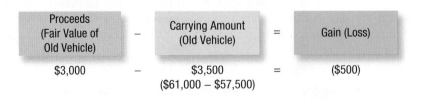

The cost of the new vehicle ($46,000) is determined by the fair value of the old vehicle ($3,000) plus the cash paid ($43,000). The entry to record the exchange of vehicles is as follows:

Oct. 1	Vehicles (cost of new vehicle)	46,000	
	Accumulated Depreciation—Vehicles (on the old vehicle)	57,500	
	Loss on Disposal	500	
	Vehicles (cost of old vehicle)		61,000
	Cash		43,000
	To record exchange of vehicles, plus cash.		

A	=	L	+	OE
+46,000				−500
+57,500				
−61,000				
−43,000				

Note that the exchange of vehicles is not netted. That is, it is shown as a separate increase and decrease to the general ledger account Vehicles. Also note that the list price of $51,000 and the trade-in allowance of $8,000 are ignored in determining the real cost of the new vehicle.

In some situations, the exchange lacks commercial substance or else the fair value of the asset acquired or the asset given up cannot be determined. In such cases, the new long-lived asset is recorded at the carrying amount of the old asset that was given up, plus any cash paid (or less any cash received). Carrying amount is used in these circumstances because the new asset is basically substituted or swapped for the old asset. As the carrying amount of the old asset is used for the carrying amount of the new asset, and the exchange has therefore not changed the operations of the business significantly, no gain or loss is recorded.

⟳ BEFORE YOU GO ON...

Do It

Overland Trucking has a truck that was purchased on January 1, 2010, for $80,000. The truck had been depreciated on a straight-line basis with an estimated residual value of $5,000 and an estimated useful life of five years. Overland has a December 31 year end. Assume each of the following four independent situations:

1. On January 1, 2015, Overland retires the truck.
2. On May 1, 2014, Overland sells the truck for $9,500 cash.
3. On October 1, 2014, Overland sells the truck for $9,500 cash.
4. On November 1, 2014, Overland exchanges the old truck, plus $60,000 cash, for a new truck. The old truck has a fair value of $9,500. The new truck has a list price of $70,000, but the dealer will give Overland a $10,000 trade-in allowance on the old truck.

Prepare the journal entry to record each of these situations.

Action Plan

- Update any unrecorded depreciation for dispositions during the fiscal year.
- Compare the proceeds with the asset's carrying amount to determine if there has been a gain or loss.
- Record any proceeds received and any gain or loss. Remove both the asset and any related accumulated depreciation from the accounts.
- Determine the cash paid in an exchange situation as the difference between the list price and the trade-in allowance.
- Record the cost of the new asset in an exchange situation as the fair value of the asset given up, plus the cash paid.

Solution

$$\frac{\$80,000 - \$5,000}{5 \text{ years}} = \$15,000 \text{ annual depreciation expense}$$

$15,000 ÷ 12 = $1,250 per month

1. Retirement of truck:

Jan. 1, 2015	Accumulated Depreciation—Vehicles ($1,250 × 60 months)	75,000	
	Loss on Disposal [$0 − ($80,000 − $75,000)]	5,000	
	Vehicles		80,000
	To record retirement of truck.		

2. Sale of truck for $9,500 on May 1, 2014:

May 1, 2014	Depreciation Expense ($1,250 × 4 months)	5,000	
	Accumulated Depreciation—Vehicles		5,000
	To record depreciation for 4 months.		
	Cash	9,500	
	Accumulated Depreciation—Vehicles ($1,250 × 52 months)	65,000	
	Loss on Disposal [$9,500 − ($80,000 − $65,000)]	5,500	
	Vehicles		80,000
	To record sale of truck at a loss.		

⊘ BEFORE YOU GO ON continued...

3. Sale of truck for $9,500 on Oct. 1, 2014:

Oct. 1, 2014	Depreciation Expense ($1,250 × 9 months)	11,250	
	Accumulated Depreciation—Vehicles		11,250
	To record depreciation for 9 months.		
	Cash	9,500	
	Accumulated Depreciation—Vehicles		
	($1,250 × 57 months)	71,250	
	Gain on Disposal [$9,500 − ($80,000 − $71,250)]		750
	Vehicles		80,000
	To record sale of truck at a gain.		

4. Exchange of truck on Nov. 1, 2014:

Nov. 1, 2014	Depreciation Expense ($1,250 × 10 months)	12,500	
	Accumulated Depreciation—Vehicles		12,500
	To record depreciation for 10 months.		
	Vehicles (cost of new) ($9,500 + $60,000)	69,500	
	Accumulated Depreciation—Vehicles		
	($1,250 × 58 months)	72,500	
	Gain on Disposal [$9,500 − ($80,000 − $72,500)]		2,000
	Vehicles (cost of old)		80,000
	Cash ($70,000 − $10,000)		60,000
	To record exchange of trucks, plus cash.		

THE NAVIGATOR

Related exercise material: BE9–12, BE9–13, BE9–14, E9–9, and E9–10.

Natural Resources

» STUDY OBJECTIVE 5

Calculate and record depreciation of natural resources.

Natural resources consist of standing timber and underground deposits of oil, gas, and minerals. Canada is rich in natural resources, ranging from the towering rainforests in coastal British Columbia to one of the world's largest nickel deposits in Voisey's Bay, Labrador. These long-lived assets have two characteristics that make them different from other long-lived assets: (1) they are physically extracted in operations such as mining, cutting, or pumping; and (2) only an act of nature can replace them. Because of these characteristics, natural resources are sometimes called *wasting assets*.

Natural resources are tangible assets, similar to property, plant, and equipment. A key distinction between natural resources and property, plant, and equipment is that natural resources physically lose substance, or deplete, as they are used. For example, there is less of a tract of timberland (a natural resource) as the timber is cut and sold. When we use equipment, its physical substance remains the same regardless of the product it produces.

COST

The cost of a natural resource is determined in the same way as the cost of property, plant, and equipment and includes all expenditures necessary in acquiring the resource and preparing it for its intended use. These costs are often referred to as acquisition, exploration, and development costs. The cost of a natural resource also includes the estimated future removal and site restoration cleanup costs, which are often large. Restoration costs are usually required in order to return the resource as closely as possible to its natural state at the end of its useful life.

As discussed earlier in the chapter, accounting for asset retirement costs and the allocation of these costs over the useful life of the natural resource is complicated. Further discussion of these concepts is left to an intermediate accounting course. Accounting for exploration and development costs is also very complex. We will, however, look at how the acquisition cost of a natural resource is allocated over its useful life in the next section.

DEPRECIATION

The units-of-production method (learned earlier in the chapter) is generally used to calculate the depreciation of wasting assets. Under the units-of-production method, the total cost of the natural resource minus its residual value is divided by the number of units estimated to be in the resource. The result is a depreciable amount per unit of product. The depreciable amount per unit is then multiplied by the number of units extracted, to determine the annual depreciation expense.

Alternative terminology Depreciation for natural resources is frequently called *depletion* because the assets physically deplete as the resource is extracted.

To illustrate, assume that Rabbit Lake Company invests $5.5 million in a mine that is estimated to have 10 million tonnes (t) of uranium and a $200,000 residual value. In the first year, 800,000 tonnes of uranium are extracted. Illustration 9-13 shows the formulas and calculations.

▶ **ILLUSTRATION 9-13**
Formula for units-of-production method for natural resources

Cost	−	Residual Value	=	Depreciable Amount
$5,500,000	−	$200,000	=	$5,300,000
Depreciable Amount	÷	Total Estimated Units of Production	=	Depreciable Amount per Unit
$5,300,000	÷	10,000,000 t	=	$0.53
Depreciable Amount per Unit	×	Number of Units Extracted and Sold During the Year	=	Annual Depreciation Expense
$0.53	×	800,000 t	=	$424,000

The depreciation expense for the amount of the resource that has been extracted is initially charged (debited) to an inventory account, a current asset. Note that this is not the same as depreciation for property, plant, and equipment, which is recorded as an expense. Depreciation on natural resources is accounted for in this way because the resource extracted is available for sale—similar to merchandise that has been purchased or manufactured for sale, as we learned in Chapter 5.

The entry to record depreciation of the uranium mine for Rabbit Lake Company's first year of operation, ended December 31, 2014, is as follows:

Dec. 31	Inventory ($0.53 × 800,000 t)	424,000	
	Accumulated Depreciation—Uranium Mine		424,000
	To record depreciation expense on uranium mine.		

```
A    =    L    +    OE
+424,000
−424,000
```
Cash flows: no effect

All costs of extracting the natural resource—both current production costs such as labour and depreciation of the natural resource—are recorded as inventory. When sold, the inventory costs are transferred to cost of goods sold and matched with the period's revenue. In other words, the depreciation is charged to the income statement only in the period in which the related goods are sold. Depreciation related to goods not yet sold remains in inventory and is reported as a current asset.

For example, assume that Rabbit Lake Company does not sell all of the 800,000 tonnes of uranium extracted in 2014. It sells 700,000 tonnes and stores 100,000 tonnes for later sale. In this situation, Rabbit Lake Company would include $371,000 (700,000 × $0.53) in the cost of the resource sold on its income statement. As mentioned before, the cost of labour and other production costs related to the goods sold would also be included in the cost of the resource sold on the income statement. The remaining depreciation of $53,000 ($424,000 − $371,000) is for the 100,000 tonnes kept for later sale and will be included in inventory in the current assets section of the company's balance sheet.

Like depreciation for property, plant, and equipment, the depreciation of a natural resource needs to be revised if there are capital expenditures during the useful life. Also, the depreciable amount per unit of a natural resource needs to be revised whenever the estimated total units of the resource have changed as a result of new information. Natural resources such as oil and gas deposits and some metals have provided the greatest challenges. Estimates of the total units (also called reserves) of these natural resources are mostly knowledgeable guesses and may be revised whenever more information becomes available.

Natural resources must also be reviewed and tested for impairment annually or more frequently whenever circumstances make this appropriate. For example, Rabbit Lake Company would need to test the uranium mine for impairment if there was a significant and permanent decline in the selling price of uranium. If there is impairment, the uranium mine must be written down to its fair value, an impairment loss must be recorded, and current and future depreciation needs to be revised accordingly.

DISPOSAL

At disposal, just as with property, plant, and equipment, any unrecorded depreciation of natural resources must be updated for the portion of the year up to the date of the disposal. Then proceeds are recorded, the cost and the accumulated depreciation of the natural resource are removed, and a gain or loss, if any, is recorded. As mentioned earlier, there may also be site restoration costs at this time, but we leave the accounting for these costs to a future accounting course.

Action Plan

- Use units-of-production depreciation for natural resources.
- Calculate the depreciable amount per unit by dividing the total cost minus the estimated residual value by the total estimated units.
- Multiply the depreciable amount per unit by the number of units cut to determine the total depreciation.
- Allocate the depreciation related to the units that have been cut but not yet sold to inventory.
- Allocate the depreciation related to the units that have been cut and sold to expense.

⊙ BEFORE YOU GO ON...

Do It

High Timber Company invests $14 million in a tract of timber land. It is estimated to have 10 million cunits (1 cunit = 100 cubic feet) of timber and a $500,000 residual value. In the first year, 40,000 cunits of timber are cut, and 30,000 of these cunits are sold. Calculate depreciation for High Timber's first year of operations and allocate it between inventory and cost of goods sold.

Solution

1. Depreciable amount per unit: ($14,000,000 − 500,000) ÷ 10,000,000 cunits = $1.35 per cunit
2. Total depreciation for the year: $1.35 per cunit × 40,000 cunits cut = $54,000
3. Depreciation allocated to inventory: $1.35 per cunit × 10,000 cunits on hand = $13,500
4. Depreciation allocated to expense: $1.35 per cunit × 30,000 cunits sold = $40,500

Related exercise material: BE9–15 and E9–11.

THE **NAVIGATOR**

Intangible Assets and Goodwill

» STUDY OBJECTIVE 6

Identify the basic accounting issues for intangible assets and goodwill.

Similar to property, plant, and equipment, and natural resources, intangible assets provide economic benefits in future periods. They are used to produce products or provide services over these periods and are not intended for sale to customers. However, unlike property, plant, and equipment, and natural resources, which are **tangible assets** because they have a physical substance, **intangible assets** involve rights, privileges, and competitive advantages that have no physical substance. In other words, they are not physical things. Many companies' most valuable assets are intangible. Some widely known intangibles are Alexander Graham Bell's patent on the telephone, the franchises of Tim Hortons, the trade name of President's Choice, and the trademark CBC. On the other hand, some organizations, such as George Brown College in the feature story, do not have intangible assets or goodwill.

An intangible asset must be identifiable, which means it must meet one of the two following criteria: (1) it can be separated from the company and sold, whether or not the company intends to do so, or

(2) it is based on contractual or legal rights, regardless of whether or not it can be separated from the company. Since goodwill cannot be separated from a company and sold, there are differences in the accounting for goodwill versus other intangible assets.

ACCOUNTING FOR INTANGIBLE ASSETS

Like tangible assets (property, plant, and equipment, and natural resources), intangible assets are recorded at cost. Cost includes all the costs of acquisition and other costs that are needed to make the intangible asset ready for its intended use—including legal fees and similar charges.

As with tangible assets, companies have a choice of following the cost model or the revaluation model when accounting for intangible assets subsequent to acquisition. The majority of companies use the cost model for all long-lived assets. So we will leave further study of the revaluation model, as it applies to intangible assets, for a later accounting course.

Under the cost model, if an intangible asset has a finite (limited) life, its cost must be systematically allocated over its useful life. We called this "depreciation" when discussing tangible assets. With intangible assets, we use the term **amortization**.

For an intangible asset with a finite life, its **amortizable amount** (cost less residual value) should be allocated over the shorter of the (1) estimated useful life and (2) legal life. Intangible assets, by their nature, rarely have any residual value, so the amortizable amount is normally equal to the cost. In addition, the useful life of an intangible asset is usually shorter than its legal life, so useful life is most often used as the amortization period.

When a company estimates the useful life of an intangible asset, it must consider factors such as how long the company expects to use the asset, obsolescence, demand, and other factors that can make the intangible asset ineffective at helping to earn revenue. For example, a patent on a computer chip may have a legal life of 20 years, but with technology changing as rapidly as it does, the chip's useful life may be only four or five years maximum.

Amortization begins as soon as the asset is ready to be used as intended by management. Similar to depreciation, the company must use the amortization method that best matches the pattern with which the asset's future economic benefits are expected to be consumed. If that pattern cannot be determined reliably, the straight-line method should be used.

Just as land is considered to have an indefinite life, there are also intangible assets with an indefinite life. An intangible asset is considered to have an indefinite (unlimited) life when, based on an analysis of all of the relevant factors, there is no foreseeable limit to the period over which the intangible asset is expected to generate net cash inflows for the company. If an intangible has an indefinite life, it is not amortized.

As with tangible assets, companies must determine if there are indicators of impairment on intangible assets' definite lives. If there are indicators, an impairment test is performed. Under IFRS, intangible assets with indefinite lives must be tested for impairment at least once a year even if no indications of impairment are evident. Under ASPE, this annual test is not required unless indicators are present.

Recall from earlier in this chapter that there is impairment if the asset's recoverable amount falls below its carrying amount. If any impairment is evident, the intangible asset is written down to its recoverable amount and an impairment loss recorded. Under IFRS, an impairment loss can be reversed for intangible assets (but not goodwill), similar to property, plant, and equipment. Under ASPE, losses cannot be reversed.

Similar to tangible assets, the amortization is revised if there are changes in cost, or useful life, or an impairment loss. The revision is accounted for in the current and future periods; retroactive adjustments are not recorded.

At disposal, just as with tangible assets, the carrying amount of the intangible asset is removed, and a gain or loss, if any, is recorded.

INTANGIBLE ASSETS WITH FINITE LIVES

Examples of intangible assets with finite lives include patents and copyrights. We also include research and development costs in this section because these costs often lead to the creation of patents and copyrights.

Patents

A **patent** is an exclusive right issued by the Canadian Intellectual Property Office of Industry Canada that allows the patent holder to manufacture, sell, or otherwise control an invention for a period of 20 years from the date of the application. A patent cannot be renewed. But the legal life of a patent may be extended if the patent holder obtains new patents for improvements or other changes in the basic design.

The initial cost of a patent is the price paid to acquire it. After it has been acquired, legal costs are often incurred. Legal costs to successfully defend a patent in an infringement suit are considered necessary to prove the patent's validity. They are added to the Patent account and amortized over the patent's remaining life.

The cost of a patent should be amortized over its 20-year legal life or its useful life, whichever is shorter. As mentioned earlier, the useful life should be carefully assessed by considering whether the patent is likely to become ineffective at contributing to revenue before the end of its legal life.

Copyrights

A **copyright** is granted by the Canadian Intellectual Property Office, giving the owner an exclusive right to reproduce and sell an artistic or published work. Copyrights extend for the life of the creator plus 50 years. Generally, a copyright's useful life is significantly shorter than its legal life.

The cost of a copyright consists of the cost of acquiring and defending it. The cost may only be the fee paid to register the copyright, or it may amount to a great deal more if a copyright infringement suit is involved.

ACCOUNTING IN ACTION
ALL ABOUT YOU INSIGHT

If you copy a song from a CD to your iPod that has a "digital lock" on it to prevent unauthorized copying, you could be liable for a fine ranging from $100 to $5,000 for breaking the digital lock and copying the CD. This is one of the provisions in Canada's new *Copyright Modernization Act*, passed in 2012. The last time the copyright laws were changed was in 1997, before the first MP3 player came on the market. Since that time, the Internet and other new technologies have changed the way we produce and access copyright material. Supporters of the law argue that companies and individuals in the entertainment and creative fields need to have their songs, videos, TV shows, software, electronic books, and other works protected in order to foster creativity and innovation. But the amendments are also intended to give more flexibility to consumers such as officially legalizing the recording of television programs to watch at their convenience.

Sources: Bea Vongdouangchanh, "Parliament Passes New Copyright Law; Geist Says Feds Caved to U.S. on Digital Locks," *The Hill Times*, July 2, 2012; CBC News, "Copyright Bill Finally Clears Commons," CBC.ca, June 19, 2012; Mary Teresa Bitti, "Chambers: Copyright Lawyers Prepare for New Rules," *Financial Post*, March 26, 2012.

Why is it important that the copyrights of artists, writers, musicians, and the entertainment industry be protected?

Research and Development Costs

Research and development (R&D) costs are not intangible assets by themselves. But they may lead to patents and copyrights, new processes, and new products. Many companies spend large sums of money on research and development in an ongoing effort to develop new products or processes.

Research and development costs present two accounting problems: (1) it is sometimes difficult to determine the costs related to specific projects; (2) it is also hard to know the extent and timing of future benefits. As a result, accounting distinguishes between research costs and development costs.

Research is original, planned investigation that is done to gain new knowledge and understanding. It is not known at this stage if a future benefit will exist as a result of the research. Therefore, all research costs should be expensed when they are incurred.

Development is the use of research findings and knowledge for a plan or design before the start of commercial production. Development costs with probable future benefits should be capitalized. All of the following criteria must be met for development costs to be capitalized:

- The project is technically feasible.
- The company plans to complete the project.
- There are adequate resources to complete the project.
- A market exists for the product.

If any of these conditions are not met, the development costs must be expensed. Illustration 9-14 shows the distinction between research and development. After development is completed, the capitalized development costs are amortized over the useful life of the project developed.

Research

Examples
- Laboratory research aimed at the discovery of new knowledge
- Searching for ways to use new research findings or other knowledge
- Forming concepts and designs of possible product or process alternatives

Development

Examples
- Testing in search or evaluation of product or process alternatives
- Design, construction, and testing of pre-production prototypes and models
- Design of tools, jigs, moulds, and dies involving new technology

▶ **ILLUSTRATION 9-14**
Distinction between research and development

INTANGIBLE ASSETS WITH INDEFINITE LIVES

An intangible asset is considered to have an indefinite life when there is no foreseeable limit to the length of time over which the asset is expected to generate cash. Examples of intangible assets with indefinite lives include trademarks and trade names, franchises, and licences. Intangible assets do not always fit perfectly in a specific category. Sometimes trademarks, trade names, franchises, or licences do have finite lives. In such cases, they would be amortized over the shorter of their legal or useful lives. It is more usual, however, for these intangible assets, along with goodwill, to have indefinite lives.

Trademarks, Trade Names, and Brands

A **trademark** or **trade name** is a word, phrase, jingle, or symbol that identifies a particular enterprise or product. Trade names like President's Choice, KFC, Nike, Tim Hortons, the Blue Jays, and TSN create immediate brand recognition and generally help the sale of a product or service. Each year, Interbrands ranks the world's best brands. In 2012, it ranked Coca-Cola as the most successful brand in the world, followed by Apple, IBM, Google, and Microsoft. In Canada, the most valuable brands in retail included lululemon and Shoppers Drug Mart.

The creator can get an exclusive legal right to the trademark or trade name by registering it with the Canadian Intellectual Property Office. This registration gives continuous protection. It may be renewed every 15 years, as long as the trademark or trade name is in use. In most cases, companies continuously renew their trademarks or trade names. In such cases, as long as the trademark or trade name continues to be marketable, it will have an indefinite useful life.

If the trademark or trade name is purchased, the cost is the purchase price. If the trademark or trade name is developed internally rather than purchased, it cannot be recognized as an intangible asset on the balance sheet. The reason is that expenditures on internally developed trademarks or brands cannot be distinguished from the cost of developing the business as a whole. The cost cannot be separately measured.

Franchises and Licences

When you purchase a Civic from a Honda dealer, fill up your gas tank at the corner Mohawk station, or buy coffee from Tim Hortons, you are dealing with franchises. A **franchise** is a contractual arrangement under which the franchisor grants the franchisee the right to sell certain products, to provide specific services, or to use certain trademarks or trade names, usually inside a specific geographic area.

Another type of franchise is granted by a government body that allows a company to use public property in performing its services. Examples are the use of city streets for a bus line or taxi service; the use of public land for telephone, power, and cable lines; and the use of airwaves for radio or TV broadcasting. Such operating rights are called **licences**.

When costs can be identified with the acquisition of the franchise or licence, an intangible asset should be recognized. These rights have indefinite lives and are not amortized. Annual payments, which are often in proportion to the franchise's total sales, are sometimes required under a franchise agreement. These payments are called **royalties** and are recorded as operating expenses in the period in which they are incurred.

GOODWILL

Unlike other assets, which can be sold individually in the marketplace, goodwill cannot be sold individually as it is part of the business as a whole. It cannot be separated from the company, nor is it based on legal rights. **Goodwill** represents the value of favourable attributes related to a business such as exceptional management, a desirable location, good customer relations, skilled employees, high-quality products, fair pricing policies, and harmonious relations with labour unions.

If goodwill can be identified only with the business as a whole, how can it be determined? An accountant could try to put a dollar value on the attributes (exceptional management, a desirable location, and so on), but the results would be very subjective. Subjective valuations would not contribute to the reliability of financial statements. For this reason, internally generated goodwill is not recognized as an asset.

Goodwill is recorded only when there is a purchase of an entire business, at which time an independent valuation can be determined. The cost of goodwill is measured by comparing the cost paid to purchase the entire business with the fair value of its net assets (assets less liabilities). If the cost is greater than these net identifiable assets, then the purchaser has paid for something that is not identifiable, that cannot be separated and sold—goodwill. In this situation, because a transaction has occurred, the cost of the purchased goodwill can be measured and therefore recorded as an asset.

 Because goodwill has an indefinite life, just as the company has an indefinite life, it is not amortized. Since goodwill is measured using the company's fair value—a value that can easily change—IFRS requires goodwill to be tested annually for impairment even if there is no indication of impairment. Under ASPE, impairment tests of goodwill are only conducted if there is an indication that impairment exists.

Impairment losses on goodwill are never reversed, even if the value of the company increases after the impairment loss has been recognized. This is applicable under both IFRS and ASPE.

↺ BEFORE YOU GO ON...

Do It

Dummies 'R' Us Company purchased a copyright to a new book series for $15,000 cash on August 1, 2013. The books are expected to have a saleable life of three years. One year later, the company spends an additional $6,000 cash to successfully defend this copyright in court. The company's year end is July 31. Record (a) the purchase of the copyright on August 1, 2013; (b) the year-end amortization at July 31, 2014; (c) the legal costs incurred on August 1, 2014; and (d) the year-end amortization at July 31, 2015.

Solution

(a)

Aug. 1, 2013	Copyrights	15,000	
	Cash		15,000
	To record purchase of copyright.		

(b)

July 31, 2014	Amortization Expense ($15,000 ÷ 3)	5,000	
	Accumulated Amortization—Copyrights		5,000
	To record amortization expense.		

(c)

Aug. 1, 2014	Copyrights	6,000	
	Cash		6,000
	To record costs incurred to defend copyright.		

(d)

July 31, 2015	Amortization Expense	8,000*	
	Accumulated Amortization—Copyrights		8,000
	To record revised amortization expensse.		

*$15,000 − $5,000 + $6,000 = $16,000 carrying amount; $16,000 carrying amount ÷ 2 years remaining = $8,000

Related exercise material: BE9–16, E9–12, E9–13, and E9–14.

Action Plan
- Amortize intangible assets with finite lives over the shorter of their useful life and legal life (the legal life of a copyright is the life of the author plus 50 years).
- Treat costs to successfully defend an intangible asset as a capital expenditure because they benefit future periods.
- Revise amortization for additions to the cost of the asset, using the carrying amount at the time of the addition and the remaining useful life.

THE **NAVIGATOR**

Statement Presentation and Analysis

PRESENTATION

Long-lived assets are normally reported in the balance sheet under the headings "property, plant, and equipment," "intangible assets," and "goodwill." Some companies combine property, plant, and equipment and intangible assets under the heading "capital assets." Goodwill must be disclosed separately.

The cost and the accumulated depreciation and/or amortization for each major class of assets are disclosed in either the balance sheet or notes. In addition, the depreciation and amortization methods that are used must be described. The amount of depreciation and amortization expense for the period should also be disclosed. As previously explained, gains or losses on disposals of long-lived assets are included in operating expenses on the income statement.

Under IFRS, companies also have to disclose if they are using the cost or the revaluation model for each class of assets, and include a reconciliation of the carrying amount at the beginning and end of the period for each class of long-lived assets in the notes to the financial statements. This means they must show all of the following for each class of long-lived assets: (1) additions, (2) disposals, (3) depreciation or amortization, (4) impairment losses, and (5) reversals of impairment losses. ASPE does not require disclosure of all of these details.

Illustration 9-15 contains an excerpt from Enerflex's 2011 balance sheet (which it calls *statement of financial position*).

» STUDY **OBJECTIVE 7**

Illustrate the reporting and analysis of long-lived assets.

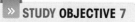

ENERFLEX LTD. Statement of Financial Position (partial) December 31, 2011 (in thousands)	**ENERFLEX**
Assets	
Property, plant, and equipment (note 10)	$123,130
Rental equipment (note 10)	101,908
Intangible assets (note 12)	31,528
Goodwill (note 13)	459,935

▶ I L L U S T R A T I O N
Presentation of long-lived assets

Enerflex provides additional details on the long-lived assets in the notes to its financial statements. For example, in note 10, Enerflex discloses the required information about all of its property, plant, and equipment, which include land, buildings, equipment, assets under construction, assets held for sale, and rental equipment.

Another note, Enerflex's summary of significant accounting policies, discloses that straight-line depreciation is used and provides information on the estimated useful lives of the company's long-lived assets. This note also states that major renewals and improvements in rental equipment and property, plant, and equipment are capitalized. It explains that significant components of property, plant, and equipment that required replacement at regular intervals are accounted for separately. The notes also include information on Enerflex's policies on testing its long-lived assets for impairment. Property, plant, and equipment, rental equipment and intangible assets are assessed for impairment whenever changes in events or changes in circumstances indicate that the asset's carrying amount may not be recovered. Goodwill is tested for impairment at least annually.

ANALYSIS

Information in the financial statements about long-lived assets allows decision makers to analyze a company's use of its total assets. We will use two ratios to analyze total assets: asset turnover and return on assets.

Asset Turnover

The **asset turnover** ratio indicates how efficiently a company uses its assets; that is, how many dollars of sales are generated by each dollar that is invested in assets. It is calculated by dividing net sales by average total assets. If a company is using its assets efficiently, each dollar of assets will create a high amount of sales. When we compare two companies in the same industry, the one with the higher asset turnover is operating more efficiently. The asset turnover ratio for fiscal 2012 for Reitmans (Canada) Limited (dollars in thousands) is calculated in Illustration 9-16.

▶ **ILLUSTRATION 9-16**
Asset turnover

Net Sales	÷	Average Total Assets	=	Asset Turnover
$1,019,397	÷	($633,861 + $659,355) ÷ 2 =		1.58 times

The asset turnover ratio shows that each dollar invested in assets produced $1.58 in sales for Reitmans. This ratio varies greatly among different industries—from those that have a large investment in assets (e.g., utility companies) to those that have much less invested in assets (e.g., service companies). Asset turnover ratios, therefore, should only be compared for companies that are in the same industry.

Return on Assets

The **return on assets** ratio measures overall profitability. This ratio is calculated by dividing profit by average total assets. The return on assets ratio indicates the amount of profit that is generated by each dollar invested in assets. A high return on assets indicates a profitable company. Illustration 9-17 shows the return on assets for Reitmans (dollars in thousands).

▶ **ILLUSTRATION 9-17**
Return on assets

Profit	÷	Average Total Assets	=	Return on Assets
$47,539	÷	($633,861 + $659,355) ÷ 2 =		7.4%

Reitmans' return on assets was 7.4% for 2012. As with other ratios, the return on assets should be compared with previous years, with other companies in the same industry, and with industry averages, to determine how well the company has performed.

BEFORE YOU GO ON...

Do It

The following information is available for Toni's Sporting Goods for three recent years:

	2014	2013	2012
Total assets	$299,650	$259,700	$223,540
Net sales	521,180	487,150	441,280
Profit	26,390	18,210	13,540

Calculate the asset turnover and return on assets ratios for Toni's Sporting Goods for 2014 and 2013 and comment on any trends.

Solution

	2014	2013
Average total assets	($299,650 + $259,700) ÷ 2 = $279,675	($259,700 + $223,540) ÷ 2 = $241,620
Asset turnover	$1.9 \text{ times} = \dfrac{\$521,180}{\$279,675}$	$2 \text{ times} = \dfrac{\$487,150}{\$241,620}$
Return on assets	$9.4\% = \dfrac{\$26,390}{\$279,675}$	$7.5\% = \dfrac{\$18,210}{\$241,620}$

In general, it is better to have a higher asset turnover and return on assets. Toni's Sporting Goods' lower asset turnover may indicate it is not using its assets as efficiently in 2014 as compared with 2013. However, the increase in the return on assets indicates improved profitability. Given the decrease in turnover, this is a positive result.

Related exercise material: BE9–17, BE9–18, BE9–19, E9–15, and E9–16.

Action Plan
- Calculate average total assets using the total assets at the beginning and end of the year.
- Divide net sales by the average total assets for that year to calculate asset turnover.
- Divide profit by the average total assets for that year to calculate return on assets.
- Recall if it is better for asset turnover and return on assets to increase or decrease.

THE NAVIGATOR

Comparing IFRS and ASPE

Key Differences	International Financial Reporting Standards (IFRS)	Accounting Standards for Private Enterprises (ASPE)
Valuing property, plant, and equipment	Choice of cost or revaluation model.	Must use cost model.
Terminology	The term "depreciation" is used for allocating the cost of property, plant, and equipment.	The term "amortization" may be used for allocating the cost of property, plant, and equipment. The term "depreciation" is also accepted.
Impairment of property, plant, and equipment, and finite-life intangible assets	Must look for indicators of impairment annually. If exist, then must test for impairment. Allow for recoveries of previously recorded impairments.	No requirement to look for indicators of impairment annually. Perform tests only if it is apparent they exist. Impairments recorded less often, but cannot later reverse an impairment loss.
Test for impairment of indefinite-life intangible assets	Must perform impairment tests annually. Allows for recoveries of previously recorded impairments.	Same approach as for property, plant, and equipment, and intangible assets with finite lives.
Test for impairment of goodwill	Must be conducted every year.	Conducted only if there is an indication of impairment.
Disclosure	Must provide a reconciliation of the opening and closing carrying amount of each class of assets.	Reconciliation not required.

THE NAVIGATOR

Demonstration Problem 1

DuPage Company purchases a factory machine at a cost of $17,500 on June 1, 2014. The machine is expected to have a residual value of $1,500 at the end of its four-year useful life on May 31, 2018. DuPage has a December 31 year end.

During its useful life, the machine is expected to be used for 10,000 hours. Actual annual use was as follows: 1,300 hours in 2014; 2,800 hours in 2015; 3,300 hours in 2016; 1,900 hours in 2017; and 700 hours in 2018.

ACTION PLAN

- Deduct the residual value in the straight-line and units-of-production methods, but not in the diminishing-balance method.
- In the diminishing-balance method, the depreciation rate is applied to the carrying amount (cost − accumulated depreciation). The residual value is not used in the calculations except to make sure the carrying amount is not reduced below the residual value.
- When the asset is purchased during the year, the first year's depreciation for the straight-line and diminishing-balance methods must be adjusted for the part of the year that the asset is owned. No adjustment is required for the units-of-production method. In the straight-line method, the final year must also be adjusted.
- Depreciation should never reduce the asset's carrying amount below its estimated residual value.

Instructions

Prepare depreciation schedules for the following methods: (a) straight-line, (b) units-of-production, and (c) diminishing-balance using double the straight-line rate.

Solution to Demonstration Problem 1

(a) Straight-line method

Year	Amount	×	Rate	=	Expense	End of Year Accumulated Depreciation	Carrying Amount
							$17,500
2014	$16,000[a]		25%[b] × 7/12		$2,333	$ 2,333	15,167
2015	16,000		25%		4,000	6,333	11,167
2016	16,000		25%		4,000	10,333	7,167
2017	16,000		25%		4,000	14,333	3,167
2018	16,000		25% × 5/12		1,667	16,000	1,500

[a] $17,500 − $1,500 = $16,000
[b] 100% ÷ 4 years = 25%

(b) Units-of-production method

Year	Units of Production	×	Depreciable Amount/Unit	=	Depreciation Expense	End of Year Accumulated Depreciation	Carrying Amount
							$17,500
2014	1,300		$1.60[a]		$2,080	$ 2,080	15,420
2015	2,800		1.60		4,480	6,560	10,940
2016	3,300		1.60		5,280	11,840	5,660
2017	1,900		1.60		3,040	14,880	2,620
2018	700		1.60		1,120	16,000	1,500

[a] $17,500 − $1,500 = $16,000 depreciable amount ÷ 10,000 total units = $1.60/unit

(c) Diminishing-balance method

Year	Carrying Amount Beginning of Year	×	Depreciation Rate (25% × 2)	=	Depreciation Expense	Accumulated Depreciation	End of Year Carrying Amounts End of Year
							$17,500
2014	$17,500		50% × 7/12		$5,104	$ 5,104	12,396
2015	12,396		50%		6,198	11,302	6,198
2016	6,198		50%		3,099	14,401	3,099
2017	3,099		50%		1,549	15,950	1,550
2018	1,550		50%		50[a]	16,000	1,500

[a] Adjusted to $50 so that the carrying amount at the end of the year is not less than the residual value.

THE NAVIGATOR

Demonstration Problem 2

On January 1, 2011, Skyline Limousine Co. purchased a specialty limo for $78,000. The vehicle is being amortized by the straight-line method using a four-year service life and a $4,000 residual value. The company's fiscal year ends on December 31.

Instructions

Prepare the journal entry or entries to record the disposal of the limo, assuming that it is:
(a) retired on January 1, 2014.
(b) sold for $15,000 on July 1, 2014.
(c) traded in on a new limousine on January 1, 2014, for a trade-in allowance of $25,000 and cash of $52,000. The fair value of the old vehicle on January 1, 2014, was $20,000.

ACTION PLAN

- Calculate the annual depreciation expense and accumulated depreciation at end of previous year.
- Update the depreciation to the date of the disposal for any partial period.
- Determine the asset's carrying amount at the time of disposal.
- Calculate any gain or loss by comparing proceeds with the carrying amount.
- Remove the asset's carrying amount by debiting accumulated depreciation (for the total depreciation to the date of disposal) and crediting the asset account for the cost of the asset. Record proceeds and any gain or loss.
- Ignore trade-in allowances.
- Record the new asset in an exchange situation at the fair value of the asset given up, plus the cash paid.

Solution to Demonstration Problem 2

$$\frac{\$78,000 - \$4,000}{4 \text{ years}} = \$18,500 \text{ annual depreciation expense}$$

Accumulated Depreciation at December 31, 2013: $18,500 \times 3$ years $= \$55,500$

(a)

Jan. 1, 2014	Accumulated Depreciation—Vehicles	55,500	
	Loss on Disposal [$0 − ($78,000 − $55,500)]	22,500	
	Vehicles		78,000
	To record retirement of limo.		

(b)

July 1, 2014	Depreciation Expense ($18,500 × 6/12)	9,250	
	Accumulated Depreciation—Vehicles		9,250
	To record depreciation for 6 months.		
	Cash	15,000	
	Accumulated Depreciation—Vehicles ($55,500 + $9,250)	64,750	
	Gain on Disposal [$15,000 − ($78,000 − $64,750)]		1,750
	Vehicles		78,000
	To record sale of limo.		

(c)

Jan. 1, 2014	Vehicles (cost of new) ($20,000 + $52,000)	72,000	
	Accumulated Depreciation—Vehicles	55,500	
	Loss on Disposal [$20,000 − ($78,000 − $55,500)]	2,500	
	Vehicles (cost of old)		78,000
	Cash		52,000
	To record exchange of limousines, plus cash.		

THE **NAVIGATOR**

▶ Summary of Study Objectives

1. **Determine the cost of property, plant, and equipment.** The cost of property, plant, and equipment includes all costs that are necessary to acquire the asset and make it ready for its intended use. All costs that benefit future periods (that is, capital expenditures) are included in the cost of the asset. When applicable, cost also includes asset retirement costs. When multiple assets are purchased in one transaction, or when an asset has significant components, the cost is allocated to each individual asset or component using their relative fair values.

2. ***Explain and calculate depreciation.*** After acquisition, assets are accounted for using the cost model or the revaluation model. Depreciation is recorded and assets are carried at cost less accumulated depreciation. Depreciation is the allocation of the cost of a long-lived asset to expense over its useful life (its service life) in a rational and systematic way. Depreciation is not a process of valuation and it does not result in an accumulation of cash. There are three commonly used depreciation methods:

Method	Effect on Annual Depreciation	Calculation
Straight-line	Constant amount	(Cost − residual value) ÷ estimated useful life (in years)
Diminishing-balance	Diminishing amount	Carrying amount at beginning of year × diminishing-balance rate
Units-of-production	Varying amount	(Cost − residual value) ÷ total estimated units of production × actual activity during the year

Each method results in the same amount of depreciation over the asset's useful life. Depreciation expense for income tax purposes is called capital cost allowance (CCA). The single diminishing-balance method is required and depreciation rates are prescribed.

3. ***Explain the factors that cause changes in periodic depreciation and calculate revisions.*** A revision to depreciation will be required if there are (a) capital expenditures during the asset's useful life, (b) impairments in the asset's fair value, (c) changes in the asset's fair value when using the revaluation model, and/or (d) changes in the appropriate depreciation method, estimated useful life, or residual value. An impairment loss must be recorded if the recoverable amount is less than the carrying amount. Only under IFRS can impairment losses be reversed in future periods if the recoverable amount increases. Revisions of periodic depreciation are made in present and future periods, not retroactively. The new annual depreciation is determined by using the depreciable amount (carrying amount less the revised residual value), and the remaining useful life, at the time of the revision.

4. ***Account for the disposal of property, plant, and equipment.*** The accounting for the disposal of a piece of property, plant, or equipment through retirement or sale is as follows:

(a) Update any unrecorded depreciation for partial periods since depreciation was last recorded.

(b) Calculate the carrying amount (cost − accumulated depreciation).

(c) Calculate any gain (proceeds > carrying amount) or loss (proceeds < carrying amount) on disposal.

(d) Remove the asset and accumulated depreciation accounts at the date of disposal. Record the proceeds received and the gain or loss, if any.

An exchange of assets is recorded as the purchase of a new asset and the sale of an old asset. The new asset is recorded at the fair value of the asset given up plus any cash paid (or less any cash received). The fair value of the asset given up is compared with its carrying amount to calculate the gain or loss. If the fair value of the new asset or the asset given up cannot be determined, the new long-lived asset is recorded at the carrying amount of the old asset that was given up, plus any cash paid (or less any cash received).

5. ***Calculate and record depreciation of natural resources.*** The units-of-production method of depreciation is generally used for natural resources. The depreciable amount per unit is calculated by dividing the total depreciable amount by the number of units estimated to be in the resource. The depreciable amount per unit is multiplied by the number of units that have been extracted to determine the annual depreciation. The depreciation and any other costs to extract the resource are recorded as inventory until the resource is sold. At that time, the costs are transferred to cost of resource sold on the income statement. Revisions to depreciation will be required for capital expenditures during the asset's useful life, for impairments, and for changes in the total estimated units of the resource.

6. ***Identify the basic accounting issues for intangible assets and goodwill.*** The accounting for tangible and intangible assets is much the same. Intangible assets are reported at cost, which includes all expenditures necessary to prepare the asset for its intended use. An intangible asset with a finite life is amortized over the shorter of its useful life or legal life, usually on a straight-line basis. The extent of the annual impairment tests depends on whether IFRS or ASPE is followed and whether the intangible asset had a finite or indefinite life. Intangible assets with indefinite lives and goodwill are not amortized and are tested at least annually for impairment. Impairment losses on goodwill are never reversed under both IFRS and ASPE. Impairment losses on intangible assets are never reversed under ASPE.

7. ***Illustrate the reporting and analysis of long-lived assets.*** It is common for property, plant, and equipment, and natural resources to be combined in financial statements under the heading "property, plant, and equipment." Intangible assets with finite and indefinite lives are sometimes combined under the heading "intangible assets" or are listed separately. Goodwill must be presented separately. Either on the balance sheet or in the notes, the cost of the major classes of long-lived assets is presented. Accumulated depreciation (if the asset is depreciable) and carrying amount must be disclosed either in the balance sheet or in the notes. The depreciation and amortization methods and rates, as well as the annual depreciation expense, must also be indicated. The company's impairment policy and any impairment losses should be described and reported. Under IFRS, companies must include a reconciliation of the carrying amount at the beginning and end of the period for each class of

long-lived assets and state whether the cost or revaluation model is used.

The asset turnover ratio (net sales ÷ average total assets) is one measure that is used by companies to show how efficiently they are using their assets to generate sales revenue. A second ratio, return on assets (profit ÷ average total assets), calculates how profitable the company is in terms of using its assets to generate profit.

Flash cards

▶ Glossary

Additions and improvements Costs that are incurred to increase the operating efficiency, productive capacity, or expected useful life of property, plant, or equipment. (p. 475)

Amortizable amount The cost minus the residual value of a finite-life intangible asset which is amortized over its useful life. (p. 489)

Amortization The systematic allocation of the amortizable amount of a finite-life intangible asset over its useful life. (p. 489)

Asset retirement costs The cost to dismantle, remove, or restore an asset when it is retired. (p. 464)

Asset turnover A measure of how efficiently a company uses its total assets to generate sales. It is calculated by dividing net sales by average total assets. (p. 494)

Basket purchase The acquisition of a group of assets for a single price. Individual asset costs are determined by allocating relative fair values. (p. 466)

Capital cost allowance (CCA) The depreciation of long-lived assets that is allowed by the *Income Tax Act* for income tax purposes. It is calculated on a class (group) basis and mainly uses the diminishing-balance method with maximum rates specified for each class of assets. (p. 474)

Capital expenditures Expenditures related to long-lived assets that benefit the company over several accounting periods. (p. 464)

Copyright An exclusive right granted by the federal government allowing the owner to reproduce and sell an artistic or published work. (p. 490)

Cost model A model of accounting for a long-lived asset that carries the asset at its cost less accumulated depreciation or amortization and any impairment losses. (p. 468)

Depreciable amount The cost of a depreciable asset (property, plant, and equipment, or natural resources) less its residual value. (p. 469)

Diminishing-balance method A depreciation method that applies a constant rate to the asset's diminishing carrying amount. This method produces a decreasing annual depreciation expense over the useful life of the asset. (p. 471)

Franchise A contractual arrangement under which the franchisor grants the franchisee the right to sell certain products, offer specific services, or use certain trademarks or trade names, usually inside a specific geographical area. (p. 492)

Goodwill The amount paid to purchase another company that is more than the fair value of the company's net identifiable assets. (p. 492)

Impairment loss The amount by which an asset's carrying amount exceeds its recoverable amount. (p. 476)

Intangible assets Rights, privileges, and competitive advantages that result from owning long-lived assets that have no physical substance. (p. 488)

Land improvements Structural additions to land that have limited useful lives, such as paving, fencing, and lighting. (p. 465)

Licences Operating rights to use public property, granted by a government agency to a company. (p. 492)

Natural resources Long-lived tangible assets, such as standing timber and underground deposits of oil, gas, and minerals, that are physically extracted and are only replaceable by an act of nature. (p. 486)

Operating expenditures Expenditures that benefit only the current period. They are immediately charged against revenues as expenses. (p. 464)

Ordinary repairs Expenditures to maintain the operating efficiency and productive life of the unit. (p. 475)

Patent An exclusive right issued by the federal government that enables the recipient to manufacture, sell, or otherwise control an invention for a period of 20 years from the date of the application. (p. 490)

Property, plant, and equipment Identifiable, long-lived tangible assets, such as land, land improvements, buildings, and equipment, that the company owns and uses for the production and sale of goods or services. (p. 464)

Recoverable amount The higher of the asset's fair value, less costs to sell, and its value in use. (p. 476)

Research and development (R&D) costs Expenditures that may lead to patents, copyrights, new processes, and new products. (p. 490)

Residual value The estimated amount that a company would currently obtain from disposing of the asset if the asset were already as old as it will be, and in the condition it is expected to be in, at the end of its useful life. (p. 469)

Return on assets An overall measure of profitability that indicates the amount of profit that is earned from each dollar

invested in assets. It is calculated by dividing profit by average total assets. (p. 494)

Revaluation model A model of accounting for a long-lived asset in which it is carried at its fair value less accumulated depreciation or amortization and any impairment losses. (p. 477)

Royalties Recurring payments that may be required under a franchise agreement and are paid by the franchisee to the franchisor for services provided (e.g., advertising, purchasing), and are often proportionate to sales. (p. 492)

Straight-line method A depreciation method in which an asset's depreciable amount is divided by its estimated useful life. This method produces the same periodic depreciation for each year of the asset's useful life. (p. 470)

Tangible assets Long-lived resources that have physical substance, are used in the operations of the business, and are not intended for sale to customers. Tangible assets include property, plant, and equipment, and natural resources. (p. 488)

Trade-in allowance A price reduction offered by the seller when a used asset is exchanged for a new asset as part of the deal. (p. 483)

Trademark (trade name) A word, phrase, jingle, or symbol that distinguishes or identifies a particular enterprise or product. (p. 491)

Units-of-production method A depreciation method in which useful life is expressed in terms of the total estimated units of production or use expected from the asset. Depreciation expense is calculated by multiplying the depreciable amount per unit (cost less residual value divided by total estimated activity) by the actual activity that occurs during the year. (p. 472)

Useful life The period of time over which an asset is expected to be available for use, or the number of units of production (such as machine hours) or units of output that are expected to be obtained from an asset. (p. 469)

▶ Self-Study Questions
Answers are at the end of the chapter.

(SO 1) AP **1.** Bulyea Company purchased equipment and incurred the following costs:

Cash price	$36,000
Freight – FOB shipping point	1,000
Insurance during transit	200
Annual licence fee	300
Annual insurance policy	500
Installation and testing	400
Total cost	$38,400

What amount should be recorded as the cost of the equipment?
(a) $36,000   (c) $37,600
(b) $36,200   (d) $38,400

(SO 1) AP **2.** Asura Company purchased land, a building, and equipment for a package price of $200,000. The land's fair value at the time of acquisition was $75,000. The building's fair value was $80,000. The equipment's fair value was $50,000. What costs should be debited to the three accounts Land, Building, and Equipment, respectively?
(a) $66,667, $66,667, and $66,666
(b) $73,171, $78,049, and $48,780
(c) $75,000, $80,000, and $50,000
(d) $200,000, $0, and $0

(SO 2) AP **3.** Cuso Company purchased equipment on January 1, 2013, at a cost of $40,000. The equipment has an estimated residual value of $10,000 and an estimated useful life of five years. If the straight-line method of depreciation is used, what is the amount of accumulated depreciation at December 31, 2014, the end of the second year of the asset's life?
(a) $6,000   (c) $18,000
(b) $12,000   (d) $24,000

(SO 2) AP **4.** Kant Enterprises purchases a truck for $33,000 on July 1, 2014. The truck has an estimated residual value of $3,000, and an estimated useful life of five years, or a total distance of 300,000 kilometres. If 50,000 kilometres are driven in 2014, what amount of depreciation expense would Kant record at December 31, 2014, assuming it uses the units-of-production method?
(a) $2,500   (c) $5,000
(b) $3,000   (d) $5,333

(SO 2) AP **5.** Refer to the data for Kant Enterprises in question 4. If Kant uses the double diminishing-balance method of depreciation, what amount of depreciation expense would it record at December 31, 2014?
(a) $6,000   (c) $12,000
(b) $6,600   (d) $13,200

(SO 3) K **6.** Which of the following is true regarding revising depreciation calculations?
(a) When the revision is the result of a change in management's estimation of the asset's useful life, past years should be corrected.
(b) Recording an impairment loss will result in an increase in the annual depreciation expense in future years.
(c) Capital expenditures during the asset's useful life do not result in a change in annual depreciation.
(d) Regardless of the reason for the change in depreciation, the revision is made for current and future years only.

(SO 3) AP **7.** Rubiat Company has equipment with an original cost of $200,000 and a residual value of $20,000. On December 31, 2014, the accumulated depreciation is $75,000 and the recoverable amount is $100,000.

What amount of an impairment loss should the company record?

(a) $0   (c) $25,000
(b) $5,000   (d) $80,000

(SO 4) AP 8. Oviatt Company sold equipment for $10,000. At that time, the equipment had a cost of $45,000 and accumulated depreciation of $30,000. Oviatt should record a:

(a) $5,000 loss on disposal.
(b) $5,000 gain on disposal.
(c) $15,000 loss on disposal.
(d) $15,000 gain on disposal.

(SO 4) AP 9. St. Laurent Company exchanged an old machine with a carrying amount of $10,000 and a fair value of $6,000 for a new machine. The new machine had a list price of $53,000. St. Laurent was offered a trade-in allowance of $11,000, and paid $42,000 cash in the exchange. At what amount should the new machine be recorded on St. Laurent's books?

(a) $42,000   (c) $52,000
(b) $48,000   (d) $53,000

(SO 5) AP 10. On April 1, 2013, Shady Tree Farm Company purchased a Christmas tree farm that has an estimated 100,000 harvestable Christmas trees. The purchase price was $500,000 and the tree

farm is expected to have an estimated residual value of $50,000. During the first year of operations, ended January 31, 2014, Shady Tree Farm cut and sold 10,000 trees. What amount of depreciation should be included in cost of goods sold for the year ended January 31?

(a) $37,500   (c) $45,000
(b) $40,500   (d) $50,000

(SO 6) AP 11. Pierce Company incurred $150,000 of research costs in its laboratory to develop a new product in January 2014. On March 31, 2014, Pierce paid $20,000 for legal fees to register the new product. On July 31, 2014, Pierce paid $35,000 for legal fees in a successful defence of the patent. The total amount debited to Patents through July 31, 2014, should be:

(a) $20,000.   (c) $170,000.
(b) $55,000.   (d) $185,000.

(SO 7) AP 12. Cross Continental Rail Services reported net sales of $2,550 million, profit of $178 million, and average total assets of $3,132 million in 2014. What are the company's return on assets and asset turnover?

(a) 0. 81% and 5.7 times
(b) 5.7% and 1.2 times
(c) 7.0% and 5.7 times
(d) 5.7% and 0.81 times

THE NAVIGATOR

▶ Questions

(SO 1) C 1. What are the three characteristics of property, plant, and equipment? In what respect are property, plant, and equipment similar to inventory? How are they different?

(SO 1) C 2. What are the three components of the cost of property, plant, and equipment?

(SO 1) C 3. Blue Hosta Company recently purchased a new vehicle. The company also had to pay for the company's logo to be painted on the vehicle, for a safety inspection, and for an annual insurance policy on the vehicle. Explain how each of these costs should be recorded and why.

(SO 1) C 4. What are land improvements? Should the cost of clearing and grading land be recorded as a land improvement cost or not? Explain.

(SO 1) C 5. Jacques asks why the total cost in a basket purchase has to be allocated to the individual assets. For example, if we purchase land and a building for $250,000, why can we not just debit an account called Land and Building for $250,000? Answer his questions.

(SO 2) C 6. Justine argues that all companies should use the revaluation model as it provides more useful information than the cost model. She is also concerned that, if companies do have a choice, they will only use the revaluation model for assets that have increased in value. Do you agree or disagree with Justine? Why?

(SO 2) C 7. What is the relationship, if any, between depreciation and (a) cost allocation, (b) asset valuation, and (c) cash?

(SO 2) K 8. Explain the factors that are used to calculate depreciation.

(SO 2) C 9. How are annual depreciation and profit different each year over the useful life of an asset, and in total at the end of its useful life, under each of the three depreciation methods?

(SO 2, 3) C 10. What factors should be considered when choosing a depreciation method? When revising a depreciation method?

(SO 2) C 11. Ralph has a plan to reduce the amount of income taxes that will have to be paid on his company's profit. He has decided to calculate depreciation expense using very low estimated useful lives on his property, plant, and equipment. Will Ralph's plan work? Why or why not?

(SO 3) C 12. Explain the difference between operating expenditures and capital expenditures during an asset's useful life and describe the accounting treatment of each.

(SO 3) C 13. Under what circumstances will depreciation need to be revised? Should these circumstances also result in the revision of previously recorded depreciation?

(SO 3) C 14. What factors contribute to an impairment loss? In what circumstances, if any, is a company allowed to write up its property, plant, and equipment?

(SO 3) C 15. In the fourth year of an asset's five-year useful life, the company decides that the asset will have an eight-year service life. Explain how this will impact the amount of depreciation recorded each year over the asset's useful life.

(SO 4) C 16. If equipment is sold in the middle of a fiscal year, why does depreciation expense have to be recorded for the partial period? Doesn't the subsequent journal entry to record the sale remove the accumulated depreciation from the books anyway?

(SO 4) C 17. Ewing Company owns a machine that is fully depreciated but is still being used. How should Ewing account for this asset and report it in the financial statements?

(SO 4) K 18. How is a gain or loss on the sale of an item of property, plant, or equipment calculated? Is the calculation the same for an exchange of a piece of property, plant, or equipment?

(SO 4) C 19. How is the carrying amount of an item of property, plant, or equipment calculated? Why does this amount NOT appear in the journal entry to record the disposition of an item of property, plant, or equipment?

(SO 5) K 20. Describe the similarities and differences between natural resources and property, plant, and equipment.

(SO 5) C 21. Why is the units-of-production method used frequently to calculate depreciation for natural resources? Why is the term "depletion" often used instead of "depreciation"?

(SO 6) C 22. What are the similarities and differences between accounting for intangible and tangible assets?

(SO 6) C 23. Under IFRS and ASPE, what are the differences between the treatment of impairment losses for (a) finite life intangible assets, (b) indefinite life intangible assets, and (c) goodwill?

(SO 6) C 24. What is goodwill? Why can it not be sold to raise cash if a company is planning to expand?

(SO 7) K 25. How should long-lived assets be reported on the balance sheet and income statement? What information should be disclosed in the notes to the financial statements?

(SO 7) C 26. Balpreet believes that when comparing the ratios for one company over a two-year period, it is more important for a company to have an improved asset turnover than it is to have an improved return on assets. Do you agree or disagree? Why?

▶ Brief Exercises

Determine cost of land and land improvements. (SO 1) AP

BE9–1 The following costs were incurred by Shumway Company in purchasing land: cash price, $85,000; legal fees, $1,500; removal of old building, $5,000; clearing and grading, $3,500; installation of a parking lot, $5,000. (a) What is the cost of the land? (b) What is the cost of the land improvements?

Determine cost of equipment. (SO 1) AP

BE9–2 Surkis Company incurs the following costs in purchasing equipment: invoice price, $40,375; transportation-in, $625; installation and testing, $1,000; one-year insurance policy, $1,750. What is the cost of the equipment?

Identify operating and capital expenditures. (SO 1) K

BE9–3 In the space provided, indicate whether each of the following items is an operating expenditure (O) or a capital expenditure (C):

(a) _____ Repaired building roof, $1,500
(b) _____ Replaced building roof, $27,500
(c) _____ Purchased building, $480,000
(d) _____ Paid insurance on equipment in transit, $550
(e) _____ Purchased supplies, $350
(f) _____ Purchased truck, $55,000
(g) _____ Purchased oil and gas for truck, $125
(h) _____ Rebuilt engine on truck, $5,000
(i) _____ Replaced tires on truck, $600
(j) _____ Estimated retirement cost of plant, $1,000,000
(k) _____ Added new wing to building, $250,000
(l) _____ Painted interior of building, $1,500
(m) _____ Replaced an elevator, $17,500

Record basket purchase. (SO 1) AP

BE9–4 Rainbow Company purchased land, a building, and equipment on January 2, 2014, for $850,000. The company paid $170,000 cash and signed a mortgage note payable for the remainder. Management's best estimate of the value of the land was $352,000; of the building, $396,000; and of the equipment, $132,000. Record the purchase.

Calculate straight-line depreciation. (SO 2) AP

BE9–5 Surkis Company acquires equipment at a cost of $42,000 on January 3, 2014. Management estimates the equipment will have a residual value of $6,000 at the end of its four-year useful life. Assume the company uses the straight-line method of depreciation. Calculate the depreciation expense (a) for each year of the equipment's life, and (b) in total over the equipment's life. Surkis has a December 31 fiscal year end.

BE9–6   Refer to the data given for Surkis Company in BE9–5. Assume instead that the company uses the diminishing-balance method and that the diminishing-balance depreciation rate is double the straight-line rate. Calculate the depreciation expense (a) for each year of the equipment's life, and (b) in total over the equipment's life.

Calculate diminishing-balance depreciation. (SO 2) AP

BE9–7   Speedy Taxi Service uses the units-of-production method in calculating depreciation on its taxicabs. Each cab is expected to be driven 550,000 kilometres. Taxi 10 cost $38,950 and is expected to have a residual value of $4,300. Taxi 10 is driven 90,000 kilometres in 2013, and 135,000 kilometres in 2014. Calculate (a) the depreciable cost per kilometre (use three decimals), and (b) the depreciation expense for 2013 and 2014.

Calculate units-of-production depreciation. (SO 2) AP

BE9–8   Refer to the data given for Surkis Company in BE9–5. Assume the equipment was purchased on April 6, 2014, and that the company pro-rates depreciation to the nearest month. Using the straight-line method, calculate the depreciation expense (a) for each year of the equipment's life, and (b) in total over the equipment's life.

Calculate partial-year straight-line depreciation. (SO 2) AP

BE9–9   Refer to the data given for Surkis Company in BE9–5. Assume the equipment was purchased on April 6, 2014, and that the company has a policy of recording a half year's depreciation in the year of acquisition and a half year's depreciation in the year of disposal. Using the double diminishing-balance method, calculate the depreciation expense (a) for each year of the equipment's life, and (b) in total over the equipment's life.

Calculate partial-year diminishing-balance depreciation.(SO 2) AP

BE9–10   Cherry Technology purchased equipment on January 4, 2012, for $250,000. The equipment had an estimated useful life of six years and a residual value of $10,000. The company has a December 31 year end and uses straight-line depreciation. On December 31, 2014, the company tests for impairment and determines that the equipment's recoverable amount is $100,000. (a) Calculate the equipment's carrying amount at December 31, 2014 (after recording the annual depreciation). (b) Record the impairment loss.

Determine carrying amount and record impairment loss. (SO 3) AP

BE9–11   Raj Cleaning Services purchased equipment for $65,000 on January 2, 2011. Management estimated the equipment would have a useful life of seven years and a residual value of $5,500. On January 3, 2014, the equipment was upgraded at a cost of $10,200. After the upgrade, management estimates that the equipment will now have a total useful life of nine years and a residual value of $3,200. The company uses straight-line depreciation and has a December 31 fiscal year end. Calculate annual depreciation expense for 2011 through 2014.

Calculate revised depreciation. (SO 3) AP

BE9–12   On January 3, 2014, Ruiz Company retires equipment, which cost $25,700. No residual value is received. Prepare journal entries to record the transaction if (a) accumulated depreciation is also $25,700 on this equipment, and (b) the accumulated depreciation is $22,500 instead of $25,700. Ruiz has a December 31 fiscal year end.

Record disposal by retirement. (SO 4) AP

BE9–13   Wilbur Company sells equipment on March 31, 2014, for $15,000 cash. The equipment was purchased on January 5, 2009, at a cost of $86,400, and had an estimated useful life of six years and a residual value of $2,200. Adjusting journal entries are made annually at the company's year end, December 31. Prepare the journal entries to (a) update depreciation to March 31, 2014, (b) record the sale of the equipment, and (c) record the sale of the equipment if Wilbur Company received $9,000 cash for it.

Record disposal by sale. (SO 4) AP

BE9–14   Subramanian Company has equipment with an original cost of $95,000 and, as at December 31, 2013, accumulated depreciation of $78,000. On January 7, 2014, Subramanian exchanges the equipment for new equipment with a list price of $110,000. The dealer gives Subramanian a $20,000 trade-in allowance on the old equipment even though its fair value is only $15,000. Record the January 7, 2014, journal entry for the equipment exchange.

Record disposal by exchange of equipment. (SO 4) AP

BE9–15   Cuono Mining Co. purchased a mine for $6.5 million that is estimated to have 25 million tonnes of ore and a residual value of $500,000. In the first year, 5 million tonnes of ore are extracted and 3 million tonnes are sold.

(a) Record the depreciation and the cost of the ore extracted for the first year, ended August 31, 2014.
(b) Show how the mine and the ore on hand are reported on the balance sheet on August 31, 2014.

Record depreciation and show balance sheet presentation for natural resources. (SO 5) AP

BE9–16   Mabasa Company purchases a patent for $150,000 cash on January 2, 2014. Its legal life is 20 years and its estimated useful life is 8 years. On January 5, 2015, Mabasa paid $30,000 cash to successfully defend the patent in court.

(a) Record the purchase of the patent on January 2, 2014.
(b) Record amortization expense for the year ended December 31, 2014.
(c) Record the legal costs on January 5, 2015.
(d) Calculate amortization expense for 2015.

Record acquisition, legal expenditure, and amortization for patent. (SO 6) AP

BE9–17   Indicate whether each of the following items is property, plant, and equipment (write "PPE"), a natural resource ("NR"), or an intangible asset ("I"). If the item does not fit any of these categories, write "NA" (not applicable) in the space provided.

Identify and classify long-lived assets. (SO 7) K

(a) _____ Building		(i) _____ Mining equipment	
(b) _____ Cost of goods sold		(j) _____ Natural gas deposit	
(c) _____ Franchise		(k) _____ Note receivable, due in 3 years	
(d) _____ Goodwill		(l) _____ Parking lot	
(e) _____ Inventory		(m) _____ Patent	
(f) _____ Land		(n) _____ Research costs	
(g) _____ Land held for resale		(o) _____ Supplies	
(h) _____ Licence right		(p) _____ Trademark	

Prepare partial balance sheet.
(SO 7) AP

BE9–18 Canadian Tire Corporation, Limited reports the following selected information about long-lived assets at December 31, 2011 (in millions):

Accumulated amortization—finite-life intangibles	$ 1.5
Accumulated depreciation—assets under finance lease	138.5
Accumulated depreciation—buildings	1,014.8
Accumulated depreciation—fixtures and equipment	545.6
Accumulated depreciation—leasehold improvements	216.5
Assets under finance lease	267.4
Buildings	2,589.6
Fixtures and equipment	826.0
Construction in progress	137.0
Goodwill	377.6
Land (net of $1.4 of impairments)	748.8
Leasehold improvements	712.5
FGL Sports finite-life intangibles	22.4
FGL Sports indefinite-life intangibles	316.8
Mark's Work Wearhouse indefinite-life intangibles	64.1

FGL Sports and Mark's Work Wearhouse indefinite-life intangibles include legal trademarks such as store brands and banners, as wells as franchise agreements. Finite-life intangibles include certain brands that management has assessed to have a limited life. Prepare a partial balance sheet for Canadian Tire.

Calculate ratios. (SO 7) AP

BE9–19 Agrium Inc., a global agricultural nutrients producer that is headquartered in Calgary, Alberta, reports the following in its 2011 financial statements (in millions of US$):

	2011	2010
Net sales	$15,470	$10,743
Profit	1,375	713
Total assets	13,140	12,892

Calculate Agrium's return on assets and asset turnover for 2011.

▶ Exercises

Classify expenditures.
(SO 1) AP

E9–1 The following expenditures related to property, plant, and equipment were made by Pascal Company:

1. Paid $400,000 for a new plant site.
2. Paid $5,000 in legal fees on the purchase of the plant site.
3. Paid $7,500 for grading the plant site.
4. Paid $4,800 to demolish an old building on the plant site; residual materials were sold for $900.
5. Paid $54,000 for a new delivery truck.
6. Paid $200 freight to have the new delivery truck delivered.
7. Paid $450 to have the company name and advertising slogan painted on the new truck.
8. Paid the $95 motor vehicle licence fee on the new truck.
9. Paid $1,900 for a one-year accident insurance policy on the new delivery truck.
10. Paid $17,500 in architect fees for work on the new plant.
11. Paid $17,500 for paving the parking lots and driveways on the plant site.

Instructions

(a) Explain what types of costs should be included in determining the cost of property, plant, and equipment.
(b) List the numbers of the preceding transactions, and beside each number write the account title that the expenditure should be debited to.

E9–2   Hohenberger Farms purchased real estate for $1,280,000, which included $5,000 in legal fees. It paid $255,000 cash and incurred a mortgage payable for the balance. The real estate included land that was appraised at $476,000, buildings appraised at $748,000, and fences and other land improvements appraised at $136,000. The buildings have an estimated useful life of 60 years and a $50,000 residual value. Land improvements have an estimated 15-year useful life and no residual value.

Record basket purchase and calculate depreciation.
(SO 1, 2) AP

Instructions

(a) Calculate the cost that should be allocated to each asset purchased.
(b) Record the purchase of the real estate.
(c) Calculate the annual depreciation expense for the buildings and land improvements assuming Hohenberger Farms uses straight-line depreciation.

E9–3   Randell Equipment Repair purchased equipment on March 15, 2014, for $75,000. The company also paid the following amounts: $1,000 for delivery charges; $200 for insurance while the machine was in transit; $1,800 for a one-year insurance policy; and $2,800 for testing and installation. The machine was ready for use on April 1, 2014, but the company did not start using it until May 1, 2014.

Calculate cost and depreciation; recommend method.
(SO 1, 2) AP

Randell will depreciate the equipment over 10 years with no residual value. It expects to consume the equipment's future economic benefits evenly over the useful life. The company has a December 31 fiscal year end.

Instructions

(a) Calculate the cost of the equipment.
(b) When should the company begin depreciating the equipment: March 15, April 1, or May 1? Why?
(c) Which depreciation method should the company use? Why?
(d) Calculate the depreciation on the equipment for 2014 and 2015.

E9–4   On June 9, 2013, Blue Ribbon Company purchased manufacturing equipment at a cost of $345,000. Blue Ribbon estimated that the equipment will produce 600,000 units over its five-year useful life, and have a residual value of $15,000. The company has a December 31 fiscal year end and has a policy of recording a half year's depreciation in the year of acquisition.

Calculate depreciation using three methods; recommend method.
(SO 2) AP

Instructions

(a) Calculate depreciation under the straight-line method for 2013 and 2014.
(b) Calculate the depreciation expense under the diminishing-balance method using double the straight-line rate, for 2013 and 2014.
(c) Calculate the depreciation expense under the units-of-production method, assuming the actual number of units produced was 71,000 in 2013 and 118,600 in 2014.
(d) In this situation, what factors should the company consider in determining which depreciation method it should use?

E9–5   On April 22, 2013, Sandstone Enterprises purchased equipment for $129,200. The company expects to use the equipment for 12,000 working hours during its four-year life and that it will have a residual value of $14,000. Sandstone has a December 31 year end and pro-rates depreciation to the nearest month. The actual machine usage was: 1,900 hours in 2013; 2,800 hours in 2014; 3,700 hours in 2015; 2,700 hours in 2016; and 1,100 hours in 2017.

Prepare depreciation schedules and answer questions.
(SO 2) AP

Instructions

(a) Prepare a depreciation schedule for the life of the asset under each of the following methods:
    1. straight-line,
    2. diminishing-balance using double the straight-line rate, and
    3. units-of-production.
(b) Which method results in the lowest profit over the life of the asset?
(c) Which method results in the least cash used for depreciation over the life of the asset?

E9–6   Bisor Company has a December 31 year end and uses straight-line depreciation for all property, plant, and equipment. On July 1, 2010, the company purchased equipment for $500,000. The equipment had an expected useful life of 10 years and no residual value.

Record depreciation and impairment. (SO 3) AP

On December 31, 2013, after recording annual depreciation, Bisor reviewed its equipment for possible impairment. Bisor determined that the equipment has a recoverable amount of $225,000. It is not known if the recoverable amount will increase or decrease in the future.

Instructions

(a) Prepare journal entries to record the purchase of the asset on July 1, 2010, and to record depreciation expense on December 31, 2010, and December 31, 2013.
(b) Determine if there is an impairment loss at December 31, 2013, and if there is, prepare a journal entry to record it.

(c) Calculate depreciation expense for 2014 and the carrying amount of the equipment at December 31, 2014.

(d) Assume that the equipment is assessed again for impairment at December 31, 2014, and that the company determines the recoverable amount is $240,000. Should Bisor make an adjustment to reflect the increase in the recoverable amount? Why or why not?

Calculate revised depreciation. (SO 3) AP

E9–7 Lindy Weink, the new controller of Lafrenière Company, has reviewed the expected useful lives and residual values of selected depreciable assets at December 31, 2014. (Depreciation for 2014 has not been recorded yet.) Her findings are as follows:

Type of Asset	Date Acquired	Cost	Total Useful Life in Years		Residual Value	
			Current	Proposed	Current	Proposed
Building	Jan. 1, 2002	$800,000	20	30	$40,000	$60,500
Equipment	Jan. 1, 2012	125,000	5	4	5,000	4,000

After discussion, management agrees to accept Lindy's proposed changes. All assets are depreciated by the straight-line method. Lafrenière Company has a December 31 year end.

Instructions

(a) For each asset, calculate the annual depreciation expense using the original estimated useful life and residual value.

(b) Calculate the carrying amount of each asset as at January 1, 2014.

(c) For each asset, calculate the revised annual depreciation expense and the carrying amount at December 31, 2014.

(d) For each asset, calculate the total depreciation expense over the life of the asset assuming the asset is used until the end of its revised useful life.

Record asset addition and revised depreciation; show balance sheet presentation. (SO 3) AP

E9–8 On October 1, 2012, Chignecto Manufacturing Company purchased a piece of high-tech equipment for $90,000 cash. Chignecto estimated the equipment would have a six-year useful life and a residual value of $9,000. The company uses straight-line depreciation and has a September 30 fiscal year end.

On October 1, 2014, Chignecto paid $15,000 cash to upgrade the equipment. It is expected that the upgrade will significantly reduce the operating costs of the equipment. Chignecto also reviewed the equipment's expected useful life and estimated that due to changing technology, the equipment's total expected useful life will be four years and its residual value will be $5,000.

Instructions

(a) Calculate the annual depreciation expense for the first two years of the equipment's life.

(b) Calculate the carrying amount of the equipment at September 30, 2014.

(c) Record the expenditure to upgrade the equipment on October 1, 2014.

(d) Record the annual depreciation of the equipment on September 30, 2015.

(e) Show the balance sheet presentation of the equipment on September 30, 2015.

Record disposal of property, plant, and equipment. (SO 4) AP

E9–9 The following are some transactions of Surendal Company for 2014. Surendal Company uses straight-line depreciation and has a December 31 year end.

Jan. 2 Scrapped a piece of equipment that originally cost $8,000 and was fully depreciated.

Apr. 1 Retired a piece of equipment that was purchased on January 1, 2005, for $45,000. The equipment had an expected useful life of 10 years with no residual value.

July 30 Sold equipment for $1,100 cash. The equipment was purchased on January 3, 2012, for $12,600 and was depreciated over an expected useful life of three years with no residual value.

Nov. 1 Traded in an old vehicle for a new vehicle, receiving a $10,000 trade-in allowance and paying $36,000 cash. The old vehicle had been purchased on November 1, 2007, at a cost of $35,000. The estimated useful life was eight years and the estimated residual value was $5,000. The fair value of the old vehicle was $7,000 on November 1, 2014.

Instructions

(a) For each of these disposals, prepare a journal entry to record depreciation from January 1, 2014, to the date of disposal, if required.

(b) For each these disposals, indicate if the disposal has increased (+) or decreased (−) Cash, Equipment, Accumulated Depreciation, total property, plant, and equipment (PP&E), and profit, and by how much. If the item is not changed, write "NE" to indicate there is no effect. Use the following format, in which the first one has been done for you as an example.

Transaction	Cash	Equipment	Accumulated Depreciation	Total PP&E	Total Assets	Owner's Equity	Profit
Jan. 2	NE	−$8,000	−$8,000	NE	NE	NE	NE

(c) Record the disposals.

E9–10   On January 3, 2011, Hamir Company purchased equipment for $48,000. Hamir planned to keep the equipment for four years, and expected the equipment would then be sold for $4,000. On January 5, 2014, Hamir sold the computer equipment for $8,000.

Instructions

(a) Calculate the depreciation expense for 2011, 2012, and 2013 under (1) the straight-line method and (2) the double diminishing-balance method.

(b) Calculate the gain or loss on disposal if Hamir had used (1) the straight-line method and (2) the double diminishing-balance method.

(c) Explain why the gain or loss on disposal is not the same under the two depreciation methods.

(d) Calculate the total depreciation expense plus the loss or minus the gain under (1) the straight-line method and (2) the double diminishing-balance method. Comment on your findings.

Calculate gain or loss on disposal under different depreciation methods and comment. (SO 4) AP

E9–11   On July 1, 2014, Phillips Exploration Inc. invests $1.3 million in a mine that is estimated to have 800,000 tonnes of ore. The company estimates that the property will be sold for $100,000 when production at the mine has ended. During the last six months of 2014, 100,000 tonnes of ore are mined and sold. Phillips has a December 31 fiscal year end.

Instructions

(a) Explain why the units-of-production method is often used for depreciating natural resources.

(b) Record the 2014 depreciation.

(c) Show how the mine and any related accounts are reported on the December 31, 2014, income statement and balance sheet.

(d) Assume that the selling price of ore has dropped significantly after December 31, 2014. By June 30, 2015, it is $1.40 per tonne. Does this indicate that the mine may be impaired? Why or why not?

Record depreciation for natural resources; show financial statement presentation; comment on potential impairment. (SO 5) AP

E9–12   An accounting co-op student encountered the following situations at Chin Company:

1. During the year, Chin Company purchased land and paid legal fees on the purchase. The land had an old building, which was demolished. The land was then cleared and graded. Construction of a new building will start next year. All of these costs were included in the cost of land. The student decided that this was incorrect, and prepared a journal entry to put the cost of removing the building and clearing and grading the land in land improvements and the legal fees in legal fee expense.

2. The student learned that Chin is depreciating its buildings and equipment, but not its land. The student could not understand why land was not included, so she prepared journal entries to depreciate all of the company's property, plant, and equipment for the current year end.

3. The student decided that Chin's amortization policy on its intangible assets is wrong. The company is currently amortizing its patents but not its trademarks. The student fixed that for the current year end by adding trademarks to her adjusting entry for amortization. She told a fellow student that she felt she had improved the consistency of the company's accounting policies by making these changes.

4. One of the buildings that Chin uses has a zero carrying amount but a substantial fair value. The co-op student felt that leaving the carrying amount at zero did not benefit the financial information's users—especially the bank—and wrote the building up to its fair value. After all, she reasoned, you write down assets if fair values are lower. She feels that writing them up if their fair value is higher is yet another example of the improved consistency that her employment has brought to the company's accounting practices.

Instructions

Explain whether or not the co-op student's accounting treatment in each of the above situations follows generally accepted accounting principles. If it does not, explain why and what the appropriate accounting treatment should be.

Apply accounting concepts. (SO 1, 2, 6) AP

E9–13   Karsch Enterprises, a public company, has a December 31 fiscal year end and uses straight-line amortization for its finite-life intangible assets. The company has provided you with the following information related to its intangible assets and goodwill during 2013 and 2014:

Record acquisition, amortization, and impairment of intangible assets. (SO 6) AP

2013

Jan.   9   Purchased a patent with an estimated useful life of five years and a legal life of 20 years for $45,000 cash.
May 15   Purchased another company and recorded goodwill of $450,000 as part of the purchase.
Dec. 31   Recorded adjusting entries as required for amortization.
Dec. 31   Tested assets for impairment and determined the patent and the goodwill's recoverable amounts were $40,000 and $400,000, respectively.

2014

Jan.   2   Incurred legal fees of $30,000 to successfully defend the patent.
Mar. 31   Incurred research costs of $175,000.

Apr. 1   Purchased a copyright for $66,000 cash. The company expects the copyright will benefit the company for 10 years.

July 1   Purchased a trademark with an indefinite expected life for $275,000 cash.

Dec. 31   Recorded adjusting entries as required for amortization.

Dec. 31   Tested assets for impairment and determined the copyright and the trademark's recoverable amounts were in excess of their cost. The patent and the goodwill's recoverable amounts were $45,000 and $425,000, respectively.

Instructions

(a) Record the transactions and adjusting entries as required.

(b) Show the balance sheet presentation of the intangible assets and goodwill at December 31, 2014.

Determine balance sheet and income statement presentation for intangible assets and goodwill.
(SO 6) AP

E9–14   Whiteway Company has a December 31 fiscal year end. Selected information follows for Whiteway Company for three independent situations as at December 3, 2014:

1. Whiteway purchased a patent from Hopkins Inc. for $400,000 on January 1, 2011. The patent expires on January 1, 2019. Whiteway has been amortizing it over its legal life. During 2014, Whiteway determined that the patent's economic benefits would not last longer than six years from the date of acquisition.

2. Whiteway has a trademark that had been purchased in 2010 for $250,000. During 2013, the company spent $50,000 on a lawsuit that successfully defended the trademark. On December 31, 2014, it was assessed for impairment and the recoverable amount was determined to be $275,000.

3. In 2012, Whiteway purchased another business and paid $70,000 in excess of the fair value of the net identifiable assets of that business. This goodwill was assessed for impairment as at December 31, 2013, and December 31, 2014. The recoverable amount was determined to be $55,000 at December 31, 2013, and $80,000 at December 31, 2014.

Instructions

(a) For each of these assets, determine the amount that will be reported on Whiteway's December 31, 2013 and 2014, balance sheets.

(b) For each of these assets, determine what, if anything, will be recorded on Whiteway's 2014 income statement. Be specific about the account name and the amount.

Classify long-lived assets; prepare partial balance sheet.
(SO 7) AP

E9–15   **Shoppers Drug Mart Corporation** reported the following selected information as at December 31, 2011 (in thousands):

Accumulated amortization—computer software	$ 136,406
Accumulated amortization—customer relationships	13,691
Accumulated amortization—other intangible assets	6,262
Accumulated amortization—prescription files	64,372
Accumulated depreciation—assets under financing leases	16,411
Accumulated depreciation—buildings	24,325
Accumulated depreciation—equipment, fixtures, and computer equipment	792,644
Accumulated depreciation—leasehold improvements	451,481
Assets under financing leases	127,034
Depreciation and amortization expense	297,682
Buildings	214,043
Computer software	308,478
Customer relationships	50,736
Equipment, fixtures, and computer equipment	1,283,062
Goodwill	2,499,722
Finance expenses	64,038
Investment property	16,372
Land	65,478
Leasehold improvements	1,291,445
Loss on disposal of property, plant, and equipment	1,498
Other non-current assets	39,289
Other intangible assets	9,267
Prescription files	133,987
Properties under development	71,342

Prescription files and customer relationships were acquired in the process of purchasing independent drug stores and are being amortized over their estimated useful lives. Computer software includes the costs of developing the software and is being amortized over its useful life.

Instructions

(a) Identify in which financial statement (balance sheet or income statement) and which section (e.g., property, plant, and equipment) each of the above items should be reported.

(b) Prepare the non-current assets section of the balance sheet as at December 31, 2011.

E9–16   Suncor Energy Inc. reported the following information for the fiscal years ended December 31, 2011, and December 31, 2010 (in millions):

Calculate asset turnover and return on assets. (SO 7) AN

	Dec. 31, 2011	Dec. 31, 2010
Net revenues	$39,337	$32,003
Profit	4,304	3,829
Total assets, end of year	74,777	68,607
Total assets, beginning of year	68,607	67,799

Instructions

(a) Calculate Suncor's asset turnover and return on assets for the two years.

(b) Comment on what the ratios reveal about Suncor Energy Inc.'s effectiveness in using its assets to generate revenues and produce profit.

▶ Problems: Set A

P9–1A   In 2014, Kadlec Company had the following transactions related to the purchase of a property. All transactions were for cash unless otherwise stated.

Record property transactions. (SO 1) AP

Jan. 12   Purchased real estate for a future plant site for $420,000, paying $95,000 cash and signing a note payable for the balance. On the site, there was an old building, and the fair values of the land and building were $400,000 and $40,000, respectively. The old building will be demolished and a new one built.

16   Paid $8,500 for legal fees on the real estate purchase.

31   Paid $25,000 to demolish the old building to make room for the new plant.

Feb. 13   Received $10,000 for residual materials from the demolished building.

28   Graded and filled the land in preparation for the construction for $9,000.

Mar. 14   Paid $38,000 in architect fees for the building plans.

31   Paid the local municipality $15,000 for building permits.

Apr. 22   Excavation costs for the new building were $17,000.

Sept. 26   The construction of the building was completed. The full cost was $750.000. Paid $150,000 cash and signed a mortgage note payable for the balance.

Sept. 30   Purchased a one-year insurance policy for the building, $4,500.

Oct. 20   Paved the parking lots, driveways, and sidewalks for $45,000.

Nov. 15   Installed a fence for $12,000.

Instructions

(a) Record the above transactions.

(b) Determine the cost of the land, land improvements, and building that will appear on Kadlec's December 31, 2014, balance sheet.

TAKING IT FURTHER   When should Kadlec start to record depreciation and on which assets?

P9–2A   In its first year of business, ChalkBoard purchased land, a building, and equipment on March 5, 2013, for $650,000 in total. The land was valued at $275,000, the building at $343,750, and the equipment at $68,750. Additional information on the depreciable assets follows:

Allocate cost and calculate partial period depreciation. (SO 1, 2) AP

Asset	Residual Value	Useful Life in Years	Depreciation Method
Building	$25,000	60	Straight-line
Equipment	5,000	8	Double diminishing-balance

Instructions

(a) Allocate the purchase cost of the land, building, and equipment to each of the assets.

(b) ChalkBoard has a December 31 fiscal year end and is trying to decide how to calculate depreciation for assets purchased during the year. Calculate depreciation expense for the building and equipment for 2013 and 2014 assuming:

1. depreciation is calculated to the nearest whole month.
2. a half year's depreciation is recorded in the year of acquisition.

(c) Which policy should ChalkBoard follow in the year of acquisition: recording depreciation to the nearest whole month or recording a half year of depreciation?

TAKING IT FURTHER   In the year the asset is purchased should ChalkBoard record depreciation for the exact number of days the asset is owned? Why or why not?

Determine cost; calculate and compare depreciation under different methods.
(SO 1, 2) AP

P9–3A   Payne Company purchased equipment on account on September 3, 2012, at an invoice price of $210,000. On September 4, 2012, it paid $4,400 for delivery of the equipment. A one-year, $1,975 insurance policy on the equipment was purchased on September 6, 2012. On September 20, 2012, Payne paid $5,600 for installation and testing of the equipment. The equipment was ready for use on October 1, 2012.

Payne estimates that the equipment's useful life will be four years, with a residual value of $13,000. It also estimates that, in terms of activity, the equipment's useful life will be 75,000 units. Payne has a September 30 fiscal year end. Assume that actual usage is as follows:

# of Units	Year Ended September 30
15,750	2013
23,900	2014
20,200	2015
15,350	2016

Instructions

(a) Determine the cost of the equipment.
(b) Prepare depreciation schedules for the life of the asset under the following depreciation methods:
   1. straight-line
   2. diminishing-balance at double the straight-line rate
   3. units-of-production
(c) Which method would result in the highest profit for the year ended September 30, 2013? Over the life of the asset?
(d) Which method would result in the least cash used for the year ended September 30, 2013? Over the life of the asset?

TAKING IT FURTHER   Assume instead that, when Payne purchased the equipment, it had a legal obligation to ensure that the equipment was recycled at the end of its useful life. Assume the cost of doing this is significant. Would this have had an impact on the answers to (a) and (b) above? Explain.

Account for operating and capital expenditures, and asset impairments.
(SO 1, 3) AP

P9–4A   Arnison Company has a December 31 fiscal year end and follows ASPE. The following selected transactions are related to its property, plant, and equipment in 2014:

Jan. 12   All of the company's light bulbs were converted to energy-efficient bulbs for $2,200. Arnison expects that this will save money on its utility bills in the future.
Feb. 6   Paid $5,400 to paint equipment that had started to rust.
Apr. 24   An air conditioning system in the factory was installed for $75,000.
May 17   Safety training was given to factory employees on using the equipment at a cost of $3,100.
July 19   Windows broken in a labour dispute (not covered by insurance) were replaced for $5,900.
Aug. 21   Paid $26,000 to convert the company's delivery vehicles from gasoline to propane. Arnison expects this will substantially reduce the vehicles' future operating costs, but it will not extend the vehicles' useful lives.
Sept. 20   The exhaust system in a delivery vehicle was repaired for $2,700.
Oct. 25   New parts were added to equipment for $20,000. Arnison expects this will increase the equipment's useful life by four years.
Dec. 31   After recording annual depreciation, Arnison reviewed its property, plant, and equipment for possible impairment. Arnison determined the following:
   1. Land that originally cost $200,000 had previously been written down to $175,000 in 2011 as a result of a decline in the recoverable amount. The current recoverable amount of the land is $220,000.
   2. The recoverable amount of equipment that originally cost $150,000 and has accumulated depreciation of $62,500 is $50,000.

Instructions

(a) For each of these transactions, indicate if the transaction has increased (+) or decreased (−) Land, Buildings, Equipment, Accumulated Depreciation, total property, plant, and equipment (PP&E), and profit, and by how much. If the item is not changed, write "NE" to indicate there is no effect. Use the following format, in which the first one has been done for you as an example.

Transaction	Land	Buildings	Equipment	Accumulated Depreciation	Total PP&E	Profit
Jan. 12	NE	NE	NE	NE	NE	−$2,200

(b) Prepare journal entries to record the above transactions. All transactions are paid in cash.

TAKING IT FURTHER   Assume that Arnison also purchases equipment with an expected useful life of 12 years. Assume also that the equipment's engine will need to be replaced every four years. Which useful life should Arnison use when calculating depreciation on the equipment? Explain.

P9–5A   Slope Style Snowboarding Company, a public company, purchased equipment on January 10, 2010, for $750,000. At that time, management estimated that the equipment would have a useful life of 10 years and a residual value of $50,000. Slope Style uses the straight-line method of depreciation and has a December 31 year end.

     Slope Style tested the equipment for impairment on December 31, 2014, after recording the annual depreciation expense. It was determined that the equipment's recoverable amount was $320,000, and that the total estimated useful life would be eight years instead of ten, with a residual value of $10,000 instead of $50,000.

Instructions

(a) Calculate the annual depreciation expense for the years 2010 to 2014 and the carrying amount at December 31, 2014.
(b) Record the impairment loss, if any, on December 31, 2014.
(c) What will appear on Slope Style's 2014 income statement and balance sheet with regard to this equipment?
(d) Assuming no further impairments or recoveries, calculate the annual depreciation expense for the years 2015 to 2017.
(e) Determine the equipment's accumulated depreciation and carrying amount at the end of its useful life.

Record impairment and calculate revised depreciation. (SO 3) AP

TAKING IT FURTHER   Suggest some possible reasons as to why companies are allowed to record recoveries of previously recorded impairments under IFRS but not under ASPE.

P9–6A   NW Tool Supply Company purchased land and a building on May 1, 2012, for $385,000. The company paid $115,000 in cash and signed a 5% note payable for the balance. At that time, it was estimated that the land was worth $150,000 and the building, $235,000. The building was estimated to have a 25-year useful life with a $35,000 residual value. The company has a December 31 year end and uses the single diminishing-balance depreciation method for buildings. The following are related transactions and adjustments during the next three years.

Record acquisition, depreciation, impairment, and disposal of land and building. (SO 2, 3, 4) AP

2012
Dec. 31   Recorded annual depreciation.
     31   Paid the interest owing on the note payable.

2013
Feb. 17   Paid $225 to have the furnace cleaned and serviced.
Dec. 31   Recorded annual depreciation.
     31   Paid the interest owing on the note payable.
     31   The land and building were tested for impairment. The land had a recoverable amount of $120,000 and the building, $240,000.

2014
Jan. 31   Sold the land and building for $320,000 cash: $110,000 for the land and $210,000 for the building.
Feb. 1   Paid the note payable and interest owing.

Instructions

(a) Record the above transactions and adjustments, including the purchase on May 1, 2012.
(b) What factors may have been responsible for the impairment?
(c) Assume instead that the company sold the land and building on October 31, 2014, for $400,000 cash: $160,000 for the land and $240,000 for the building. Record the journal entries to record the sale.

TAKING IT FURTHER   How might management determine the recoverable amount of the land and building at each year end? Would the company need to test the assets for impairment every year?

P9–7A   On December 27, 2011, Wolcott Windows purchased a piece of equipment for $107,500. The estimated useful life of the equipment is either three years or 60,000 units, with a residual value of $10,500. The company has a December 31 fiscal year end and normally uses straight-line depreciation. Management is considering the merits

Calculate and compare depreciation and gain or loss on disposal under three methods of depreciation. (SO 2, 4) AP

of using the units-of-production or diminishing-balance method of depreciation instead of the straight-line method. The actual numbers of units produced by the equipment were 10,000 in 2012, 20,000 in 2013, and 29,000 in 2014. The equipment was sold on January 5, 2015, for $15,000.

Instructions

(a) Calculate the actual cost of owning this equipment.
(b) Calculate the depreciation for the equipment for 2012 to 2014 under (1) the straight-line method, (2) the diminishing-balance method, using a 40% rate, and (3) units-of-production. (*Hint:* Round the depreciable cost per unit to three decimal places.)
(c) Calculate the gain or loss on the sale of the equipment under each of the three methods.
(d) Calculate the total depreciation expense plus the loss on sale (or minus the gain on sale) under each of the three depreciation methods. Compare these totals with your answer in (a) above. Comment on your results.

TAKING IT FURTHER The owner of Wolcott Windows believes that having a gain or loss on sale indicates the company had made a mistake in calculating depreciation. Do you agree or disagree? Explain.

Record acquisition, depreciation, and disposal of equipment. (SO 2, 4) AP

P9–8A Express Co. purchased equipment on March 1, 2012, for $95,000 on account. The equipment had an estimated useful life of five years, with a residual value of $5,000. The equipment is disposed of on February 1, 2015. Express Co. uses the diminishing-balance method of depreciation with a 20% rate and calculates depreciation for partial periods to the nearest month. The company has an August 31 year end.

Instructions

(a) Record the acquisition of the equipment on March 1, 2012.
(b) Record depreciation at August 31, 2012, 2013, and 2014.
(c) Record the disposal on February 1, 2015, under the following assumptions:
   1. It was scrapped with no residual value.
   2. It was sold for $55,000.
   3. It was sold for $45,000.
   4. It was traded for new equipment with a list price of $97,000. Express was given a trade-in allowance of $52,000 on the old equipment and paid the balance in cash. Express determined the old equipment's fair value to be $47,000 at the date of the exchange.

TAKING IT FURTHER What are the arguments in favour of recording gains and losses on disposals of property, plant, and equipment as part of profit from operations? What are the arguments in favour of recording them as non-operating items?

Record property, plant, and equipment transactions; prepare partial financial statements. (SO 2, 4, 7) AP

P9–9A At January 1, 2014, Hamsmith Corporation reported the following property, plant, and equipment accounts:

Accumulated depreciation—buildings	$31,100,000
Accumulated depreciation—equipment	27,000,000
Buildings	48,700,000
Equipment	75,000,000
Land	10,000,000

Hamsmith uses straight-line depreciation for buildings and equipment and its fiscal year end is December 31. The buildings are estimated to have a 50-year useful life and no residual value; the equipment is estimated to have a 10-year useful life and no residual value. Interest on the notes is payable or collectible annually on the anniversary date of the issue.

During 2014, the following selected transactions occurred:

Apr.	1	Purchased land for $2.2 million. Paid $550,000 cash and issued a three-year, 6% note for the balance.
May	1	Sold equipment for $150,000 cash. The equipment cost $1.4 million when originally purchased on January 1, 2006.
June	1	Sold land for $1.8 million. Received $450,000 cash and accepted a three-year, 5% note for the balance. The land cost $700,000.
July	1	Purchased equipment for $1.1 million cash.
Dec. 31		Retired equipment that cost $500,000 when purchased on December 31, 2004.

Instructions

(a) Record the above transactions.
(b) Record any adjusting entries required at December 31, 2014.
(c) Prepare the property, plant, and equipment section of Hamsmith's balance sheet at December 31, 2014.

<u>TAKING IT FURTHER</u>   The owner of Hamsmith suggests the company should start using the revaluation model, not the cost model, for property, plant, and equipment now that it is following IFRS. Comment on this suggestion.

P9–10A   Due to rapid turnover in the accounting department, several transactions involving intangible assets were improperly recorded by Riley Co. in the year ended December 31, 2014:

Correct errors in recording intangible asset transactions.
(SO 6) AP

1. Riley developed a new manufacturing process early in the year, incurring research and development costs of $160,000. Of this amount, 45% was considered to be development costs that could be capitalized. Riley recorded the entire $160,000 in the Patents account and amortized it using a 15-year estimated useful life.
2. On July 1, 2014, Riley purchased a small company and, as a result of the purchase, recorded goodwill of $400,000. Riley recorded a half year's amortization on the goodwill in 2014 based on a 40-year useful life.
3. The company purchased a trademark for $47,500. Shortly thereafter, it was sued for trademark infringement. At the end of the year, Riley determined that the recoverable amount of the trademark was $35,000. Riley did not record an impairment loss because it is hopeful that the recoverable amount will rebound next year after the conclusion of a legal case defending the company's right to use this trademark.
4. Several years ago, Riley paid $70,000 for a licence to be the exclusive Canadian distributor of a Danish beer. In 2011, Riley determined there was an impairment of $40,000 in the value of the licence and recorded the loss. In 2014, because of a change in consumer tastes, the value of the licence increased to $80,000. Riley recorded the $50,000 increase in the licence's value by crediting Impairment Loss and debiting the licence account. Management felt the company should consistently record increases and decreases in value.
5. The company made an $8,000 charitable donation on December 31, 2014, which it debited to goodwill.

Instructions

Assuming that Riley reports under IFRS, prepare the journal entries that are needed to correct the errors made during 2014.

<u>TAKING IT FURTHER</u>   The majority of the intangible assets reported on a balance sheet have been purchased as opposed to being internally generated. Why? What happens to the cost of an internally generated intangible asset if it is not recorded as an asset?

P9–11A   The intangible assets reported by Ip Company at December 31, 2013, follow:

Record intangible asset transactions; prepare partial balance sheet. (SO 6, 7) AP

Patent #1	$80,000	
Less: Accumulated amortization	16,000	$ 64,000
Copyright #1	$48,000	
Less: Accumulated amortization	28,800	19,200
Goodwill		220,000
Total		$303,200

Patent #1 was acquired in January 2012 and has an estimated useful life of 10 years. Copyright #1 was acquired in January 2008 and also has an estimated useful life of 10 years. The following cash transactions may have affected intangible assets and goodwill during the year 2014:

Jan.   2   Paid $23,200 of legal costs to successfully defend Patent #1 against infringement by another company.
June 30   Developed a new product, incurring $180,000 in research costs and $60,000 in development costs, which were paid in cash. Patent #2 was granted for the product on July 1. Its estimated useful life is equal to its legal life of 20 years.
Sept. 1   Paid $12,000 to an Olympic athlete to appear in commercials advertising the company's products. The commercials will air in September.
Oct.   1   Acquired a second copyright for $18,000 cash. Copyright #2 has an estimated useful life of six years.
Dec. 31   Determined the recoverable amount of the goodwill to be $240,000. The company had originally paid $250,000 for the goodwill in 2011. In 2012, the company had recorded a $30,000 impairment loss on the goodwill. There is no indication that the patents and copyrights were impaired.

Instructions

(a) Record the above transactions.
(b) Prepare any adjusting journal entries required at December 31, 2014, the company's year end.
(c) Show how the intangible assets and goodwill will be reported on the balance sheet at December 31, 2014.

<u>TAKING IT FURTHER</u>   Since intangible assets do not have physical substance, why are they considered to be assets?

Record natural resource transactions; prepare partial financial statements. (SO 3, 5, 7) AP

P9–12A Yount Mining Company has a December 31 fiscal year end. The following information relates to its Gough Alexander mine:

1. Yount purchased the Gough Alexander mine on March 31, 2013, for $2.6 million cash. On the same day, modernization of the mine was completed at a cash cost of $260,000. It is estimated that this mine will yield 560,000 tonnes of ore. The mine's estimated residual value is $200,000. Yount expects it will extract all the ore, and then close and sell the mine site in four years.
2. During 2013, Yount extracted and sold 120,000 tonnes of ore from the mine.
3. At the beginning of 2014, Yount reassessed its estimate of the remaining ore in the mine. Yount estimates that there is still 550,000 tonnes of ore in the mine at January 1, 2014. The estimated residual value remains at $200,000.
4. During 2014, Yount extracted and sold 100,000 tonnes of ore from the mine.

Instructions

(a) Prepare the 2013 and 2014 journal entries for the above, including any year-end adjustments.
(b) Show how the Gough Alexander mine will be reported on Yount's December 31, 2014, income statement and balance sheet.

TAKING IT FURTHER If the total estimated amount of units that will be produced (extracted) changes during the life of the natural resource, is it still appropriate to use the units-of-production method? Explain.

Calculate ratios and comment. (SO 7) AN

P9–13A Andruski Company and Brar Company both manufacture school science equipment. The following financial information is for three years ended December 31 (in thousands):

Andruski Company	2014	2013	2012
Net sales	$552.0	$515.9	$469.0
Profit	21.4	20.6	18.7
Total assets	702.5	662.8	602.5

Brar Company	2014	2013	2012
Net sales	$1,762.9	$1,588.2	$1,484.3
Profit	96.5	85.4	79.8
Total assets	1,523.5	1,410.7	1,318.4

Instructions

(a) Calculate the asset turnover and return on assets ratios for both companies for 2013 and 2014. Round your answers to two decimal points.
(b) Comment on how effective each of the companies is at using its assets to generate sales and produce profit.

TAKING IT FURTHER After reading the notes to the financial statements, you have determined that Andruski Company uses diminishing-balance depreciation and Brar uses straight-line. Does this affect your ability to compare these two companies?

▶ Problems: Set B

Record property transactions. (SO 1) AP

P9–1B In 2014, Weisman Company had the following transactions related to the purchase of a property. All transactions are for cash unless otherwise stated.

Feb. 7 Purchased real estate for $575,000, paying $115,000 cash and signing a note payable for the balance. The site had an old building on it and the fair value of the land and building were $555,000 and $30,000, respectively. Weisman intends to demolish the old building and construct a new apartment building on the site.

9 Paid legal fees of $7,500 on the real estate purchase on February 7.

15 Paid $19,000 to demolish the old building and make the land ready for the construction of the apartment building.

17 Received $8,500 from the sale of material from the demolished building.

25 Graded and filled the land in preparation for the building construction at a cost of $10,500.

Mar. 2 Architect's fees on the apartment building were $28,000.

15 Excavation costs were $18,000. Construction began on March 20.

Aug. 31   The apartment building was completed. The full cost of construction was $850,000. Paid $170,000 cash and signed a note payable for the balance.

Sept. 3   Paid $40,000 for sidewalks and a parking lot for the building.

     10   Purchased a one-year insurance policy on the finished building for $3,750.

Oct. 31   Paid $37,750 for landscaping.

Instructions

(a) Record the above transactions.

(b) Determine the cost of the land, land improvements, and building that will appear on Weisman's December 31, 2014, balance sheet.

TAKING IT FURTHER   When should Weisman begin recording depreciation on this property and on which assets?

P9–2B   In its first year of business, Solinger Company purchased land, a building, and equipment on November 5, 2013, for $700,000 in total. The land was valued at $262,500, the building at $337,500, and the equipment at $150,000. Additional information on the depreciable assets follows:

Allocate cost and calculate partial period depreciation. (SO 1, 2) AP

Asset	Residual Value	Useful Life in Years	Depreciation Method
Building	$15,000	60	Straight-line
Equipment	15,000	8	Double diminishing-balance

Instructions

(a) Allocate the purchase cost of the land, building, and equipment to each of the assets.

(b) Solinger has a December 31 fiscal year end and is trying to decide how to calculate depreciation for assets purchased during the year. Calculate depreciation expense for the building and equipment for 2013 and 2014 assuming:

   1. depreciation is calculated to the nearest whole month.
   2. a half year's depreciation is recorded in the year of acquisition.

(c) Which policy should Solinger follow in the year of acquisition: recording depreciation to the nearest whole month or recording a half year of depreciation?

TAKING IT FURTHER   Suppose that Solinger decided to use the units-of-production depreciation method instead of diminishing-balance for its equipment. How would this affect your answer to (c) above?

P9–3B   Glans Company purchased equipment on account on April 6, 2012, at an invoice price of $442,000. On April 7, 2012, it paid $4,000 for delivery of the equipment. A one-year, $3,000 insurance policy on the equipment was purchased on April 9, 2012. On April 22, 2012, Glans paid $6,000 for installation and testing of the equipment. The equipment was ready for use on May 1, 2012.

Determine cost; calculate and compare depreciation under different methods. (SO 1, 2) AP

   Glans estimates that the equipment's useful life will be four years, with a residual value of $20,000. It also estimates that, in terms of activity, the equipment's useful life will be 150,000 units. Glans has an April 30 fiscal year end. Assume that actual usage is as follows:

# of Units	Year Ended April 30
22,600	2013
45,600	2014
49,700	2015
32,200	2016

Instructions

(a) Determine the cost of the equipment.

(b) Prepare depreciation schedules for the life of the asset under the following depreciation methods:

   1. straight-line
   2. diminishing-balance at double the straight-line rate
   3. units-of-production

(c) Which method would result in the highest profit for the year ended April 30, 2013? Over the life of the asset?

(d) Which method would result in the least cash used for the year ended April 30, 2013? Over the life of the asset?

TAKING IT FURTHER   Assume instead that at the time Glans purchased the equipment, it had a legal obligation to ensure that the equipment was recycled at the end of its useful life. Assume the cost of doing this is significant. Would this have had an impact on the answers to (a) and (b) above? Explain.

Account for operating and capital expenditures and asset impairments. (SO 1, 3) AP

P9–4B Sugden Company has a December 31 fiscal year end and follows IFRS. The following selected transactions are related to its property, plant, and equipment in 2014:

Jan. 22   Performed an annual safety inspection on the equipment for $4,600.

Apr. 10   Installed a conveyor belt system in the factory for $95,000, which is expected to increase efficiency and allow the company to produce more products each year.

May 6   Painted the interior of the entire building at a cost of $30,500.

July 20   Repaired a machine for $10,000. An employee had used incorrect material in the machine, which resulted in a complete mechanical breakdown.

Aug. 7   Overhauled equipment that originally cost $100,000 for $35,000. This increased the equipment's expected useful life by three years.

15   Trained several new employees to operate the company's equipment at a cost of $1,900.

Oct. 25   Paid $16,700 for the purchase of new equipment and $1,500 to a consultant for testing and installing the equipment.

Nov. 6   Added an elevator and ramps to a building owned by the company to make it wheelchair accessible for $120,000.

Dec. 31   After recording annual depreciation, Sugden reviewed its property, plant, and equipment for possible impairment. Sugden determined the following:

     1. The recoverable amount of equipment that originally cost $250,000 and has accumulated depreciation of $75,000 is $90,000.

     2. Land that originally cost $575,000 had previously been written down to $500,000 as a result of an impairment in 2011. Circumstances have changed, and the land's recoverable amount is now $600,000.

Instructions

(a) For each of these transactions, indicate if the transaction has increased (+) or decreased (−) Land, Buildings, Equipment, Accumulated Depreciation, total property, plant, and equipment (PP&E), and profit, and by how much. If the item is not changed, write "NE" to indicate there is no effect. Use the following format, in which the first one has been done for you as an example.

Transaction	Land	Buildings	Equipment	Accumulated Depreciation	Total PP&E	Profit
Jan. 22	NE	NE	NE	NE	NE	−$4,600

(b) Prepare journal entries to record the above transactions. All transactions are on account.

TAKING IT FURTHER   Assume that Sugden also purchased equipment with an expected useful life of 15 years and that the equipment's engine will need to be replaced every five years. Which useful life should Sugden use when calculating depreciation on the equipment? Explain.

Record impairment and calculate revised depreciation. (SO 3) AP

P9–5B   Short Track Speed Skating, a public company, purchased equipment on January 10, 2010, for $600,000. At that time, management estimated that the equipment would have a useful life of 10 years and a residual value of $25,000. Short Track uses the straight-line method of depreciation and has a December 31 year end.

Short Track tested the equipment for impairment on December 31, 2014, after recording the annual depreciation expense. It was determined that the equipment's recoverable amount was $260,000, and that the total estimated useful life would be seven years instead of ten, with a residual value of $10,000 instead of $25,000.

Instructions

(a) Calculate the annual depreciation expense for the years 2010 to 2014 and the carrying amount at December 31, 2014.

(b) Record the impairment loss, if any, on December 31, 2014.

(c) What will appear on Short Track's 2014 income statement and balance sheet with regard to this equipment?

(d) Assuming no further impairments or recoveries, calculate the annual depreciation expense for the years 2015 and 2016.

(e) Determine the equipment's accumulated depreciation and carrying amount at the end of its useful life.

TAKING IT FURTHER   Suggest some possible reasons as to why the IFRS accounting standards result in recording impairments of long-lived assets more frequently than ASPE.

Record acquisition, depreciation, impairment, and disposal of land and buildings. (SO 1, 2, 3, 4) AP

P9–6B   SE Parts Supply Company purchased land and a building on August 1, 2012, for $595,000. It paid $200,000 in cash and signed a 5% note payable for the balance. The company estimated the land was worth $340,000 and the building, $255,000. The building was estimated to have a 40-year useful life with a $15,000 residual value. The company has a December 31 year end and uses the straight-line depreciation method for buildings. The following are related transactions and adjustments during the next three years.

2012

Dec. 31   Recorded annual depreciation.
    31   Paid the interest owing on the note payable.

2013

May 21   Paid $2,000 to fix the roof.
Dec. 31   Recorded annual depreciation.
    31   Paid the interest owing on the note payable.
    31   The land and building were tested for impairment. The land had a recoverable amount of $280,000 and the building, $249,000.

2014

Mar. 31   Sold the land and building for $480,000 cash: $250,000 for the land and $230,000 for the building.
Apr. 1   Paid the note payable and interest owing.

Instructions

(a) Record the above transactions and adjustments, including the acquisition on August 1, 2012.
(b) What factors may have been responsible for the impairment?
(c) Assume instead that the company sold the land and building on November 30, 2014, for $650,000 cash: $390,000 for the land and $260,000 for the building. Record the journal entries to record the sale.

TAKING IT FURTHER   How might management determine the recoverable amount of the land and building at each year end? Does the company need to test the assets for impairment every year?

P9–7B   On January 3, 2013, Ajax Adanacs purchased a piece of equipment for $125,000. The equipment's estimated useful life is either three years or 12,000 units, with a residual value of $18,000. The company has a December 31 fiscal year end and normally uses straight-line depreciation. Management is considering the merits of using the units-of-production or diminishing-balance method of depreciation instead of the straight-line method. The actual numbers of units produced by the equipment were 6,000 in 2013, 2,000 in 2014, and 3,800 in 2015. The equipment was sold on January 5, 2016, for $21,000.

Calculate and compare depreciation and gain or loss on disposal under three methods of depreciation. (SO 2, 4) AP

Instructions

(a) Calculate the actual cost of owning this equipment.
(b) Calculate the depreciation for the equipment for 2013 to 2015 under (1) the straight-line method, (2) the diminishing-balance method, using a 45% rate, and (3) units-of-production. (*Hint:* Round the depreciable cost per unit to three decimal places.)
(c) Calculate the gain or loss on the sale of the equipment under each of the three methods.
(d) Calculate the total depreciation expense plus the loss on sale (or minus the gain on sale) under each of the three depreciation methods. Compare these totals with your answer in (a) above. Comment on your results.

TAKING IT FURTHER   The owner of Ajax Adanacs believes that having a gain or loss on sale indicates the company had made a mistake in calculating depreciation. Do you agree or disagree? Explain.

P9–8B   Walker Co. purchased furniture on February 4, 2012, for $70,000 on account. At that time, it was expected to have a useful life of five years and a $1,000 residual value. The furniture was disposed of on January 26, 2015, when the company moved to new premises. Walker Co. uses the diminishing-balance method of depreciation with a 20% rate and calculates depreciation for partial periods to the nearest month. The company has a September 30 year end.

Record acquisition, depreciation, and disposal of furniture. (SO 2, 4) AP

Instructions

(a) Record the acquisition of the furniture on February 4, 2012.
(b) Record depreciation for each of 2012, 2013, and 2014.
(c) Record the disposal on January 26, 2015, under the following assumptions:
    1. It was scrapped and has no residual value.
    2. It was sold for $30,000.
    3. It was sold for $40,000.
    4. It was traded for new furniture with a catalogue price of $115,000. Walker Co. was given a trade-in allowance of $45,000 on the old furniture and paid the balance in cash. Walker Co. determined that the old furniture's fair value was $30,000 at the date of the exchange.

TAKING IT FURTHER   What are the arguments in favour of recording gains and losses on disposals of property, plant, and equipment as part of profit from operations? What are the arguments in favour of recording them as non-operating items?

Record property, plant, and equipment transactions; prepare partial financial statements. (SO 2, 4, 7) AP

P9–9B At January 1, 2014, Jaina Company reported the following property, plant, and equipment accounts:

Accumulated depreciation—buildings	$12,100,000
Accumulated depreciation—equipment	15,000,000
Buildings	28,500,000
Equipment	48,000,000
Land	4,000,000

Jaina uses straight-line depreciation for buildings and equipment, and its fiscal year end is December 31. The buildings are estimated to have a 50-year life and no residual value; the equipment is estimated to have a 10-year useful life and no residual value. Interest on all notes is payable or collectible at maturity on the anniversary date of the issue.

During 2014, the following selected transactions occurred:

Apr. 1   Purchased land for $1.9 million. Paid $475,000 cash and issued a 10-year, 6% note for the balance.
May 1   Sold equipment that cost $750,000 when purchased on January 1, 2007. The equipment was sold for $350,000 cash.
June 1   Sold land purchased on June 1, 1996, for $1.2 million. Received $380,000 cash and accepted a 6% note for the balance. The land cost $300,000.
July 1   Purchased equipment for $1 million on account, terms n/60.
Dec. 31   Retired equipment that cost $470,000 when purchased on December 31, 2004.

Instructions

(a) Record the above transactions.
(b) Record any adjusting entries required at December 31, 2014.
(c) Prepare the property, plant, and equipment section of Jaina's balance sheet at December 31, 2014.

TAKING IT FURTHER   The owner of Jaina Company suggests the company should start using the revaluation model, not the cost model, for property, plant, and equipment now that it is following IFRS. Comment on this suggestion.

Correct errors in recording intangible asset transactions. (SO 6) AP

P9–10B   Due to rapid employee turnover in the accounting department, the following transactions involving intangible assets were recorded in a questionable way by Hahn Company in the year ended August 31, 2014:

1. Hahn developed an electronic monitoring device for running shoes. It incurred research costs of $70,000 and development costs with probable future benefits of $45,000. It recorded all of these costs in the Patent account.
2. The company registered the patent for the monitoring device developed in transaction 1. Legal fees and registration costs totalled $21,000. These costs were recorded in the Professional Fees Expense account.
3. The company successfully fought a competitor in court, defending its patent. It incurred $38,000 of legal fees. These costs were recorded in the Legal Fees Expense account.
4. The company recorded $5,750 of annual amortization on the patent over its legal life of 20 years [($70,000 + $45,000 = $115,000) ÷ 20 years]. The patent's expected economic life is five years. Assume that for amortization purposes, all costs occurred at the beginning of the year.
5. At the end of the year, Hahn tested the patent for impairment and found that its recoverable amount of $110,000 exceeded its carrying amount of $109,250 ($115,000 − $5,750). Since Hahn follows the cost model, it did not record an entry.

Instructions

Assuming Hahn reports under ASPE, prepare the journal entries that are needed to correct the errors made during 2014.

TAKING IT FURTHER   The majority of the intangible assets reported on a balance sheet have been purchased as opposed to being internally generated. Why? What happens to the cost of an internally generated intangible asset if it is not recorded as an asset?

Record intangible asset transactions; prepare partial balance sheet. (SO 6, 7) AP

P9–11B   The intangible assets section of Ghani Corporation's balance sheet at December 31, 2013, is as follows:

Copyright #1	$36,000	
Less: Accumulated amortization	24,000	$ 12,000
Trademark		52,000
Goodwill		150,000
Total		$214,000

The copyright was acquired in January 2012 and has an estimated useful life of three years. The trademark was acquired in January 2010 and is expected to have an indefinite useful life. The following cash transactions may have affected intangible assets during 2014:

Jan. 2   Paid $7,000 in legal costs to successfully defend the trademark against infringement by another company.

July 1   Developed a new product, incurring $275,000 in research costs and $50,000 in development costs. A patent was granted for the product on July 1, and its useful life is equal to its legal life.

Aug. 1   Paid $45,000 to a popular hockey player to appear in commercials advertising the company's products. The commercials will air in September and October.

Oct. 1   Acquired a second copyright for $168,000. The new copyright has an estimated useful life of six years.

Dec. 31   The company determined the recoverable amount of the trademark and goodwill to be $50,000 and $170,000, respectively. There was no indication that any of the patents or copyrights were impaired.

Instructions

(a) Prepare journal entries to record the transactions.

(b) Prepare any adjusting journal entries required at December 31, 2014, the company's year end.

(c) Show how the intangible assets and goodwill will be presented on the balance sheet at December 31, 2014.

TAKING IT FURTHER   Since intangible assets do not have physical substance, why are they considered to be assets?

P9–12B   Cypress Timber Company has a December 31 fiscal year end. The following information is related to its Westerlund tract of timber land:

Record equipment, note payable, and natural resource transactions; prepare partial financial statements. (SO 2, 5, 7) AP

1. Cypress purchased a 50,000-hectare tract of timber land at Westerlund on June 7, 2013, for $50 million, paying $10 million cash and signing a 7% mortgage payable for the balance. Principal payments of $8 million and the annual interest on the mortgage are due each December 31. It is estimated that this tract will yield 1 million tonnes of timber. The timber tract's estimated residual value is $2 million. Cypress expects it will cut all the trees and then sell the Westerlund site in seven years.

2. On June 26, 2013, Cypress purchased and installed equipment at the Westerlund timber site for $196,000 cash. The equipment will be amortized on a straight-line basis over an estimated useful life of seven years with no residual value. Cypress has a policy of recording depreciation for partial periods to the nearest month. The equipment will be scrapped after the Westerlund site is harvested.

3. In 2013, Cypress cut and sold 110,000 tonnes of timber.

4. In 2014, Cypress cut and sold 240,000 tonnes of timber.

Instructions

(a) Prepare the 2013 and 2014 journal entries for the above, including any year-end adjustments.

(b) Show how property, plant, and equipment, natural resources, and related accounts will be reported on Cypress's December 31, 2014, income statement and balance sheet.

TAKING IT FURTHER   If the total estimated amount of units that will be produced (extracted) changes during the life of the natural resource, is it still appropriate to use the units-of-production method? Explain.

P9–13B   Mock Orange Company and Cotoneaster Company both manufacture pruning shears. The following financial information is for three years ended December 31 (in thousands):

Calculate ratios and comment. (SO 7) AN

Mock Orange Company	2014	2013	2012
Net sales	$9,428.0	$8,894.3	$8,235.5
Profit	627.7	597.8	553.5
Total assets	5,829.1	5,771.4	5,343.9

Cotoneaster Company	2014	2013	2012
Net sales	$3,839.8	$3,656.9	$3,417.7
Profit	143.4	137.9	128.9
Total assets	2,754.5	2,504.1	2,340.3

Instructions

(a) Calculate the asset turnover and return on assets ratios for both companies for 2013 and 2014. Round your answers to two decimal points.

(b) Comment on how effective each of the companies is at using its assets to generate sales and produce profit.

TAKING IT FURTHER   After reading the notes to the financial statements, you have determined that Mock Orange Company uses straight-line depreciation and Cotoneaster uses diminishing-balance. Does this affect your ability to compare these two companies?

● Continuing Cookie Chronicle

(*Note:* This is a continuation of the Cookie Chronicle from Chapters 1 through 8.)

Natalie is thinking of buying a van that will be used only for business. She estimates that she can buy the van for $28,400. Natalie would spend an additional $3,000 to have the van painted. As well, she wants the back seat of the van removed so that she will have lots of room to transport her mixer inventory and baking supplies. The cost of taking out the back seat and installing shelving units is estimated at $1,600. She expects the van to last about five years and to be driven for 200,000 km. The annual cost of vehicle insurance will be $1,440. Natalie estimates that at the end of the five-year useful life, the van will sell for $5,000. Assume that she will buy the van on April 15, 2014, and it will be ready for use on May 1, 2014.

Natalie is concerned about the impact of the van's cost and related depreciation on Cookie Creations' income statement and balance sheet.

Instructions

(a) Determine the cost of the van.
(b) Prepare depreciation schedules for the life of the van under the following depreciation methods:
    1. straight-line.
    2. diminishing-balance at double the straight-line rate.
    3. units-of-production. It is estimated that the van will be driven as follows: 30,000 km in 2014, 37,500 km in 2015, 40,000 km in 2016, 47,500 km in 2017, 35,000 km in 2018, and 10,000 km in 2019.
    Recall that Cookie Creations has a December 31 year end.
(c) Which method of depreciation would result in the highest profit for the year ended December 31, 2014? Over the life of the asset?
(d) Which method would result in the van's highest carrying amount for the year ended December 31, 2014? Over the life of the asset?
(e) Which method would result in the least cash used for the year ended December 31, 2014? Over the life of the asset?
(f) Which method of depreciation would you recommend that Natalie use? Why?

CHAPTER 9 | BROADENING YOUR PERSPECTIVE

● Financial Reporting and Analysis

Financial Reporting Problem

BYP9–1 Refer to the financial statements and the Notes to Consolidated Statements for **Reitmans (Canada) Limited**, which are reproduced in Appendix A.

Instructions

(a) For each type of property and equipment that Reitmans reports in note 8 to its balance sheet, identify the following amounts at January 28, 2012: (1) cost, (2) accumulated depreciation and impairment losses, and (3) net carrying amount.
(b) For the intangible assets and goodwill that Reitmans reports in note 9 and in its balance sheet, identify the following amounts at January 28, 2012: (1) cost, (2) accumulated amortization, and (3) net carrying amount.
(c) Did Reitmans have any impairment losses or reversals of impairment losses in the year ended January 28, 2012? How does Reitmans determine if an impairment loss needs to be recorded?
(d) Depreciation and amortization expense are not disclosed separately on the statement of earnings. Where are they included? What were the amounts for fiscal 2012? (See notes 8 and 9.)
(e) What was the amount of cash used to buy property and equipment and intangible assets during the 2012 fiscal year? (*Hint:* Look at the statement of cash flows to determine this amount.)
(f) What depreciation methods are used by Reitmans for financial reporting purposes? (See note 3 to the financial statements.) What expected useful life does the company use to calculate the depreciation on its property and equipment? On its intangible assets?

Interpreting Financial Statements

BYP9-2   WestJet Airlines Ltd. is one of Canada's leading airlines, offering service to destinations in Canada, the United States, Mexico, and the Caribbean. The following is a partial extract from its December 31, 2011, notes to the financial statements:

Note. 1 (j) Statement of Significant Accounting Policies — Property and Equipment

Property and equipment is stated at cost and depreciated to its estimated residual value.

Asset class	Basis	Rate
Aircraft, net of estimated residual value	Straight-line	20 years
Engine, airframe and landing gear overhaul	Straight-line	8 to 15 years
Buildings	Straight-line	40 years
Leasehold improvements	Straight-line	Term of lease
Assets under finance leases	Straight-line	Term of lease

Major overhaul expenditures are capitalized and depreciated over the expected life between overhauls. All other costs relating to the maintenance of fleet assets are charged to the consolidated statement of earnings on consumption or as incurred.

Instructions

(a) WestJet uses straight-line depreciation for all of its depreciable property and equipment. For which of the assets shown above might WestJet consider using units-of-production instead of straight-line depreciation? Should WestJet use units-of-production for those assets?

(b) According to this note, major overhaul expenditures are treated differently than other fleet maintenance costs. Explain how WestJet records these items. Is this appropriate? Why or why not?

(c) WestJet depreciates the cost of leasehold improvements, and assets under finance leases over the terms of the leases. Is this appropriate? Are these terms the same as the physical lives of these assets?

(d) Does WestJet use component depreciation for any of its property and equipment assets? Should it?

⊙ Critical Thinking

Collaborative Learning Activity

Note to instructor: Additional instructions and material for this group activity can be found on the Instructor Resource Site and in *WileyPLUS*.

BYP9-3   In this group activity, you will work in two groups to improve your understanding of the different depreciation methods. First you will work in "expert" groups in which you will ensure that each group member thoroughly understands one method of depreciation. Then you will move to a second group consisting of one student from each of the three expert groups, and take turns teaching each other the different depreciation methods.

Communication Activity

BYP9-4   Long Trucking Corporation is a medium-sized publicly owned trucking company with trucks that are driven across North America. The company owns large garages and equipment to repair and maintain the trucks. Ken Bond, the controller, knows that long-lived assets are reviewed annually for impairment. Ken records an impairment loss of $100,000 and the loss appears on the income statement for the current fiscal year. Jason Long, the company president, reviews the financial statements and wants more information from Ken about the impairment loss.

Instructions

Write an e-mail to Jason Long that explains (1) what might have caused the impairment loss, (2) the journal entry required for the impairment loss, and (3) how this writedown will affect Long Trucking's balance sheet and income statement in future years.

Ethics Case

BYP9-5   Finney Container Company has been seeing sales go down for its main product, non-biodegradable plastic cartons. Although some expenses have also reduced in line with the reduced revenues, there has been a decrease in profit because some expenses, such as depreciation, have not declined. The company uses the straight-line depreciation method.

The president, Philip Shapiro, recalling his college accounting classes, instructs his controller to lengthen the estimated asset lives used for depreciation calculations in order to reduce annual depreciation expense and increase profit. The president's compensation includes an annual bonus based on the amount of net profit reported in the income statement.

A processing line of automated plastic-extruding equipment that was purchased for $2.9 million in January 2012 was originally estimated to have a useful life between five and nine years. Therefore, the company used the middle of that estimate, or seven years, as the useful life, and a residual value of $100,000, to calculate the annual straight-line depreciation for the first two years. However, the president now wants the equipment's estimated useful life to be changed to nine years (total), and to continue using the straight-line method.

The controller is hesitant to make the change, believing it is unethical to increase profit in this way. The president says, "Hey, the useful life is only an estimate. Besides, I've heard that our competition uses a nine-year estimated life on its production equipment. You want the company results to be competitive, don't you? So maybe we were wrong the first time and now we are getting it right. Or you can tell the auditors that we think may be the equipment will last longer now that we are not using it as much."

Instructions

(a) Who are the stakeholders in this situation?
(b) Is the suggested change in asset life unethical, or simply a shrewd business practice by a sharp president?
(c) What would be the impact of the president's proposed change on profit in the year of the change?

"All About You" Activity

BYP9–6 In the "All About You" feature, you learned about actions that have been taken to strengthen Canada's copyright law and the radical changes in technology that are driving the need to update the law. You have recently graduated from a music program and have composed two songs that you believe a recording artist may produce. You are wondering how you can best get copyright protection for your songs.

Instructions

Go to the Canadian Intellectual Property Office website at http://www.cipo.ic.gc.ca and search for its publication "A Guide to Copyrights."

Answer the following questions:

(a) What is a copyright and to what does copyright apply?
(b) How can you obtain a copyright for your songs and what do you have to do to be protected?
(c) What are the benefits to you of getting copyright registration for your songs?
(d) How and where do you register a copyright?
(e) When you register a copyright you are required to pay a fee for the registration. Should the registration fee for the copyright be recorded as an asset or an expense?
(f) Go to the glossary in "A Guide to Copyrights." What is infringement of copyright? Provide a specific example of infringement.
(g) Go to frequently asked questions in "A Guide to Copyrights." Whose responsibility is it for monitoring the use of your songs once you have registered the copyright?

ANSWERS TO CHAPTER QUESTIONS

ANSWERS TO ACCOUNTING IN ACTION INSIGHT QUESTIONS

Business Insight, p. 474

Q: Is the units-of-production method the best depreciation method for Morris Formal Wear to use for its tuxedos or would you recommend another method?

A: Since Morris Formal Wear wants to track wear and tear on each of its tuxedos, the units-of-production depreciation method is the best choice. Rental tuxedos are the type of long-lived asset that will physically wear out with use much faster than they would become obsolete due to changing tuxedo styles. By keeping track of how many times each tuxedo has been used, instead of just how old they are, the company can make better decisions about when to replace the tuxedos.

All About You Insight, p. 490

Q: Why is it important that the copyrights of artists, writers, musicians, and the entertainment industry be protected?

A: Just as it is important that you as an individual be compensated in your career, it is important that individuals in artistic, music, entertainment, and literary careers be compensated fairly for their creativity. Without fair compensation, Canada's creativity and innovation will be discouraged. Without copyright protection, it may be difficult to ensure that appropriate individuals are fairly compensated and companies may not be willing to invest in creative ventures if the work is not protected.

ANSWERS TO SELF-STUDY QUESTIONS

1. c   2. b   3. b   4. c   5. b   6. d   7. c   8. a   9. b   10. c   11. b   12. d

Remember to go back to the beginning of the chapter to check off your completed work!

←

CURRENT LIABILITIES AND PAYROLL

THE **NAVIGATOR**

- ☐ Understand *Concepts for Review*
- ☐ Read *Feature Story*
- ☐ Scan *Study Objectives*
- ☐ Read *Chapter Preview*
- ☐ Read text and answer *Before You Go On*
- ☐ Review *Comparing IFRS and ASPE*
- ☐ Work *Demonstration Problem*
- ☐ Review *Summary of Study Objectives*
- ☐ Answer *Self-Study Questions*
- ☐ Complete assignments
- ☐ Go to *WileyPLUS* for practice and tutorials

CONCEPTS FOR **REVIEW**

Before studying this chapter, you should understand or, if necessary, review:

a. How to make adjusting entries for unearned revenue (Ch. 3, pp. 120–121) and accrued expenses. (Ch. 3, pp. 124–127)

b. The importance of liquidity in evaluating the financial position of a company. (Ch. 4, pp. 193– 195)

c. How to account for sales discounts. (Ch. 5, p. 246–247)

d. Accounting for notes receivable. (Ch. 8, pp. 427–430)

EVEN SMALL COMPANIES HAVE BIG PAYROLL OBLIGATIONS

TORONTO, Ont.—A big portion of any organization's current liabilities is its payroll obligations: employees' salaries or wages, and any related deductions for things like the Canada Pension Plan (CPP), Employment Insurance (EI), and income taxes. Then there are health care taxes, workers' compensation premiums, and any taxable benefits the employer offers. Depending on the business size and reach, there are more than 190 different pieces of legislation and regulations that a payroll person has to keep up to date with, points out Steven Van Alstine, Vice President, Education, at the Canadian Payroll Association. This includes the federal *Income Tax Act*, *Employment Insurance Act*, and *Canada Pension Plan Act*, along with provincial workers' compensation regulations, employment standards, health tax acts, and so on. "It is difficult, certainly if you're a new small business, being faced with myriad different requirements or legislation," he says. "It is a little daunting when you think, as a new business owner, 'What do I have to do?'"

No doubt, accounting for this liability can be a challenge for smaller businesses. Of the association's 18,000 members, 65% to 70% are organizations with 200 or fewer employees, says Mr. Van Alstine. For about one-third of people working in payroll, it is their sole responsibility, he continues. But for the remaining two-thirds, it's only a part of their responsibilities, which likely include such functions as human resources or accounts payable. The association can help small businesses and people who don't handle payroll full-time. "We are a support for those individuals who may be the sole payroll person within the organization," he

says. Consultants are on hand to guide payroll staff through the process by phone.

The association offers a certification program for payroll professionals. In addition, it offers "Learning Payroll" professional development seminars. The association also has a "Setting Up a New Payroll" checklist with various resources and forms an employer may need and where to locate them, including those specific to provinces.

The Canada Revenue Agency also has tools available to help employers with their payroll, including an on-line payroll deduction calculator, which many may think does the job for them. However, as Mr. Van Alstine points out, "The employer needs to know that those are the deductions for the employee." Among other things, employers also have to contribute to CPP and EI for their employees.

Those lacking the necessary qualifications and skills to properly account for payroll may hire a Canadian Payroll Association–certified professional, a bookkeeper, or an accounting firm to take over the paperwork. Or employers may outsource the whole payroll function to a service provider like Ceridian or ADP, which is a growing trend. "Because there is all this legislation to keep up with, they feel that it's better to totally outsource this function," Mr. Van Alstine says. The benefits to employers include reduced costs, partly because they use the service provider's technology rather than setting up their own system.

Payroll is a liability that needs proper administration no matter what the size of the business is. After all, a company's employees are its greatest asset.

THE **NAVIGATOR**

» STUDY **OBJECTIVES**

After studying this chapter, you should be able to:

1. Account for determinable or certain current liabilities.

2. Account for estimated liabilities.

3. Account for contingencies.

4. Determine payroll costs and record payroll transactions.

5. Prepare the current liabilities section of the balance sheet.

6. Calculate mandatory payroll deductions (Appendix 10A).

THE **NAVIGATOR**

Whether it is a huge company such as one of Canada's chartered banks, or a small business such as your local convenience store, every company has current liabilities. As explained in Chapter 4, current liabilities are obligations that are expected to be settled within one year from the balance sheet date or in the company's normal operating cycle. Obligations that are expected to be paid after one year or longer are classified as non-current liabilities. We explain current liabilities in this chapter and non-current liabilities in Chapter 15. Payroll creates current liabilities and affects almost every company. It is also explained in this chapter.

The chapter is organized as follows:

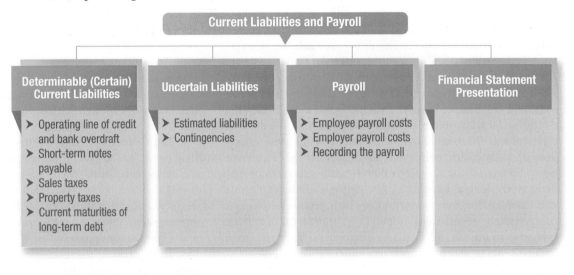

Determinable (Certain) Current Liabilities

» **STUDY OBJECTIVE 1**

Account for determinable or certain current liabilities.

Helpful hint Gift cards are an example of an unearned revenue liability where it is necessary to estimate the liability. These are discussed in the next section of this chapter.

Alternative terminology Determinable liabilities are also referred to as *certain liabilities* or *known liabilities*.

In Chapter 1, we defined liabilities as present obligations, arising from past events, to make future payments of assets or services. A future commitment is not considered a liability unless an obligation also exists. For example, a company may have made a commitment to purchase an asset in the future, but the obligation normally arises only when the goods are delivered or if the company has entered into an irrevocable agreement. Thus, an essential characteristic of a liability is the existence of a *present* obligation.

Sometimes there is a great deal of uncertainty regarding whether or not a liability exists. Even if it is certain that the liability exists, sometimes we are not certain as to whom we owe, how much we owe, or when we owe. We will discuss this type of liability in the sections on estimated liabilities and contingencies.

In this section of the chapter, we will discuss liabilities where there is no uncertainty about their existence, amount, or timing. Liabilities with a known amount, payee, and due date are often referred to as **determinable liabilities**.

Examples of determinable current liabilities include bank indebtedness from operating lines of credit, and notes payable, accounts payable, sales taxes payable, unearned revenue, and current maturities of long-term debt. This category also includes accrued liabilities such as property taxes, payroll, and interest payable.

Accounts payable, or trade accounts payable, are often the largest current liability on a company's balance sheet. For example, as shown on Reitmans' balance sheet in Appendix A, its trade and other payables amount to $63,875 thousand, which is almost 72% of its total current liabilities.

The entries for accounts payable and determinable unearned revenues have been explained in previous chapters, and are not included in this section. We will discuss the accounting for other types of current liabilities in this section, including bank indebtedness from an operating line of credit, notes payable, sales taxes payable, property taxes payable, and current maturities of long-term debt. Payroll and employee benefits payable are also examples of determinable liabilities, but as the accounting for payroll is complex, we discuss it in a separate section of this chapter.

OPERATING LINE OF CREDIT AND BANK OVERDRAFT

Operating Line of Credit

Current assets (such as accounts receivable) do not always turn into cash at the exact time that current liabilities (such as accounts payable) must be paid. Consequently, most companies have an **operating line of credit** at their bank to help them manage temporary cash shortfalls. This means that the company has been pre-authorized by the bank to borrow money when it is needed, up to a pre-set limit.

Security, called **collateral**, is usually required by the bank as protection in case the company is unable to repay the loan. Collateral normally includes some, or all, of the company's current assets (e.g., accounts receivable or inventories); investments; or property, plant, and equipment.

Money borrowed through a line of credit is normally borrowed on a short-term basis, and is repayable immediately upon request—that is, on demand—by the bank. In reality, repayment is rarely demanded without notice. A line of credit makes it very easy for a company to borrow money. It does not have to make a call or visit its bank to actually arrange the transaction. The bank simply covers any cheques written in excess of the bank account balance, up to the approved credit limit.

Bank Overdraft

Some companies have a negative (credit), or overdrawn, cash balance at year end. This amount is usually called *bank indebtedness, bank overdraft,* or *bank advances.* No special entry or account is required to record the overdrawn amount. The Cash account has a credit balance because the dollar amount of cheques written exceeded the dollar amount of deposits. The credit balance in Cash is reported as a current liability with an appropriate note disclosure.

Interest is usually charged on the overdrawn amount at a floating rate, such as prime plus a specified percentage. The **prime rate** is the interest rate that banks charge their best customers. This rate is usually increased by a specified percentage according to the company's risk profile.

SHORT-TERM NOTES PAYABLE

The line of credit described above is similar to a **note payable**. Notes payable are obligations in the form of written promissory notes. In Chapter 8, we discussed notes receivable and included an illustration of a promissory note. You will recall that the payee has a note receivable and the maker of the note has a note payable.

Notes payable may be used instead of accounts payable. This gives the lender proof of the obligation in case legal action is needed to collect the debt. Accounts and notes payable that result from purchase transactions (i.e., amounts owed to suppliers) are often called **trade payables**. Notes payable are also frequently issued to meet short-term financing needs.

Helpful hint Notes payable are the opposite of notes receivable, and the accounting is similar.

Notes are issued for varying periods. If they are due for payment within one year of the balance sheet date, they are classified as current liabilities. Most notes are interest-bearing, with interest due monthly or at maturity.

To illustrate the accounting for notes payable, assume that Kok Co. borrows $100,000 from the local caisse populaire (credit union) on March 1 for four months, at an interest rate of 6%. The note matures on July 1 and interest, along with the note's principal amount, is payable at maturity.

Kok makes the following journal entry when it signs the note and receives the $100,000:

Mar. 1	Cash	100,000	
	Notes Payable		100,000
	To record issue of four-month, 6% note to		
	Caisse Populaire Dumoulin.		

A = L + OE
+100,000 +100,000

↑ Cash flows: +100,000

Interest accrues over the life of the note; therefore, interest expense must be recorded in the period when the borrowed money is used. Also, at year end, all liabilities (all obligations) must be recorded. If Kok Co. has a March 31 year end, then the interest owing at the end of March must be recorded. An adjusting entry is made to recognize interest expense and interest payable of $500 ($100,000 × 6% × $\frac{1}{12}$)

Helpful hint Interest is normally calculated using the number of days. In this textbook, we use months in order to simplify the calculations.

Helpful hint Interest rates are always expressed as annual rates, not the rate for the duration of the note.

at March 31. Recall from Chapter 3 that interest is calculated by multiplying the principal amount by the annual interest rate by the fraction of the year in the accrual.

The adjusting entry is:

A	=	L	+	OE
		+500		−500

Cash flows: no effect

Mar. 31	Interest Expense		500	
	Interest Payable			500
	To accrue interest to March 31.			

In the March 31 financial statements, the current liabilities section of the balance sheet will show notes payable of $100,000 and interest payable of $500. In addition, interest expense of $500 will be reported as other expenses in the income statement. **Interest payable is shown separately from the note payable.**

At maturity (July 1), Kok Co. must pay the face value of the note ($100,000) plus $2,000 interest ($100,000 × 6% × $^4/_{12}$). One month ($500) of this interest has already been accrued. Interest must also be updated for $1,500 ($100,000 × 6% × $^3/_{12}$) for the three additional months—April through June—since interest was last recorded. This can be done in one compound entry or in separate journal entries as follows:

A	=	L	+	OE
		+1,500		−1,500

Cash flows: no effect

A	=	L	+	OE
−102,000		−100,000		
		−2,000		

↓ Cash flows: −102,000

July 1	Interest Expense		1,500	
	Interest Payable			1,500
	To accrue interest for April, May, and June.			
1	Notes Payable		100,000	
	Interest Payable ($500 + $1,500)		2,000	
	Cash ($100,000 + $2,000)			102,000
	To record payment of Caisse Populaire			
	Dumoulin note and accrued interest.			

SALES TAXES

As a consumer, you are well aware that you pay sales taxes on many products and services. For the business, sales taxes collected from customers are a liability because the company has an obligation to pay the amount collected to the appropriate government body.

Sales taxes are expressed as a percentage of the sales price. As discussed in earlier chapters and in Appendix B, sales taxes usually take the form of the federal Goods and Services Tax (GST) and Provincial Sales Tax (PST). The GST is 5% across Canada. Provincial sales tax rates vary from 0% to 9.975% across the country.

In Ontario, Newfoundland and Labrador, Nova Scotia, and New Brunswick, the PST and GST have been combined into one 13% Harmonized Sales Tax (HST). Prince Edward Island introduced a 14% HST on April 1, 2013, the same day that British Columbia abolished HST and reintroduced PST. When this textbook went to press, Quebec was considering combining its provincial sales tax, the Quebec Sales Tax (QST), and the GST into the HST. Alberta, Yukon, Northwest Territories, and Nunavut do not have PST.

Whether GST, PST, or HST, the business collects the tax from the customer when the sale occurs. The business then pays (remits) the sales taxes collected to the designated federal and provincial collecting authorities. In the case of GST, HST, and QST, collections may be offset against sales taxes paid by the business on its purchases. In such cases, only the net amount owing or recoverable must be paid or refunded. Depending on the size of the business, the sales taxes must be sent to the government monthly, quarterly, or, for very small companies, annually.

The amount of the sale and the amount of the sales tax collected are usually rung up separately on the cash register. The cash register readings are then used to credit sales or services and the correct sales taxes payable accounts. For example, if the March 25 cash register reading for Comeau Company, in New Brunswick, shows sales of $10,000 and Harmonized Sales Tax of $1,300 ($10,000 × 13% HST rate), the entry is as follows:

Mar. 25	Cash	11,300	
	Sales		10,000
	HST Payable		1,300
	To record sales and sales taxes.		

A = L + OE
+11,300 +1,300 +10,000
↑ Cash flows: +11,300

Comeau Company does not report the sales taxes collected from customers as revenue; sales taxes collected from customers are a liability. Comeau Company serves only as a collection agent for the government. When the company remits (pays) these sales taxes to the appropriate government collecting authorities, the HST Payable account is debited and Cash is credited.

Some businesses include sales taxes in the selling price. They do not separate sales taxes from the price of the goods sold. In these businesses, however, sales taxes must still be recorded separately from sales revenues. To find the sales amount, the total receipts are divided by 100% plus the sales tax percentage.

To illustrate, assume that Comeau Company's total receipts of $11,300 include HST. In this case you divide the total receipts from the sale by 100% plus 13% (which is equal to 1.13) to determine the sales revenue. Thus the sales amount of $10,000 is calculated as follows: $11,300 ÷ 1.13 = $10,000. The HST of $1,300 can be found by multiplying the sales amount by the sales tax rate ($10,000 × 13% = $1,300).

Helpful hint If sales taxes are included in the sales price, then the sales tax collected is equal to the selling price × the sales tax percentage *divided by 100% plus the sales tax percentage.*

PROPERTY TAXES

Businesses that own property pay property taxes. These taxes are charged by the municipal governments, and are calculated at a specified rate for every $100 of assessed value of property (land and buildings). Property taxes generally cover a full calendar year, although bills are not issued until the spring of each year.

To illustrate, assume that Tantramar Management owns land and a building in the city of Regina. Tantramar's year end is December 31 and it makes adjusting entries annually. On March 1, it receives its property tax bill of $6,000 for the calendar year, which is due to be paid on May 31.

In March, when Tantramar receives the property tax bill for the calendar year, two months of that year have passed. The company records the property tax expense for the months of January and February and the liability owed at that point as follows:

Mar. 1	Property Tax Expense ($6,000 × 2/12)	1,000	
	Property Tax Payable		1,000
	To record property tax expense for January and February and amount owing.		

A = L + OE
+1,000 −1,000
Cash flows: no effect

On May 31, when Tantramar pays the property tax bill, the company records the payment of the liability recorded on March 1. It also records the expense incurred to date for the months of March, April, and May. As at May 31, five months have passed and should be recorded as property tax expense. The remaining seven months of the year are recorded as a prepayment, as shown in the following entry:

May 31	Property Tax Payable	1,000	
	Property Tax Expense ($6,000 × 3/12)	1,500	
	Prepaid Property Tax ($6,000 × 7/12)	3,500	
	Cash		6,000
	To record payment of property tax expense for March through May, and amount prepaid for June through December.		

A = L + OE
+3,500 −1,000 −1,500
−6,000
↓ Cash flows: −6,000

After the payment of the property tax, Tantramar has a zero balance in its liability account but still has a prepayment. Since Tantramar only makes adjusting entries annually, it would not adjust the prepaid property tax account until year end, December 31. At that time, it would make the following entry:

A	=	L	+	OE
−3,500				−3,500

Cash flows: no effect

Dec. 31	Property Tax Expense	3,500	
	Prepaid Property Tax		3,500
	To record property tax expense for June through December.		

There are other acceptable ways to record and adjust property taxes. Some companies would debit Property Tax Expense when the bill is recorded on March 1 and avoid a later adjusting entry. In addition, companies may prepare monthly or quarterly adjusting entries. Whatever way is used, at year end, the companies would have the same ending balances. In this case, the accounts Prepaid Property Tax and Property Tax Payable should each have a zero balance and Property Tax Expense should have a balance of $6,000.

CURRENT MATURITIES OF LONG-TERM DEBT

Companies often have a portion of long-term debt that will be due in the current year. That amount is considered a current liability. Assume that on January 1, 2014, Cudini Construction issues a $25,000, five-year note payable. Each January 1, starting on January 1, 2015, $5,000 of the note will be repaid. When financial statements are prepared on December 31, 2014, $5,000 should be reported on the balance sheet as a current liability and the remaining $20,000 of the note should be reported as a long-term liability.

It is not necessary to prepare an adjusting entry to recognize the current maturity of long-term debt. The proper statement classification of each liability account is recognized when the balance sheet is prepared. Reitmans reports $1,474 thousand as the "current portion of long-term debt" in the current liabilities section of its balance sheet.

BEFORE YOU GO ON...

Do It

Prepare the journal entries to record the following transactions for DiMaria Enterprises. Round any calculations to the nearest dollar.

1. Accrue interest on January 31 (the company's year end) for a $10,000, 30-month, 8% note payable issued on December 1. Interest is payable the first of each month, beginning January 1.
2. The cash register total for sales on April 2 is $280,500. This total includes sales taxes. The HST tax rate is 13%. Record the sales and sales taxes.
3. A property tax bill of $12,000 for the calendar year is received on May 1 and is due on June 30. Record the entry on May 1, assuming the company has a January 31 year end.

Action Plan

- The formula for interest is as follows: principal (face) value × annual interest rate × time.
- Record sales separately from sales taxes. To calculate sales, divide the total proceeds by 100% plus the sales tax rates. Then calculate HST by multiplying sales by the appropriate rate.
- Record the property tax expense and the property tax payable for amounts incurred (owed) to date.

Solution

Jan. 31	Interest Expense ($10,000 × 8% × $1/12$)	67	
	Interest Payable		67
	To accrue interest on note payable.		
Apr. 2	Cash	282,500	
	Sales ($282,500 ÷ 113%)		250,000
	HST Payable ($250,000 × 13%)		32,500
	To record sales and sales taxes.		
May 1	Property Tax Expense ($12,000 × $3/12$)	3,000	
	Property Tax Payable		3,000
	To record property tax for February, March, and April.		

Related exercise material: BE10–1, BE10–2, BE10–3, BE10–4, E10–1, E10–2, E10–3, and E10–4.

THE NAVIGATOR

Uncertain Liabilities

In the previous section, we discussed current liabilities where there was a high degree of certainty with regard to whom an amount is owed to, when it is owed, and how much is owed. There was no uncertainty about the liability's existence, amount, or timing. In this section, we will discuss liabilities that have a lower degree of certainty but are still likely to occur. We will then discuss situations where there is an even greater degree of uncertainty if an obligation exists, or where the existence of a liability depends on the outcome of a future event.

ESTIMATED LIABILITIES

An **estimated liability** is a liability that is known to exist but whose amount and timing are uncertain. We know we owe someone, but are not necessarily sure how much and when. We may not even know whom we owe. There is a lower degree of certainty than in determinable liabilities, but as long as it is *likely* the company will have to settle the obligation, and the company can reasonably estimate the amount, the liability is recognized. Common estimated liabilities include product warranties, customer loyalty programs, and gift cards. We discuss these three examples in the following sections.

> » **STUDY OBJECTIVE 2**
>
> Account for estimated liabilities.

Alternative terminology Estimated liabilities are also known as *provisions*.

Product Warranties

Product warranties are promises made by the seller to a buyer to repair or replace the product if it is defective or does not perform as intended. Warranties (also known as guarantees) are usually issued by manufacturers. For a specified period of time after the item was sold, a manufacturer may promise to repair the item, replace it, or refund the buyer's money under certain conditions. As a buyer, it is important to read all warranty contracts carefully because the promises they make can be quite different.

Warranties will lead to future costs for the manufacturer for the repair or replacement of defective units. At the time of the sale, it is not known which units will become defective, so it is not known in advance whom the company will have to pay, or when it will be paid. But the liability still exists even if the payee and timing are unknown.

There are two possible approaches to accounting for product warranties. Historically, an expense approach has been used to account for the warranty liability. But changes in accounting standards have led some companies to use what is known as a revenue approach. In this chapter, we will illustrate the expense approach. The revenue approach is explained in an intermediate accounting textbook.

Under the expense approach, the warranty liability is measured using the estimated future cost of servicing (honouring) the product's warranty. At the time the product is sold, the costs are not known, but based on their previous experience with a particular product, it is usually not that hard for most companies to estimate it.

This process will also result in the warranty expense being recorded at the same time as the liability. Recognizing both an expense and a liability in the period where the sale occurs also ensures that companies have recognized the full cost of the sale in the period in which the sale occurs. Recall that this is known as matching expenses with revenues. As the actual costs are incurred in subsequent periods, the liability is reduced.

To illustrate the expense approach of accounting for warranty liabilities, assume that Hermann Company sells 10,000 washers and dryers at an average price of $600 in the year ended December 31, 2014. The selling price includes a one-year warranty on parts. Based on past experience, it is expected that 500 units (5%) will be defective, and that warranty repair costs will average $100 per unit.

At December 31, it is necessary to accrue the estimated warranty costs for the 2014 sales. The calculation is as follows:

Number of units sold	10,000
Estimated rate of defective units	× 5%
Total estimated defective units	500
Average warranty repair cost	× $100
Estimated product warranty liability	$50,000

The adjusting entry is:

A	=	L	+	OE
		+50,000		−50,000

Cash flows: no effect

Dec. 31	Warranty Expense	50,000	
	Warranty Liability		50,000
	To accrue estimated warranty costs.		

In 2014, warranty contracts were honoured on 300 units at a total cost of $30,000. These costs are recorded when they are incurred, but for our illustration they are being recorded in one summary journal entry for the year:

A	=	L	+	OE
−30,000		−30,000		

Cash flows: no effect

Dec. 31	Warranty Liability	30,000	
	Repair Parts Inventory (and/or Wages Payable)		30,000
	To record honouring of 300 warranty contracts on 2014 sales.		

In 2014, a warranty expense of $50,000 is reported as an operating expense in the income statement. The estimated warranty liability of $20,000 ($50,000 − $30,000) is classified as a current liability on the balance sheet.

In 2015, all costs incurred to honour warranty contracts on 2014 sales should be debited to the Warranty Liability account, like what was shown above for the 2014 sales. The Warranty Liability account will be carried forward from year to year—increased by the current year's estimated expense and decreased by the actual warranty costs incurred. It is quite likely that the actual expenses will not exactly equal the estimated liability amount. Every year, as is done with accounts receivable and the allowance for doubtful accounts, the warranty liability is reviewed and adjusted if necessary.

Customer Loyalty Programs

Alternative terminology Customer loyalty programs are also called *promotions* or *incentive programs*.

To attract or keep customers, many companies offer **customer loyalty programs** that result in future savings for the customers on the merchandise or services the company sells. These customer loyalty programs take varying forms. For example, the program may require customers to collect points. A common example of that is airline frequent flyer programs. Or the programs may involve a credit reward that gives a cash discount on future sales. Loyalty programs are designed to increase sales and are important for many businesses.

The most successful loyalty program in Canadian retail history is Canadian Tire "money" (CTM), first introduced in 1958. The "money" resembles real currency (although the bills are considerably smaller than Bank of Canada notes) and is issued with no expiry date. CTM is given out by the cashiers for purchases paid for by cash, debit card, or Canadian Tire Options MasterCard credit card. Customers can use CTM to buy anything at a Canadian Tire store. In fact, some privately owned businesses in Canada also accept CTM as payment since the owners of many of these businesses shop at Canadian Tire.

Customer loyalty programs result in a liability to the business equal to the future savings that customers will receive when they use their points or credit awards. There has been some debate about whether the cost of such programs should be recorded as an expense (similar to the expense approach illustrated earlier in the chapter for warranties) or as a decrease in revenue. While there are a few exceptions, accountants have decided that, when a loyalty program results in a reduced future selling price, it should be accounted for as a decrease in revenue and not as an expense.

The liability for customer loyalty programs must be estimated because at the time of the sale, it is not known if or when customers will redeem the reward. But as long as some redemptions are likely, and can be reasonably estimated based on past experience, the decrease in revenue and a related liability should be recorded in the period when the reward was issued to ensure that liabilities are correctly recognized.

To illustrate, assume that Greenville Co-op has a rewards program whereby Greenville Co-op Gas Bar customers get a redemption reward of 3 cents per litre of gasoline that can be used in Greenville Co-op Food Stores on the purchase of groceries. Assume that during January, the gas bar sells 99,000 litres of gasoline. Greenville Co-op estimates that 90% of the rewards issued will be redeemed. At January 31, Greenville will record the following for the redemption rewards issued during January:

Jan. 31	Sales Discount for Redemption Rewards Issued (99,000 × 90% × $0.03)	2,673	
	Redemption Rewards Liability		2,673
	To record the estimated rewards from January sales that will be redeemed.		

$$A = L + OE$$
$$+2,673 \quad -2,673$$
Cash flows: no effect

The account Sales Discount for Redemption Rewards Issued is a contra sales account, and is deducted from sales to give net sales in the same way that sales returns and allowances are deducted from sales, as we learned in Chapter 5. The company could debit sales, but instead a contra revenue account is used to allow the company to track the redemption rewards. The Redemption Rewards Liability is reported as a current liability on the balance sheet.

Helpful hint Reductions in revenue are recorded in the period in which the reward is issued, not when it is redeemed.

To illustrate what happens when the rewards are redeemed, assume that on February 1, customers redeem $100 of the rewards in the Greenville Co-op Food Store when purchasing $7,500 of groceries. Greenville Co-op makes the following entry that day (ignoring the cost of sales):

Feb. 1	Rewards Redemption Liability	100	
	Cash ($7,500 − $100)	7,400	
	Grocery Sales Revenue		7,500
	To record grocery sales and the redemption of rewards.		

$$A = L + OE$$
$$+7,400 \quad -100 \quad +7,500$$
↑ Cash flows: +7,400

Note that when the rewards are redeemed, the amount of cash collected is less than the sales revenue recognized. The liability account is reduced by the difference between the sales revenue and cash collected, which is the amount of the redemption. The liability account should be reviewed periodically and adjusted based on the company's experience with redemption rates.

Gift Cards

Gift cards or gift certificates have become an increasingly popular source of revenue for many companies. They are unearned revenues in that the company receives cash in advance of providing the goods or the services. Thus, when gift cards are issued, the Unearned Revenue account (liability) is recorded. When the gift card is redeemed (used), the company will then record the sales or service revenue and reduce or debit the Unearned Revenue account.

Alternative terminology Unearned revenue is sometimes called *deferred revenue.*

As with customer loyalty programs, the difficulty with gift cards is that it is unknown when and even if the card will be redeemed. Typically, the longer a gift card is outstanding, the less likely it is to be redeemed for merchandise. Similarly, gift cards that have been used but have relatively small remaining balances are less likely to be redeemed than newer, high-balance gift cards.

If it is unlikely that the company will have to settle a portion of the liability, then an obligation no longer exists. As with warranties and customer loyalty programs, a company with a gift card program will need to use past experience to estimate the appropriate balance for the liability.

As shown in Reitmans' financial statements in Appendix A, the company has a deferred liability on its balance sheet for both a customer loyalty program as well as gift cards.

BEFORE YOU GO ON...

Do It

Hockey Gear Company sells hockey skates with a two-year warranty against defects. The company expects that of the units sold each year, 5% will be returned in the first year after they are sold and 2% will be returned in the second year. The average cost to repair or replace a defective unit under warranty is $50. The company reported the following sales and warranty cost information:

	Units Sold	Actual Warranty Costs Incurred
2013	10,000	$20,000
2014	15,000	45,000

Calculate the balance in the Warranty Expense and Warranty Liability accounts at the end of 2014.

Solution

2013: Total defective units = 5% + 2% = 7%
   10,000 × 7% = 700 × $50 = $35,000

Warranty Expense		Warranty Liability			
35,000		Actual	20,000	Estimate	35,000
				Bal. Dec. 31, 2013	15,000

2014: 15,000 × 7% = 1,050 × $50 = $52,500

Warranty Expense		Warranty Liability			
52,500		Actual	20,000	Estimate	35,000
				Bal. Dec. 31, 2013	15,000
		Actual	45,000	Estimate	52,500
				Bal. Dec. 31, 2013	22,500

Related exercise material: BE10–5, BE10–6, BE10–7, BE10–8, E10–6, E10–7, and E10–8.

Action Plan

- Calculate the warranty expense by multiplying the number of units sold by the percentage that is expected to be returned and by the average warranty cost.
- Record warranty expenses in the period of the sale.
- The warranty liability is increased by the expense in each period and decreased by the actual costs of repairs and replacements.

THE **NAVIGATOR**

CONTINGENCIES

» **STUDY OBJECTIVE 3**

Account for contingencies.

The current liabilities discussed earlier in this chapter were either definitely determinable or estimable. While it might have been necessary to estimate the timing or amount, in both cases there was no uncertainty about their existence. With contingencies there is much more uncertainty about the timing and the amount and even the existence of a liability.

In general, a **contingency** can be defined as an existing condition or situation that is uncertain, where it cannot be known if a loss (and a related liability) will result from the situation until one or more future events happen or do not happen. In some situations, a gain (and a related asset) may arise from the contingency. But assets that are contingent on the outcome of an event are never recorded, and are not discussed in this textbook.

Lawsuits are good examples of contingencies. The existence of a loss and the related liability depend on the outcome of the lawsuit. The settlement of the lawsuit will confirm the existence of the liability, the amount payable, the payee, and/or the date payable. Under ASPE, a liability for a contingent loss is recorded if **both** of the following conditions are met:

1. The contingency is *likely* (the chance of occurrence is high).
2. The amount of the contingency can be *reasonably estimated*.

Therefore, if it is likely that the company will lose a lawsuit, and if the amount can be reliably estimated, then the company must record the loss and the liability. Under IFRS, a liability is recorded if the chance of occurrence is "probable" as opposed to "likely." Probable events are defined as being "more likely than not." Thus IFRS is generally regarded as having a lower threshold for recognizing these liabilities. Under ASPE, only highly likely contingent losses are recognized.

Under ASPE, these liabilities are called **contingent liabilities**, and under IFRS, these liabilities are called **provisions**. Under IFRS, a provision is a liability of uncertain timing or amount. The term "provisions" is often used for other uncertain liabilities, such as warranties, as discussed in the previous section of this chapter.

When a contingent loss is likely, but cannot be reasonably estimated, or if its likelihood of occurrence is not determinable, it is necessary only to disclose the contingency in the notes to the financial statements. In that case, a liability is not recorded.

If a contingency is unlikely—the chance of occurrence is small—it should still be disclosed if the event could have a substantial negative effect on the company's financial position. Otherwise, it does not need to be disclosed. A loan guarantee is an example of a contingency that should be disclosed even if the chance of having to pay is small. General risk contingencies that can affect anyone who is operating a business, such as the possibility of a war, strike, or recession, are not reported in the notes to the financial statements.

ACCOUNTING IN ACTION
BUSINESS INSIGHT

There are many contingencies in the real world. Lawsuits are the most common type of contingency, followed by environmental contingencies. Environmental contingencies generally relate to liabilities that could be incurred in order to clean up environmental problems.

The Canadian National Railway Company discloses the following information in the notes to its consolidated financial statements: "A risk of environmental liability is inherent in railroad and related transportation operations..." the Company goes on to say, "the magnitude of such... liabilities and the costs of complying with future environmental laws and containing or remediating contamination cannot be reasonably estimated... there can thus be no assurance that liabilities or costs related to environmental matters will not be incurred in the future, or will not have a material adverse effect on the Company's financial position or results of operations in a particular quarter or fiscal year, or that the Company's liquidity will not be adversely impacted by such environmental liabilities or costs."

Source: Canadian National Railway Company, 2011 Annual Information Form.

Environmental contingencies are generally considered to be harder to estimate than contingencies from lawsuits. What might be the reason for this difference?

BEFORE YOU GO ON...

Do It

A list of possible contingencies follows. Identify whether each of the following should be recorded, disclosed, or not reported:

1. A factory risks being damaged by floods. The building is located on a flood plain but has never experienced any damage from flooding in the past.
2. The government may expropriate a company's assets so that a new highway can be built. So far, there have been no discussions about how much the government might pay the company.
3. A public company is being sued for $1 million for unlawful termination of a company executive.
4. A company has guaranteed other companies' loans but the guarantees are unlikely to result in any payments.
5. A private company following ASPE is being sued for negligence and damages by a customer who slipped and broke a leg in the company's store.

Action Plan
- Recall that under ASPE, contingent liabilities are recorded if they are likely and can be reasonably estimated.
- Under IFRS, contingent liabilities (called provisions) are accrued when they are probable (more likely than not) and estimable.
- If the amounts cannot be estimated, they are only disclosed. Contingencies are not disclosed if they are unlikely.

BEFORE YOU GO ON continued...

Solution

1. No disclosure required.
2. Disclosure required.
3. If it is probable that the company will lose and the amount can be reasonably estimated, then this would be recorded as a provision; otherwise, just disclose.
4. Disclosure required.
5. If it is likely that the company will lose and the amount can be reasonably estimated, then this is recorded as a contingent liability; otherwise, just disclose.

Related exercise material: BE10–9, BE10–10, E10–9, and E10–10.

THE **NAVIGATOR**

Payroll

> **STUDY OBJECTIVE 4**

Determine payroll costs and record payroll transactions.

Payroll accounting involves more than just paying employee salaries and wages. In addition to paying salaries and wages, companies are required by law to have payroll records for each employee, to report and remit payroll deductions, and to respect provincial and federal laws on employee compensation. As mentioned in our feature story, there are up to 190 different pieces of legislation and regulations that employers have to consider when doing payroll. In this section, we will discuss some of the basic issues regarding payroll costs, journalizing payroll, and payroll records. In the appendix to this chapter, we explain calculating mandatory payroll deductions.

There are two types of payroll costs to a company: employee costs and employer costs. The first type, employee costs, involves the gross amount earned by employees. The second type, employer costs, involves amounts paid by the employer on behalf of the employee (employee benefits). We will explore employee and employer payroll costs in the following sections.

EMPLOYEE PAYROLL COSTS

Accounting for employee payroll costs involves calculating (1) gross pay, (2) payroll deductions, and (3) net pay.

Gross Pay

Gross pay, or earnings, is the total compensation earned by an employee. It consists of salaries or wages, plus any bonuses and commissions. The terms "salaries" and "wages" are often used interchangeably and the total amount of salaries or wages earned by the employee is called **gross pay**, or gross earnings.

In addition to the hourly pay rate, most companies are required by law to pay hourly workers for overtime work at the rate of at least one and one-half times the government-regulated minimum hourly wage. The number of hours that need to be worked before overtime becomes payable is based on a standard workweek. A 44-hour standard workweek is fairly common but this will vary by industry and occupation. Most employees in executive, managerial, and administrative positions do not earn overtime pay.

To illustrate gross pay, assume that Mark Jordan works for Academy Company as a shipping clerk. His authorized pay rate is $20 per hour. The calculation of Mark's gross pay for the 48 hours shown on his time card for the weekly pay period ending June 20, 2012, is as follows:

Type of Pay	Hours	×	Rate	=	Gross Pay
Regular	44	×	$20	=	$ 880
Overtime	4	×	30	=	120
Total	48				$1,000

This calculation assumes that Mark receives one and one-half times his regular hourly rate ($20 × 1.5) for any hours worked in excess of 44 hours per week (overtime). Overtime rates can be as much as twice the regular rates.

Payroll Deductions

As anyone who has received a paycheque knows, gross pay is usually very different from the amount that is actually received. The difference is referred to as **payroll deductions**. Payroll deductions are also frequently called "withholdings" because these are the amounts that the employer withholds or holds back from the employee. Payroll deductions may be mandatory or voluntary. Illustration 10-1 shows the types of payroll deductions that most employers usually make.

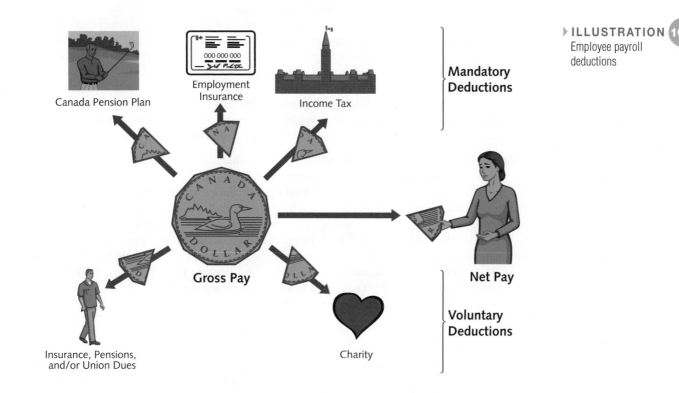

▶ ILLUSTRATION 10-1
Employee payroll deductions

Payroll deductions do not result in an expense for the employer. The employer is only a collection agent. The mandatory deductions are later paid to the government (for deductions such as Canada Pension Plan, Employment Insurance, and income tax). The voluntary deductions are later paid to some other agency (such as a union, an insurance company, or the United Way). The designated collection agency for the federal government is the Canada Revenue Agency (CRA), which collects money on behalf of the Receiver General for Canada, the cabinet minister responsible for accepting payments to the Government of Canada.

Mandatory Payroll Deductions. Mandatory deductions are required by law and include Canada Pension Plan contributions, Employment Insurance premiums, and personal income tax. We will discuss these three deductions in the following sections.

Canada Pension Plan. All employees between the ages of 18 and 70, except those employed in the province of Quebec, must contribute to the **Canada Pension Plan (CPP)**. Quebec has its own similar program, the Quebec Pension Plan (QPP). These mandatory plans give disability, retirement, and death benefits to qualifying Canadians.

Contribution rates are set by the federal government and are adjusted every January if there are increases in the cost of living. We will show how to calculate CPP contributions in Appendix 10A. For now, assume that Mark Jordan's CPP contribution for the weekly pay period ending June 20, 2012, is $46.17.

Employment Insurance. The *Employment Insurance Act* requires all Canadian workers who are not self-employed to pay **Employment Insurance (EI)** premiums. Employment insurance is designed to give income protection (in the form of payments representing a portion of one's earnings) for a limited period of time to employees who are temporarily laid off, who are on parental leave, or who lose their jobs. Starting January 2013, self-employed individuals may choose to pay EI to qualify for special benefits such as maternity or parental benefits. But this will not qualify them for employment insurance if they are not able to work.

Each year, the federal government determines the contribution rate and the maximum amount of premiums for the year. We will show how to calculate EI premiums in Appendix 10A. For now, assume that Mark Jordan's EI premium for the weekly pay period ending June 20, 2012, is $18.30.

Personal Income Tax. Under the *Income Tax Act*, employers are required to withhold income tax from employees for each pay period. The amount to be withheld is determined by three variables: (1) the employee's gross pay, (2) the number of credits claimed by the employee, and (3) the length of the pay period. The amount of provincial income taxes also depends on the province in which the employee works. There is no limit on the amount of gross pay that is subject to income tax withholdings. The higher the pay or earnings, the higher the amount of taxes withheld.

The calculation of personal income tax withholdings is complicated and is best done using payroll deduction tables supplied by the CRA. We will show this in Appendix 10A. For now, assume that Mark Jordan's federal income tax is $118.85 and provincial income tax is $60.45, for a total income tax owed of $179.30 on his gross pay of $1,000 for the weekly pay period ending June 20, 2012.

Voluntary Payroll Deductions. Unlike mandatory payroll deductions, which are required by law, voluntary payroll deductions are chosen by the employee.

Employees may choose to authorize withholdings for charitable, retirement, and other purposes. All voluntary deductions from gross pay should be authorized in writing by the employee. The authorization may be made individually or as part of a group plan. Deductions for charitable organizations, such as the United Way, or for financial arrangements, such as Canada Savings Bonds and the repayment of loans from company credit unions, are determined by each employee. In contrast, deductions for union dues, extended health insurance, life insurance, and pension plans are often determined on a group basis. In the calculation of net pay in the next section, we assume that Mark Jordan has voluntary deductions of $10 for the United Way and $5 for union dues.

Net Pay

The difference between an employee's gross pay, or total earnings, less any employee payroll deductions withheld from the earnings is known as **net pay**. This is the amount that the employer must pay to the employee.

Net pay is determined by subtracting payroll deductions from gross pay. For Mark Jordan, net pay for the weekly pay period ending June 20, 2012, is $741.23, as shown in Illustration 10-2.

▶ **ILLUSTRATION 10-2**
Employee payroll deductions

Gross pay		$1,000.00
Payroll deductions:		
CPP	$ 46.17	
EI	18.30	
Income tax (federal and provincial)	179.30	
United Way	10.00	
Union dues	5.00	258.77
Net pay		$ 741.23

Before we learn how to record employee payroll costs and deductions, we will turn our attention to *employer* payroll costs. After this discussion, we will record the total employee and employer payroll costs for Academy Company, where Mark Jordan works.

EMPLOYER PAYROLL COSTS

Employer payroll costs are amounts that the federal and provincial governments require employers to pay. The federal government requires CPP and EI contributions from employers. The provincial governments require employers to fund a workplace health, safety, and compensation plan. These contributions, plus such items as paid vacations and pensions, are referred to as **employee benefits**. Employer payroll costs are not debited to the Salaries Expense account, but rather to a separate Employee Benefits Expense account.

Canada Pension Plan

Employers must also contribute to the CPP. For each dollar withheld from the employee's gross pay, the employer must contribute an equal amount. The CPP Payable account is credited for both the employees' and employer's CPP contributions.

Employment Insurance

Employers are required to contribute 1.4 times an employee's EI premiums. The EI Payable account is credited for both the employees' and employer's EI premiums.

Workplace Health, Safety, and Compensation

Each provincial workplace health, safety, and compensation plan gives benefits to workers who are injured or disabled on the job. The cost of this program is paid entirely by the employer; employees do not make contributions to these plans. Employers are assessed a rate—usually between 0.25% and 10% of their gross payroll—based on the risk of injury to employees in their industry and past experience.

> **Helpful hint** CPP contributions and EI premiums are paid by both the employer and the employee. Workers' compensation premiums are paid entirely by the employer.

Additional Employee Benefits

In addition to the three employer payroll costs described above, employers have other employee benefit costs. Two of the most important are paid absences and post-employment benefits. We will describe these briefly here, but leave further details to an intermediate accounting course.

Paid Absences. Employees have the right to receive compensation for absences under certain conditions. The compensation may be for paid vacations, sick pay benefits, and paid statutory holidays. A liability should be estimated and accrued for future paid absences. Ordinarily, vacation pay is the only paid absence that is accrued. Other types of paid absences are disclosed only in notes to the statements.

Post-Employment Benefits. Post-employment benefits are payments by employers to retired or terminated employees. These payments are for (1) pensions, and (2) supplemental health care, dental care, and life insurance. Employers must use the accrual basis in accounting for post-employment benefits. It is important to match the cost of these benefits with the periods where the employer benefits from the services of the employee.

RECORDING THE PAYROLL

Recording the payroll involves maintaining payroll records, recording payroll expenses and liabilities, paying the payroll, and filing and remitting payroll deductions.

Payroll Records

A separate record of an employee's gross pay, payroll deductions, and net pay for the calendar year is kept for each employee and updated after each pay period. It is called the **employee earnings record** and its cumulative payroll data are used by the employer to (1) determine when an employee has reached the maximum earnings subject to CPP and EI premiums, (2) file information returns with the CRA (as explained later in this section), and (3) give each employee a statement of gross pay and withholdings for the year.

An extract from Mark Jordan's employee earnings record for the month of June is shown in Illustration 10-3. This record includes the pay details shown in Illustration 10-2 for the weekly pay period ending June 20, 2012, highlighted in red.

ACADEMY COMPANY
Employee Earnings Record
Year Ending December 31, 2012

Name	Mark Jordan	Address	162 Bowood Avenue
Social Insurance Number	113-114-496		Toronto
Date of Birth	December 24, 1985		Ontario, M4N 1Y6
Date Employed	September 1, 2010	Telephone	416-486-0669
Date Employment Ended		E-mail	jordan@sympatico.ca
Job Title	Shipping Clerk	Claim Code	1

2012 Period Ending	Total Hours	Gross Pay				Deductions						Payment	
		Regular	Overtime	Total	Cumulative	CPP	EI	Income Tax	United Way	Union Dues	Total	Net Amount	Cheque #
June 6	46	880.00	60.00	940.00	19,940.00	43.20	17.20	161.35	10.00	5.00	236.75	703.25	974
13	47	880.00	90.00	970.00	20,910.00	44.68	17.75	169.30	10.00	5.00	246.73	723.27	1028
20	48	880.00	120.00	1,000.00	21,910.00	46.17	18.30	179.30	10.00	5.00	258.77	741.23	1077
27	46	880.00	60.00	940.00	22,850.00	43.20	17.20	161.35	10.00	5.00	236.75	703.25	1133
June Total		3,520.00	330.00	3,850.00		177.25	70.45	671.30	40.00	20.00	979.00	2,871.00	

▶ **ILLUSTRATION 10-3**
Employee earnings record

In addition to employee earnings records, many companies find it useful to prepare a **payroll register**. This record accumulates the gross pay, deductions, and net pay per employee for each pay period and becomes the documentation for preparing paycheques for each employee. Academy Company's payroll register for the weekly pay period ended June 20, 2012, is presented in Illustration 10-4. It shows the data for Mark Jordan in the wages section, highlighted in red. In this example, Academy Company's total payroll is $34,420, as shown in the gross pay column.

ACADEMY COMPANY
Payroll Register
Week Ending June 20, 2012

Employee	Total Hours	Gross Pay				Deductions						Payment	
		Regular	Overtime	Gross	CPP	EI	Income Tax	United Way	Union Dues	Total	Net Pay	Cheque #
Aung, Ng	44	1,276.00		1,276.00	59.83	23.35	266.80	15.00		364.98	911.02	998
Canton, Mathilda	44	1,298.00		1,298.00	60.92	23.75	270.55	20.00		375.22	922.78	999
Caron, William	44	1,166.00		1,166.00	54.39	21.34	229.40	11.00		316.13	849.87	1000
Deol, Réjean	44	880.00	60.00	940.00	43.20	17.20	161.35	10.00	5.00	236.75	703.25	1001
Jordan, Mark	48	880.00	120.00	1,000.00	46.17	18.30	179.30	10.00	5.00	258.77	741.23	1077
Milroy, Lee	47	880.00	90.00	970.00	44.68	17.75	169.30	10.00	5.00	246.73	723.27	1078
Total		32,400.00	2,020.00	34,420.00	1,497.28	629.89	6,722.86	480.00	150.00	9,480.03	24,939.97	

▶ **ILLUSTRATION 10-4**
Payroll register

Note that this record is a listing of each employee's payroll data for the June 20, 2012, pay period. In some companies, the payroll register is a special journal. Postings are made directly to ledger accounts. In other companies, the payroll register is a supplementary record that gives the data for a general journal entry and later posting to the ledger accounts. At Academy Company, the second procedure is used.

Recording Payroll Expenses and Liabilities

Payroll expenses are equal to the employees' gross salaries and wages plus the employer's payroll costs. Typically, as shown in the following entry, employee payroll costs and employer's payroll costs are recorded in separate journal entries.

Employee Payroll Costs. A journal entry is made to record the employee portion of the payroll. For the week ending June 20, the entry for Academy Company, using total amounts from the company's payroll register for the period, as shown in Illustration 10-4, is as follows:

June 20	Salaries Expense	34,420.00	
	CPP Payable		1,497.28
	EI Payable		629.89
	Income Tax Payable		6,722.86
	United Way Payable		480.00
	Union Dues Payable		150.00
	Salaries Payable		24,939.97
	To record payroll for week ending June 20.		

```
A     =    L     +   OE
     +1,497.28 −34,420.00
       +629.89
     +6,722.86
       +480.00
       +150.00
    +24,939.97
Cash flows: no effect
```

The above journal entry records the gross pay of $34,420 in Academy Company's Salaries Expense account. Separate expense accounts may be used for gross pay for office workers, on salary, and other employees, paid an hourly rate. For example, a company may use the account Wages Expense for its hourly workers. The net pay of $24,939.97 that is owed to employees is recorded in the Salaries Payable account. This is equal to the sum of the individual cheques that the employees will receive when the payroll is paid. Academy Company uses separate liability accounts for the amounts that it owes for its employee payroll deductions to the government for CPP, EI, and income tax, and amounts owed to third parties like United Way and for union dues.

Employer Payroll Costs. Employer payroll costs are usually recorded when the payroll is journalized. The entire amount of gross pay is subject to four of the employer payroll costs mentioned earlier: CPP, EI, workers' compensation, and vacation pay. For the June 20 payroll, Academy Company's CPP is $1,497.28 ($1,497.28 × 1). Its EI premium is $881.85 ($629.89 × 1.4).

Assume that Academy Company is also assessed for workers' compensation at a rate of 1%. Its expense for the week would therefore be $344.20 ($34,420 × 1%). For vacation pay, assume that Academy Company employees accrue vacation days at an average rate of 4% of the gross payroll (equivalent to two weeks of vacation). The accrual for vacation benefits in one pay period—one week—is therefore $1,376.80 ($34,420 × 4%).

Some provinces, including the Province of Ontario, require an additional employer payroll cost—an employer health tax to help fund health care. The maximum health tax in the Province of Ontario is 1.95% of payroll, but the tax rate varies by the amount of payroll. For simplicity, we will assume that Academy is exempt from this health tax.

Accordingly, the entry to record the employer payroll costs or employee benefits associated with the June 20 payroll is as follows:

June 20	Employee Benefits Expense	4,100.13	
	CPP Payable		1,497.28
	EI Payable		881.85
	Workers' Compensation Payable		344.20
	Vacation Pay Payable		1,376.80
	To record employer payroll costs on June 20 payroll.		

```
A     =    L     +   OE
     +1,497.28 −4,100.13
       +881.85
       +344.20
     +1,376.80
Cash flows: no effect
```

Employer payroll costs are debited to a separate expense account, normally called Employee Benefits Expense, so the employer can keep track of these costs. It is combined with Salaries Expense on the income statement. The liability accounts are classified as current liabilities since they will be paid within the next year.

Recording Payment of the Payroll

Payment of the payroll by cheque or electronic funds transfer (EFT) is made from either the employer's regular bank account or a payroll bank account. Each paycheque or EFT is usually accompanied by a statement of earnings document. This shows the employee's gross pay, payroll deductions, and net pay for the period and for the year to date.

After the payroll has been paid, the cheque numbers are entered in the payroll register. The entry to record payment of the payroll for Academy Company follows:

	A	=	L	+	OE
	−24,939.97		−24,939.97		

↓ Cash flows: −24,939.97

June 20	Salaries Payable	24,939.97	
	Cash		24,939.97
	To record payment of payroll.		

Note that Academy Company is only recording payments to its employees in this entry and not its payroll deductions. Employee and employer deductions will be remitted to government authorities or other third parties when they are due later in the month.

Many companies use a separate bank account for payroll. Only the total amount of each period's payroll is transferred, or deposited, into that account before it is distributed. This helps the company determine if there are any unclaimed amounts.

When companies report and remit their payroll deductions, they combine withholdings of CPP, EI, and income tax. Generally, the withholdings must be reported and remitted monthly on a Statement of Account for Current Source Deductions (known by the CRA as the PD7A remittance form), and no later than the 15th day of the month following the month's pay period. Depending on the size of the payroll deductions, however, the employer's payment deadline could be different. For example, large employers must remit more often than once a month, and small employers with perfect payroll deduction remittance records can remit quarterly.

Workplace health, safety, and compensation costs are remitted quarterly to the provincial workers' compensation commission or board. Remittances can be made by mail or through deposits at any Canadian financial institution. When payroll deductions are remitted, payroll liability accounts are debited and Cash is credited.

The entry to record the remittance of payroll deductions by Academy Company in the following month is as follows:

	A	=	L	+	OE
	−12,203.36		−2,994.56		
			−1,511.74		
			−6,722.86		
			−480.00		
			−150.00		
			−344.20		

↓ Cash flows: −12,203.36

July 13	CPP Payable ($1,497.28 + $1,497.28)	2,994.56	
	EI Payable ($629.89 + $881.85)	1,511.74	
	Income Tax Payable	6,722.86	
	United Way Payable	480.00	
	Union Dues Payable	150.00	
	Workers' Compensation Payable	344.20	
	Cash		12,203.36
	To record payment of payroll deductions for		
	June 20 payroll.		

Note that the vacation pay liability recorded on June 20 is not debited or "paid" until the employees actually take their vacation.

Other payroll information returns or forms must be filed by the employer with the government by the last day of February each year. In addition, as noted previously, employers must give employees a Statement of Remuneration Paid (called a T4 slip by the CRA) by the same date.

ACCOUNTING IN ACTION
ALL ABOUT YOU INSIGHT

Employers are required by law each month to remit to the CRA mandatory payroll deductions as well as the employer's share of CPP and EI. Failure to do so can lead to interest and stiff penalties.

What happens if you are self-employed and providing consulting services to a company? If you are self-employed, you are required to pay CPP equal to both the employee's and employer's share, and you are also responsible for paying income tax. If you are self-employed, you can choose to pay EI to qualify for special benefits such as maternity or sickness benefits. But this will not qualify you for employment insurance if you are not able to work. If you choose to pay EI, you will not be required to pay the employer's portion of the EI premium.

It may seem beneficial to some companies to hire consultants and avoid paying the employer's share of CPP and EI as well as other benefits. However, the CRA has strict guidelines as to whether an individual is considered an employee or a self-employed consultant. If a company inappropriately treats an individual as self-employed and fails to deduct CPP and EI, the company will be required to pay both the employer's and employee's share of CPP and EI as well as penalties and interest.

Sources: Service Canada website, "Frequently Asked Questions: Employment Insurance (EI) Special Benefits for Self-Employed People," available at http://www.servicecanada.gc.ca/eng/sc/ei/sew/faq.shtml; Canada Revenue Agency website, "Payroll," available at http://www.cra-arc.gc.ca/tx/bsnss/tpcs/pyrll/menu-eng.html; Canada Revenue Agency, "Employee or Self-Employed?", available at http://www.cra-arc.gc.ca/E/pub/tg/rc4110/rc4110-11e.pdf.

If you are providing services to a company, what are the advantages and disadvantages of being a self-employed consultant versus an employee of the company?

BEFORE YOU GO ON...

Do It

Prepare the journal entries to record the following transactions. Round any calculations to the nearest dollar.

1. A company's gross salaries amount to $10,000 for the week ended July 11. The following amounts are deducted from the employees' wages: CPP of $495; EI of $183; income tax of $3,965; and health insurance of $950. Assume employees are paid in cash on July 11.
2. The company accrues employer's payroll costs on the same day as it records payroll. Assume vacation days are accrued at an average rate of 4% of the gross payroll and that the health insurance is 100% funded by the employees.
3. Record the payment of the mandatory payroll deductions from the July 11 payroll on August 15.

Action Plan

- Record both the employees' portion of the payroll and the benefits owed by the employer.
- Employee deductions are not an expense to the employer.
- The vacation pay liability is not "paid" until the employees actually take their vacation.

Solution

July 11	Salaries Expense	10,000	
	CPP Payable		495
	EI Payable		183
	Income Tax Payable		3,965
	Health Insurance Payable		950
	Cash		4,407
	To record payment of wages for week ending July 11.		
July 11	Employee Benefits Expense	1,151	
	CPP Payable		495
	EI Payable ($183 × 1.4)		256
	Vacation Pay Payable ($10,000 × 4%)		400
	To record employer's payroll costs on July 11 payroll.		

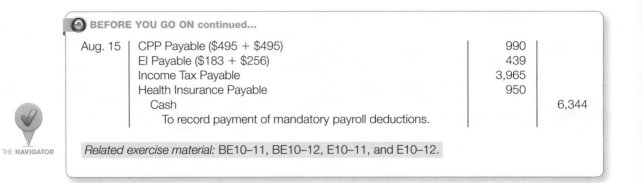

BEFORE YOU GO ON continued...

Aug. 15	CPP Payable ($495 + $495)	990	
	EI Payable ($183 + $256)	439	
	Income Tax Payable	3,965	
	Health Insurance Payable	950	
	Cash		6,344
	To record payment of mandatory payroll deductions.		

Related exercise material: BE10–11, BE10–12, E10–11, and E10–12.

THE NAVIGATOR

Financial Statement Presentation

» **STUDY OBJECTIVE 5**

Prepare the current liabilities section of the balance sheet.

Current liabilities are generally reported as the first category in the liabilities section of the balance sheet. Each of the main types of current liabilities is listed separately. In addition, the terms of operating lines of credit and notes payable and other information about the individual items are disclosed in the notes to the financial statements.

Similar to current assets, current liabilities are generally listed in order of liquidity (by maturity date). However, this is not always possible, because of the varying maturity dates that may exist for specific obligations such as notes payable. Many companies show bank loans, notes payable, and accounts payable first.

As discussed in Chapter 4, international companies often choose to order their current liabilities in order of reverse liquidity. They also often choose to present their current liabilities following the non-current liabilities.

Illustration 10-5 shows how Shoppers Drug Mart presents its current liabilities in traditional order in its balance sheet.

▶ **ILLUSTRATION 10-5**
Presentation of current liabilities

SHOPPERS DRUG MART CORPORATION
Balance Sheet (partial)
December 31, 2011
(in thousands)

SHOPPERS DRUG MART

Current liabilities	
Bank indebtedness	$ 172,262
Accounts payable and accrued liabilities	1,109,444
Income taxes payable	26,538
Dividends payable	53,119
Current portion of long-term debt	249,971
Provisions	12,024
Associate interest	152,880
Total current liabilities	$1,776,238

Income taxes payable and dividends payable are accounts that are used only by corporations and you will learn about these in Chapters 13 and 14. Associate interest is the amount that Shoppers Drug Mart would owe to its associates (owners of the Shoppers Drug Mart stores) if its associate agreements were terminated. Shoppers Drug Mart explains in its notes to its financial statements that it does not expect to pay this amount in the next 12 months, but because it doesn't have the unconditional right to defer settlement of the liability for at least 12 months, under IFRS, the company must report this amount in current liabilities.

Shoppers Drug Mart also discloses information about its provisions and contingencies in the notes to its financial statements, as shown in Illustration 10-6.

SHOPPERS DRUG MART CORPORATION
Notes to Consolidated Financial Statements (partial)
December 31, 2011

SHOPPERS DRUG MART

Note 22 PROVISIONS

	2011	2010
Balance, beginning of the financial year	$14,414	$12,071
Provisions made	8,980	12,341
Provisions used	(9,907)	(9,817)
Provisions reversed	(192)	(306)
Unwind of discount	430	125
Balance, end of the financial year	$13,725	$14,414
Balance, end of the financial year, presented as follows:		
Current liabilities	$12,024	$12,562
Long-term liabilities	1,701	1,852
	$13,725	$14,414

(a) The Company has been served with a Statement of Claim in a proposed class proceeding that has been filed in the Ontario Superior Court of Justice by two of its licensed Associate-owners, claiming various declarations and damages of $1,000,000 on behalf of a proposed class comprised of all of its current and former licensed Associate-owners resident in Canada, other than in Québec. The claim alleges, among other things, that Shoppers Drug Mart and two of its affiliates breached contractual and other duties to its Associate-owners by collecting, receiving and/or retaining funds and/or benefits that are in excess of those permitted to be collected, received and/or retained by the applicable agreements. The Company believes that the claim is without merit and will vigorously defend the claim. However, there can be no assurance that the outcome of this claim will be favourable to the Company or that it will not have a material adverse impact on the Company's financial position. The amount payable, if any, is not reasonably determinable at this time.

(b) In addition, the Company is involved in certain legal claims arising in the normal course of business. In the opinion of the Company's management, the eventual settlement of such claims will not have a significant effect on the Company's financial position or results of operations. Management has recorded a provision for these claims based on its best estimate of the final settlements.

Notice that Shoppers Drug Mart is following the procedures for contingencies discussed earlier in the chapter. For the lawsuits or statements of claim by two of its licensed associate-members [see (a) in Illustration 10-6], the company is unable to reasonably estimate a probable loss. Therefore, it is only disclosed in this note. For the lawsuits or legal claims [see (b) in Illustration 10-6], where it is probable a loss will be incurred, and where the amount can be reasonably measured, the company has recorded a provision in the amounts shown in the note. In addition, Shoppers Drug Mart explains in Note 19 that it has entered into agreements with banks to guarantee a total of $520,000 thousand of its Associate-owned stores' bank lines of credit.

Companies must carefully monitor the relationship of current liabilities to current assets. This relationship is critical in evaluating a company's short-term ability to pay debt. There is usually concern when a company has more current liabilities than current assets, because it may not be able to make its payments when they become due.

Shoppers Drug Mart has current assets of $2,695,647 at December 31, 2011, which results in a positive current ratio. You will recall from Chapter 4 that the current ratio is calculated by dividing current assets by current liabilities. Shoppers Drug Mart's current ratio is 1.52:1 ($2,695,647 ÷ $1,776,238), which indicates that Shoppers Drug Mart has enough current assets to cover its current liabilities.

Recall also that the current ratio should never be interpreted without also looking at the receivables and inventory turnover ratios to ensure that all of the current assets are indeed liquid. It is also important to look at the acid-test ratio. If we wanted to do a more complete analysis of Shoppers Drug Mart's liquidity, we would need additional information.

BEFORE YOU GO ON...

Do It

The following selected items were included in EastBoat Enterprises' adjusted trial balance at November 30, 2014:

Accounts payable	$52,775
Accounts receivable	30,250
Accrued liabilities	18,350
Bank indebtedness	10,400
Merchandise inventory	85,900
Notes payable	100,000
Prepaid expenses	12,000
Unearned revenue	6,500
Warranty liability	8,825

Action Plan

- Determine which items are liabilities.
- Recall that current liabilities are payable within one year of the balance sheet date.

Additional information:

The $100,000 balance in notes payable consisted of: (1) a six-month, 5%, $25,000 note payable due on March 31, 2015; (2) a two-year, 5.5%, $15,000 note payable due on October 31, 2015; and (3) a three-year, 4.5%, $60,000 note payable due on September 30, 2016.

Prepare the current liabilities section of the balance sheet.

Solution

<table>
<tr><td colspan="2" align="center">EASTBOAT ENTERPRISES
Balance Sheet (partial)
November 30, 2014</td></tr>
<tr><td>Current liabilities</td><td></td></tr>
<tr><td>   Bank indebtedness</td><td align="right">$ 10,400</td></tr>
<tr><td>   Accounts payable</td><td align="right">52,775</td></tr>
<tr><td>   Accrued liabilities</td><td align="right">18,350</td></tr>
<tr><td>   Unearned revenue</td><td align="right">6,500</td></tr>
<tr><td>   Warranty liability</td><td align="right">8,825</td></tr>
<tr><td>   Notes payable</td><td align="right">40,000</td></tr>
<tr><td>   Total current liabilities</td><td align="right">136,850</td></tr>
</table>

THE NAVIGATOR

Related exercise material: BE10–13, BE10–14, BE10–15, E10–5, E10-13, and E10–14.

APPENDIX 10A | PAYROLL DEDUCTIONS

MANDATORY PAYROLL DEDUCTIONS

» STUDY OBJECTIVE 6

Calculate mandatory payroll deductions.

As discussed in the chapter, payroll deductions may be mandatory or voluntary. Mandatory deductions are required by law and include Canada Pension Plan contributions, Employment Insurance premiums, and income tax. We discuss how to calculate these in the following sections.

Canada Pension Plan (CPP)

CPP contributions are based on a maximum ceiling or limit (called the maximum pensionable earnings) less a basic yearly exemption, and on the contribution rate set each year by the federal government. **Pensionable earnings** are gross earnings less the basic yearly exemption.

As of January 1, 2012, the following amounts were in effect:

Maximum pensionable earnings	$50,100
Basic yearly exemption	$3,500
CPP contribution rate	4.95%
Maximum annual employee CPP contribution	$2,306.70

Illustration 10A-1 shows the formulas and calculations used to determine Mark Jordan's CPP contribution on his gross pay of $1,000 for the weekly pay period ending June 20, 2012.

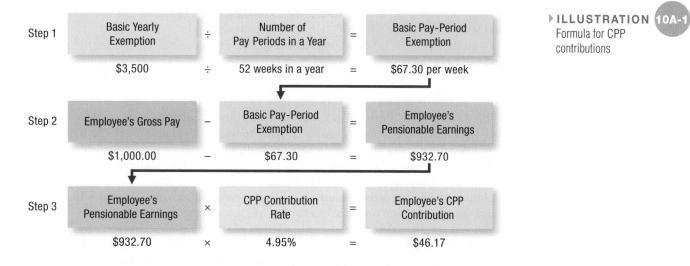

▶ **ILLUSTRATION 10A-1**
Formula for CPP contributions

Note that the basic pay-period exemption of $67.30 is a per-week exemption and is used in this case because Academy Company pays its employees weekly. If a company pays its employees monthly, the basic pay-period exemption would be $291.67 ($3,500 ÷ 12).

An employer stops deducting CPP contributions if and when the employee's earnings are greater than the maximum pensionable earnings. In this way, the employee's CPP contributions will not be greater than the maximum annual CPP contribution. Self-employed individuals pay both the employee and employer share of CPP.

Employment Insurance (EI)

EI calculations are based on a maximum earnings ceiling (called the maximum annual insurable earnings) and the contribution rate set by the federal government each year. Different from CPP, there is no basic yearly exemption. For 2012, the following amounts were in effect:

Maximum insurable earnings	$45,900
EI contribution rate	1.83%
Maximum annual employee EI premium	$839.97

In most cases, **insurable earnings** are gross earnings.

The required EI premium is calculated by multiplying the employee's insurable earnings by the EI contribution rate. Illustration 10A-2 shows the formula and calculations to determine Mark Jordan's EI premium on his gross pay of $1,000 for the pay period ending June 20, 2012.

Employee's Insurable Earnings	×	EI Contribution Rate	=	Employee's EI Premium
$1,000	×	1.83%	=	$18.30

▶ **ILLUSTRATION 10A-2**
Formula for EI premiums

An employer stops deducting EI premiums if and when the employee's earnings are greater than the maximum insurable earnings. In this way, the employee's EI premiums will not be greater than the maximum annual EI premium. Self-employed individuals who have chosen to pay EI pay only the employee's share of EI.

Personal Income Tax

Income tax deductions are based on income tax rates set by the federal and provincial governments. The federal government uses a progressive tax scheme when calculating income taxes. Basically, this means that the higher the pay or earnings, the higher the income tax percentage, and thus the higher the amount of taxes withheld. For example, effective January 1, 2012, the federal tax rates were:

- 15% **on the first** $42,707 of taxable income, plus
- 22% **on the next** $42,707 of taxable income (on the portion of taxable income between $42,707 and $85,414), plus
- 26% **on the next** $46,992 of taxable income (on the portion of taxable income between $85,414 and $132,406), plus
- 29% of taxable income **over** $132,406.

Taxable income is determined by the employee's gross pay and the amount of personal tax credits claimed by the employee. **Personal tax credits** are amounts deducted from an individual's income taxes and determine the amount of income taxes to be withheld. To indicate to the Canada Revenue Agency (CRA) which credits he or she wants to claim, the employee must complete a Personal Tax Credits Return (known as a TD1 form). In 2012, all individuals were entitled to a minimum personal credit (called the basic personal credit) of $10,822.

In addition, provincial income taxes must be calculated. All provinces, except Alberta, also use a progressive tax scheme. Each province has its own specific tax rates and calculations.

As you can see, the calculation of personal income tax deductions is very complicated. Consequently it is best done using one of the many payroll accounting programs that are available or by using the payroll deduction tools provided by the CRA. These tools include payroll deduction tables and the Payroll Deductions Online Calculator. We will illustrate how to use the payroll deduction tables.

USING PAYROLL DEDUCTION TABLES

Payroll deduction tables are prepared by the CRA and can be easily downloaded from the CRA website (go to www.cra-arc.gc.ca and click on Businesses, then Payroll). There are separate payroll deduction tables for determining federal tax deductions, provincial tax deductions, Canada Pension Plan contributions, and Employment Insurance premiums.

These tables are updated at least once a year on January 1 to reflect the new rates for that year. Income tax tables are also reissued during the year if the federal or provincial governments make changes to income tax rates during the year. It is important to make sure you have the tables that are in effect during the payroll period for which you are calculating deductions.

There are separate sections of the federal and provincial income tax and the CPP tables for weekly, biweekly, semi-monthly, and monthly pay periods. Thus, when determining these amounts, it is important to make sure you are using the table prepared for the company's pay period. The Academy Company would use the weekly tables.

Illustration 10A-3 shows excerpts from the CPP, EI, and federal and Ontario income tax tables effective January 1, 2012. You can use these tables to determine the appropriate deductions for Mark Jordan's gross pay of $1,000 during the pay period ended June 20, 2012.

In the CPP table, under the Pay column, find $1,000. The CPP deduction for the pay range $993.57 to $1,003.56 is $46.10. Earlier in the appendix, we showed how to calculate Mark Jordan's CPP and determined it was $46.17. Why the difference? The amount shown in the table is calculated using the mid-point in the range. As the mid-point is less than $1,000, the amount in the table is less than the calculated amount. Both ways of determining the CPP contribution are correct—the table is just slightly less precise than the calculation. The Academy Company could have used either amount.

In the EI table, under the Insurable Earnings column, find $1,000. The EI deduction in the pay range $999.73 to $1,000.27 is $18.30. This is exactly the same amount we calculated earlier in the appendix because Mark Jordan's pay of $1,000 is the mid-point of this range. As with CPP, companies

Canada Pension Plan Contributions
Weekly (52 pay periods a year)

Cotisations au Régime de pensions du Canada
Hebdomadaire (52 périodes de paie par année)

▶ILLUSTRATION 10A-3
Excerpts from CPP, EI, and income tax deduction tables prepared by the Canada Revenue Agency, effective January 1, 2012

Pay Rémunération From - De	To - À	CPP RPC	Pay Rémunération From - De	To - À	CPP RPC	Pay Rémunération From - De	To - À	CPP RPC	Pay Rémunération From - De	To - À	CPP RPC
949.02 -	949.21	43.65	963.57 -	973.56	44.61	1683.57 -	1693.56	80.25	2403.57 -	2413.56	115.89
949.22 -	949.42	43.66	973.57 -	983.56	45.11	1693.57 -	1703.56	80.75	2413.57 -	2423.56	116.39
949.43 -	949.62	43.67	983.57 -	993.56	45.60	1703.57 -	1713.56	81.24	2423.57 -	2433.56	116.88
949.63 -	949.82	43.68	993.57 -	1003.56	46.10	1713.57 -	1723.56	81.74	2433.57 -	2443.56	117.38
949.83 -	950.02	43.69	1003.57 -	1013.56	46.59	1723.57 -	1733.56	82.23	2443.57 -	2453.56	117.87
950.03 -	950.22	43.70	1013.57 -	1023.56	47.09	1733.57 -	1743.56	82.73	2453.57 -	2463.56	118.37
950.23 -	950.43	43.71	1023.57 -	1033.56	47.58	1743.57 -	1753.56	83.22	2463.57 -	2473.56	118.86
950.44 -	950.63	43.72	1033.57 -	1043.56	48.08	1753.57 -	1763.56	83.72	2473.57 -	2483.56	119.36
950.64 -	950.83	43.73	1043.57 -	1053.56	48.57	1763.57 -	1773.56	84.21	2483.57 -	2493.56	119.85
950.84 -	951.03	43.74	1053.57 -	1063.56	49.07	1773.57 -	1783.56	84.71	2493.57 -	2503.56	120.35
951.04 -	951.23	43.75	1063.57 -	1073.56	49.56	1783.57 -	1793.56	85.20	2503.57 -	2513.56	120.84
951.24 -	951.44	43.76	1073.57 -	1083.56	50.06	1793.57 -	1803.56	85.70	2513.57 -	2523.56	121.34
951.45 -	951.64	43.77	1083.57 -	1093.56	50.55	1803.57 -	1813.56	86.19	2523.57 -	2533.56	121.83
951.65 -	951.84	43.78	1093.57 -	1103.56	51.05	1813.57 -	1823.56	86.69	2533.57 -	2543.56	122.33
951.85 -	952.04	43.79	1103.57 -	1113.56	51.54	1823.57 -	1833.56	87.18	2543.57 -	2553.56	122.82
952.05 -	952.24	43.80	1113.57 -	1123.56	52.04	1833.57 -	1843.56	87.68	2553.57 -	2563.56	123.32
952.25 -	952.45	43.81	1123.57 -	1133.56	52.53	1843.57 -	1853.56	88.17	2563.57 -	2573.56	123.81
952.46 -	952.65	43.82	1133.57 -	1143.56	53.03	1853.57 -	1863.56	88.67	2573.57 -	2583.56	124.31

Employment Insurance Premiums

Cotisations à l'assurance-emploi

Insurable Earnings Rémunération assurable From - De	To - À	EI premium Cotisation d'AE	Insurable Earnings Rémunération assurable From - De	To - À	EI premium Cotisation d'AE	Insurable Earnings Rémunération assurable From - De	To - À	EI premium Cotisation d'AE	Insurable Earnings Rémunération assurable From - De	To - À	EI premium Cotisation d'AE
949.46 -	949.99	17.38	988.80 -	989.34	18.10	1028.15 -	1028.68	18.82	1067.49 -	1068.03	19.54
950.00 -	950.54	17.39	989.35 -	989.89	18.11	1028.69 -	1029.23	18.83	1068.04 -	1068.57	19.55
950.55 -	951.09	17.40	989.90 -	990.43	18.12	1029.24 -	1029.78	18.84	1068.58 -	1069.12	19.56
951.10 -	951.63	17.41	990.44 -	990.98	18.13	1029.79 -	1030.32	18.85	1069.13 -	1069.67	19.57
951.64 -	952.18	17.42	990.99 -	991.53	18.14	1030.33 -	1030.87	18.86	1069.68 -	1070.21	19.58
952.19 -	952.73	17.43	991.54 -	992.07	18.15	1030.88 -	1031.42	18.87	1070.22 -	1070.76	19.59
952.74 -	953.27	17.44	992.08 -	992.62	18.16	1031.43 -	1031.96	18.88	1070.77 -	1071.31	19.60
953.28 -	953.82	17.45	992.63 -	993.16	18.17	1031.97 -	1032.51	18.89	1071.32 -	1071.85	19.61
953.83 -	954.37	17.46	993.17 -	993.71	18.18	1032.52 -	1033.06	18.90	1071.86 -	1072.40	19.62
954.38 -	954.91	17.47	993.72 -	994.26	18.19	1033.07 -	1033.60	18.91	1072.41 -	1072.95	19.63
954.92 -	955.46	17.48	994.27 -	994.80	18.20	1033.61 -	1034.15	18.92	1072.96 -	1073.49	19.64
955.47 -	956.01	17.49	994.81 -	995.35	18.21	1034.16 -	1034.69	18.93	1073.50 -	1074.04	19.65
956.02 -	956.55	17.50	995.36 -	995.90	18.22	1034.70 -	1035.24	18.94	1074.05 -	1074.59	19.66
956.56 -	957.10	17.51	995.91 -	996.44	18.23	1035.25 -	1035.79	18.95	1074.60 -	1075.13	19.67
957.11 -	957.65	17.52	996.45 -	996.99	18.24	1035.80 -	1036.33	18.96	1075.14 -	1075.68	19.68
957.66 -	958.19	17.53	997.00 -	997.54	18.25	1036.34 -	1036.88	18.97	1075.69 -	1076.22	19.69
958.20 -	958.74	17.54	997.55 -	998.08	18.26	1036.89 -	1037.43	18.98	1076.23 -	1076.77	19.70
958.75 -	959.28	17.55	998.09 -	998.63	18.27	1037.44 -	1037.97	18.99	1076.78 -	1077.32	19.71
959.29 -	959.83	17.56	998.64 -	999.18	18.28	1037.98 -	1038.52	19.00	1077.33 -	1077.86	19.72
959.84 -	960.38	17.57	999.19 -	999.72	18.29	1038.53 -	1039.07	19.01	1077.87 -	1078.41	19.73
960.39 -	960.92	17.58	999.73 -	1000.27	18.30	1039.08 -	1039.61	19.02	1078.42 -	1078.96	19.74
960.93 -	961.47	17.59	1000.28 -	1000.81	18.31	1039.62 -	1040.16	19.03	1078.97 -	1079.50	19.75
961.48 -	962.02	17.60	1000.82 -	1001.36	18.32	1040.17 -	1040.71	19.04	1079.51 -	1080.05	19.76
962.03 -	962.56	17.61	1001.37 -	1001.91	18.33	1040.72 -	1041.25	19.05	1080.06 -	1080.60	19.77
962.57 -	963.11	17.62	1001.92 -	1002.45	18.34	1041.26 -	1041.80	19.06	1080.61 -	1081.14	19.78
963.12 -	963.66	17.63	1002.46 -	1003.00	18.35	1041.81 -	1042.34	19.07	1081.15 -	1081.69	19.79
963.67 -	964.20	17.64	1003.01 -	1003.55	18.36	1042.35 -	1042.89	19.08	1081.70 -	1082.24	19.80

Federal tax deductions
Effective January 1, 2012
Weekly (52 pay periods a year)
Also look up the tax deductions
in the provincial table

Retenues d'impôt fédéral
En vigueur le 1er janvier 2012
Hebdomadaire (52 périodes de paie par année)
Cherchez aussi les retenues d'impôt
dans la table provinciale

Pay Rémunération From De	Less than Moins de	Federal claim codes/Codes de demande fédéraux 0	1	2	3	4	5	6	7	8	9	10
		Deduct from each pay Retenez sur chaque paie										
931 -	939	136.20	105.00	102.00	96.05	90.05	84.10	78.15	72.15	66.20	60.25	54.25
939 -	947	137.90	106.70	103.70	97.75	91.75	85.80	79.85	73.85	67.90	61.95	55.95
947 -	955	139.60	108.40	105.40	99.45	93.45	87.50	81.55	75.55	69.60	63.65	57.65
955 -	963	141.30	110.10	107.10	101.15	95.15	89.20	83.25	77.25	71.30	65.35	59.35
963 -	971	143.00	111.80	108.80	102.85	96.90	90.95	84.95	79.00	73.05	67.05	61.10
971 -	979	144.80	113.55	110.60	104.60	98.65	92.70	86.70	80.75	74.80	68.85	62.85
979 -	987	146.55	115.35	112.35	106.40	100.40	94.45	88.50	82.50	76.55	70.60	64.60
987 -	995	148.30	117.10	114.10	108.15	102.15	96.20	90.25	84.30	78.30	72.35	66.40
995 -	1003	150.05	118.85	115.85	109.90	103.95	97.95	92.00	86.05	80.05	74.10	68.15
1003 -	1011	151.80	120.60	117.60	111.65	105.70	99.75	93.75	87.80	81.85	75.85	69.90
1011 -	1023	154.00	122.80	119.80	113.85	107.90	101.95	95.95	90.00	84.05	78.05	72.10
1023 -	1035	156.65	125.45	122.45	116.50	110.55	104.55	98.60	92.65	86.65	80.70	74.75
1035 -	1047	159.30	128.10	125.10	119.15	113.15	107.20	101.25	95.30	89.30	83.35	77.40
1047 -	1059	161.95	130.75	127.75	121.80	115.80	109.85	103.90	97.90	91.95	86.00	80.00
1059 -	1071	164.60	133.35	130.40	124.40	118.45	112.50	106.50	100.55	94.60	88.65	82.65
1071 -	1083	167.20	136.00	133.00	127.05	121.10	115.15	109.15	103.20	97.25	91.25	85.30
1083 -	1095	169.85	138.65	135.65	129.70	123.75	117.75	111.80	105.85	99.85	93.90	87.95
1095 -	1107	172.50	141.30	138.30	132.35	126.35	120.40	114.45	108.50	102.50	96.55	90.60
1107 -	1119	175.15	143.95	140.95	135.00	129.00	123.05	117.10	111.10	105.15	99.20	93.20
1119 -	1131	177.80	146.55	143.60	137.60	131.65	125.70	119.70	113.75	107.80	101.85	95.85

▶ **ILLUSTRATION 10A-3**

Excerpts from CPP, EI, and income tax deduction tables prepared by the Canada Revenue Agency, effective January 1, 2012 (*continued*)

Ontario provincial tax deductions
Effective January 1, 2012
Weekly (52 pay periods a year)
Also look up the tax deductions in the federal table

Retenues d'impôt provincial de l'Ontario
En vigueur le 1er janvier 2012
Hebdomadaire (52 périodes de paie par année)
Cherchez aussi les retenues d'impôt dans la table fédérale

Pay Rémunération		Provincial claim codes/Codes de demande provinciaux										
		0	1	2	3	4	5	6	7	8	9	10
From De	Less than Moins de	Deduct from each pay / Retenez sur chaque paie										
928 -	936	62.40	53.30	52.30	50.35	48.35	46.40	44.45	42.45	40.50	38.55	36.55
936 -	944	63.80	54.65	53.65	51.70	49.75	47.75	45.80	43.85	41.85	39.90	37.90
944 -	952	64.50	55.35	54.40	52.40	50.45	48.45	46.50	44.55	42.55	40.60	38.65
952 -	960	65.20	56.05	55.10	53.10	51.15	49.20	47.20	45.25	43.30	41.30	39.35
960 -	968	65.90	56.80	55.80	53.85	51.85	49.90	47.95	45.95	44.00	42.05	40.05
968 -	976	66.65	57.50	56.55	54.55	52.60	50.65	48.65	46.70	44.75	42.75	40.80
976 -	984	67.40	58.25	57.25	55.30	53.35	51.35	49.40	47.45	45.45	43.50	41.55
984 -	992	68.10	59.00	58.00	56.05	54.05	52.10	50.15	48.15	46.20	44.20	42.25
992 -	1000	68.85	59.70	58.75	56.75	54.80	52.85	50.85	48.90	46.90	44.95	43.00
1000 -	1008	69.60	60.45	59.45	57.50	55.55	53.55	51.60	49.60	47.65	45.70	43.70
1008 -	1016	70.30	61.20	60.20	58.25	56.25	54.30	52.30	50.35	48.40	46.40	44.45
1016 -	1024	71.05	61.90	60.95	58.95	57.00	55.00	53.05	51.10	49.10	47.15	45.20
1024 -	1032	71.80	62.65	61.65	59.70	57.70	55.75	53.80	51.80	49.85	47.90	45.90
1032 -	1040	72.50	63.35	62.40	60.40	58.45	56.50	54.50	52.55	50.60	48.60	46.65
1040 -	1048	73.25	64.10	63.10	61.15	59.20	57.20	55.25	53.30	51.30	49.35	47.40
1048 -	1060	74.15	65.00	64.05	62.05	60.10	58.15	56.15	54.20	52.25	50.25	48.30
1060 -	1072	75.25	66.10	65.15	63.15	61.20	59.25	57.25	55.30	53.35	51.35	49.40
1072 -	1084	76.35	67.20	66.25	64.25	62.30	60.35	58.35	56.40	54.45	52.45	50.50
1084 -	1096	77.45	68.30	67.35	65.35	63.40	61.45	59.45	57.50	55.55	53.55	51.60
1096 -	1108	78.55	69.40	68.45	66.45	64.50	62.55	60.55	58.60	56.60	54.65	52.70
1108 -	1120	79.65	70.50	69.55	67.55	65.60	63.60	61.65	59.70	57.70	55.75	53.80
1120 -	1132	80.75	71.60	70.60	68.65	66.70	64.70	62.75	60.80	58.80	56.85	54.90
1132 -	1144	81.85	72.70	71.70	69.75	67.80	65.80	63.85	61.90	59.90	57.95	56.00
1144 -	1156	82.95	73.80	72.80	70.85	68.90	66.90	64.95	63.00	61.00	59.05	57.10
1156 -	1168	84.05	74.90	73.90	71.95	70.00	68.00	66.05	64.10	62.10	60.15	58.20

Source: T4032 Payroll Deduction Tables, Effective July 1, 2012. Pages: B-15, C-7, E-3, D3-D4; http://www.cra-arc.gc.ca/tx/bsnss/tpcs/pyrll/t4032/jn12/menu-eng.html

can either calculate the EI as shown earlier, or use the tables. Both amounts are correct—the table is just slightly less precise than the calculation.

In the federal tax deduction table, first find $1,000 in the Pay column. Now follow across the table to the Federal Claim Code 1 column. The federal tax deduction in the "from" $995 to "less than" $1,003 range, claim code 1, is $118.85. The same process is used in the Ontario provincial tax deduction table. In the "from" $1,000 to "less than" $1,008 range, provincial claim code 1, the provincial tax deduction is $60.45. The total of these amounts of $179.30 ($118.85 + $60.45) agree with the amounts given for Mark Jordan's income tax deduction earlier in the chapter.

Claim code 1 is used for individuals who qualify for only the basic personal credit on the TD1 form discussed earlier in the appendix. You will notice on the federal and provincial tax deduction tables that the higher the claim code, the lower the income tax deduction. These claim codes can be used for employees who will have more personal tax credits. We have assumed that Mark Jordan will qualify for only the basic personal credit.

As mentioned earlier, employers may also use the payroll software packages or the CRA's Payroll Deductions Online Calculator to determine payroll deductions. All of these methods will provide correct deductions as long as the correct dates, gross pay, pay period, and claim codes are used.

⊙ BEFORE YOU GO ON...

Do It

Action Plan
- The CPP basic pay-period deduction is the annual basic deduction divided by the number of pay periods in a year.
- CPP deductions are equal to an employee's pensionable earnings times the CPP contribution rate.

Highland Company pays salaries on a weekly basis. The payroll for the week ended May 29, 2012, includes three employees as follows:

Employee Name	Weekly Earnings	Claim Code
Hudson, James	$975	4
Randell, Findley	$975	2
Jaegeun, Kim	$1,125	1

Determine the appropriate mandatory payroll deductions and net pay for each employee. Calculate the CPP and EI deductions using the formula provided in Appendix 10A. Use the tables in Illustration 10A-3 to determine federal and provincial income taxes.

Solution

Employee	Gross Pay	Deductions						Net Pay
		CPP	EI	Federal Income Tax	Provincial Income Tax	Total		
Hudson, James	$ 975.00	44.93[1]	17.84[3]	98.65	52.60	214.02		760.98
Randell, Findley	975.00	44.93	17.84	110.60	56.55	229.92		745.08
Jaegeun, Kim	1,125.00	52.36[2]	20.59[4]	146.55	71.60	291.10		833.90

Calculations:
Note: CPP basic pay period deduction = $3,500 ÷ 52 = $67.30
[1] ($975.00 − $67.30) × 4.95% = $44.93
[2] ($1,125.00 − $67.30) × 4.95% = $52.36
[3] $975.00 × 1.83% = $17.84
[4] $1,125.00 × 1.83% = $20.59

Related exercise material: *BE10–16, *BE10–17, *BE10–18, *E10–15, and *E10–16.   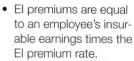 THE **NAVIGATOR**

- EI premiums are equal to an employee's insurable earnings times the EI premium rate.
- The federal tax deduction is the amount in the correct Pay range and Claim Code column on the federal tax deduction table.
- The provincial tax deduction is the amount in the correct Pay range and Claim Code column on the provincial tax deduction table.

■Comparing IFRS and ASPE ■

Key Differences	International Financial Reporting Standards (IFRS)	Accounting Standards for Private Enterprises (ASPE)
Conditions necessary to record a liability for a contingent loss.	Chance of occurrence is "probable" or "more likely than not."	Chance of occurrence is "likely."
Terminology	A liability related to a contingent loss is called a "provision."	A liability related to a contingent loss is called a "contingent liability."

THE **NAVIGATOR**

Demonstration Problem

Benoit Company has the following selected transactions:

Feb. 1   Signed a $50,000, six-month, 7% note payable to the Central Canadian Bank, receiving $50,000 in cash. Interest is payable at maturity.

10   Cash register receipts totalled $37,565, plus 13% HST.

28   The payroll for the month is salaries of $50,000. CPP contributions and EI premiums withheld are $2,475 and $915, respectively. A total of $15,000 in income taxes is withheld. The salaries are paid on March 1.

The following adjustment data are noted at the end of the month:

1. Interest expense should be accrued on the note.
2. Employer payroll costs are recorded. In addition to mandatory costs, the company also pays $800 a month for a dental plan for all its employees.
3. Some sales were made under warranty. Of the units sold under warranty this month, 350 are expected to become defective. Repair costs are estimated to be $40 per defective unit.

Instructions

(a) Record the February transactions. Round your calculations to the nearest dollar.
(b) Record the adjusting entries at February 28.

ACTION PLAN

• Remember that interest rates are annual rates and must be adjusted for periods of time less than one year.

• Remember that sales taxes collected must be sent to the government and are not part of sales revenue.

• Remember that employee deductions for CPP, EI, and income tax reduce the salaries payable.

• Employer contributions to CPP, EI, and the dental plan create an additional expense.

• Warranty costs are expensed in the period when the sales occur.

Solution to Demonstration Problem

(a)

Feb. 1	Cash		50,000	
	Notes Payable			50,000
	Issued six-month, 7% note.			
10	Cash ($37,565 + $4,883)		42,448	
	Sales			37,565
	HST Payable ($37,565 × 13%)			4,883
	To record sales and sales tax payable.			
28	Salaries Expense		50,000	
	Income Taxes Payable			15,000
	CPP Payable			2,475
	EI Payable			915
	Salaries Payable			31,610
	To record February salaries.			

(b)

Feb. 28	Interest Expense ($50,000 × 7% × $^{1}/_{12}$)		292	
	Interest Payable			292
	To record accrued interest for February.			
28	Employee Benefits Expense		4,556	
	CPP Payable ($2,475 × 1)			2,475
	EI Payable ($915 × 1.4)			1,281
	Dental Plan Payable			800
	To record employee benefit costs for February.			
28	Warranty Expense (350 × $40)		14,000	
	Warranty Liability			14,000
	To record estimated product warranty liability.			

THE NAVIGATOR

▶ Summary of Study Objectives

1. ***Account for determinable or certain current liabilities.*** Liabilities are present obligations arising from past events, to make future payments of assets or services. Determinable liabilities have certainty about their existence, amount, and timing—in other words, they have a known amount, payee, and due date. Examples of determinable current liabilities include operating lines of credit, notes payable, accounts payable, sales taxes, unearned revenue, current maturities of long-term debt, and accrued liabilities such as property taxes, payroll, and interest.

2. ***Account for estimated liabilities.*** Estimated liabilities exist, but their amount or timing is uncertain. As long as it is *likely* the company will have to settle the obligation, and the company can reasonably estimate the amount, the liability is recognized. Product warranties, customer loyalty programs, and gift cards result in liabilities that must be estimated. They are recorded either as an expense (or as a decrease in revenue) and a liability in the period when the sales occur. These liabilities are reduced when repairs under warranty or redemptions occur. Gift cards are a type of unearned revenue as they result in a liability until

the gift card is redeemed. As some cards are never redeemed, it is necessary to estimate the liability and make adjustments.

3. ***Account for contingencies.*** A contingency is an existing condition or situation that is uncertain, where it cannot be known if a loss (and a related liability) will result until a future event happens, or does not happen. Under ASPE, a liability for a contingent loss is recorded if it is it likely a loss will occur and the amount of the contingency can be reasonably estimated. Under IFRS, the threshold for recording the loss is lower. It is recorded if a loss is probable. Under ASPE, these liabilities are called contingent liabilities, and under IFRS, these liabilities are called provisions. If it is not possible to estimate the amount, these liabilities are only disclosed. They are not disclosed if they are unlikely.

4. ***Determine payroll costs and record payroll transactions.*** Payroll costs consist of employee and employer payroll costs. In recording employee costs, Salaries Expense is debited for the gross pay, individual liability accounts are credited for payroll deductions, and Salaries Payable is

credited for net pay. In recording employer payroll costs, Employee Benefits Expense is debited for the employer's share of CPP, EI, workers' compensation, vacation pay, and any other deductions or benefits provided. Each benefit is credited to its specific current liability account.

5. *Prepare the current liabilities section of the balance sheet.* The nature and amount of each current liability and contingency should be reported in the balance sheet or in the notes accompanying the financial statements. Traditionally, current liabilities are reported first and in order of liquidity. International companies sometimes report current liabilities on the lower section of the balance sheet and in reverse order of liquidity.

6. *Calculate mandatory payroll deductions (Appendix 10A).* Mandatory payroll deductions include CPP, EI, and income taxes. CPP is calculated by multiplying pensionable earnings (gross pay minus the pay period exemption) by the CPP contribution rate. EI is calculated by multiplying insurable earnings by the EI contribution rate. Federal and provincial income taxes are calculated using a progressive tax scheme and are based on taxable earnings and personal tax credits. The calculations are very complex and it is best to use one of the CRA income tax calculation tools such as payroll deduction tables.

THE NAVIGATOR

Flash cards

▶ Glossary

Canada Pension Plan (CPP)   A mandatory federal plan that gives disability, retirement, and death benefits to qualifying Canadians. (p. 537)

Collateral   Property pledged as security for a loan. (p. 527)

Contingency   An existing condition or situation that is uncertain, where it cannot be known if a loss (and a related liability) will result from the situation until one or more future events happen or do not happen. (p. 534)

Contingent liability   A liability whose existence will be confirmed only by the occurrence or non-occurrence of a future event. (p. 535)

Customer loyalty programs   Programs that result in future savings for the customers on the merchandise or services the company sells. (p. 532)

Determinable liability   A liability whose existence, amount, and timing are known with certainty. (p. 526)

Employee benefits   Payments made by an employer, in addition to wages and salaries, to give pension, insurance, medical, or other benefits to its employees. (p. 539)

Employee earnings record   A separate record of an employee's gross pay, payroll deductions, and net pay for the calendar year. (p. 539)

Employment Insurance (EI)   A federal mandatory insurance program designed to give income protection for a limited period of time to employees who are temporarily laid off, who are on parental leave, or who lose their jobs. (p. 538)

Estimated liability   A liability that is known to exist but whose amount or timing is uncertain. (p. 531)

Gross pay   Total compensation earned by an employee. Also known as gross earnings. (p. 536)

Insurable earnings   Gross earnings used to calculate EI deductions. There is a maximum amount of insurable earnings set each year by the government. (p. 547)

Net pay   Gross pay less payroll deductions. (p. 538)

Notes payable   Obligations in the form of written promissory notes. (p. 527)

Operating line of credit   Pre-authorized approval to borrow money at a bank when it is needed, up to a pre-set limit. (p. 527)

Payroll deductions   Deductions from gross pay to determine the amount of a paycheque. (p. 537)

Payroll register   A record that accumulates the gross pay, deductions, and net pay per employee for each pay period and becomes the documentation for preparing a paycheque for each employee. (p. 540)

Pensionable earnings   Gross earnings less the basic yearly exemption. There is a maximum amount of pensionable earnings set each year by the government. (p. 546)

Personal tax credits   Amounts deducted from an individual's income taxes that determine the amount of income taxes to be withheld. (p. 548)

Prime rate   The interest rate banks charge their best customers. (p. 527)

Product warranties   Promises made by the seller to a buyer to repair or replace a product if it is defective or does not perform as intended. (p. 531)

Provisions   Liabilities of uncertain timing or amount. (p. 535)

Trade payables   Accounts and notes payable that result from purchase transactions with suppliers. (p. 527)

Note: All questions, exercises, and problems below with an asterisk (*) relate to material in Appendix 10A.

▶ Self-Study Questions

Answers are at the end of the chapter.

(SO 1) C 1. Which of the following statements is the best description of a liability?
    (a) A liability is a commitment to pay an amount in the future.
    (b) A liability arises when an expense is incurred.
    (c) A liability is an amount that should have been paid in the past.
    (d) A liability is a present obligation, arising from past events, to make future payments of assets or services.

(SO 1) AP 2. Gibraltar Company borrows $55,200 on July 31, 2014, from the East Coast Bank by signing a seven-month, 5% note. Interest is payable at maturity. Assuming Gibraltar has a December 31 fiscal year end, how much interest expense will Gibraltar record in 2014 and in 2015?

	2014	2015
(a)	$ 0	$1,610
(b)	$1,150	$ 460
(c)	$1,380	$ 230
(d)	$1,971	$ 789

(SO 1) AP 3. RedEarth Company, located in Ontario, has $5,007 of sales, which included 13% HST. What are the amounts (rounded to the nearest dollar) that should be credited to Sales and to HST Payable?

	Sales	HST Payable
(a)	$5,007	$651
(b)	$4,356	$651
(c)	$4,431	$576
(d)	$5,007	$576

(SO 1) AP 4. On March 1, Swift Current Company receives its property tax assessment of $13,200 for the 2014 calendar year. The property tax bill is due May 1. If Swift Current prepares quarterly financial statements, how much property tax expense should the company report for the quarter ended March 31, 2014?
    (a) $3,300
    (b) $4,400
    (c) $1,100
    (d) $13,200

(SO 2) AP 5. Big Al's Appliance Store offers a two-year warranty on all appliances sold. The company estimates that 5% of all appliances sold need to be serviced at an average cost of $100 each. At December 31, 2013, the Warranty Liability account had a balance of $20,000. During 2014, the store spends $14,500 repairing 145 appliances. An additional 4,500 appliances are sold in 2014. On the 2014 income statement, warranty expense will be:
    (a) $28,000.
    (b) $22,500.
    (c) $14,500.
    (d) $20,000.

(SO 2) K 6. Friendly Department Store has a customer loyalty program in which customers receive points when they make a purchase. The points can be redeemed on future purchases. The value of the points issued should be recorded as:
    (a) a contra revenue when the points are issued.
    (b) an expense when the points are issued.
    (c) a contra revenue when the points are redeemed.
    (d) an expense when the points are redeemed.

(SO 3) K 7. Under IFRS, a contingent loss and the related liability should be recorded in the accounts when:
    (a) it is probable the contingency will happen, but the amount cannot be reasonably estimated.
    (b) it is probable the contingency will happen, and the amount can be reasonably estimated.
    (c) it is highly unlikely the contingency will happen, but the amount can be reasonably estimated.
    (d) it is unlikely that the users of the financial statements will read the notes.

(SO 4) AP 8. In a recent pay period, Blue Company employees have gross salaries of $17,250. Total deductions are: CPP $866, EI $316, and income taxes $4,312. What is Blue Company's total payroll expense for this pay period? Ignore vacation benefits and workers' compensation premiums.
    (a) $17,250
    (b) $18,558
    (c) $11,765
    (d) $18,432

(SO 5) K 9. On November 1, 2014, SSNL Company borrows $120,000 cash from the bank and issues a two-year, 4% note payable. SSNL must make payments of $5,000 plus interest at the end of each month. On December 31, 2014, what amount will be included in current and in non-current liabilities on the balance sheet?

	Current Liabilities	Non-Current Liabilities
(a)	$60,000	$ 50,000
(b)	$60,000	$ 60,000
(c)	$10,000	$100,000
(d)	$50,000	$ 70,000

(SO 4, 6) *10. During the first week of May 2012, Emily Marquette
AP   worked 40 hours at an hourly wage of $25.75 per hour for an employer in Ontario. Using the payroll deduction tables in Appendix 10A, what was her net pay, assuming her only personal tax credit is the basic personal amount?
    (a) $1,030.00
    (b) $775.47
    (c) $841.90
    (d) $735.87

THE NAVIGATOR

ⓞ Questions

(SO 1) K   1. What is a determinable liability? List some examples.

(SO 1) K   2. Why is a present commitment to purchase an asset in the future not recorded as a liability?

(SO 1) K   3. How is interest calculated on a note payable? How is the amount of interest payable at the fiscal year end calculated?

(SO 1) K   4. What is the difference between an operating line of credit and a bank overdraft?

(SO 1) C   5. A friend is opening a retail store and doesn't understand how to calculate the amount of sales tax collected if the sales tax is included in the selling price. Explain how to do this and provide an example. Assume the company must collect the 13% HST from its customers.

(SO 1) C   6. Your roommate argues that since property taxes are unavoidable, a company should record the full year's worth of property taxes as an expense when it is paid. Is your roommate correct? Explain.

(SO 1) C   7. Laurel Hyatt believes that if a company has a long-term liability, the entire amount should be classified as non-current liabilities. Is Laurel correct? Explain.

(SO 2) C   8. The accountant for Amiable Appliances feels that warranty expense should not be recorded unless an appliance is returned for repair. "Otherwise, how do you know if the appliance will be returned, and if so, how much it will cost to fix?" he says. Do you agree? Explain.

(SO 2) C   9. Why does issuing a customer some form of future savings, when the customer purchases goods or services, result in a liability for the business?

(SO 2) C   10. A restaurant recently started a customer loyalty program. For all bills in excess of $100, the customer receives a 2-for-1 voucher for an appetizer for future meals. How should the restaurant account for the vouchers?

(SO 2) C   11. In what respects are gift cards similar to unearned revenues and why are they classified as a liability? How is a gift card different than an airline's unearned passenger revenue for flights paid in advance?

(SO 1, 2, 3) K   12. What are the differences between determinable, estimated, and contingent liabilities?

(SO 3) C   13. What is a contingency? How is it different from an estimated liability?

(SO 3) C   14. If a company is using ASPE, under what circumstances are a contingent loss and the related liability recorded in the accounts? Under what circumstances are they disclosed only in the notes to the financial statements?

(SO 3) C   15. If a company is using IFRS, under what circumstances are a contingent loss and the related liability recorded in the accounts? How is IFRS different from ASPE in this respect?

(SO 3) C   16. When is it necessary to disclose a contingency even if the chance of occurrence is small?

(SO 4) C   17. What is gross pay? How is it different than net pay? Which amount (gross or net) should a company record as salaries expense?

(SO 4) C   18. Explain the different types of employee and employer payroll deductions, and give examples of each.

(SO 4) K   19. What are an employee earnings record and a payroll register?

(SO 4) C   20. To whom, and how often, are payroll deductions remitted?

(SO 4) K   21. What are some additional employee benefits paid by employers? How are they accounted for?

(SO 5) K   22. In what order are current liabilities generally reported in the balance sheet? Why might this method not always be possible?

(SO 5) K   23. What information about current liabilities should be reported in the notes to the financial statements?

(SO 5) K   24. How can a company determine if its current liabilities are too high?

(SO 6) K *25. Explain how CPP and EI are calculated.

(SO 6) K *26. How is the amount deducted from an employee's wages for income tax determined?

ⓞ Brief Exercises

BE10–1   Rabbitt Enterprises borrows $10,500 from LowLand Trust Co. on May 1, 2014, signing a 10-month, 4% note payable. Interest is payable the first of each month, starting June 1. Prepare journal entries for Rabbitt Enterprises to record: (a) the receipt of the proceeds of the note; (b) the first interest payment; (c) an adjusting entry, if required, at Rabbitt's year end, August 31, 2014; and (d) the payment of the note at maturity.

Record note payable. (SO 1) AP

BE10–2   Blue Robin Retail has one store in Ottawa, Ontario, and one in Gatineau, Quebec. All sales in Ontario are subject to 13% HST; all sales in Quebec are subject to 5% GST and 9.975% QST. On March 12, 2013, the Ottawa store reports cash sales of $7,200 and the Gatineau store reports cash sales of $8,400. (a) Calculate the sales taxes each store charged for these sales (Note: sales taxes are not included in these amounts.) (b) Prepare a journal entry for each store to record the sales on March 12, 2013.

Calculate sales taxes and record sales. (SO 1) AP

Calculate HST and record sales. (SO 1) AP

BE10–3 Backyard Shed Solutions sells its largest shed for $1,500 plus HST of 13%. On May 10, 2014, it sold 10 of these sheds. In order to increase sales the following weekend, the company offered to sell these sheds for $1,500, sales tax included. On May 17, 2014, the company sold 20 of these sheds. All sales are cash sales. For each day's sales, (a) calculate the HST, and (b) prepare a journal entry to record the sales.

Record property tax. (SO 1) AP

BE10–4 Dresner Company has a December 31 fiscal year end. It receives a $7,860 property tax bill for the 2014 calendar year on March 31, 2014. The bill is payable on June 30. Prepare entries for March 31, June 30, and December 31, assuming the company adjusts its accounts annually.

Record warranty. (SO 2) AP

BE10–5 In 2014, Song Company introduces a new product that includes a two-year warranty on parts. During 2014, 2,500 units are sold for $400 each. The cost of each unit was $175. The company estimates 5% of the units will be defective and that the average warranty cost will be $85 per unit. The company has a December 31 fiscal year end and prepares adjusting entries on an annual basis. (a) Prepare an adjusting entry at December 31, 2014, to accrue the estimated warranty cost. (b) Assume that the warranty contract was honoured on 25 units during 2014 for a total cost of $2,125 to replace defective parts. Prepare an entry dated December 31 to record honouring these warranties. (c) Calculate the profit earned by the company during 2014 on this new product.

Record loyalty rewards issued and redeemed. (SO 2) AP

BE10–6 One-Stop Department Store has a loyalty program where customers are given One-Stop "Money" for cash or debit card purchases. The amount they receive is equal to 2% of the pre-tax sales total. Customers can use the One-Stop Money to pay for part or all of their next purchase at One-Stop Department Store. On July 3, 2014, Judy Wishloff purchases merchandise for $150. She uses $20 of One-Stop Money that she has from earlier purchases, and pays for the rest of the purchase with cash. What entry or entries will One-Stop Department Store record for this transaction? Ignore taxes.

Record estimated liability for cash rebate program. (SO 2) AP

BE10–7 Metropolis Books sold 50,000 copies of a best-selling novel in July for $8 each. Included in each book was a $2 mail-in rebate if the customer sends in proof of purchase with a completed rebate form. Metropolis estimates that 10% of the purchasers will claim the rebate. (a) Calculate the net sales revenue Metropolis earned in July on this book. (b) Prepare an adjusting entry at July 31 to accrue the estimated rebate liability. (c) Assume in August that 1,000 rebate forms are received and processed. Prepare one journal entry to record processing the rebate forms.

Record gift cards issued and redeemed. (SO 2) AP

BE10–8 Rikard's Menswear sells $4,750 of gift cards for cash in December 2014. Rikard's has a December 31 fiscal year end and uses a perpetual inventory system. In January 2015, $2,425 of the gift cards are redeemed for merchandise, with a cost of $1,070. Prepare journal entries for Rikard's for December 2014 and January 2015.

Account for contingencies. (SO 3) C

BE10–9 For each of the following independent situations, indicate whether it should be (1) recorded, (2) disclosed, or (3) neither recorded nor disclosed. Explain your reasoning and indicate if the accounting treatment would be the same or different under IFRS and ASPE.

(a) A customer has sued a company for $1 million. Currently the company is unable to determine if it will win or lose the lawsuit.
(b) A customer has sued a company for $1 million. The company will likely lose the lawsuit.
(c) A competitor has sued a company for $2 million. The lawyers have advised that there is a 55% chance that the company will lose the lawsuit.
(d) A company has guaranteed a $300,000 loan for one of its key suppliers. The supplier has a good credit rating and is not expected to default on the loan.

Discuss contingency. (SO 3) AP

BE10–10 Athabasca Toil & Oil Company, a public company, is a defendant in a lawsuit for improper discharge of pollutants and waste into the Athabasca River. Athabasca's lawyers have advised that it is probable the company will lose this lawsuit and that it could settle out of court for $50,000. Should Athabasca record anything with regard to this lawsuit? Or should it disclose it in the notes to the financial statements? Explain.

Calculate gross, net pay, and employer costs. (SO 4) AP

BE10–11 Becky Sherrick's regular hourly wage rate is $18, and she is paid time and a half for work over 40 hours per week. In the pay period ended March 16, Becky worked 45 hours. Becky's CPP deductions total $38.99, EI deductions total $15.65, and her income tax withholdings are $132.00. (a) Calculate Becky's gross and net pay for the pay period. (b) What are Becky's employer's costs for CPP, EI, and income tax?

Record payroll (SO 4) AP

BE10–12 Bri Company's gross pay for the week ended August 22 totalled $70,000, from which $3,330 was deducted for CPP, $1,281 for EI, and $19,360 for income tax. Prepare the entries to record (a) the employee payroll costs, assuming salaries were paid August 22, and (b) the employer payroll costs, assuming these will not be paid until September.

Identify current liabilities. (SO 1, 2, 3, 4, 5) K

BE10–13 Identify which of the following items should be classified as a current liability. For those that are not current liabilities, identify where they should be classified.

(a) A product warranty
(b) Cash received in advance for airline tickets

(c) HST collected on sales

(d) Bank indebtedness

(e) Interest owing on an overdue account payable

(f) Interest due on an overdue account receivable

(g) A lawsuit pending against a company. The company is not sure of the likely outcome.

(h) Amounts withheld from the employees' weekly pay

(i) Prepaid property tax

(j) A $75,000 mortgage payable, of which $5,000 is due in the next year

BE10–14 Diamond Dealers has two notes payable outstanding on December 31, 2014, as follows:

(a) A five-year, 5.5%, $60,000 note payable issued on August 31, 2014. Diamond Dealers is required to pay $12,000 plus interest on August 31 each year starting in 2015.

(b) A four-year, 4.5%, $96,000 note payable issued on September 30, 2014. Diamond Dealers is required to pay $2,000 plus interest at the end of each month starting on October 31, 2014. All payments are up to date.

Calculate the amount of each note to be included in current and non-current liabilities on Diamond Dealers' December 31, 2014, balance sheet. Ignore interest.

Calculate current and non-current portion of notes payable. (SO 1, 5) AP

BE10–15 **Suncor Energy Inc.** reported the following current assets and current liabilities (in millions) at December 31, 2011:

Accounts payable and accrued liabilities	$7,755
Accounts receivable	5,412
Cash and cash equivalents	3,803
Current portion of long-term debt	12
Current portion of provisions	811
Income taxes payable	969
Income taxes receivable	704
Inventories	4,205
Short-term debt	763

Prepare current liabilities section and calculate ratios. (SO 5) AP

(a) Prepare the current liabilities section of the balance sheet.

(b) Calculate the current and acid-test ratios.

*BE10–16 Cecilia Hernandez earned $60,100 in 2012 and was paid monthly. She worked for HillSide Tours for all of 2012. What were her CPP and EI deductions in (a) January 2012 and (b) December 2012?

Calculate CPP and EI deductions. (SO 6) AP

*BE10–17 In 2012, Viktor Petska was paid a gross salary of $1,075 on a weekly basis. For the week ended May 11, 2012: (a) calculate his CPP and EI deductions and (b) use the excerpts in Illustration 10A-3 to determine his income tax deductions assuming his TD1 claim code is 1.

Calculate payroll deductions. (SO 6) AP

*BE10–18 Augustus Jackson earns $860 for a 40-hour week and is paid time and a half for hours above 40. During the week ended April 27, 2012, he worked 48 hours. (a) Calculate his gross pay for the week. (b) Calculate his CPP and EI deductions. (c) Use the excerpts in Illustration 10A-3 to determine his income tax deductions assuming his TD1 claim code is 2. (d) Calculate his net pay.

Calculate gross pay, payroll deductions, and net pay. (SO 4, 6) AP

▶ Exercises

E10–1 On June 1, 2014, Novack Company purchases equipment on account from Moleski Manufacturers for $50,000. Novack is unable to pay its account on July 1, 2014, so Moleski agrees to accept a three-month, 7% note payable from Novack. Interest is payable the first of each month, starting August 1, 2014. Novack has an August 31 fiscal year end. Moleski has a December 31 fiscal year end. Both companies adjust their accounts on an annual basis. Novack honours the note at maturity.

Record note payable and note receivable; interest paid monthly. (SO 1) AP

Instructions

(a) Record all transactions related to the note for Novack Company.

(b) Record all transactions related to the note for Moleski Manufacturers. Assume the cost of the equipment to Moleski was $30,000.

E10–2 On March 1, 2014, Tundra Trees Company purchased equipment from Edworthy Equipment Dealership in exchange for a seven-month, 8%, $30,000 note payable. Interest is due at maturity. Tundra Trees has a July 31 fiscal year end. Edworthy has a May 31 fiscal year end. Both companies adjust their accounts annually. Tundra honours the note at maturity.

Record note payable and note receivable; interest paid at maturity. (SO 1) AP

Instructions

(a) For Tundra Trees, record all transactions related to the note.

(b) For Edworthy Equipment, record all transactions related to the note. Assume the cost of the equipment to Edworthy was $18,000.

Record sales taxes.
(SO 1) AP

E10-3 In providing accounting services to small businesses, you encounter the following independent situations:

1. Sainsbury Company rang up $13,200 of sales, plus HST of 13%, on its cash register on April 10.
2. Hockenstein Company prices its merchandise with sales taxes included. Its register total for April 15 is $35,595, which includes 13% HST.
3. Montgomery Company rang up $30,000 of sales, before sales taxes, on its cash register on April 21. The company charges 5% GST and no PST.
4. Winslow Co. charges 5% GST and 7% PST on all sales. On April 27, the company collected $25,100 sales in cash plus sales taxes.

Instructions

Record the sales transactions and related taxes for each client.

Account for unearned
revenue. (SO 1) AP

E10-4 Charleswood Musical Theatre's season begins in November and ends in April with a different play each month. In October 2014, Charleswood sold 150 season tickets for the 2014–15 season, which sold for $210 each. Charleswood records all season ticket sales as unearned revenue and adjusts its accounts on a monthly basis. The company has a March 31 fiscal year end.

Instructions

(a) Prepare the entry for sale of the season tickets. Date the entry October 31.

(b) Prepare any required adjusting entries on:
   1. November 30, 2014
   2. March 31, 2015
   3. April 30, 2015

(c) Determine the balance (after any required adjustments) in Unearned Revenue on:
   1. November 30, 2014
   2. December 31, 2014
   3. March 31, 2015

Record property tax;
determine financial statement
impact. (SO 1, 5) AP

E10-5 Seaboard Company receives its annual property tax bill of $18,660 for the 2014 calendar year on May 31, 2014, and it is payable on July 31, 2014. Seaboard has a December 31 fiscal year end.

Instructions

(a) Prepare the journal entries for Seaboard on May 31, July 31, and December 31, 2014, assuming that the company makes monthly adjusting entries. (Assume property tax expense in 2013 was $1,475 per month.)

(b) What is recorded on Seaboard's December 31, 2014, balance sheet and income statement for the year ended December 31, 2014, in regard to property taxes?

Record warranty costs.
(SO 2) AP

E10-6 Castellitto Company began selling blenders on November 1, 2014. The company offers a 75-day warranty for defective merchandise. Based on past experience with other similar products, Castellitto estimates that 2.5% of the units sold will become defective in the warranty period, and that the average cost of replacing or repairing a defective unit is $20. In November, Castellitto sold 30,000 units and 450 defective units were returned. In December, Castellitto sold 32,000 units and 630 defective units were returned. The actual cost of replacing the defective units was $21,600.

Instructions

(a) Prepare a journal entry to accrue for the estimated warranty costs for the November and December sales at December 31, 2014.

(b) Prepare one summary journal entry at December 31, 2014, to record the cost of replacing the defective blenders returned during November and December.

(c) What amounts will be included in Castellitto's 2014 income statement and balance sheet at December 31, 2014, with regard to the warranty?

Calculate warranty costs for
multiple years. (SO 2) AP

E10-7 Silver Cloud Company manufactures and sells computers for $2,000 each, with a two-year parts and labour warranty. Based on prior experience, the company expects, on average, to incur warranty costs equal to 5% of sales. The company reports the following sales and warranty cost information:

	Sales (units)	Actual Warranty Costs
2012	500	$30,000
2013	600	46,000
2014	525	53,500

Instructions

(a) Calculate the warranty expense for each year.
(b) Calculate the warranty liability at the end of each year.

E10–8   Steig's Sports Store has a customer loyalty program in which it issues points to customers for every cash purchase that can be applied to future purchases. For every dollar spent, a customer receives three points. Each point is worth one cent. There is no expiry date on the points. Steig's estimates that 35% of the points issued will eventually be redeemed. Steig's has a December 31 year end.

Calculate customer loyalty program liability. (SO 2) AP

The program was started in 2014. During 2014, 900,000 points were issued. In 2015, 1.2 million points were issued. Redemptions total 225,000 points in 2014 and 336,000 in 2015.

Instructions

(a) What amount should be recorded as contra revenue (sales discounts for redemption rewards issued) in 2014? In 2015?
(b) What was the value of the points redeemed in 2014? In 2015?
(c) What is the redemption rewards liability that should be reported at December 31, 2014? At December 31, 2015?
(d) When the points are redeemed, how is this accounted for? What is the impact of the point redemptions on profit?

E10–9   A list of possible liabilities follows:

Identify type of liability. (SO 1, 2, 3) C

1. An automobile company recalled a particular car model because of a possible problem with the brakes. The company will pay to replace the brakes.
2. A large retail store has a policy of refunding purchases to dissatisfied customers under a widely advertised "money-back, no questions asked" guarantee.
3. A manufacturer offers a three-year warranty at the time of sale.
4. To promote sales, a company offers prizes (such as a chance to win a trip) in return for a specific type of bottle cap.
5. A local community has filed suit against a chemical company for contamination of drinking water. The community is demanding compensation, and the amount is uncertain. The company is vigorously defending itself.

Instructions

(a) State whether you believe each of the above liabilities is determinable, estimable, or contingent, and explain why.
(b) If you identify the liability as contingent in part (a), state what factors should be considered in determining if it should be recorded, disclosed, or neither recorded nor disclosed in the financial statements.

E10–10   Sleep-a-Bye Baby Company, a public company, is the defendant in a lawsuit alleging that its portable baby cribs are unsafe. The company has offered to replace the cribs free of charge for any concerned parent. Nonetheless, it has been sued for damages and distress amounting to $1.5 million. The company plans to vigorously defend its product safety record in court.

Analyze contingency. (SO 3) AP

Instructions

(a) What should the company record or report in its financial statements for this situation? Explain why.
(b) What if Sleep-a-Bye Baby Company's lawyers advise that it is likely the company will have to pay damages of $100,000? Does this change what should be recorded or reported in the financial statements? Explain.
(c) How would your answers to (a) and (b) change if Sleep-a-Bye Baby Company were a private company that had chosen to follow ASPE?

E10–11   Hidden Dragon Restaurant's gross payroll for April is $45,500. The company deducted $2,108 for CPP, $833 for EI, and $8,798 for income taxes from the employees' cheques. Employees are paid monthly at the end of each month.

Record payroll. (SO 4) AP

Instructions

(a) Prepare a journal entry for Hidden Dragon on April 30 to record the payment of the April payroll to employees.
(b) Prepare a journal entry on April 30 to accrue Hidden Dragon's employer payroll costs. Assume that Hidden Dragon is assessed workers' compensation premiums at a rate of 1% per month and accrues for vacation pay at a rate of 4% per month.
(c) On May 15, Hidden Dragon pays the government the correct amounts for April's payroll. Prepare a journal entry to record this remittance.

E10–12   Ahmad Company has the following data for the weekly payroll ending May 31:

Calculate gross pay; prepare payroll register, and record payroll. (SO 4) AP

Employee	M	Tu	W	Th	F	S	Hourly Rate	CPP Deduction	Income Tax Withheld	Health Insurance
A. Kassam	9	8	9	8	10	3	$13	$29.17	$ 85.55	$10
H. Faas	8	8	8	8	8	5	14	29.59	87.10	15
G. Labute	9	10	9	10	8	0	15	33.05	102.55	15

Employees are paid 1.5 times the regular hourly rate for all hours worked over 40 hours per week. Ahmad Company must make payments to the workers' compensation plan equal to 2% of the gross payroll. In addition, Ahmad matches the employees' health insurance contributions and accrues vacation pay at a rate of 4%.

Instructions

(a) Prepare the payroll register for the weekly payroll. Calculate each employee's EI deduction at a rate of 1.83% of gross pay.

(b) Record the payroll and Ahmad Company's employee benefits.

Calculate current and non-current portion of notes payable, and interest payable. (SO 1, 5) AP

E10–13   Emerald Enterprises has three notes payable outstanding on December 31, 2014, as follows:

1. A six-year, 6%, $60,000 note payable issued on March 31, 2014. Emerald Enterprises is required to pay $10,000 plus interest on March 31 each year starting in 2015.
2. A seven-month, 4%, $30,000 note payable issued on July 1, 2014. Interest and principal are payable at maturity.
3. A 30-month, 5%, $120,000 note payable issued on September 1, 2014. Emerald Enterprises is required to pay $4,000 plus interest on the first day of each month starting on October 1, 2014. All payments are up to date.

Instructions

(a) Calculate the current portion of each note payable.
(b) Calculate the non-current portion of each note payable.
(c) Calculate any interest payable at December 31, 2014.

Prepare current liabilities section of balance sheet. Calculate current and acid-test ratios. (SO 5) AP

E10–14   The following selected account balances are from LightHouse Distributors' adjusted trial balance at September 30, 2014:

Accounts payable	$ 90,000
Accounts receivable	182,000
Bank overdraft	62,500
CPP payable	7,500
EI payable	3,750
HST payable	15,000
Income tax payable	35,000
Interest payable	10,000
Merchandise inventory	275,000
Mortgage payable	150,000
Notes payable	100,000
Prepaid expenses	12,500
Property taxes payable	10,000
Redemption rewards liability	5,000
Unearned gift card revenue	30,000
Vacation pay payable	13,500
Warranty liability	22,500
Workers' compensation payable	1,250

Additional information:

1. On September 30, 2014, the unused operating line of credit is $75,000.
2. Redemption rewards, warranties, and gift cards are expected to be redeemed within one year.
3. Of the mortgage, $10,000 is due each year.
4. Of the note payable, $1,000 is due at the end of each month.

Instructions

(a) Prepare the current liabilities section of the balance sheet.
(b) Calculate LightHouse's current ratio and acid-test ratio.
(c) Explain why the company did not report any cash as part of its current assets.

Calculate gross pay and payroll deductions; record payroll. (SO 4, 6) AP

*E10–15   Kate Gough's regular hourly wage rate is $22.60, and she receives a wage of 1.5 times the regular hourly rate for work over 40 hours per week. For the weekly pay period ended June 15, 2012, Kate worked 44 hours. Kate lives in Ontario and has a claim code of 1 for tax deductions.

Instructions

(a) Calculate Kate's gross pay, payroll deductions, and net pay. Use Illustration 10A-3 to determine her income tax deductions.
(b) Record Kate's salary on June 15, assuming it was also paid on this date.
(c) Record the employer's related payroll costs on June 15, assuming they were not paid on this date.

*E10–16   In 2012, Donald Green worked for the Green Red Company and earned a gross salary of $57,000 for the year ($4,750 per month). He was paid once a month at the end of each month.

Calculate gross pay and payroll deductions.
(SO 6) AP

Instructions

Calculate Donald's CPP and EI deductions for the following:

(a) September 2012
(b) October 2012
(c) November 2012
(d) December 2012
(e) In total for 2012

▶ Problems: Set A

P10–1A   Crab Apple Tree Farm has a December 31 fiscal year end. The company has six notes payable outstanding on December 31, 2014, as follows:

Calculate current and non-current portion of notes payable, and interest payable.
(SO 1, 5) AP

1. A 10-month, 5%, $35,000 note payable issued on August 1, 2014. Interest is payable monthly on the first day of each month starting on September 1.
2. A four-month, 4%, $15,000 note payable issued on September 1, 2014. Interest and principal are payable at maturity.
3. A six-month, 4.5%, $26,000 note payable issued on November 1, 2014. Interest and principal are payable at maturity.
4. A five-year, 3.5%, $60,000 note payable issued on March 31, 2014. Crab Apple Tree Farm is required to pay $12,000 plus interest on March 31 each year starting in 2015.
5. A six-year, 5%, $100,000 note payable issued on October 1, 2014. Crab Apple Tree Farm is required to pay $2,000 plus interest on the first day of each month starting on November 1, 2014. All payments are up to date.
6. A four-year, 5%, $40,000 note payable issued on January 31, 2013. Crab Apple Tree Farm is required to pay $10,000 every January 31 starting in 2014. Interest is payable monthly on the last day of each month, starting on February 28, 2013.

Instructions

(a) Calculate the current portion of each note payable.
(b) Calculate the non-current portion of each note payable.
(c) Calculate any interest payable at December 31, 2014.

TAKING IT FURTHER   What are the costs and benefits to the maker and the payee of the note of using a note payable in place of an account payable?

P10–2A   The current liabilities section of the December 31, 2013, balance sheet of Learnstream Company included notes payable of $14,000 and interest payable of $490. The note payable was issued to Tanner Company on June 30, 2013. Interest of 7% is payable at maturity, March 31, 2014.
The following selected transactions occurred in the year ended December 31, 2014:

Record note transactions; show financial statement presentation.
(SO 1, 5) AP

Jan. 12   Purchased merchandise on account from McCoy Company for $20,000, terms n/30. Learnstream uses a perpetual inventory system.
      31   Issued a $20,000, three-month, 5% note to McCoy Company in payment of its account. Interest is payable monthly.
Feb. 28   Paid interest on the McCoy note (see January 31 transaction).
Mar. 31   Paid the Tanner note, plus interest.
      31   Paid interest on the McCoy note (see January 31 transaction).
Apr. 30   Paid the McCoy note, plus one month's interest (see January 31 transaction).
Aug. 1   Purchased equipment from Drouin Equipment by paying $11,000 cash and signing a $30,000, 10-month, 6% note. Interest is payable at maturity.
Sept. 30   Borrowed $100,000 cash from the First Interprovincial Bank by signing a 10-year, 5% note payable. Interest is payable quarterly on December 31, March 31, June 30, and September 30. Of the principal, $10,000 must be paid each September 30.
Dec. 31   Paid interest on the First Interprovincial Bank note (see September 30 transaction).

Instructions

(a) Record the transactions and any adjustments required at December 31.
(b) Show the balance sheet presentation of notes payable and interest payable at December 31.
(c) Show the income statement presentation of interest expense for the year.

TAKING IT FURTHER   Why is it important to correctly classify notes payable as either current or non-current in the balance sheet?

Record current liability transactions; prepare current liabilities section.
(SO 1, 2, 4, 5) AP

P10–3A   On January 1, 2014, Shumway Software Company's general ledger contained these liability accounts:

Accounts payable	$37,900
Redemption rewards liability	4,500
CPP payable	1,580
EI payable	730
HST payable	9,230
Income tax payable	3,367
Unearned revenue	15,000
Vacation pay payable	9,035

In January, the following selected transactions occurred:

Jan.	2	Issued a $50,000, four-month, 7% note. Interest is payable at maturity.
	5	Sold merchandise for $8,800 cash, plus 13% HST. The cost of this sale was $4,600. Shumway Software uses a perpetual inventory system.
	12	Provided services for customers who had paid $8,500 cash in advance. (*Hint:* Part of this is HST and the remaining amount is Service Revenue.)
	14	Paid the Receiver General (federal government) for sales taxes collected in December 2013.
	15	Paid the Receiver General for amounts owing from the December payroll for CPP, EI, and income tax.
	17	Paid $15,000 to creditors on account.
	20	Sold 500 units of a new product on account for $55 per unit, plus 13% HST. This new product has a one-year warranty. It is estimated that 9% of the units sold will be returned for repair at an average cost of $10 per unit. The cost of this sale was $25 per unit.
	29	During the month, provided $2,300 of services for customers who redeemed their customer loyalty rewards. Assume that HST of 13% is included in $2,300.
	31	Issued 30,000 loyalty rewards points worth $1 each. Based on past experience, 20% of these points are expected to be redeemed.
	31	Recorded and paid the monthly payroll. Gross salaries were $17,500. Amounts withheld included CPP of $809, EI of $320, and income tax of $3,544.

Instructions

(a) Record the transactions.
(b) Record adjusting entries for the following:
    1. Interest on the note payable
    2. The estimated warranty liability
    3. Employee benefits for CPP, EI, and vacation pay (accrued at a rate of 4%)
    4. Estimated property taxes of $8,940 for the 2014 calendar year
(c) Prepare the current liabilities section of the balance sheet at January 31.

TAKING IT FURTHER   Explain how and when the Vacation Pay Payable account balance is paid.

Record warranty transactions.
(SO 2) AP

P10–4A   On January 1, 2012, Hopewell Company began a warranty program to stimulate sales. It is estimated that 5% of the units sold will be returned for repair at an estimated cost of $30 per unit. Sales and warranty figures for the three years ended December 31 are as follows:

	2012	2013	2014
Sales (units)	1,500	1,700	1,800
Sales price per unit	$150	$120	$125
Units returned for repair under warranty	75	90	105
Actual warranty costs	$2,250	$2,400	$2,640

Instructions

(a) Calculate the warranty expense for each year and warranty liability at the end of each year.
(b) Record the warranty transactions for each year. Credit Repair Parts Inventory for the actual warranty costs.
(c) To date, what percentage of the units sold have been returned for repair under warranty? What has been the average actual warranty cost per unit for the three-year period?

TAKING IT FURTHER   Assume that at December 31, 2014, management reassesses its original estimates and decides that it is more likely that the company will have to service 7% of the units sold in 2014. Management also determines that the average actual cost per unit incurred to date (as calculated in [c] above) is more reasonable than its original estimate. What should be the balance in the warranty liability account at December 31, 2014?

P10–5A   Save-Always Stores started a customer loyalty program at the beginning of 2013 in which customers making cash purchases of gasoline at Save-Always Gas Bars are issued rewards in the form of grocery coupons. For each litre of gasoline purchased, the customer gets a grocery coupon for 3.5 cents that can be redeemed in Save-Always Food Stores. The coupons have no expiry date. Save-Always Stores began selling gift cards in 2014 that do not have expiry dates.

Record customer loyalty program and gift card transactions; determine impact on financial statements. (SO 2) AP

The following are selected transactions in 2013 and 2014:

1. In 2013, the Gas Bars sold 3.5 million litres of gasoline, issuing grocery coupons for these sales.
2. In 2013, customers redeemed $45,000 of the grocery coupons in the Food Stores while purchasing $1.8 million of groceries, paying the balance in cash.
3. In 2014, the Gas Bars sold 4,250,000 litres of gasoline, issuing grocery coupons for these sales.
4. In 2014, customers redeemed $52,500 of the grocery coupons in the Food Stores while purchasing $2,230,000 of groceries, paying for the balance in cash.
5. In 2014, customers purchased $75,000 of gift cards, and $45,400 of the cards were redeemed by the end of the year.

Instructions

(a) Indicate if the following activities will increase, decrease, or have no effect on each of revenues, expenses, and profit:
   1. Issuing grocery coupons
   2. Redeeming grocery coupons
   3. Issuing gift cards
   4. Redeeming gift cards
(b) Record the above transactions.
(c) What balances will be included in current liabilities at December 31, 2013 and 2014, regarding the customer loyalty program and gift cards?

TAKING IT FURTHER   What factors should management consider in determining if current liabilities are correctly valued at December 31, 2014?

P10–6A   Mega Company, a public company, is preparing its financial statements for the year ended December 31, 2014. It is now January 31, 2015, and the following situations are being reviewed to determine the appropriate accounting treatment:

Discuss reporting of contingencies and record provisions. (SO 3, 5) AP

1. Mega Company is being sued for $4 million for a possible malfunction of one of its products. In July 2014, a customer suffered a serious injury while operating the product. The company is vigorously defending itself as it is clear the customer was intoxicated when using the product.
2. In a separate lawsuit, Mega is being sued for $3 million by an employee who was injured on the job in February 2014. It is likely that the company will lose this lawsuit, but a reasonable estimate cannot be made of the amount of the expected settlement.
3. Since June 2012, Mega has guaranteed a $1-million bank loan for one of its main suppliers. In September 2014, the supplier started experiencing financial difficulties, which have continued. On December 16, 2014, the bank called Mega Company to confirm that if the supplier is unable repay the loan in January 2015, the bank will be seeking payment from Mega Company under the guarantee.
4. On December 7, 2014, a potential customer injured himself when he slipped on the floor in the foyer of Mega Company's office building. Mega Company did not have appropriate floor mats in place and melting snow from the customer's boots made the floor very dangerous. Mega has negotiated a potential settlement of $200,000 with the individual's lawyer.

Instructions

For each of the above situations, recommend whether Mega Company should (1) make an accrual in its December 31, 2014, financial statements; (2) disclose the situation in the notes to the financial statements; or (3) not report it. Provide a rationale for your recommendations.

TAKING IT FURTHER   What are the potential benefits and costs of making an accrual for a contingency as opposed to only disclosing it in the notes to the financial statements?

Prepare payroll register and record payroll. (SO 4) AP

P10–7A Sure Value Hardware has four employees who are paid on an hourly basis, plus time and a half for hours worked in excess of 40 hours a week. Payroll data for the week ended March 14, 2014, follow:

Employee	Total Hours	Hourly Rate	CPP	EI	Income Tax	United Way
I. Dahl	37.5	$17.00	$29.22	$11.67	$ 82.25	$ 7.50
F. Gualtieri	42	16.00	30.72	12.59	91.20	8.00
G. Ho	44	15.50	31.96	13.05	97.50	5.00
A. Israeli	46	15.50	34.26	13.90	107.75	10.00

Instructions

(a) Prepare a payroll register for the weekly payroll.
(b) Record the payroll on March 14 and the accrual of employee benefits expense. Assume the company accrues 4% for vacation pay.
(c) Record the payment of the payroll on March 14.
(d) Record the payment of employee benefits on April 15.

TAKING IT FURTHER Does the owner of a proprietorship need to deduct CPP, EI, and income taxes on his or her drawings?

Record payroll transactions and calculate balances in payroll liability accounts. (SO 4) AP

P10–8A On January 31, 2014, Cardston Company had the following payroll liability accounts in its ledger:

Canada Pension Plan payable	$ 7,887	Life insurance payable	$ 855
Disability insurance payable	1,280	Union dues payable	1,450
Employment Insurance payable	3,755	Vacation pay payable	20,520
Income tax payable	16,252	Workers' compensation payable	4,275

In February, the following transactions occurred:

Feb.	4	Sent a cheque to the union treasurer for union dues.
	7	Sent a cheque to the insurance company for the disability and life insurance.
	13	Issued a cheque to the Receiver General for the amounts due for CPP, EI, and income tax.
	20	Paid the amount due to the workers' compensation plan.
	28	Completed the monthly payroll register, which shows gross salaries $92,600; CPP withheld $4,281; EI withheld $1,695; income tax withheld $17,595; union dues withheld $1,574; and long-term disability insurance premiums $1,380.
	28	Prepared payroll cheques for the February net pay and distributed the cheques to the employees.
	28	Recorded an adjusting journal entry to record February employee benefits for CPP, EI, workers' compensation at 5% of gross pay, vacation pay at 4% of gross pay, and life insurance at 1% of gross pay.

Instructions

(a) Journalize the February transactions and adjustments.
(b) Calculate the balances in each of the payroll liability accounts at February 28, 2014.

TAKING IT FURTHER Why do employers need an employee earnings record for each employee as well as a payroll register?

Prepare current liabilities section; calculate and comment on ratios. (SO 5) AP

P10–9A Maple Leaf Foods Inc. reports the following current assets and current liabilities at December 31, 2011 (in thousands):

Accounts payable and accruals	$482,059
Accounts receivable	133,504
Bank indebtedness	36,404
Biological assets	49,265
Current portion of long-term debt	5,618
Income and other taxes recoverable	43,789
Inventories	293,231
Notes receivable	98,545
Other current liabilities	20,409
Prepaid expenses and other assets	24,688
Provisions	44,255

Instructions

(a) Prepare the current liabilities section of the balance sheet.

(b) Calculate the current and acid-test ratios.

(c) At December 31, 2010, Maple Leaf Foods Inc. had current assets of $583,557 thousand, cash, short-term investments plus receivables of $217,751 thousand, and current liabilities of $1,091,960 thousand. Did the current and acid-test ratios improve or weaken in 2011?

TAKING IT FURTHER   What other factors should be considered in assessing Maple Leaf Foods' liquidity?

*P10–10A   Western Electric Company pays its support staff weekly and its electricians on a semi-monthly basis. The following support staff payroll information is available for the week ended June 8, 2012:   *Calculate payroll deductions; prepare payroll register. (SO 6) AP*

Employee Name	Weekly Earnings	Claim Code
Chris Tanm	$ 945	2
Terry Ng	1,130	4
Olga Stavtech	1,130	1
Alana Mandell	1,067	1

The electricians' salaries are based on their experience in the field, as well as the number of years they have worked for the company. All three electricians have been with the company more than two years. The annual salaries of these employees are as follows:

Employee Name	Annual Salary for 2012
Sam Goodspeed	$43,440
Marino Giancarlo	64,770
Hillary Ridley	76,880

Instructions

(a) Prepare a payroll register for June 8, 2012, weekly payroll for the support staff. Calculate the CPP and EI deductions using the formula provided in Appendix 10A. Use the tables in Illustration 10A-3 to determine federal and provincial income taxes.

(b) Calculate the CPP and EI deductions for each of the electricians for their June 15, 2012, semi-monthly payroll.

(c) In which semi-monthly pay period will each of the electricians reach their maximum CPP and EI payments for 2012?

TAKING IT FURTHER   Why are there separate payroll deduction tables for determining weekly, semi-monthly, and monthly income tax deductions?

▶ Problems: Set B

P10–1B   Juniper Bush Farm has a December 31 fiscal year end. The company has six notes payable outstanding on December 31, 2014, as follows: *Calculate current and non-current portion of notes payable, and interest payable. (SO 1, 5) AP*

1. A nine-month, 5%, $25,000 note payable issued on July 1, 2014. Interest is payable monthly on the first day of each month starting on August 1.

2. A six-month, 4%, $10,000 note payable issued on September 1, 2014. Interest and principal are payable at maturity.

3. A seven-month, 4.5%, $40,000 note payable issued on November 1, 2014. Interest and principal are payable at maturity.

4. A five-year, 3.75%, $80,000 note payable issued on May 31, 2014. Juniper Bush Farm is required to pay $16,000 plus interest on May 31 each year starting in 2015.

5. A three-year, 4.25%, $126,000 note payable issued on October 1, 2014. Juniper Bush Farm is required to pay $3,500 plus interest on the first day of each month starting on November 1, 2014. All payments are up to date.

6. A four-year, 5%, $50,000 note payable issued on March 31, 2013. Juniper Bush Farm is required to pay $12,500 every March 31 starting in 2014. Interest is payable monthly at the end of the month, starting on April 30, 2013.

Instructions

(a) Calculate the current portion of each note payable.

(b) Calculate the non-current portion of each note payable.

(c) Calculate any interest payable at December 31, 2014.

TAKING IT FURTHER   What are the costs and benefits to the maker and the payee of the note of using a note payable in place of an account payable?

Record note transactions; show financial statement presentation. (SO 1, 5) AP

P10–2B   MileHi Mountain Bikes markets mountain-bike tours to clients vacationing in various locations in the mountains of British Columbia. The current liabilities section of the October 31, 2013, balance sheet included notes payable of $15,000 and interest payable of $375 related to a six-month, 6% note payable to Eifert Company on December 1, 2013.

During the year ended October 31, 2014, MileHi had the following transactions related to notes payable:

2013

Dec. 1   Paid the $15,000 Eifert note, plus interest.

2014

Apr. 1   Issued a $75,000, nine-month, 7% note to Mountain Real Estate for the purchase of additional mountain property on which to build bike trails. Interest is payable quarterly on July 1, October 1, and at maturity on January 1, 2015.

    30   Purchased Mongoose bikes to use as rentals for $8,000, terms n/30.

May 31   Issued Mongoose an $8,000, three-month, 8% note payable in settlement of its account (see April 30 transaction). Interest is payable at maturity.

July 1   Paid interest on the Mountain Real Estate note (see April 1 transaction).

Aug. 31   Paid the Mongoose note, plus interest (see May 31 transaction).

Oct. 1   Paid interest on the Mountain Real Estate note (see April 1 transaction).

    1   Borrowed $90,000 cash from Western Bank by issuing a five-year, 6% note. Interest is payable monthly on the first of the month. Principal payments of $18,000 must be made on the anniversary of the note each year.

Instructions

(a) Record the transactions and any adjustments required at October 31, 2014.

(b) Show the balance sheet presentation of notes payable and interest payable at October 31, 2014.

(c) Show the income statement presentation of interest expense for the year.

TAKING IT FURTHER   Why is it important to correctly classify notes payable as either current or non-current in the balance sheet?

Record current liability transactions; prepare current liabilities section. (SO 1, 2, 4, 5) AP

P10–3B   On January 1, 2014, Zaur Company's general ledger had these liability accounts:

Accounts payable	$63,700
Redemption rewards liability	2,150
CPP payable	2,152
EI payable	1,019
HST payable	11,390
Income tax payable	4,563
Unearned revenue	16,000
Vacation pay payable	9,120
Warranty liability	5,750

In January, the following selected transactions occurred:

Jan. 5   Sold merchandise for $15,800 cash, plus 13% HST. Zaur uses a periodic inventory system.

    12   Provided services for customers who had previously made advance payments of $7,000. (*Hint:* Part of this is HST and the remaining amount is Service Revenue.)

    14   Paid the Receiver General (federal government) sales taxes collected in December 2013.

    15   Paid the Receiver General for amounts owing from the December payroll for CPP, EI, and income tax.

    16   Borrowed $18,000 from Second National Bank on a three-month, 6% note. Interest is payable monthly on the 15th day of the month.

    17   Paid $35,000 to creditors on account.

    20   Sold 500 units of a new product on account for $60 per unit, plus 13% HST. This new product has a two-year warranty. It is expected that 6% of the units sold will be returned for repair at an average cost of $10 per unit.

    30   Customers redeemed $1,750 of loyalty rewards in exchange for services. Assume that HST of 13% is included in this amount.

    31   Issued 50,000 loyalty points worth $1 each. Based on past experience, 10% of these points are expected to be redeemed.

    31   Determined that the company had used $875 of parts inventory in January to honour warranty contracts.

    31   Recorded and paid the monthly payroll. Gross salaries were $25,350. Amounts withheld include CPP of $1,183, EI of $464, and income tax of $4,563.

Instructions

(a) Record the transactions.

(b) Record adjusting entries for the following:
   1. Interest on the note payable for half a month
   2. The estimated warranty liability
   3. Employee benefits, which include CPP, EI, and vacation pay that is accrued at a rate of 4%

(c) Prepare the current liabilities section of the balance sheet at January 31.

TAKING IT FURTHER   Explain how and when the Vacation Pay Payable account balance is paid.

P10–4B   On January 1, 2012, Logue Company began a warranty program to stimulate sales. It is estimated that 5% of the units sold will be returned for repair at an estimated cost of $25 per unit. Sales and warranty figures for the three years ended December 31 are as follows:

Record warranty transactions. (SO 2) AP

	2012	2013	2014
Sales (units)	1,200	1,320	1,420
Sales price per unit	$100	$105	$110
Units returned for repair under warranty	60	70	80
Actual warranty costs	$1,275	$1,600	$1,960

Instructions

(a) Calculate the warranty expense for each year and warranty liability at the end of each year.

(b) Record the warranty transactions for each year. Credit Repair Parts Inventory for the actual warranty costs.

(c) To date, what percentage of the units sold have been returned for repair under warranty? What has been the average actual warranty cost per unit for the three-year period?

TAKING IT FURTHER   Suppose at December 31, 2014, management reassesses its original estimates and decides that it is more likely that the company will have to service 7% of the units sold in 2014. Management also determines that the original estimate of the cost per unit is the appropriate cost to use for future repair work. What should be the balance in the warranty liability account at December 31, 2014?

P10–5B   Caribou County Service Station started a customer loyalty program at the beginning of 2013 in which customers making cash purchases of gasoline at the gas bar are issued rewards in the form of coupons. For each litre of gasoline purchased, the customer gets a coupon for 2.5 cents that can be redeemed in the service department toward such things as oil changes or repairs. The coupons have no expiry date. Caribou County Service Station began selling gift cards in 2014 that do not have expiry dates.
   The following are selected transactions in 2013 and 2014:

Record customer loyalty program and gift card transactions; determine impact on financial statements. (SO 2) AP

1. In 2013, the gas bar sold 750,000 litres of gasoline, issuing coupons for these sales.
2. In 2013, customers redeemed $5,950 of the coupons in the service department while purchasing $23,800 of repair services for their vehicles, paying the balance in cash.
3. In 2014, the gas bar sold 810,000 litres of gasoline, issuing coupons for these sales.
4. In 2014, customers redeemed $9,500 of the coupons in the service department while purchasing $30,230 of repair services for their vehicles, paying for the balance in cash.
5. In 2014, customers purchased $3,950 of gift cards, and $1,500 of the cards were redeemed by the end of the year.

Instructions

(a) Indicate if the following items will increase, decrease, or have no effect on each of revenues, expenses, and profit:
   1. Issuing coupons
   2. Redeeming coupons
   3. Issuing gift cards
   4. Redeeming gift cards

(b) Record the above transactions.

(c) What balances will be included in current liabilities at December 31, 2013 and 2014, regarding the customer loyalty program and gift cards?

TAKING IT FURTHER   What factors should management consider in determining if current liabilities are correctly valued at December 31, 2014?

P10–6B   Big Fork Company, a private company that follows ASPE, is preparing its financial statements for the year ended December 31, 2014. It is now February 15, 2015, and the following situations are being reviewed to determine the appropriate accounting treatment:

Discuss reporting of contingencies and record provisions. (SO 3, 5) AP

1. Since 2007, Big Fork has guaranteed a $250,000 bank loan for one of its main customers, Little Fork. Little Fork has always made all of its payments in a timely fashion.

2. Big Fork is being sued for $3 million for a possible malfunction of one of its products. In March 2014, a customer suffered a serious injury while operating the product. The company is defending itself but it is clear that there was an error in the published operations manual for the product. It is likely that the company will lose this lawsuit, but it is unlikely it will have to pay the full $3 million. At this point, a reasonable estimate cannot be made of the amount of the expected settlement.

3. Big Fork is being sued for $1.5 million by an employee for wrongful dismissal and defamation of character. The employee was fired on August 2, 2014. The company is vigorously defending itself because the employee had a documented history of poor performance at work.

4. On December 16, 2014, a sales representative from one of the company's suppliers injured herself on a visit to Big Fork's offices. She tripped over equipment that had not been properly stored and will be unable to work for several months as a result of her injuries. A $250,000 claim against Big Fork has been filed by the sales representative's insurance company.

Instructions

For each of the above situations, recommend whether Big Fork Company should (1) make an accrual in its December 31, 2014, financial statements; (2) disclose the situation in the notes to the financial statements; or (3) not report it. Provide a rationale for your recommendations.

TAKING IT FURTHER   What are the potential benefits and costs of making an accrual for a contingency as opposed to only disclosing it in the notes to the financial statements?

Prepare payroll register and record payroll. (SO 4) AP

P10–7B   Scoot Scooters has four employees who are paid on an hourly basis, plus time and a half for hours in excess of 40 hours a week. Payroll data for the week ended February 17, 2012, follow:

Employee	Total Hours	Hourly Rate	CPP	EI	Income Tax	United Way
P. Kilchyk	40	$15.25	$26.86	$11.16	$76.60	$5.00
B. Quon	42	15.00	28.60	11.80	83.70	7.25
C. Pospisil	40	16.25	28.84	11.90	84.10	5.50
B. Verwey	44	14.50	29.68	12.21	87.10	8.25

Instructions

(a) Prepare a payroll register for the weekly payroll.

(b) Record the payroll on February 15 and the accrual of employee benefits expense. Assume the company accrues 4% for vacation pay.

(c) Record the payment of the payroll on February 17.

(d) Record the payment of the employee benefits on March 15.

TAKING IT FURTHER   Does the owner of a proprietorship have to deduct CPP, EI, and income taxes from his or her own drawings?

Record payroll transactions and calculate balances in payroll liability accounts. (SO 4) AP

P10–8B   On March 31, 2014, Babb Company had the following payroll liability accounts in its ledger:

Canada Pension Plan payable	$ 6,907	Life insurance payable	$ 756
Disability insurance payable	1,134	Union dues payable	1,285
Employment Insurance payable	3,320	Vacation pay payable	3,024
Income tax payable	14,364	Workers' compensation payable	3,780

In April, the following transactions occurred:

Apr.	4	Sent a cheque to the union treasurer for union dues.
	7	Sent a cheque to the insurance company for the disability and life insurance.
	13	Issued a cheque to the Receiver General for the amounts due for CPP, EI, and income tax.
	20	Paid the amount due to the workers' compensation plan.
	28	Completed the monthly payroll register, which shows gross salaries $83,160; CPP withheld $3,799; EI withheld $1,522; income tax withheld $15,800; union dues withheld $1,414; and long-term disability insurance premiums $1,247.
	28	Prepared payroll cheques for the April net pay and distributed the cheques to the employees.
	28	Recorded an adjusting journal entry to record April employee benefits for CPP, EI, workers' compensation at 5% of gross pay, vacation pay at 4% of gross pay, and life insurance at 1% of gross pay.

Instructions

(a) Journalize the April transactions and adjustments.

(b) Calculate the balances in each of the payroll liability accounts at April 30, 2014.

<u>**TAKING IT FURTHER**</u>   Why do employers need an employee earnings record for each employee as well as a payroll register?

P10–9B   BCE Inc., more commonly known as Bell Canada, reports the following current assets and current liabilities at December 31, 2011 (in millions of dollars):

Prepare current liabilities section; calculate and comment on ratios.
(SO 5) AP

Cash	$ 130
Cash equivalents	45
Current tax liabilities	47
Debt due within one year	2,106
Dividends payable	415
Interest payable	134
Inventory	427
Other current assets	152
Prepaid expenses	262
Trade and other receivables	3,162
Trade payables and other liabilities	4,056

Instructions

(a) Prepare the current liabilities section of the balance sheet.
(b) Calculate the current and the acid-test ratio.
(c) On December 31, 2010, BCE Inc. had current assets of $4,655 million, cash and cash equivalents plus trade and other receivables of $3,795 million, and current liabilities of $6,954 million. Did the current and acid-test ratios improve or weaken in 2011?

<u>**TAKING IT FURTHER**</u>   What other factors should be considered in assessing BCE Inc.'s liquidity?

*P10–10B   Slovak Plumbing Company pays its support staff weekly and its plumbers on a semi-monthly basis. The following support staff payroll information is available for the week ended May 11, 2012:

Calculate payroll deductions and prepare payroll register.
(SO 6) AP

Employee Name	Weekly Earnings	Claim Code
Dan Quinn	$ 985	1
Karol Holub	1,037	3
Al Lowhorn	1,080	1
Irina Kostra	950	4

The plumbers' salaries are based on their experience in the field, as well as the number of years they have worked for the company. All three plumbers have been with the company more than two years. The annual salary of these employees is as follows:

Employee Name	Annual Salary for 2012
Branislav Dolina	$80,700
Henrietta Koleno	62,500
Aida Krneta	44,120

Instructions

(a) Prepare a payroll register for May 11, 2012, weekly payroll for the support staff. Calculate the CPP and EI deductions using the formula provided in Appendix 10A. Use the tables in Illustration 10A-3 to determine federal and provincial income taxes.
(b) Calculate the CPP and EI deductions for each of the plumbers for their May 15, 2012, semi-monthly payroll.
(c) In which semi-monthly pay period will each of the plumbers reach their maximum CPP and EI payments for 2012?

<u>**TAKING IT FURTHER**</u>   Why are there separate payroll deduction tables for determining income tax deductions for weekly, semi-monthly, and monthly pay periods?

▶ Continuing Cookie Chronicle

(***Note:*** This is a continuation of the Cookie Chronicle from Chapters 1 through 9.)

Natalie has had much success with her cookie-making lessons over the last number of months. A few parents who have attended have shown interest in purchasing gift certificates from Natalie. Natalie is considering a gift certificate that would include a one-hour cookie-making lesson and all of the supplies needed to create two dozen cookies.

Natalie wants to make sure that she has considered all of the risks and rewards of issuing gift certificates. She has come to you with the following questions:

1. From what I understand, if I sell a gift certificate, I need to be recording the money received as "unearned revenue." I am a little confused. How is the use of this account the same as the money that I received from schools that have paid me a deposit for pre-booked cookie-making lessons?
2. What if I record the sale of gift certificates as revenue instead of unearned revenue? Technically, I have made a sale of a gift certificate and therefore should be recording amounts received as revenue for the sale of a gift certificate. What if a gift certificate is never used? Does this not justify a sale being recorded?
3. How do I make sure that the gift certificates that I have sold are in fact used? How do I make sure that the ones that I have sold have not been duplicated and used again?

Instructions

Answer Natalie's questions.

Cumulative Coverage—Chapters 3 to 10

The unadjusted trial balance of LeBrun Company at its year end, July 31, 2014, is as follows:

LEBRUN COMPANY
Trial Balance
July 31, 2014

	Debit	Credit
Cash	$ 16,550	
Petty cash	200	
Accounts receivable	38,500	
Allowance for doubtful accounts		$ 2,000
Note receivable (due December 31, 2014)	10,000	
Merchandise inventory	45,900	
Prepaid expenses	16,000	
Land	50,000	
Building	155,000	
Accumulated depreciation—building		10,800
Equipment	25,000	
Accumulated depreciation—equipment		12,200
Patent	75,000	
Accumulated amortization—patent		15,000
Accounts payable		78,900
Warranty liability		6,000
Notes payable (due August 1, 2029)		124,200
S. LeBrun, capital		124,700
S. LeBrun, drawings	54,000	
Sales		750,000
Cost of goods sold	450,000	
Operating expenses	181,220	
Interest revenue		400
Interest expense	6,830	
Totals	$1,124,200	$1,124,200

Adjustment information:

1. The July 31 bank statement reported debit memos for service charges of $50 and a $650 NSF (not sufficient funds) cheque that had been received from a customer for the purchase of merchandise in July.
2. Estimated uncollectible accounts receivable at July 31 are $3,850.
3. The note receivable bears interest of 8% and was issued on December 31, 2013. Interest is payable the first of each month.
4. A physical count of inventory determined that $39,200 of inventory was actually on hand.
5. Prepaid expenses of $5,500 expired in the year (use the account Operating Expenses).
6. Depreciation is calculated on the long-lived assets using the following methods and useful lives:

> Building: straight-line, 25 years, $15,000 residual value
> Equipment: double diminishing-balance, five years, $2,500 residual value
> Patent: straight-line, five years, no residual value

7. The 6% note payable was issued on August 1, 2004. Interest is paid monthly at the beginning of each month for the previous month's interest. Of the note principal, $1,680 is currently due.
8. Estimated warranty costs for July are $1,975 (use Operating Expenses).

Instructions

(a) Prepare the adjusting journal entries required at July 31. (Round your calculations to the nearest dollar.)
(b) Prepare an adjusted trial balance at July 31.
(c) Prepare a multiple-step income statement and statement of owner's equity for the year and a balance sheet at July 31.

BROADENING YOUR PERSPECTIVE | CHAPTER 10

▶ Financial Reporting and Analysis

Financial Reporting Problem

BYP10–1 Refer to the financial statements of **Reitmans (Canada) Limited** and the Notes to the Financial Statements in Appendix A.

Instructions

Answer the following questions about the company's current and contingent liabilities:

(a) What were Reitmans' total current liabilities at January 28, 2012? What was the increase (decrease) in total current liabilities from the previous year?
(b) Which specific current liabilities and in what order did Reitmans present on the January 28, 2012, balance sheet?
(c) Calculate Reitmans' current ratio, acid-test ratio, receivables, and inventory turnover ratios, and operating cycle for 2012 and 2011. Comment on Reitmans' overall liquidity.
(d) Does Reitmans report any contingencies? If so, where are they disclosed? Explain the nature, amount, and significance of Reitmans' contingencies, if any.

Interpreting Financial Statements

BYP10–2 **Canadian Tire Corporation, Limited** reported the following information about contingencies in the notes to its December 31, 2011, financial statements:

CANADIAN TIRE CORPORATION, LIMITED
Notes to the Consolidated Financial Statements
December 31, 2011

23. Contingencies

Legal matters

The Company and certain of its subsidiaries are party to a number of legal proceedings. The Company has determined that each such proceeding constitutes a routine legal matter incidental to the business conducted by the Company and that the ultimate disposition of the proceedings will not have a material effect on its consolidated earnings, cash flows, or financial position.

The Canadian Tire Bank (a wholly-owned subsidiary) is the subject of two class action proceedings regarding allegations that certain fees charged on the Bank issued credit cards are not permitted under the Quebec Consumer Protection Act. The Bank has determined that it has a solid defense to both actions on the basis that banking and cost of borrowing disclosure is a matter of exclusive federal jurisdiction. Accordingly, no provision has been made for amounts, if any, that would be payable in the event of an adverse outcome. If adversely decided, the total aggregate exposure to the Company would have been approximately $24.4 million at December 31, 2011.

Instructions

(a) Why would Canadian Tire disclose information about these legal disputes, including reporting the amount of the potential loss, in the notes to the financial statements instead of accruing an amount for these as liabilities in its accounting records?

(b) Canadian Tire also discloses that it has made "provisions for the cost of legal issues that have not yet been settled. The provisions are based on the Company's best estimate of the expected settlement amount. The amount of the provisions for legal issues is $11.1 million at December 31, 2011 (2010 − $0.3 million)." Why would Canadian Tire accrue for this amount when it hasn't made an accrual for the related legal dispute?

▶ Critical Thinking

Collaborative Learning Activity

Note to instructor: Additional instructions and material for this group activity can be found on the Instructor Resource Site and in *WileyPLUS*.

BYP10–3 In this group activity, your group must decide on the best accounting treatment for a contingency. Your instructor will provide the class with a scenario and each group will be required to decide if an accrual should be made and, if so, for how much. Groups will simultaneously report to the class and will be required to defend their decisions.

Communication Activity

BYP10–4 The Show Time movie theatre sells thousands of gift certificates every year. The certificates can be redeemed at any time since they have no expiry date. Some of them may never be redeemed (because they are lost or forgotten, for example). The owner of the theatre has raised some questions about the accounting for these gift certificates.

Instructions

Write an e-mail to answer the following questions from the owner:

(a) Why is a liability recorded when these certificates are sold? After all, they bring customers into the theatre, where they spend money on snacks and drinks. Why should something that helps generate additional revenue be treated as a liability?

(b) How should the gift certificates that are never redeemed be treated? At some point in the future, can the liability related to them be eliminated? If so, what type of journal entry would be made?

Ethics Case

BYP10–5 Nice Nuke Corporation, which owns and operates a nuclear plant, recently received notice from the provincial government that it has to find a new disposal site for its radioactive waste. The company was also told that it is responsible for the environmental cleanup of the old site. The vice-president of engineering and the vice-president of finance meet to discuss the situation. The engineer says that it could take many years to clean up the site and that the cost could be considerable—a minimum of $50 million and perhaps as much as $100 million.

The vice-president of finance says that there is no way that the company can afford to record this liability. He says he is not even sure that he wants to disclose the potential liability, because of how this could affect the company's share price.

Instructions

(a) Who are the stakeholders in this situation?
(b) What are the alternative reporting options that the company can use?
(c) What is the likely impact of each alternative on the company's financial position?
(d) Is there anything unethical in what the vice-president of finance suggests doing about this potential liability?
(e) What do you recommend the company do?

"All About You" Activity

BYP10–6 In the "All About You" feature, you learned who is responsible for remitting income tax, CPP, and EI to the CRA if you are an employee or self-employed. You also learned that the CRA has strict guidelines as to whether someone is self-employed or an employee.

Assume that as a new graduate you are accepting a position where you will be providing consulting services to a company. You have agreed to provide the services for $3,000 a month. The company's manager of human resources suggests that you may want to be considered self-employed rather than an employee of the company. Before you make your decision, you need to better understand the CRA's guidelines and the financial implications.

Instructions

(a) Go to the Canada Revenue Agency's website at www.cra-arc.gc.ca and search for document RC4110 "Employee or Self-Employed?" What are the factors that should be considered when determining if a worker is an employee or self-employed?

(b) Assume you are an employee and you are paid monthly and that the following is deducted from your gross earnings: (*Note: The following deductions are based on the 2012 payroll tables for Ontario.*)

CPP	$134.06
EI	54.90
Income tax	407.95

What is the amount of cash you will receive each month? What is the total amount of cash you will receive in a year?

(c) Based on the information in (b), what is the total CPP you will pay in a year? What is the total EI you will pay in a year?

(d) Assume you are self-employed, and you have chosen to pay EI. What is the amount of cash you will receive each month from the company? What is the total CPP you will have to pay in a year? What is the total EI you will have to pay in a year?

(e) Assuming that you will pay the same amount of income tax as you would if you were an employee, calculate the amount of cash you will receive for the year if you are self-employed.

(f) Based on your answers to (c) and (e), do you want to be self-employed or an employee of the company? Explain.

(g) If you had the opportunity to provide consulting services to another company in your spare time, would your answer in (f) be different? Explain.

ANSWERS TO CHAPTER QUESTIONS

ANSWERS TO ACCOUNTING IN ACTION INSIGHT QUESTIONS

Business Insight, p. 535

Q: Environmental contingencies are generally considered to be harder to estimate than contingencies from lawsuits. What might be the reason for this difference?

A: The requirement to account for environmental contingencies is relatively new compared with the requirement to account for contingencies from lawsuits. Although it is difficult to predict whether the company will win or lose a lawsuit and what type of settlement may be involved, there is a vast history of case law that can be used to help a company form an opinion. Environmental regulations, in contrast, are still evolving and there is often no system (e.g., regulatory compliance audits or environmental site assessment data) that would help a company estimate the possible cost, or even the existence, of environmental contingencies for many years.

All About You Insight, p. 543

Q: If you are providing services to a company, what are the advantages and disadvantages of being a self-employed consultant versus an employee of the company?

A: As a self-employed individual, your monthly cash received from the company would be higher as no CPP, EI, and income tax will be deducted. On the other hand, you will have to make quarterly instalment payments of CPP, EI (if you choose to pay it), and income taxes. If you are self-employed, you may be able to deduct certain expenses to reduce your income tax.

However, some individuals may not manage their cash properly and may be unable to make the remittances when required. In addition, you will have to pay twice as much for CPP and you will not qualify for EI benefits. If you are self-employed, you would not qualify for other benefits offered to employees by the company, either.

ANSWERS TO SELF-STUDY QUESTIONS

1. d   2. b   3. c   4. a   5. b   6. a   7. b   8. b   9. a   *10. b

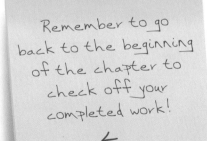

Remember to go back to the beginning of the chapter to check off your completed work!

←

Photo Credits

Logos are registered trademarks of the respective companies and are reprinted with permission.

Chapter 1 Opener: The Canadian Press Images-Mario Beauregard; Page 5: © istockphoto.com/Andreas Rodriguez; Page 26: © istockphoto.com/Jacob Wackerhausen. **Chapter 2** Opener: Courtesy Prestige Dance Academy; Page 63: ©iStockphoto.com/ NevinGiesbrecht; Page 76: ©iStockphoto.com/mihalec. **Chapter 3** Opener: Courtesy Seneca College of Applied Arts and Technology; Page 114: ©iStockphoto.com/Ashwin82; Page 122: ©iStockphoto.com/spxChrome. **Chapter 4** Opener: Courtesy Laurel Hyatt; Page 186: Copied with the permission of Canada Post Corporation; Page 187: Adapted and reprinted with the permission of Empire Company Limited; Page 188: BlackBerry®, RIM®, Research In Motion® and related trademarks, names and logos are the property of Research In Motion Limited and are registered and/or used in the U.S. and countries around the world. Used under license from Research In Motion Limited; Page 189: Used with permission of Sears Canada Inc; Page 189: Canadian National Railway Company ("CN"), reproduced by authorization of CN; Page 192: © iStockphoto.com/WillSelarep. **Chapter 5** Opener: Courtesy Moulé; Page 249: © iStockphoto.com/Leah-Anne Thompson. **Chapter 6** Opener: Courtesy Gravitypope/Louise Dirks; Page 304: ©istockphoto. com/SimplyCreativePhotography; Page 319: © istockphoto.com/Lewis Wright. **Chapter 7** Opener: © Barrett & MacKay Photo; Page 365: © istockphoto.com/Peter Garbet; Page 368: © istockphoto.comARICAN. **Chapter 8** Opener: Cindy Wilson/ Telegraph-Journal; Page 419: ©iStockphoto.com/Marcus Clackson; Page 434: AP/Charles Krupa/The Canadian Press. **Chapter 9** Opener: Courtesy George Brown College; Page 474: ©istockphoto/DNY59; Page 490: ©istockphoto/Chris Reed. **Chapter 10** Page 524: © istockphoto.com/GRAZVYDAS; Page 535: The Canadian Press/Marcos Townsend; Page 543: istockphoto.com/Morgan Lane Studios. Pages 544 and 555: Shoppers Drug Mart Corporation.

Reitmans (Canada) Limited

In this appendix, we illustrate current financial reporting with a comprehensive set of corporate financial statements that are prepared in accordance with International Financial Reporting Standards (IFRS). We are grateful for permission to use the actual financial statements of Reitmans (Canada) Ltd.—Canada's largest women's specialty clothing retailer.

Reitman's financial statement package features a statement of earnings, statement of comprehensive income, balance sheets, statement of changes in shareholders' equity, statement of cash flows, and notes to the financial statements. The financial statements are preceded by two reports: a statement of management's responsibilities for financial reporting and the independent auditors' report.

We encourage students to use these financial statements in conjunction with the relevant material in the textbook. As well, these statements can be used to solve the Financial Reporting Problem in the Broadening Your Perspective section of the end-of-chapter material.

Annual reports, including the financial statements, are reviewed in detail in *WileyPLUS* and on the companion website to this textbook.

MANAGEMENT'S RESPONSIBILITY FOR FINANCIAL STATEMENTS

The accompanying financial statements and all the information in the annual report are the responsibility of management and have been approved by the Board of Directors of Reitmans (Canada) Limited.

These financial statements have been prepared by management in conformity with International Financial Reporting Standards and include amounts that are based on best estimates and judgments. The financial information used elsewhere in the annual report is consistent with that in the financial statements.

Management of the Company has developed and maintains a system of internal accounting controls. Management believes that this system of internal accounting controls provides reasonable assurances that financial records are reliable and form a proper basis for the preparation of the financial statements and that assets are properly accounted for and safeguarded.

The Board of Directors carries out its responsibility for the financial statements in this annual report principally through its Audit Committee, consisting of all outside directors. The Audit Committee reviews the Company's annual financial statements and recommends their approval to the Board of Directors. The auditors appointed by the shareholders have full access to the Audit Committee, with and without management being present.

These financial statements have been examined by the auditors appointed by the shareholders, KPMG LLP, Chartered Accountants and their report is presented hereafter.

(signed) Jeremy H. Reitman
Chairman and
Chief Executive Officer

(signed) Eric Williams, CA
Vice-President, Finance and
Chief Financial Officer

March 28, 2012

INDEPENDENT AUDITORS' REPORT

To the Shareholders of Reitmans (Canada) Limited

We have audited the accompanying financial statements of Reitmans (Canada) Limited, which comprise the balance sheets as at January 28, 2012, January 29, 2011 and January 31, 2010, the statements of earnings, comprehensive income, changes in shareholders' equity and cash flows for the years ended January 28, 2012 and January 29, 2011, and notes, comprising a summary of significant accounting policies and other explanatory information.

Management's Responsibility for the Financial Statements

Management is responsible for the preparation and fair presentation of these financial statements in accordance with International Financial Reporting Standards, and for such internal control as management determines is necessary to enable the preparation of financial statements that are free from material misstatement, whether due to fraud or error.

Auditors' Responsibility

Our responsibility is to express an opinion on these financial statements based on our audits. We conducted our audits in accordance with Canadian generally accepted auditing standards. Those standards require that we comply with ethical requirements and plan and perform the audit to obtain reasonable assurance about whether the financial statements are free from material misstatement.

An audit involves performing procedures to obtain audit evidence about the amounts and disclosures in the financial statements. The procedures selected depend on our judgment, including the assessment of the risks of material misstatement of the financial statements, whether due to fraud or error. In making those risk assessments, we consider internal control relevant to the entity's preparation and fair presentation of the financial statements in order to design audit procedures that are appropriate in the circumstances, but not for the purpose of expressing an opinion on the effectiveness of the entity's internal control. An audit also includes evaluating the appropriateness of accounting policies used and the reasonableness of accounting estimates made by management, as well as evaluating the overall presentation of the financial statements.

We believe that the audit evidence we have obtained in our audits is sufficient and appropriate to provide a basis for our audit opinion.

Opinion

In our opinion, the financial statements present fairly, in all material respects, the financial position of Reitmans (Canada) Limited as at January 28, 2012, January 29, 2011 and January 31, 2010, and its financial performance and its cash flows for the years ended January 28, 2012 and January 29, 2011 in accordance with International Financial Reporting Standards.

*KPMG LLP**

Chartered Accountants

Montréal, Canada
March 28, 2012

* CA Auditor Permit no. 23443

KPMG LLP is a Canadian limited liability partnership and a member firm of the KPMG network of independent member firms affiliated with KPMG International Cooperative ("KPMG International"), a Swiss entity.
KPMG Canada provides services to KPMG LLP.

REITMANS (CANADA) LIMITED
STATEMENTS OF EARNINGS
(in thousands of Canadian dollars except per share amounts)

| | For the years ended | |
	January 28, 2012	January 29, 2011
Sales	$ 1,019,397	$ 1,059,000
Cost of goods sold (note 7)	363,333	350,671
Gross profit	656,064	708,329
Selling and distribution expenses	547,367	528,676
Administrative expenses	46,878	55,511
Results from operating activities	61,819	124,142
Finance income (note 19)	5,562	4,505
Finance costs (note 19)	1,509	845
Earnings before income taxes	65,872	127,802
Income taxes (note 11)	18,333	38,817
Net earnings	$ 47,539	$ 88,985
Earnings per share (note 20):		
Basic	$ 0.72	$ 1.33
Diluted	0.72	1.32

The accompanying notes are an integral part of these financial statements.

REITMANS (CANADA) LIMITED
STATEMENTS OF COMPREHENSIVE INCOME
(in thousands of Canadian dollars)

	For the years ended	
	January 28, 2012	**January 29, 2011**
Net earnings	$ **47,539**	$ 88,985
Other comprehensive income:		
Net change in fair value of available-for-sale financial assets (net of tax of $79; 2011 - $427) (note 19)	**530**	2,866
Reclassification of realized gains on available-for-sale financial assets to net earnings (net of tax of $22) (note 19)	**-**	(145)
Reclassification of impairment loss on available-for-sale financial assets to net earnings (net of tax of $9; 2011 - $11) (note 19)	**64**	67
Defined benefit actuarial losses (net of tax of $1,041; 2011 - $272) (note 15)	**(2,965)**	(777)
Total comprehensive income	$ **45,168**	$ 90,996

The accompanying notes are an integral part of these financial statements.

REITMANS (CANADA) LIMITED
BALANCE SHEETS
(in thousands of Canadian dollars)

	January 28, 2012	January 29, 2011	January 31, 2010
ASSETS			
CURRENT ASSETS			
Cash and cash equivalents (note 5)	$ **196,835**	$ 230,034	$ 228,577
Marketable securities	**71,442**	70,413	48,026
Trade and other receivables	**3,033**	2,866	2,926
Derivative financial asset (note 6)	**751**	-	-
Income taxes recoverable	**4,735**	-	-
Inventories (note 7)	**78,285**	73,201	63,127
Prepaid expenses	**11,902**	12,491	11,010
Total Current Assets	**366,983**	389,005	353,666
NON-CURRENT ASSETS			
Property and equipment (note 8)	**184,221**	193,064	208,362
Intangible assets (note 9)	**17,057**	13,841	9,964
Goodwill (note 10)	**42,426**	42,426	42,426
Deferred income taxes (note 11)	**23,174**	21,021	18,313
Total Non-Current Assets	**266,878**	270,352	279,065
TOTAL ASSETS	$ **633,861**	$ 659,357	$ 632,731
LIABILITIES AND SHAREHOLDERS' EQUITY			
CURRENT LIABILITIES			
Trade and other payables (note 12)	$ **63,875**	$ 64,093	$ 54,684
Derivative financial liability (note 6)	**1,505**	-	-
Deferred revenue (note 13)	**22,278**	19,834	18,122
Income taxes payable	**-**	5,998	4,677
Current portion of long-term debt (note 14)	**1,474**	1,384	1,300
Total Current Liabilities	**89,132**	91,309	78,783
NON-CURRENT LIABILITIES			
Other payables (note 12)	**11,110**	10,180	9,105
Deferred revenue (note 13)	**-**	2,384	2,686
Deferred lease credits	**17,317**	19,011	20,609
Long-term debt (note 14)	**8,573**	10,047	11,431
Pension liability (note 15)	**14,877**	13,626	11,865
Total Non-Current Liabilities	**51,877**	55,248	55,696
SHAREHOLDERS' EQUITY			
Share capital (note 16)	**39,890**	29,614	25,888
Contributed surplus	**5,158**	6,266	5,164
Retained earnings	**439,067**	468,777	461,845
Accumulated other comprehensive income (note 16)	**8,737**	8,143	5,355
Total Shareholders' Equity	**492,852**	512,800	498,252
TOTAL LIABILITIES AND SHAREHOLDERS' EQUITY	$ **633,861**	$ 659,357	$ 632,731

Commitments (note 18)

The accompanying notes are an integral part of these financial statements.

On behalf of the Board,

(signed) Jeremy H. Reitman, Director   (signed) Stephen J. Kauser, Director

REITMANS (CANADA) LIMITED
STATEMENTS OF CHANGES IN SHAREHOLDERS' EQUITY
(in thousands of Canadian dollars)

	For the years ended	
	January 28, 2012	**January 29, 2011**
SHARE CAPITAL		
Balance, beginning of the year	$ **29,614**	$ 25,888
Cash consideration on exercise of share options (note 16)	**8,828**	3,569
Ascribed value credited to share capital from exercise of share options (note 16)	**2,228**	888
Cancellation of shares pursuant to share repurchase program (note 16)	**(780)**	(731)
Balance, end of the year	**39,890**	29,614
CONTRIBUTED SURPLUS		
Balance, beginning of the year	**6,266**	5,164
Share-based compensation costs (note 17)	**1,120**	1,990
Ascribed value credited to share capital from exercise of share options (note 16)	**(2,228)**	(888)
Balance, end of the year	**5,158**	6,266
RETAINED EARNINGS		
Balance, beginning of the year	**468,777**	461,845
Net earnings	**47,539**	88,985
Dividends (note 16)	**(52,654)**	(51,895)
Premium on repurchase of Class A non-voting shares (note 16)	**(21,630)**	(29,381)
Defined benefit actuarial losses (net of tax of $1,041; 2011 - $272) (note 15)	**(2,965)**	(777)
Balance, end of the year	**439,067**	468,777
ACCUMULATED OTHER COMPREHENSIVE INCOME		
Balance, beginning of the year	**8,143**	5,355
Net change in fair value of available-for-sale financial assets (net of tax of $79; 2011 - $427) (note 19)	**530**	2,866
Reclassification of realized gains on available-for-sale financial assets to net earnings (net of tax of $22) (note 19)	**-**	(145)
Reclassification of impairment loss on available-for-sale financial assets to net earnings (net of tax of $9; 2011 - $11) (note 19)	**64**	67
Balance, end of the year (note 16)	**8,737**	8,143
Total Shareholders' Equity	$ **492,852**	$ 512,800

The accompanying notes are an integral part of these financial statements.

REITMANS (CANADA) LIMITED
STATEMENTS OF CASH FLOWS
(in thousands of Canadian dollars)

| | For the years ended | |
	January 28, 2012	January 29, 2011
CASH FLOWS FROM (USED IN) OPERATING ACTIVITIES		
Net earnings	$ 47,539	$ 88,985
Adjustments for:		
Depreciation, amortization and impairment losses	64,990	59,754
Share-based compensation costs	1,120	1,990
Amortization of deferred lease credits	(4,635)	(4,956)
Deferred lease credits	2,941	3,358
Pension contribution	(4,245)	(629)
Pension expense	1,490	1,341
Realized gain on sale of marketable securities	-	(167)
Impairment loss on available-for-sale financial assets	73	78
Net change in fair value of derivatives	754	-
Foreign exchange loss (gain)	2,942	(31)
Interest and dividend income, net	(4,147)	(3,068)
Interest paid	(682)	(797)
Interest received	1,316	1,273
Dividends received	3,460	2,546
Income taxes	18,333	38,817
	131,249	188,494
Changes in:		
Trade and other receivables	(114)	106
Inventories	(5,084)	(10,074)
Prepaid expenses	589	(1,481)
Trade and other payables	504	9,073
Deferred revenue	60	1,410
Cash generated from operating activities	127,204	187,528
Income taxes received	793	6,040
Income taxes paid	(31,060)	(46,388)
Net cash flows from operating activities	96,937	147,180
CASH FLOWS (USED IN) FROM INVESTING ACTIVITIES		
Purchases of marketable securities	(420)	(20,803)
Proceeds on sale of marketable securities	-	1,709
Additions to property and equipment and intangible assets	(59,154)	(46,922)
Cash flows used in investing activities	(59,574)	(66,016)
CASH FLOWS (USED IN) FROM FINANCING ACTIVITIES		
Dividends paid	(52,654)	(51,895)
Purchase of Class A non-voting shares for cancellation	(22,410)	(30,112)
Repayment of long-term debt	(1,384)	(1,300)
Proceeds from exercise of share options	8,828	3,569
Cash flows used in financing activities	(67,620)	(79,738)
FOREIGN EXCHANGE (LOSS) GAIN ON CASH HELD IN FOREIGN CURRENCY	(2,942)	31
NET (DECREASE) INCREASE IN CASH AND CASH EQUIVALENTS	(33,199)	1,457
CASH AND CASH EQUIVALENTS, BEGINNING OF THE YEAR	230,034	228,577
CASH AND CASH EQUIVALENTS, END OF THE YEAR	$ 196,835	$ 230,034

Supplementary cash flow information (note 25)
The accompanying notes are an integral part of these financial statements.

REITMANS (CANADA) LIMITED
NOTES TO THE FINANCIAL STATEMENTS
(all amounts in thousands of Canadian dollars except per share amounts)

1. REPORTING ENTITY

Reitmans (Canada) Limited (the "Company") is a company domiciled in Canada and is incorporated under the Canada Business Corporations Act. The address of the Company's registered office is 3300 Highway #7 West, Suite 702, Vaughan, Ontario L4K 4M3. The principal business activity of the Company is the sale of women's wear at retail.

2. BASIS OF PRESENTATION

a) Statement of Compliance

These financial statements have been prepared in accordance with International Financial Reporting Standards ("IFRS") as issued by the International Accounting Standards Board ("IASB"). These are the Company's first annual financial statements prepared under IFRS in accordance with IFRS 1, *First-time adoption of IFRS*. The first date at which IFRS was applied was January 31, 2010 ("Transition Date"). In accordance with IFRS 1, the Company has:

- Provided comparative financial information

- Applied the same accounting policies throughout all periods presented

- Retroactively applied all effective IFRS standards as at January 28, 2012, as required; and

- Applied certain optional exemptions and certain mandatory exceptions as applicable for first-time IFRS adopters.

The Company's financial statements were previously prepared in accordance with accounting principles generally accepted in Canada ("Canadian GAAP"). An explanation of how the transition from Canadian GAAP to IFRS as at the transition date has affected the reported earnings, balance sheet and cash flows for the Company, including the mandatory exception and optional exemptions under IFRS 1, is provided in note 29.

These financial statements were authorized for issue by the Board of Directors on March 28, 2012.

b) Basis of Measurement

These financial statements have been prepared on the historical cost basis except for the following material items:

- available-for-sale financial assets are measured at fair value through other comprehensive income;

- the pension liability is recognized as the present value of the defined benefit obligation less the total of the fair value of the plan assets and the unrecognized past service cost; and

- derivative financial instruments are measured at fair value.

c) Functional and Presentation Currency

These financial statements are presented in Canadian dollars, which is the Company's functional currency. All financial information presented in Canadian dollars has been rounded to the nearest thousand, except per share amounts.

d) Estimates, Judgments and Assumptions

The preparation of the financial statements in accordance with IFRS requires management to make judgments, estimates and assumptions that affect the application of accounting policies and the reported amounts of assets, liabilities, the disclosure of contingent assets and contingent liabilities at the date of the financial statements and reported amounts of revenues and expenses during the period. These estimates and assumptions are based on historical experience, other relevant factors and expectations of the future and are reviewed regularly. Revisions to accounting estimates are recognized in the period in which the estimates are revised and in any future periods affected. Actual results may differ from these estimates.

The following is a summary of areas involving a higher degree of judgment or complexity, or areas where assumptions and estimates are significant to the financial statements:

Deferred Income Tax Assets

Management is required to make subjective assessments to determine the amount of deferred income tax assets to be recognized. Deferred income tax assets are recorded to the extent that it is probable that there will be adequate taxable income in the future against which they can be utilized.

Pension Plans

The cost of defined benefit pension plans is determined by means of actuarial valuations, which involve making assumptions about discount rates, the expected long-term rate of return on plan assets, future salary increases, mortality rates and the future increases in pensions. Because of the long-term nature of the plans, such estimates are subject to a high degree of uncertainty.

Sales Returns

The Company provides for the possibility that merchandise already sold may be returned by customers. To this end, the Company has made certain assumptions based on the quantity of merchandise returned in the past.

Share-Based Compensation

In computing the compensation cost related to share option awards under the fair value based method, various assumptions are used to determine the expected option life, risk-free interest rate, expected share price volatility and average dividend yield. The use of different assumptions could result in a share compensation expense that differs from that which the Company has recorded.

Gift Cards / Loyalty Points and Awards

Gift cards sold are recorded as deferred revenue and revenue is recognized when the gift cards are redeemed. An estimate is made of gift cards not expected to be redeemed based on the terms of the gift cards and historical redemption patterns. Loyalty points and awards granted under customer loyalty programs are recognized as a separate component of revenue and are deferred at the date of initial sale. Revenue is recognized when the loyalty points and awards are redeemed and the Company has fulfilled its obligation. The amount of revenue deferred is measured based on the fair value of loyalty points and awards granted, taking into consideration the estimated redemption percentage.

Slow-Moving Inventory

The Company has set up provisions for merchandise in inventory that may have to be sold below cost. For this purpose, the Company has developed assumptions regarding the quantity of merchandise sold below cost.

Asset Impairment

The Company must assess the possibility that the carrying amounts of tangible and intangible assets may not be recoverable. Management is required to make significant judgments related to future cash flows to determine the amount of asset impairment that should be recognized.

Fair value of derivative financial instruments

Derivative financial instruments are carried in the balance sheet at fair value estimated by using valuation techniques.

3. SIGNIFICANT ACCOUNTING POLICIES

The accounting policies set out below have been applied consistently to all periods presented in these financial statements.

a) Foreign Currency Translation

Monetary assets and liabilities denominated in foreign currencies at the reporting date are translated into the functional currency at the exchange rate at that date. Other balance sheet items denominated in foreign currencies are translated into Canadian dollars at the exchange rates prevailing at the respective transaction dates. Revenues and expenses denominated in foreign currencies are translated into Canadian dollars at average rates of exchange prevailing during the period. The resulting gains or losses on translation are included in the determination of net earnings.

b) Cash and Cash Equivalents

Cash and cash equivalents consist of cash on hand, bank balances and short-term deposits with original maturities of three months or less.

c) Financial Instruments

All financial instruments are classified into one of the following five categories: financial assets and financial liabilities at fair value through profit or loss, held-to-maturity investments, loans and receivables, available-for-sale financial assets or other financial liabilities. All financial instruments, including derivatives, are included on the balance sheet and are initially measured at fair value. The Company accounts for transaction costs related to financial instruments, other than those classified as fair value through profit or loss and for derivative instruments, in the initial measurement of the instrument. Subsequent measurement depends on their initial classification. Financial instruments and financial liabilities classified as financial assets and liabilities at fair value through profit or loss are subsequently measured at fair value and all gains and losses are included in net earnings in the period in which they arise. Available-for-sale financial instruments are subsequently measured at fair value and changes therein, other than impairment losses, are recognized in other comprehensive income. When an investment is derecognized, the cumulative gain or loss in other comprehensive income is transferred to net earnings. Loans and receivables, held-to-maturity investments and other

financial liabilities, are subsequently measured at amortized cost using the effective interest rate method, less impairment losses.

Financial assets and liabilities measured at fair value use a fair value hierarchy to prioritize the inputs used in measuring fair value. Level 1, defined as observable inputs such as quoted prices in active markets; Level 2, defined as inputs other than quoted prices in active markets that are either directly or indirectly observable; and Level 3, defined as unobservable inputs in which little or no market data exists, therefore requiring an entity to develop its own assumptions.

The Company has classified its cash and cash equivalents and its trade and other receivables as loans and receivables and its marketable securities as available-for-sale financial assets. Trade and other payables and long-term debt have been classified as other financial liabilities and are measured at amortized cost.

Financial assets and liabilities are offset and the net amount is presented in the balance sheet when, and only when, the Company has a legal right to offset the amounts and intends either to settle on a net basis or to realize the asset and settle the liability simultaneously.

Derivative instruments are recorded at their fair value except under the own use exemption. Certain derivatives embedded in other contracts must also be measured at fair value. All changes in the fair value of derivatives are recognized in net earnings unless specific hedge criteria are met, which requires that a company must formally document, designate and assess the effectiveness of transactions that receive hedge accounting.

The Company considers the use of foreign currency option contracts, with maturities not exceeding six months, to manage its US dollar exposure. Foreign currency option contracts are not designated as hedges. Derivative financial instruments are not used for trading or speculative purposes.

d) Property and Equipment

Items of property and equipment are measured at cost less accumulated depreciation and accumulated impairment losses. Cost includes expenditures that are directly attributable to the acquisition of the asset, including any costs directly attributable to bringing the asset to a working condition for its intended use. Purchased software that is integral to the functionality of the related equipment is capitalized as part of that equipment.

When parts of an item of property and equipment have different useful lives, they are accounted for as separate items (major components) of property and equipment.

Depreciation is recognized in net earnings on a straight-line basis over the estimated useful lives of each component of an item of property and equipment. Land is not depreciated. Leasehold improvements are depreciated over the lesser of the estimated useful life of the asset and the lease term. Assets not in service include expenditures incurred to-date for equipment not yet available for use. Depreciation of assets not in service begins when they are ready for their intended use. Depreciation is calculated over the depreciable amount, which is the cost of an asset, less its residual value.

The estimated useful lives for the current and comparative periods are as follows:

- Buildings   10 to 50 years
- Fixtures and equipment   3 to 20 years
- Leasehold improvements   6.7 to 10 years

estimated costs necessary to make the sale, taking into consideration fluctuations of retail prices due to seasonality.

i) Impairment

(i) Non-Financial Assets

All non-financial assets are reviewed at each reporting date for indications that the carrying amount may not be recoverable. When there is evidence of impairment, an impairment test is carried out. Goodwill is tested for impairment at least annually at the year-end reporting date, and whenever there is an indication that the asset may be impaired. For the purpose of impairment testing, assets that cannot be tested individually are grouped together into the smallest group of assets that generates cash inflows from continuing use that are largely independent of the cash inflows of other assets or groups of assets (defined as "cash-generating unit" or "CGU"). Impairment losses recognized in respect of CGUs are allocated first to reduce the carrying amount of any goodwill allocated to the CGU, and then to reduce the carrying amount of the other assets in the CGU.

An impairment loss is recognized in net earnings if the carrying amount of an asset or its related CGU exceeds its estimated recoverable amount. The recoverable amount is the higher of the value-in-use and the fair value less costs to sell. The value-in-use is the present value of estimated future cash flows, using a pre-tax discount rate that reflects current market assessments of the time value of money and the risks specific to the asset or CGU. The fair value less costs to sell is the amount for which an asset or CGU can be sold in a transaction under normal market conditions between knowledgeable and willing contracting parties, less costs to sell.

For the purposes of impairment testing, goodwill acquired in a business combination is allocated to the CGUs that are expected to benefit from the synergies of the combination. This allocation reflects the lowest level at which goodwill is monitored for internal reporting purposes.

The Company's corporate assets do not generate separate cash inflows. If there is an indication that a corporate asset may be impaired, then the recoverable amount is determined for the CGUs to which the corporate asset belongs.

An impairment loss in respect of goodwill is not reversed. In respect of other assets, an impairment loss is reversed if there has been a change in the estimates used to determine the recoverable amount. An impairment loss is reversed only to the extent that the asset's carrying amount does not exceed the carrying amount that would have been determined, net of depreciation or amortization, if no impairment loss had been recognized.

(ii) Financial Assets

For an investment in an equity security, a significant or prolonged decline in its fair value below cost is objective evidence of impairment. Impairment losses on available-for-sale financial assets are recognized by reclassifying losses accumulated in accumulated other comprehensive income to net earnings. The cumulative loss that is reclassified from accumulated other comprehensive income is the difference between the acquisition cost and the current fair value, less any impairment losses recognized previously in net earnings.

Depreciation methods, useful lives and residual values are reviewed at each annual reporting date and adjusted prospectively, if appropriate.

Gains and losses on disposal of items of property and equipment are recognized in net earnings.

e) Goodwill

Goodwill is measured at the acquisition date as the fair value of the consideration transferred less the net identifiable assets of the acquired company or business activities. Goodwill is not amortized and is carried at cost less accumulated impairment losses.

f) Intangible Assets

Intangible assets that are acquired by the Company and have finite useful lives are measured at cost less accumulated amortization and accumulated impairment losses.

Amortization is calculated over the cost of the asset less its residual value. Amortization is recognized in net earnings on a straight-line basis over the estimated useful lives of the intangible assets. Amortization of intangible assets not in service begins when they are ready for their intended use.

The estimated useful lives for the current and comparative periods are as follows:

Software   3 to 5 years

Amortization methods, useful lives and residual values are reviewed at each annual reporting date and adjusted prospectively, if appropriate.

g) Leased Assets

Leases are classified as either operating or finance, based on the substance of the transaction at inception of the lease. Classification is re-assessed if the terms of the lease are changed.

Leases in which a significant portion of the risks and rewards of ownership are not assumed by the Company are classified as operating leases. The Company carries on its operations in premises under leases of varying terms, which are accounted for as operating leases. Payments under an operating lease are recognized in net earnings on a straight-line basis over the term of the lease. When a lease contains a predetermined fixed escalation of the minimum rent, the Company recognizes the related rent expense on a straight-line basis and, consequently, records the difference between the recognized rental expense and the amounts payable under the lease as deferred rent, which is included in trade and other payables on the balance sheet. Contingent (sales-based) rentals are recognized in net earnings in the period in which they are incurred.

Tenant allowances are recorded as deferred lease credits and amortized as a reduction of rent expense over the term of the related leases.

h) Inventories

Merchandise inventories are measured at the lower of cost, determined on an average basis using the retail inventory method, and net realizable value. Costs include the cost of purchase, transportation costs that are directly incurred to bring inventories to their present location and condition, and certain distribution centre costs related to inventories. The Company estimates net realizable value as the amount that inventories are expected to be sold, in the ordinary course of business, less the

Any subsequent recovery in the fair value of an impaired available-for-sale equity security is recognized in other comprehensive income.

j) Employee Benefits

(i) Pension Benefit Plans

The Company maintains a contributory defined benefit plan ("Plan") that provides benefits to employees based on length of service and average earnings in the best five consecutive years of employment. The Company also sponsors a Supplemental Executive Retirement Plan ("SERP"), which is neither registered nor pre-funded. The costs of these retirement benefit plans are determined periodically by independent actuaries.

Benefits are also given to employees through defined contribution plans administered by the Federal and Québec governments. Company contributions to these plans are recognized in the periods when the services are rendered.

Pension expense/income is included in the determination of net earnings according to the following policies:

- The present value of the defined benefit obligation is actuarially determined using the projected unit credit method.

- For the purpose of calculating expected return on plan assets, the valuation of those assets is based on quoted market values at the year-end date.

- The discount rate used to value the defined benefit obligation is the yield at the reporting date on AA credit-rated bonds that have maturity dates approximating the terms of the Company's obligations and that are denominated in the same currency in which the benefits are expected to be paid.

- Unrecognized past service costs related to benefits are amortized on a straight-line basis over the average period until vesting. To the extent that the benefits vest immediately, the expense is recognized immediately in net earnings.

The Company recognizes all actuarial gains and losses from the Plan and SERP immediately in other comprehensive income, and reports them in retained earnings. Expenses related to defined contribution plans are recognized in net earnings in the periods in which they occur. The net obligation in respect of the Plan and SERP is the amount of future benefits that members have earned in return for their service in the current and prior periods discounted to its present value, less any unrecognized past service costs and the fair value of the plan assets.

(ii) Short-Term Employee Benefits

Short-term employee benefit obligations, which include wages, salaries, compensated absences and bonuses, are measured on an undiscounted basis and are expensed as the related service is provided.

A liability is recognized for the amount expected to be paid under short-term cash bonus or profit sharing plans if the Company has a present legal or constructive obligation to pay this amount as a result of past service provided by the employee, and the obligation can be estimated reliably.

(iii) Share-Based Compensation

Some employees receive part of their compensation in the form of share-based payments which are recognised as an employee expense, with a corresponding increase in equity, over the period that the employees unconditionally become entitled to the awards. The Company accounts for share-based compensation using the fair value based method. Compensation expense is measured at the fair value at the date of grant and the fair value of each award is recognized over its respective vesting period, which is normally five years. The amount recognized as an expense is adjusted to reflect the number of awards for which the related service conditions are expected to be met.

k) Provisions

A provision is recognized if, as a result of a past event, the Company has a present legal or constructive obligation that can be estimated reliably, and it is probable that an outflow of economic benefits will be required to settle the obligation. If the effect of the time value of money is material, provisions are determined by discounting the expected future cash flows at a pre-tax rate that reflects current market assessments of the time value of money and the risks specific to the liability. Where discounting is used, the unwinding of the discount is recognized as finance cost.

l) Revenue

Revenue is recognized from the sale of merchandise when a customer purchases and takes delivery of the merchandise. Reported sales are net of returns and estimated possible returns and exclude sales taxes.

Gift cards sold are recorded as deferred revenue and revenue is recognized when the gift cards are redeemed. An estimate is made of gift cards not expected to be redeemed based on the terms of the gift cards and historical redemption patterns.

Loyalty points and awards granted under customer loyalty programs are recognized as a separate component of revenue, and are deferred at the date of initial sale. Revenue is recognized when the loyalty points and awards are redeemed and the Company has fulfilled its obligation. The amount of revenue deferred is measured based on the fair value of loyalty points and awards granted, taking into consideration the estimated redemption percentage.

m) Finance Income and Finance Costs

Finance income comprises interest and dividend income, realized gains on sale of marketable securities, changes in the fair value of derivatives as well as foreign exchange gains. Finance costs comprise interest expense, realized losses on sale of marketable securities, changes in the fair value of derivatives as well as foreign exchange losses. Interest income is recognized on an accrual basis and interest expense is recorded using the effective interest method. Dividend income is recognized when the right to receive payment is established. Foreign exchange gains and losses and changes in the fair value of derivatives are reported on a net basis.

n) Income Tax

Income tax expense comprises current and deferred taxes. Current income taxes and deferred income taxes are recognized in net earnings except for items recognized directly in equity or in other comprehensive income.

The Company's income tax expense is based on tax rules and regulations that are subject to interpretation and require estimates and assumptions that may be challenged by taxation authorities. Current income tax is the expected tax payable or receivable on the taxable income or loss for the period, using tax rates enacted or substantively enacted at the reporting date, and any adjustment to taxes payable in respect of previous years. The Company's estimates of current income tax assets and liabilities are periodically reviewed and adjusted as circumstances warrant, such as for changes to tax laws and administrative guidance, and the resolution of uncertainties through either the final conclusion of tax audits or expiration of prescribed time limits within the relevant statutes. The final results of government tax audits and other events may vary materially compared to estimates and assumptions used by management in determining the income tax expense and in measuring current income tax assets and liabilities.

Deferred income tax is recognized in respect of temporary differences between the carrying amounts of assets and liabilities for financial reporting purposes and the amounts used for taxation purposes. Deferred income tax assets and liabilities are measured using enacted or substantively enacted income tax rates expected to apply to taxable income in the years in which temporary differences are expected to be recovered or settled. The effect on deferred income tax assets and liabilities of a change in tax rates is included in net earnings in the period that includes the enactment date, except to the extent that it relates to an item recognized either in other comprehensive income or directly in equity in the current or in a previous period.

The Company only offsets income tax assets and liabilities if it has a legally enforceable right to offset the recognized amounts and intends either to settle on a net basis, or to realize the asset and settle the liability simultaneously.

A deferred income tax asset is recognized to the extent that it is probable that future taxable profits will be available against which they can be utilized. Deferred income tax assets are reviewed at each reporting date and are reduced to the extent that it is no longer probable that the related tax benefit will be realized.

Deferred income tax assets and liabilities are recognized on the balance sheet under non-current assets or liabilities, irrespective of the expected date of realization or settlement.

o) Earnings per Share

The Company presents basic and diluted earnings per share ("EPS") data for its shares.

Basic EPS is calculated by dividing the net earnings of the Company by the weighted average number of Class A non-voting and Common shares outstanding during the period.

Diluted EPS is determined by adjusting the weighted average number of shares outstanding to include additional shares issued from the assumed exercise of share options, if dilutive. The number of additional shares is calculated by assuming that the proceeds from such exercises, as well as the amount of unrecognized share-based compensation, are used to purchase Class A non-voting shares at the average market share price during the reporting period.

p) Share Capital

Class A non-voting shares and Common shares are classified as equity. Incremental costs directly attributable to the issue of these shares and share options are recognized as a deduction from equity, net of any tax effects.

When share capital recognized as equity is purchased for cancellation, the amount of the consideration paid, which includes directly attributable costs, net of any tax effects, is recognized as a deduction from equity. The excess of the purchase price over the carrying amount of the shares is charged to retained earnings.

q) New Standards and Interpretations Not Yet Adopted

A number of new standards, and amendments to standards and interpretations, are not yet effective for the year ended January 28, 2012 and have not been applied in preparing these financial statements. New standards and amendments to standards and interpretations that are currently under review include:

IFRS 9 - Financial Instruments

This standard becomes mandatory for the years commencing on or after January 1, 2015 with earlier application permitted. IFRS 9 is a new standard which will ultimately replace IAS 39, *Financial Instruments: Recognition and Measurement*.

IFRS 13 – Fair Value Measurement

This standard provides new guidance on fair value measurement and disclosure requirements, which becomes effective for annual periods commencing on or after January 1, 2013.

IAS 1 - Presentation of Financial Statements

Amendments to IAS 1, *Presentation of Financial Statements* enhance the presentation of Other Comprehensive Income ("OCI") in the financial statements, primarily by requiring the components of OCI to be presented separately for items that may be reclassified to the statement of earnings in the future from those that would never be reclassified to the statement of earnings. The amendments are effective for annual periods beginning on or after July 1, 2012

IAS 19 - Employee Benefits

Amendments to IAS 19, Employee Benefits include the elimination of the option to defer the recognition of gains and losses, enhancing the guidance around measurement of plan assets and defined benefit obligations, streamlining the presentation of changes in assets and liabilities arising from defined benefit plans and the introduction of enhanced disclosures for defined benefit plans. The amendments are effective for annual periods beginning on or after January 1, 2013.

The extent of the impact of adoption of the above noted standards and interpretations on the financial statements of the Company has not yet been determined.

5. CASH AND CASH EQUIVALENTS

	January 28, 2012	January 29, 2011	January 31, 2010
Cash on hand and with banks	$ 12,563	$ 4,634	$ 4,677
Short-term deposits, bearing interest at 0.9% (January 29, 2011 - 0.7%; January 31, 2010 - 0.3%)	184,272	225,400	223,900
	$ 196,835	$ 230,034	$ 228,577

6. FINANCIAL INSTRUMENTS

Derivative financial instruments

During the year, the Company entered into transactions with its bank whereby it purchased call options and sold put options, both on the US dollar ("USD"). These option contracts extend over a period of six months. Purchased call options and sold put options expiring on the same date have the same strike price.

Details of the foreign currency option contracts outstanding as at January 28, 2012 are as follow:

	Notional Amount in USD	Derivative Asset	Derivative Liability	Net
Put options sold	$ 44,000	$ 751	$ -	$ 751
Call options purchased	(100,000)	-	(1,505)	(1,505)
	$ (56,000)	$ 751	$ (1,505)	$ (754)

As at January 29, 2011 and January 31, 2010, there were no foreign currency option contracts outstanding.

7. INVENTORIES

During the year ended January 28, 2012, inventories recognized as cost of goods sold amounted to $361,319 (January 29, 2011 - $348,716). In addition, $2,014 (January 29, 2011 - $1,955) of write-downs of inventory as a result of net realizable value being lower than cost was recognized in cost of goods sold, and no inventory write-downs recognized in previous periods were reversed.

4. DETERMINATION OF FAIR VALUES

A number of the Company's accounting policies and disclosures require the determination of fair value, for both financial and non-financial assets and liabilities. Fair value estimates are made at a specific point in time, using available information about the asset or liability. These estimates are subjective in nature and often cannot be determined with precision. Fair values have been determined for measurement and/or disclosure purposes based on the following methods. When applicable, further information about the assumptions made in determining fair values is disclosed in the notes specific to that asset or liability.

a) Financial Assets

The Company has determined that the carrying amount of its short-term financial assets approximates fair value at the reporting date due to the short-term maturity of these instruments. The fair value of the Company's available-for-sale financial assets is determined by reference to their quoted closing prices in active markets at the reporting date, which is considered Level 1 input in the fair value hierarchy.

b) Non-Derivative Financial Liabilities

The fair value of the Company's long-term debt bearing interest at a fixed rate, which is determined for disclosure purposes, is calculated using the present value of future payments of principal and interest discounted at the current market rates of interest available to the Company for the same or similar debt instruments with the same remaining maturity.

c) Deferred Revenue

The amount of revenue deferred with respect to the Company's customer loyalty reward programs is estimated by reference to the fair value of the merchandise for which the loyalty rewards could be redeemed. The fair value takes into account the expected redemption rate and the timing of such expected redemptions.

d) Derivative Financial Instruments

The fair value of foreign currency option contracts is determined through a standard option valuation technique used by the counterparty based on Level 2 inputs.

e) Share-based Payment Transactions

The fair values of the employee share options are measured based on the Black-Scholes valuation model. Measurement inputs include share price on measurement date, exercise price of the share option, expected volatility (based on weighted average historic volatility adjusted for changes expected due to publicly available information), weighted average expected life of the share option (based on historic experience and general option holder behaviour), expected dividends, and risk-free interest rate (based on government bonds).

8. PROPERTY AND EQUIPMENT

	Land	Buildings	Fixtures and Equipment	Leasehold Improvements	Total
Cost					
Balance at January 31, 2010	$ 5,860	$ 52,411	$ 177,874	$ 194,782	$430,927
Additions	-	400	19,107	21,591	41,098
Disposals	-	(886)	(21,595)	(21,468)	(43,949)
Balance at January 29, 2011	$ 5,860	$ 51,925	$ 175,386	$ 194,905	$428,076
Balance at January 30, 2011	$ 5,860	$ 51,925	$ 175,386	$ 194,905	$428,076
Additions	-	2,291	25,079	24,818	52,188
Disposals	-	(53)	(37,346)	(37,650)	(75,049)
Balance at January 28, 2012	$ 5,860	$ 54,163	$ 163,119	$ 182,073	$405,215
Accumulated depreciation and impairment losses					
Balance at January 31, 2010	$ -	$ 17,946	$ 97,398	$ 107,221	$222,565
Depreciation	-	2,410	26,062	26,708	55,180
Impairment loss	-	-	-	1,724	1,724
Reversal of impairment loss	-	-	-	(779)	(779)
Disposals	-	(886)	(21,580)	(21,212)	(43,678)
Balance at January 29, 2011	$ -	$ 19,470	$ 101,880	$ 113,662	$235,012
Balance at January 30, 2011	$ -	$ 19,470	$ 101,880	$ 113,662	$235,012
Depreciation	-	2,601	25,599	26,699	54,899
Impairment loss	-	-	2,296	4,427	6,723
Reversal of impairment loss	-	-	-	(591)	(591)
Disposals	-	(53)	(37,346)	(37,650)	(75,049)
Balance at January 28, 2012	$ -	$ 22,018	$ 92,429	$ 106,547	$220,994
Net carrying amounts					
At January 31, 2010	$ 5,860	$ 34,465	$ 80,476	$ 87,561	$208,362
At January 29, 2011	$ 5,860	$ 32,455	$ 73,506	$ 81,243	$193,064
At January 28, 2012	$ 5,860	$ 32,145	$ 70,690	$ 75,526	$184,221

During the year, the Company tested for impairment certain items of property and equipment for which there were indications that their carrying amounts may not be recoverable and recognized an impairment loss of $6,723 (January 29, 2011 - $1,724). The recoverable amounts of the CGUs tested for impairment were based on their value-in-use which was determined using a pre-tax discount rate of 11% (January 29, 2011 - 12%). During the year, $591 of impairment losses were reversed following an improvement in the profitability of certain CGUs (January 29, 2011 - $779).

Depreciation expense and net impairment losses for the year have been recorded in selling and distribution expenses and administrative expenses in the statements of earnings.

Property and equipment includes an amount of $8,414 (January 29, 2011 - $3,548) that is not being depreciated. Depreciation will begin when the assets have been available for use.

9. INTANGIBLE ASSETS

	Cost	Accumulated amortization	Net carrying amounts
Balance at January 31, 2010	$ 17,072	$ 7,108	$ 9,964
Additions / amortization	7,506	3,629	3,877
Disposals	(2,394)	(2,394)	-
Balance at January 29, 2011	$ 22,184	$ 8,343	$ 13,841
Balance at January 30, 2011	$ 22,184	$ 8,343	$ 13,841
Additions / amortization	7,175	3,959	3,216
Disposals	(1,105)	(1,105)	-
Balance at January 28, 2012	$ 28,254	$ 11,197	$ 17,057

The amortization of intangibles has been recorded in selling and distribution expenses and administrative expenses in the statements of earnings.

Software includes an amount of $10,846 (January 29, 2011 - $6,930) that is not being amortized. Amortization will begin when the software has been put into service.

10. GOODWILL

Goodwill is tested for impairment as described in note 3(i). For impairment testing purposes the Company uses the value-in-use approach. Value-in-use is determined by discounting the future cash flows generated from the continuing use of the respective CGU.

Management's key assumptions for cash flow projections are based on the most recent annualized operating results, assuming a series of cash flows in perpetuity. Projected cash flows are discounted using a pre-tax rate of 10% (January 29, 2011 - 11%) which reflects the specific risks and weighted average cost of capital for a company of similar size and industry.

Based upon the impairment tests as at January 28, 2012, January 29, 2011 and January 31, 2010, the value-in-use was determined to be higher than the carrying values. As a result, no impairment losses were recognized.

11. INCOME TAX

Income tax expense

The Company's income tax expense is comprised as follows:

	For the years ended	
	January 28, 2012	January 29, 2011
Current tax expense		
Current period	$ 19,840	$ 42,409
Adjustment for prior years	(307)	(740)
Current tax expense	19,533	41,669
Deferred tax expense		
Recognition and reversal of temporary differences	(1,771)	(3,990)
Changes in tax rates	319	494
Adjustment for prior years	252	644
Deferred tax expense	(1,200)	(2,852)
Total income tax expense	$ 18,333	$ 38,817

Income tax recognized in other comprehensive income

	For the year ended January 28, 2012			For the year ended January 29, 2011		
	Before Tax	Tax (expense) benefit	Net of Tax (expense)	Before Tax	Tax (expense) benefit	Net of Tax (expense)
Available-for-sale financial assets	$ 682	$ (88)	$ 594	$ 3,204	$ (416)	$ 2,788
Defined benefit plan actuarial losses	(4,006)	1,041	(2,965)	(1,049)	272	(777)
	$ (3,324)	$ 953	$ (2,371)	$ 2,155	$ (144)	$ 2,011

Reconciliation of effective tax rate

	For the years ended			
	January 28, 2012		January 29, 2011	
Earnings before income taxes	$ 65,872		$127,802	
Income tax using the Company's statutory tax rate	18,642	28.30%	38,583	30.19%
Changes in tax rates	319	0.48%	391	0.31%
Non-deductible expenses and other adjustments	393	0.60%	658	0.51%
Tax exempt income	(966)	(1.47%)	(719)	(0.56%)
Over provided in prior periods	(55)	(0.08%)	(96)	(0.08%)
	$ 18,333	27.83%	$ 38,817	30.37%

Recognized deferred tax assets and liabilities

Deferred tax assets and liabilities are attributable to the following:

	Assets		Liabilities		Net	
	January 28, 2012	January 29, 2011	January 28, 2012	January 29, 2011	January 28, 2012	January 29, 2011
Property, equipment and intangible assets	$ 17,364	$ 12,984	$ -	$ -	$ 17,364	$ 12,984
Prepaid expenses	-	214	-	-	-	214
Marketable securities	-	-	379	299	(379)	(299)
Inventories	-	-	1,144	1,082	(1,144)	(1,082)
Trade and other payables	3,461	5,644	-	-	3,461	5,644
Pension liability	3,868	3,534	-	-	3,868	3,534
Other	42	46	38	20	4	26
	$ 24,735	$ 22,422	$ 1,561	$ 1,401	$ 23,174	$ 21,021

Changes in deferred tax balances during the year

	Balance January 31, 2010	Recognized in Net Earnings	Recognized in Other Comprehensive Income	Balance January 29, 2011	Recognized in Net Earnings	Recognized in Other Comprehensive Income	Balance January 28, 2012
Property, equipment and intangible assets	$ 10,626	$ 2,358	$ -	$ 12,984	$ 4,380	$ -	$ 17,364
Prepaid expenses	257	(43)	-	214	(214)	-	-
Marketable securities	121	(4)	(416)	(299)	8	(88)	(379)
Inventories	(1,039)	(43)	-	(1,082)	(62)	-	(1,144)
Trade and other payables	5,260	384	-	5,644	(2,183)	-	3,461
Pension liability	3,076	186	272	3,534	(707)	1,041	3,868
Other	12	14	-	26	(22)	-	4
	$ 18,313	$ 2,852	$ (144)	$ 21,021	$ 1,200	$ 953	$ 23,174

12. TRADE AND OTHER PAYABLES

	January 28, 2012	January 29, 2011	January 31, 2010
Trade payables	$ 26,155	$ 16,457	$ 15,148
Non-trade payables due to related parties	56	66	90
Other non-trade payables	10,553	11,817	4,437
Personnel liabilities	23,053	31,457	30,615
Payables relating to premises	14,398	13,630	12,630
Provision for sales returns	770	846	869
	74,985	74,273	63,789
Less non-current portion	11,110	10,180	9,105
	$ 63,875	$ 64,093	$ 54,684

The non-current portion of trade and other payables, which is included in payables relating to premises, represents the portion of deferred rent to be amortized beyond the next twelve months.

15. PENSION LIABILITY

The following tables present reconciliations of the pension obligations, the plan assets and the funded status of the retirement benefit plans:

Funded Status

	Fair value of plan assets	Defined benefit obligation	Funded status	Unamortized non-vested past service cost	Pension asset (liability)
As at January 28, 2012					
Plan	$ 15,727	$ 15,318	$ 409	$ -	$ 409
SERP	-	15,540	(15,540)	254	(15,286)
Total	$ 15,727	$ 30,858	$ (15,131)	$ 254	$ (14,877)
As at January 29, 2011					
Plan	$ 11,936	$ 12,717	$ (781)	$ -	$ (781)
SERP	-	13,184	(13,184)	339	(12,845)
Total	$ 11,936	$ 25,901	$ (13,965)	$ 339	$ (13,626)
As at January 31, 2010					
Plan	$ 10,369	$ 11,399	$ (1,030)	$ -	$ (1,030)
SERP	-	11,259	(11,259)	424	(10,835)
Total	$ 10,369	$ 22,658	$ (12,289)	$ 424	$ (11,865)

13. DEFERRED REVENUE

Deferred revenue consists of the following:

	January 28, 2012	January 29, 2011	January 31, 2010
Loyalty points and awards granted under loyalty programs	$ 10,979	$ 10,984	$ 10,142
Unredeemed gift cards	11,299	11,234	10,666
	22,278	22,218	20,808
Less amounts expected to be redeemed in the next twelve months	22,278	19,834	18,122
Deferred revenue – non-current	$ -	$ 2,384	$ 2,686

14. LONG-TERM DEBT

	January 28, 2012	January 29, 2011	January 31, 2010
Mortgage payable	$ 10,047	$ 11,431	$ 12,731
Less current portion	1,474	1,384	1,300
	$ 8,573	$ 10,047	$ 11,431

The mortgage, bearing interest at 6.40%, is payable in monthly instalments of principal and interest of $172. It is due November 2017 and is secured by the Company's distribution centre having a carrying value of $18,306 (January 29, 2011 - $19,282; January 31, 2010 - $20,304).

As at January 28, 2012, principal repayments on long-term debt are as follows:

Within 1 year	$ 1,474
Within 2 years	1,570
Within 3 years	1,672
Within 4 years	1,780
Within 5 years	1,896
Subsequent years	1,655
	$ 10,047

As at January 28, 2012, the fair value of long-term debt was $10,882 (January 29, 2011 - $12,247; January 31, 2010 - $13,045) compared to its carrying value of $10,047 (January 29, 2011 - $11,431; January 31, 2010 - $12,731).

The asset allocation of the major asset categories in the Plan for each of the years was as follows:

	January 28, 2012	January 29, 2011	January 31, 2010
Equity securities	60%	62%	61%
Debt securities	38%	36%	37%
Cash and cash equivalents	2%	2%	2%
	100%	100%	100%

The Company's pension expense was as follows:

	For the year ended January 28, 2012			For the year ended January 29, 2011		
	Plan	SERP	Total	Plan	SERP	Total
Pension costs recognized in net earnings						
Current service cost	$ 596	$ 239	$ 835	$ 480	$ 232	$ 712
Interest cost	684	695	1,379	646	628	1,274
Expected return on plan assets	(808)	-	(808)	(729)	-	(729)
Past service cost	-	84	84	-	84	84
Pension expense	$ 472	$ 1,018	$ 1,490	$ 397	$ 944	$ 1,341

Pension expense is recognized in administration expenses in the statements of earnings.

The following table presents the change in the actuarial gains and losses recognized in other comprehensive income:

	For the year ended January 28, 2012			For the year ended January 29, 2011		
	Plan	SERP	Total	Plan	SERP	Total
Cumulative amount in retained earnings at the beginning of the year	$ (144)	$ 1,193	$ 1,049	$ -	$ -	$ -
Recognized during the year	2,456	1,550	4,006	(144)	1,193	1,049
Cumulative amount in retained earnings at the end of the year	$ 2,312	$ 2,743	$ 5,055	$ (144)	$ 1,193	$ 1,049
Recognized during the year net of tax			$ 2,965			$ 777

	For the year ended January 28, 2012			For the year ended January 29, 2011		
	Plan	SERP	Total	Plan	SERP	Total
Movement in the present value of the defined benefit obligation						
Defined benefit obligation, beginning of year	$12,717	$ 13,184	$ 25,901	$ 11,399	$ 11,259	$ 22,658
Current service cost	596	239	835	480	232	712
Interest cost	684	695	1,379	646	628	1,274
Employee contributions	144	-	144	140	-	140
Actuarial losses	1,778	1,550	3,328	567	1,193	1,760
Benefits paid	(601)	(128)	(729)	(515)	(128)	(643)
Defined benefit obligation, end of year	$15,318	$ 15,540	$ 30,858	$12,717	$ 13,184	$ 25,901
Movement in the fair value of plan assets						
Fair value of plan assets, beginning of year	$11,936	-	$ 11,936	$10,369	$ -	$ 10,369
Expected return on assets	808	-	808	729	-	729
Investment (loss) gain	(677)	-	(677)	712	-	712
Employer contributions	4,117	128	4,245	501	128	629
Employee contributions	144	-	144	140	-	140
Benefits paid	(601)	(128)	(729)	(515)	(128)	(643)
Fair value of plan assets, end of year	$15,727	$ -	$ 15,727	$11,936	$ -	$ 11,936

The Company has determined that, in accordance with the terms and conditions of the defined benefit plan, and in accordance with statutory requirements (such as minimum funding requirements) of the plans of the respective jurisdictions, the present value of refunds or reductions in the future contributions is not lower than the balance of the total fair value of the plan assets less the total present value of the obligations. As such, no decrease in the defined benefit plan asset is necessary at January 28, 2012 (January 29, 2011 and January 31, 2010 - no decrease in defined benefit asset).

The Common shares and Class A non-voting shares of the Company rank equally and pari passu with respect to the right to receive dividends and upon any distribution of the assets of the Company. However, in the case of share dividends, the holders of Class A non-voting shares shall have the right to receive Class A non-voting shares and the holders of Common shares shall have the right to receive Common shares.

Issuance of Class A Non-Voting Shares

During the year ended January 28, 2012, a total of 722 (January 29, 2011- 292) Class A non-voting shares were issued as a result of the exercise of vested options arising from the Company's share option program. The amounts credited to share capital from the exercise of share options include a cash consideration of $8,828 (January 29, 2011- $3,569), as well as an ascribed value from contributed surplus of $2,228 (January 29, 2011- $888).

Purchase of Shares for Cancellation

For the year ended January 28, 2012, the Company purchased, under the prior year's normal course issuer bid, 1,445 (January 29, 2011 – 1,583) Class A non-voting shares having a book value of $780 (January 29, 2011 - $731) for a total cash consideration of $22,410 (January 29, 2011 - $30,112). The excess of the purchase price over the book value of the shares in the amount of $21,630 (January 29, 2011 - $29,381) was charged to retained earnings.

In November 2011, the Company received approval from the Toronto Stock Exchange to proceed with a normal course issuer bid. Under the bid, the Company may purchase up to 2,580 Class A non-voting shares of the Company, representing 5% of the issued and outstanding Class A non-voting shares as at November 14, 2011. The bid commenced on November 28, 2011 and may continue to November 27, 2012. No Class A non-voting shares were purchased under this new program.

Accumulated Other Comprehensive Income ("AOCI")

AOCI is comprised of the following:

	January 28, 2012	January 29, 2011	January 31, 2010
Net change in fair value of available-for-sale financial assets, net of taxes	$ 8,737	$ 8,143	$ 5,355

Dividends

The following dividends were declared and paid by the Company:

	For the years ended	
	January 28, 2012	January 29, 2011
Common shares and Class A non-voting shares	$ 52,654	$ 51,895

Actuarial assumptions

Principal actuarial assumptions used were as follows:

	For the years ended	
	January 28, 2012	January 29, 2011
Accrued benefit obligation:		
Discount rate	4.30%	5.20%
Salary increase	5.00%	3.00%
Employee benefit expense:		
Discount rate	5.20%	5.50%
Expected return on plan assets	6.50%	7.00%
Salary increase	3.00%	3.00%

Expected rates of return on plan assets are based on external historical and forecast market information.

The Company expects $1,046 in employer contributions to be paid to the Plan and SERP in the year ending February 2, 2013.

The Company measures its accrued benefit obligations and the fair value of plan assets for accounting purposes at year-end. The most recent actuarial valuation for funding purposes was as of December 31, 2010 and the next required valuation will be as of December 31, 2011.

16. SHARE CAPITAL AND OTHER COMPONENTS OF EQUITY

The change in share capital for each of the periods listed was as follows:

	For the years ended			
	January 28, 2012		January 29, 2011	
	Number of shares	Carrying amount	Number of shares	Carrying amount
Common shares				
Balance at beginning and end of the year	13,440	$ 482	13,440	$ 482
Class A non-voting shares				
Balance at beginning of the year	52,869	$29,132	54,160	$25,406
Shares issued pursuant to exercise of share options	722	11,056	292	4,457
Shares purchased under issuer bid	(1,445)	(780)	(1,583)	(731)
Balance at end of the year	52,146	$39,408	52,869	$29,132
Total share capital	65,586	$39,890	66,309	$29,614

Authorized Share Capital

The Company has authorized for issuance an unlimited number of Common shares and Class A non-voting shares. Both Common shares and Class A non-voting shares have no par value. All issued shares are fully paid.

17. SHARE-BASED PAYMENTS

a) Description of the Share-Based Payment Arrangements

The Company has a share option plan that provides that up to 10% of the Class A non-voting shares outstanding, from time to time, may be issued pursuant to the exercise of options granted under the plan to key management and employees. The granting of options and the related vesting period, which is normally up to 5 years, are at the discretion of the Board of Directors and the options have a maximum term of 10 years. The exercise price payable for each Class A non-voting share covered by a share option is determined by the Board of Directors at the date of grant, but may not be less than the closing price of the Company's shares on the trading day immediately preceding the effective date of the grant.

b) Disclosure of Equity-settled Share Option Plan

Changes in outstanding share options were as follows:

	For the years ended			
	January 28, 2012		January 29, 2011	
	Options	Weighted Average Exercise Price	Options	Weighted Average Exercise Price
Outstanding, at beginning of year	3,095	$ 14.58	3,207	$ 14.14
Granted	-	-	215	18.02
Exercised	(722)	12.23	(292)	12.23
Forfeited	(428)	16.33	(35)	14.50
Outstanding, at end of year	1,945	$ 15.07	3,095	$ 14.58
Options exercisable, at end of year	238	$ 18.81	935	$ 13.74

The weighted average share price at the date of exercise for share options exercised in the year was $15.44 (January 29, 2011 - $18.21)

There were no share option awards granted during the year ended January 28, 2012. Compensation cost related to share option awards granted during the year ended January 29, 2011 under the fair value based approach was calculated using the following assumptions:

	For the year ended January 29, 2011		
	100 Options Granted April 7, 2010	15 Options Granted June 2, 2010	100 Options Granted January 14, 2011
Expected option life	6.5 years	4.9 years	6.5 years
Risk-free interest rate	3.59%	2.44%	2.90%
Expected stock price volatility	47.18%	37.40%	33.52%
Average dividend yield	4.00%	4.38%	4.44%
Weighted average fair value of options granted	$6.22	$4.25	$4.05
Share price at grant date	$18.00	$18.26	$18.00

The following table summarizes information about share options outstanding at January 28, 2012:

	Options Outstanding			Options Exercisable	
Range of Exercise Prices	Number Outstanding	Weighted Average Remaining Contractual Life	Weighted Average Exercise Price	Number Exercisable	Weighted Average Exercise Price
$14.50	1,675	5.0 years	$ 14.50	-	$ -
$15.90 - $18.26	115	2.4	16.75	83	16.58
$19.23 - $22.02	155	0.7	20.00	155	20.00
	1,945	4.5 years	$ 15.07	238	$ 18.81

c) Employee Expense

For the year ended January 28, 2012, the Company recognized compensation costs of $1,120 relating to share-based payment arrangements ($1,990 for the year ended January 29, 2011), with a corresponding credit to contributed surplus.

18. COMMITMENTS

As at January 28, 2012, financial commitments for minimum lease payments under operating leases for retail stores, offices, automobiles and equipment, as well as amounts pertaining to agreements to purchase goods or services that are enforceable and legally binding on the Company, exclusive of additional amounts based on sales, taxes and other costs are payable as follows:

	Store and Office Operating Leases	Purchases Obligations	Other Operating Leases	Total
Within 1 year	$ 99,202	$102,637	$ 4,498	$ 206,337
Within 2 years	88,467	326	3,723	92,516
Within 3 years	77,563	117	2,672	80,352
Within 4 years	66,012	-	2,477	68,489
Within 5 years	49,802	-	8	49,810
Subsequent years	89,873	-	-	89,873
Total	$ 470,919	$103,080	$ 13,378	$ 587,377

The Company leases retail stores and offices under operating leases. The Company does not sublet any of its leased properties. The leases have varying terms, escalation clauses and renewal rights. Generally, the leases run for a period that does not exceed 10 years, with options to renew that do not exceed 5 years, if at all. The majority of the leases require additional payments for the cost of insurance, taxes, maintenance and utilities. Certain rental agreements include contingent rent, which is generally based on revenue exceeding a minimum amount.

For the year ended January 28, 2012, $181,998 was recognized as an expense in net earnings with respect to operating leases ($181,868 for the year ended January 29, 2011), of which $179,149 ($179,328 for the year ended January 29, 2011) represents minimum lease payments and $2,849 ($2,540 for the year ended January 29, 2011) represents contingent rents.

19. FINANCE INCOME AND FINANCE COSTS

Recognized in Net Earnings

	For the years ended	
	January 28, 2012	January 29, 2011
Dividend income from available-for-sale financial assets	$ 3,462	$ 2,640
Interest income from loans and receivables	1,367	1,225
Realized gain on disposal of available-for-sale financial assets	-	167
Foreign exchange gain	733	473
Finance income	5,562	4,505
Interest expense - mortgage	682	767
Net change in fair value of derivatives (note 6)	754	-
Impairment loss on available-for-sale financial assets	73	78
Finance costs	1,509	845
Net finance income recognized in net earnings	$ 4,053	$ 3,660

Recognized in Other Comprehensive Income

	For the years ended	
	January 28, 2012	January 29, 2011
Net change in fair value of available-for-sale financial assets arising during the year (net of tax of $ 79; 2011 - $427)	$ 530	$ 2,866
Finance income recognized in other comprehensive income (net of tax)	$ 530	$ 2,866

20. EARNINGS PER SHARE

The calculation of basic and diluted earnings per share is based on net earnings for the year ended January 28, 2012 of $47,539 ($88,985 for the year ended January 29, 2011).

The number of shares used in the earnings per share calculation is as follows:

	For the years ended	
	January 28, 2012	January 29, 2011
Weighted average number of shares per basic earnings per share calculations	65,975	66,771
Effect of dilutive share options outstanding	126	484
Weighted average number of shares per diluted earnings per share calculations	66,101	67,255

As at January 28, 2012, a total of 1,945 (January 29, 2011– 398) share options were excluded from the calculation of diluted earnings per share as these options were deemed to be anti-dilutive, because the exercise prices were greater than the average market price of the shares during the period.

The average market value of the Company's shares for purposes of calculating the dilutive effect of share options was based on quoted market prices for the period during which the options were outstanding.

21. RELATED PARTIES

Transactions with Key Management Personnel

Only members of the Board of Directors are deemed to be key management personnel. It is the Board who has the responsibility for planning, directing and controlling the activities of the Company. The Directors participate in the share option plan, as described in note 17. Compensation expense for key management personnel is as follows:

	For the years ended	
	January 28, 2012	January 29, 2011
Salaries and short-term benefits	$ 2,088	$ 2,899
Post-employment benefits	(63)	178
Share-based compensation costs	190	200
	$ 2,215	$ 3,277

Further information about the remuneration of individual Directors is provided in the annual Management Proxy Circular.

Other Related-Party Transactions

The Company leases two retail locations which are owned by companies controlled by the major shareholders of the Company. For the year ended January 28, 2012, the rent expense under these leases was, in the aggregate, approximately $198 (January 29, 2011- $190).

The Company incurred $584 in the year ended January 28, 2012 (January 29, 2011- $606) with professional service firms connected to outside directors of the Company for fees in conjunction with general legal advice and other consultation.

These transactions are recorded at the amount of consideration paid as established and agreed to by the related parties.

22. PERSONNEL EXPENSES

	For the years ended	
	January 28, 2012	January 29, 2011
Wages, salaries and employee benefits	$ 248,208	$ 251,702
Expenses related to defined benefit plans	1,490	1,341
Share-based compensation costs	1,120	1,990
	$ 250,818	$ 255,033

23. CREDIT FACILITY

At January 28, 2012, the Company had unsecured operating lines of credit available with Canadian chartered banks to a maximum of $125,000 or its US dollar equivalent. As at January 28, 2012, $52,187 (January 29, 2011 - $60,888) of the operating lines of credit were committed for documentary and standby letters of credit.

24. GUARANTEES

The Company has granted irrevocable standby letters of credit, issued by highly-rated financial institutions, to third parties to indemnify them in the event the Company does not perform its contractual obligations. As at January 28, 2012, the maximum potential liability under these guarantees was $5,083 (January 29, 2011 - $5,060). The standby letters of credit mature at various dates during year ending February 2, 2013. The contingent portion of the guarantee is recorded when the Company considers it probable that a payment relating to the guarantee has to be made to the other party of the contract or guarantee. The Company has recorded no liability with respect to these guarantees as the Company does not expect to make any payments for these items. Management believes that the fair value of the non-contingent obligations requiring performance under the guarantees in the event that specified triggering events or conditions occur approximates the cost of obtaining the standby letters of credit.

25. SUPPLEMENTARY CASH FLOW INFORMATION

	January 28, 2012	January 29, 2011
Non-cash transactions:		
Additions to property and equipment and intangible assets included in trade and other payables	$ 3,028	$ 2,819
Ascribed value credited to share capital from exercise of share options	$ 2,228	$ 888

26. FINANCIAL RISK MANAGEMENT

The Company's risk management policies are established to identify and analyze the risks faced by the Company, to set appropriate risk limits and controls, and to monitor risks and adherence to limits. Risk management policies and systems are reviewed regularly to reflect changes in market conditions and the Company's activities. Disclosures relating to the Company's exposure to risks, in particular credit risk, liquidity risk, foreign currency risk, interest rate risk and equity price risk are provided below.

Credit Risk

Credit risk is the risk of an unexpected loss if a customer or counterparty to a financial instrument fails to meet its contractual obligations. The Company's financial instruments that are exposed to concentrations of credit risk are primarily cash and cash equivalents, marketable securities, trade and other receivables and foreign currency option contracts. The Company limits its exposure to credit risk with respect to cash and cash equivalents by investing available cash in short-term deposits with Canadian financial institutions and commercial paper with a rating not less than R1. Marketable securities consist primarily of preferred shares of highly-rated Canadian public companies. The Company's trade and other receivables consist primarily of credit card receivables from the last few days of the fiscal year, which are settled within the first days of the next fiscal year.

As at January 28, 2012, the Company's maximum exposure to credit risk for these financial instruments was as follows:

Cash and cash equivalents	$ 196,835
Marketable securities	71,442
Trade and other receivables	3,033
	$ 271,310

Liquidity Risk

Liquidity risk is the risk that the Company will not be able to meet its financial obligations as they fall due. The Company's approach to managing liquidity risk is to ensure, as far as possible, that it will always have sufficient liquidity to meet liabilities when due. The contractual maturity of the majority of trade and other payables is within six months. As at January 28, 2012, the Company had a high degree of liquidity with $268,277 in cash and cash equivalents, and marketable securities. In addition, the Company has unsecured credit facilities of $125,000 subject to annual renewals. The Company has financed its store expansion through internally-generated funds and its unsecured credit facilities are used to finance seasonal working capital requirements for US dollar merchandise purchases. The Company's long-term debt consists of a mortgage bearing interest at 6.40%, due November 2017, which is secured by the Company's distribution centre.

Foreign Currency Risk

The Company purchases a significant amount of its merchandise with US dollars and as such significant volatility in the US dollar vis-à-vis the Canadian dollar can have an adverse impact on the Company's gross margin. The Company has a variety of alternatives that it considers to manage its foreign currency exposure on cash flows related to these purchases. This includes, but is not limited to, various styles of foreign currency option or forward contracts, not to exceed six months, and spot rate purchases. A foreign currency option contract represents an option or obligation to buy a foreign currency from a counterparty. Credit risks exist in the event of failure by a counterparty to fulfill its

Equity Price Risk

Equity price risk arises from available-for-sale equity securities. The Company monitors the mix of equity securities in its investment portfolio based on market expectations. Material investments within the portfolio are managed on an individual basis and all buy and sell decisions are approved by the Chief Executive Officer.

The Company has performed a sensitivity analysis on equity price risk at January 28, 2012, to determine how a change in the market price of the Company's marketable securities would impact equity and other comprehensive income. The Company's equity investments consist principally of preferred shares of Canadian public companies. The Company believes that changes in interest rates influence the market price of these securities. A 5% increase or decrease in the market price of the securities at January 28, 2012, would result in a $3,036 increase or decrease, respectively, in equity and other comprehensive income for the year ended January 28, 2012. The Company's equity securities are subject to market risk and, as a result, the impact on equity and other comprehensive income may ultimately be greater than that indicated above.

27. CAPITAL MANAGEMENT

The Company's objectives in managing capital are:

- to ensure sufficient liquidity to enable the internal financing of capital projects thereby facilitating its expansion;
- to maintain a strong capital base so as to maintain investor, creditor and market confidence;
- to provide an adequate return to shareholders.

The Company's capital is composed of long-term debt, including the current portion and shareholders' equity. The Company's primary uses of capital are to finance increases in non-cash working capital along with capital expenditures for new store additions, existing store renovation projects and office and distribution centre improvements. The Company currently funds these requirements out of its internally-generated cash flows. The Company's long-term debt constitutes a mortgage on the distribution centre facility. The Company maintains unsecured operating lines of credit that it uses to satisfy commitments for US dollar denominated merchandise purchases. The Company does not have any long-term debt, other than the mortgage related to the distribution centre, and therefore net earnings generated from operations are available for reinvestment in the Company or distribution to the Company's shareholders. The Board of Directors does not establish quantitative return on capital criteria for management, but rather promotes year over year sustainable profitable growth. On a quarterly basis, the Board of Directors also reviews the level of dividends paid to the Company's shareholders and monitors the share repurchase program activities. The Company does not have a defined share repurchase plan and decisions are made on a specific transaction basis and depend on market prices and regulatory restrictions. The Company is not subject to any externally imposed capital requirements.

---

obligations. The Company reduces this risk by dealing only with highly-rated counterparties, normally major Canadian financial institutions. For the year ended January 28, 2012, the Company satisfied its US dollar requirements primarily through spot rate purchases.

The Company has performed a sensitivity analysis on its US dollar denominated financial instruments, which consist principally of cash and cash equivalents of $27,547 and trade payables of $3,840 to determine how a change in the US dollar exchange rate would impact net earnings. On January 28, 2012, a 1% rise or fall in the Canadian dollar against the US dollar, assuming that all other variables, in particular interest rates, had remained the same, would have resulted in a $166 decrease or increase, respectively, in the Company's net earnings for the year ended January 28, 2012.

The Company has performed a sensitivity analysis on its derivative financial instruments, a series of call and put options on US dollars, to determine how a change in the US dollar exchange rate would impact net earnings. On January 28, 2012, a 1% rise or fall in the Canadian dollar against the US dollar, assuming that all other variables had remained the same, would have resulted in a $580 decrease or increase, respectively, in the Company's net earnings for the year ended January 28, 2012.

Interest Rate Risk

Interest rate risk exists in relation to the Company's cash and cash equivalents, defined benefit pension plan and SERP. Market fluctuations in interest rates impacts the Company's earnings with respect to interest earned on cash and cash equivalents that are invested in bank bearer deposit notes and bank term deposits with major Canadian financial institutions and commercial paper with a rating not less than R1. Overall return in the capital markets and the level of interest rates affect the funded status of the Company's pension plans. Adverse changes with respect to pension plan returns and the level of interest rates from the date of the last actuarial valuation may have a material adverse effect on the funded status of the retirement benefit plans and on the Company's results of operations. The Company has unsecured borrowing and working capital credit facilities available up to an amount of $125,000 or its US dollar equivalent that it utilizes for documentary and standby letters of credit, and the Company funds the drawings on these facilities as the payments are due.

The Company has performed a sensitivity analysis on interest rate risk at January 28, 2012 to determine how a change in interest rates would impact equity and net earnings. For the year ended January 28, 2012, the Company earned interest income of $1,367 on its cash and cash equivalents. An increase or decrease of 25 basis points in the average interest rate earned during the year would have increased equity and net earnings by $321 or decreased equity and net earnings by $235, respectively. This analysis assumes that all other variables, in particular foreign currency rates, remain constant.

The Company has performed a sensitivity analysis at January 28, 2012 to determine how a change in interest rates, in relation to the Company's retirement benefit plans, would impact the benefit costs included in other comprehensive income. A one percentage point decrease in the year-end discount rate would have resulted in an increase of approximately $4,300 in benefit costs included in other comprehensive income for the year ended January 28, 2012, whereas a one percentage point increase would have resulted in a decrease of approximately $3,800. The Company's expected long-term rate of return on Plan assets reflects management's view of long-term investment returns. The effect of a 1% variation in such rate of return would have a nominal impact on the total benefit costs included in net earnings and total comprehensive income.

(ii) Employee Benefits

IFRS 1 provides the option to apply IAS 19 *Employee Benefits* paragraph 120A(p), retrospectively or prospectively from the Transition Date. The retrospective basis would require the disclosure of selected information of the defined benefit plans for the current annual period and previous four annual periods. The Company elected to disclose the amounts required by paragraph 120A(p) of IAS 19 as the amounts are determined for each accounting period prospectively from the Transition Date to IFRS.

28. COMPARATIVE FIGURES

Certain comparative figures have been reclassified to conform to the current year's presentation.

29. EXPLANATION OF TRANSITION TO IFRS

As stated in note 2 (a), these are the Company's first annual financial statements prepared in accordance with IFRS. The Company has applied IFRS 1 and the accounting policies set out in note 3 have been applied in preparing the financial statements for the year ended January 28, 2012, the comparative information presented in these financial statements for the year ended January 29, 2011 and in the preparation of the opening IFRS balance sheet at January 31, 2010, which is the Company's date of transition.

In preparing these financial statements in accordance with IFRS 1, the Company has adjusted amounts reported previously in the financial statements prepared in accordance with Canadian GAAP. An explanation of how the transition from Canadian GAAP to IFRS has affected the Company's previously published financial statements as at and for the year ended January 29, 2011 and as at January 31, 2010 is set out in the following tables and the notes that accompany the tables.

IFRS 1 requires first-time adopters to retrospectively apply all effective IFRS standards as of the reporting date of its first annual financial statements. However, it also provides for certain optional exemptions and prescribes certain mandatory exceptions for first-time adopters. Set forth below are the IFRS 1 applicable exemptions and exceptions applied in the Company's conversion from Canadian GAAP to IFRS.

a) IFRS Exemption Options

(i) Business Combinations

The Company elected not to retrospectively apply IFRS 3 *Business Combinations* to business combinations that occurred prior to its Transition Date and such business combinations have not been restated. Under the business combinations exemption, the carrying amounts of the assets acquired and liabilities assumed under Canadian GAAP at the date of the acquisition became their deemed carrying amounts under IFRS at that date.

Notwithstanding this exemption, the Company was required at the Transition Date, to evaluate whether the assets acquired and liabilities assumed meet the recognition criteria in the relevant IFRS, and whether there are any assets acquired or liabilities assumed that were not recognized under Canadian GAAP for which recognition would be required under IFRS. The requirements of IFRS were then applied to the assets acquired and liabilities assumed from the date of acquisition to the Transition Date. The application of this exemption did not result in an IFRS transition adjustment to the opening balance sheet at January 31, 2010. In addition, under the business combinations exemption, the Company tested goodwill for impairment at the Transition Date and determined that there was no impairment of the carrying value of goodwill as of that date.

APPENDIX B ▸ SALES TAXES

All companies operating in Canada need to understand how sales taxes apply to their particular business in their province or territory. Sales taxes may take the form of the Goods and Services Tax (GST), Provincial Sales Tax (PST), or Harmonized Sales Tax (HST). GST is levied by the federal government. PST is levied by the provinces, with the exception of Alberta, the Northwest Territories, Nunavut, and Yukon, where no PST is charged. Ontario, Nova Scotia, New Brunswick, Newfoundland and Labrador, and recently Prince Edward Island (effective April 1, 2013) have combined the GST and PST into one Harmonized Sales Tax. At the point of writing this textbook, Quebec announced that it was also considering moving to combining its provincial sales tax, the Quebec Sales Tax (QST), and the GST into the HST.

A business is considered an agent of the federal and provincial governments and is therefore required to collect sales taxes on the sale of certain goods and services. In addition, businesses pay sales taxes on most payments. We will discuss the collection, payment, recording, and remittance of each of these types of sales taxes in the following sections.

Types of Sales Taxes

GOODS AND SERVICES TAX

The GST is a federal sales tax on most goods and services provided in Canada. A business must register for the GST if it provides taxable goods or services in Canada and if it has revenues of more than $30,000 in any year. Businesses that have to or decide to voluntarily register for the GST are called registrants. Registrants can claim a credit—called an input tax credit (ITC)—for the amount of GST they pay or owe on purchases of goods or services against the GST they collect or are owed. GST returns are submitted quarterly for most registrants (monthly for large registrants) to the Canada Revenue Agency. The taxes are payable to the Receiver General, who is the collection agent for the federal government.

> **STUDY OBJECTIVE 1**
>
> Explain the different types of sales tax.

For those provinces that have adopted the Harmonized Sales Tax, where the PST and GST have been combined into one tax, the Receiver General is the collection agent for both the federal and provincial governments.

The GST applies at a rate of 5% on most transactions (13%, 14%, or 15% in the case of HST, depending on the province). Transactions subject to GST/HST are called taxable supplies. There are two other categories of goods and services with respect to the GST/HST:

- zero-rated supplies, such as basic groceries and prescription drugs
- exempt supplies, such as educational services, health care services, and financial services

No GST/HST applies to zero-rated or exempt supplies. However, zero-rated suppliers can claim input tax credits.

Illustration B-1 provides the GST/HST status of some typical goods and services.

Taxable Supplies	Zero-Rated Supplies	Exempt Supplies
Building materials	Prescription drugs	Used house
Ready-to-eat pizza	Uncooked pizza	Dental services
Two doughnuts	Six or more doughnuts	Insurance policy

▸**ILLUSTRATION**  **B-1**
Examples of GST/HST status

The reason ready-to-eat pizza and two doughnuts have GST/HST added to the purchase price is because they are considered convenience items, which are taxable, and not basic groceries, which are not taxable.

PROVINCIAL SALES TAX

Provincial sales taxes are charged on retail sales of certain goods and services. As of April 1, 2013, there are only four provinces that charge a separate Provincial Sales Tax: British Columbia, Saskatchewan, Manitoba, and Quebec. For businesses that operate in several provinces, the amount of PST they need to charge will depend on where the goods are being shipped. Consequently, a business could have several PST payable accounts while operating out of a province where only HST applies to sales. Provincial sales taxes are remitted periodically to the Minister of Finance in each province. PST rates vary by province and can change with each provincial budget. Certain goods are exempt, such as children's clothing, textbooks, and residential rent, and may be purchased with no PST. Examples of exempt services that are not taxable include personal services such as dental and medical services. Because rates and exemptions vary by province, it is important, when starting a business, to check with provincial officials for details on how to calculate the provincial tax that must be applied to sales.

HARMONIZED SALES TAX

The provinces of Ontario, Nova Scotia, New Brunswick, Newfoundland and Labrador, and most recently Prince Edward Island charge Harmonized Sales Tax, or HST. Instead of charging GST and PST separately, only the HST is charged at a combined rate. British Columbia also charged HST, but effective April 1, 2013, it reverted from the combined HST to the original separate GST and PST taxes.

To summarize, four provinces—British Columbia, Manitoba, Quebec, and Saskatchewan—apply both PST and GST to the selling price of a taxable good or service. The provincial tax rates used by these four provinces vary but the GST is consistent at the rate of 5%. Five provinces charge a combined HST: New Brunswick, Newfoundland and Labrador, and Ontario charge 13%; Nova Scotia uses 15%; and Prince Edward Island applies 14% HST on the selling price of goods and services. Four provinces and territories charge only the GST: Alberta, the Northwest Territories, Nunavut, and Yukon. The rates of sales tax in each province and territory are shown in Illustration B-2.

▶ **ILLUSTRATION B-2**
Sales tax rates

Province/Territory	GST (HST) Rate	PST Rate	Combined Rate[1]
Alberta	5.0%	0.0%	5.0%
British Columbia	5.0%	7.0%	12.0%
Manitoba	5.0%	7.0%	12.0%
New Brunswick	13.0%	N/A	13.0%
Newfoundland and Labrador	13.0%	N/A	13.0%
Northwest Territories	5.0%	0.0%	5.0%
Nova Scotia	15.0%	N/A	15.0%
Nunavut	5.0%	0.0%	5.0%
Ontario	13.0%	N/A	13.0%
Prince Edward Island	14.0%	N/A	14.0%
Quebec	5.0%	9.975%	14.975%
Saskatchewan	5.0%	5.0%	10.0%
Yukon	5.0%	0.0%	5.0%

[1]These rates are in effect as of April 1, 2013, and are subject to change. Nova Scotia planned to reduce the HST to 14% (from 15%) on July 1, 2014, and to 13% (from 14%) on July 1, 2015.

Similar to GST, HST returns are submitted quarterly for most registrants (monthly for large registrants) to the Receiver General for Canada. The federal government then gives the provincial portion of the tax to the province.

Sales Taxes Collected on Receipts

Sales taxes are collected by businesses from consumers on taxable goods and services. It is important to understand that sales taxes are not a source of revenue for a company. They are collected by a company on behalf of the federal and provincial governments. Consequently, collected sales tax is a current liability to the company until remitted to the respective government at regular intervals.

» STUDY OBJECTIVE 2

Record sales taxes collected by businesses on goods and services.

SERVICES

Now let's look at how service companies record sales taxes on the services they provide.

Services with PST

Assume that $250.00 of cleaning services were provided by a company in Manitoba for cash on July 24. These services are subject to both PST (7%) and GST (5%), and would be recorded as follows:

Date	Account	Debit	Credit
July 24	Cash	280.00	
	Service Revenue		250.00
	PST Payable ($250 × 7%)		17.50
	GST Payable ($250 × 5%)		12.50
	To record cleaning service revenue.		

A = L + OE
+280.00   +17.50   +250.00
           +12.50
↑ Cash flows: +280.00

Note that the revenue recorded is $250.00, and not $280.00. The service revenue is exclusive of the GST and PST amounts collected, which are recorded as current liabilities.

Services with HST

Assume now that these same services were provided by a company in New Brunswick, where HST is 13%. The entry would be as follows:

Date	Account	Debit	Credit
July 24	Cash	282.50	
	Service Revenue		250.00
	HST Payable ($250.00 × 13%)		32.50
	To record cleaning service revenue.		

A = L + OE
+282.50   +32.50   +250.00
↑ Cash flows: +282.50

MERCHANDISE

Entries are needed to record the sales taxes owed when merchandise inventory (goods) is sold, or to reduce sales taxes payable when merchandise inventory is returned.

Sales with PST

Assume that Staples sells $1,000 of office furniture, on account, in the province of Manitoba, where PST is 7%. GST is 5%. Staples uses a perpetual inventory system and the cost of the furniture to Staples was $800. Staples will make the following two entries to record the sale and the cost of the sale on May 20:

Date	Account	Debit	Credit
May 20	Accounts Receivable	1,120	
	Sales		1,000
	GST Payable ($1,000 × 5%)		50
	PST Payable ($1,000 × 7%)		70
	To record sale of merchandise on account.		
20	Cost of Goods Sold	800	
	Merchandise Inventory		800
	To record cost of merchandise sold.		

A = L + OE
+1,120   +50   +1,000
          +70
Cash flows: no effect

A = L + OE
−800   −800
Cash flows: no effect

The merchandise inventory does not include any sales taxes that may have been paid when the company purchased the merchandise. We will learn more about that in the next section of this appendix.

Under a periodic inventory system, the second entry would not be recorded.

Sales Returns and Allowances with PST

If a $300 sales return and allowance were granted by Staples on May 25 for returned merchandise from the above sale, Staples' entries to record the sales return would appear as follows:

	A	=	L	+	OE
	−336		−15		−300
			−21		

Cash flows: no effect

	A	=	L	+	OE
	+240				+240

Cash flows: no effect

May 25	Sales Returns and Allowances	300	
	GST Payable ($300 × 5%)	15	
	PST Payable ($300 × 7%)	21	
	Accounts Receivable		336
	To record credit for returned merchandise.		
25	Merchandise Inventory ($300 ÷ $1,000 × $800)	240	
	Cost of Goods Sold		240
	To record cost of merchandise returned.		

Note that the GST and PST payable accounts, rather than a receivable account, are debited, to indicate that this is a return of previously collected sales tax. The second entry assumes that the merchandise was in good condition and returned to inventory.

Under a periodic inventory system, the second entry would not be recorded.

Sales with HST

Assume now that Staples sells the same $1,000 of office furniture, on account, in the province of Ontario, where there is no PST and where HST is 13%. Staples uses a perpetual inventory system and the cost of the furniture to Staples was $800. Staples will record the following two entries to record the sale and the cost of the sale on May 20:

	A	=	L	+	OE
	+1,130		+130		+1,000

Cash flows: no effect

	A	=	L	+	OE
	−800				−800

Cash flows: no effect

May 20	Accounts Receivable	1,130	
	Sales		1,000
	HST Payable ($1,000 × 13%)		130
	To record sale of merchandise on account.		
20	Cost of Goods Sold	800	
	Merchandise Inventory		800
	To record cost of merchandise sold.		

Under a periodic inventory system, the second entry would not be recorded.

Sales Returns and Allowances with HST

Assume the same $300 sales returns and allowances were granted by Staples on May 25 for returned merchandise from the above sale. Staples' entries to record the sales return would appear as follows:

	A	=	L	+	OE
	−339		−39		−300

Cash flows: no effect

	A	=	L	+	OE
	+240				+240

Cash flows: no effect

May 25	Sales Returns and Allowances	300	
	HST Payable ($300 × 13%)	39	
	Accounts Receivable		339
	To record credit for returned merchandise.		
25	Merchandise Inventory ($300 ÷ $1,000 × $800)	240	
	Cost of Goods Sold		240
	To record cost of merchandise returned.		

Under a periodic inventory system, the second entry would not be recorded.

Sales Taxes Paid on Payments

Businesses, similar to consumers, must pay the applicable PST and GST or HST charged by their suppliers on taxable goods and services.

» **STUDY OBJECTIVE 3**

Record sales taxes paid on the purchase of goods and services.

PURCHASE OF MERCHANDISE FOR RESALE

When purchasing merchandise for resale, the treatment of the PST is different than that of the GST. PST is a single-stage tax collected from the final consumers of taxable goods and services. Consequently, wholesalers do not charge provincial sales tax to the retailer, who will in turn resell the merchandise, at a higher price, to the final consumer. By presenting a vendor licence number, retailers are able to buy merchandise for resale, exempt of the PST.

Businesses must pay GST/HST on the purchase of merchandise but can then offset the GST/HST paid against any GST/HST collected. Consequently, when merchandise is purchased, the GST/HST paid by a business is **not** part of the inventory cost. The GST/HST paid on purchases is debited to an account called GST or HST Recoverable and is called an input tax credit.

Purchases with GST

The following is an entry to record the purchase of merchandise for resale in the province of Manitoba on May 4 at a price of $4,000, on account, using a perpetual inventory system:

May 4	Merchandise Inventory	4,000	
	GST Recoverable ($4,000 × 5%)	200	
	Accounts Payable		4,200
	To record merchandise purchased on account.		

A   = L + OE
+4,000 +4,200
+200

Cash flows: no effect

As previously discussed, the cost of the merchandise, $4,000, is not affected by the GST, which is recorded as a receivable.

Under a periodic inventory system, the $4,000 debit would have been recorded to the Purchases account.

Purchase Returns and Allowances with GST

The entry to record a $300 return of merchandise on May 8 is as follows:

May 8	Accounts Payable	315	
	GST Recoverable ($300 × 5%)		15
	Merchandise Inventory		300
	To record the return of merchandise.		

A   = L + OE
−15 −315
−300

Cash flows: no effect

Note that the GST Recoverable account is credited instead of the GST Payable account because this is a reduction of the previously recorded GST.

Under a periodic inventory system, the credit of $300 would have been recorded to the Purchase Returns and Allowances account.

To summarize, PST is not paid on purchases of merchandise for resale. GST paid on purchases is recoverable and recorded as a current asset in the GST Recoverable account. Purchase returns and allowances require an adjustment of GST only, since PST was not paid on the original purchase.

Purchases with HST

The following is an entry to record the purchase of merchandise for resale in the province of Prince Edward Island, where the HST rate is 14%, on May 4 at a price of $4,000, on account, using a perpetual inventory system:

A	=	L	+	OE
+4,000		+4,560		
+560				

Cash flows: no effect

May 4	Merchandise Inventory	4,000	
	HST Recoverable ($4,000 × 14%)	560	
	Accounts Payable		4,560
	To record merchandise purchased on account.		

The cost of the merchandise, $4,000, is not affected by the HST, which is recorded as a receivable. Under a periodic inventory system, the $4,000 debit would have been recorded to the Purchases account.

Purchase Returns and Allowances with HST

The entry to record a $300 return of merchandise in the province of Prince Edward Island, where the HST rate is 14%, on May 8 is as follows:

A	=	L	+	OE
−42		−342		
−300				

Cash flows: no effect

May 8	Accounts Payable	342	
	HST Recoverable ($300 × 14%)		42
	Merchandise Inventory		300
	To record the return of merchandise.		

Note that the HST Recoverable account is credited instead of the HST Payable account because this is a reduction of the previously recorded HST.

Under a periodic inventory system, the credit of $300 would have been recorded to the Purchase Returns and Allowances account.

To summarize, HST paid on purchases is recoverable and recorded as a current asset in the HST Recoverable account.

OPERATING EXPENSES

The accounting treatment of sales taxes incurred on operating expenses depends on the type of sales taxes that the company is charged.

Operating Expenses with PST

Although PST is not charged on goods purchased for resale, it is charged to businesses that use taxable goods and services in their operations. For example, a business must pay GST and PST when it buys office supplies. As with all purchases made by a business that is a registrant, the GST is recoverable (can be offset as an input tax credit against GST collected). Because the PST is not recoverable, the PST forms part of the cost of the asset or expense that is being acquired.

The following is the entry for a cash purchase of office supplies on May 18 in the amount of $200 in the province of Saskatchewan, where PST is 5% and GST is 5%:

A	=	L	+	OE
+210				
+10				
−220				

↓ Cash flows: −220

May 18	Supplies ($200 + $10* PST)	210	
	GST Recoverable ($200 × 5%)	10	
	Cash		220
	To record purchase of office supplies.		

*$200 × 5% = $10

In this situation, the cost of the supplies includes both the supplies and the PST. Because GST is recoverable, it does not form part of the asset cost.

This same purchase would be recorded as follows if it occurred in the province of Quebec, where PST is 9.975% and GST is 5%:

May 18	Supplies ($200.00 + $19.95* PST)	219.95	
	GST Recoverable ($200.00 × 5%)	10.00	
	Cash		229.95
	To record purchase of office supplies.		

*$200.00 × 9.975% = $19.95

A	=	L	+	OE
+219.95				
+10.00				
−229.95				

↓ Cash flows: −229.95

Operating Expenses with HST

When HST is applied, it is treated in the same manner as GST. HST is recoverable and does not form part of the cost of the item purchased. The purchase of office supplies would be recorded as follows if it had occurred in the province of Ontario, where HST is 13%:

May 18	Supplies	200	
	HST Recoverable ($200 × 13%)	26	
	Cash		226
	To record purchase of office supplies.		

A	=	L	+	OE
+200				
+26				
−226				

↓ Cash flows: −226

Note that the type and amount of sales tax paid changes the amount recorded as the cost of office supplies in each province: $210.00 in Saskatchewan, $219.95 in Quebec, and $200.00 in Ontario.

PROPERTY, PLANT, AND EQUIPMENT

The PST and GST or HST apply to other purchases, such as the purchase of property, plant, and equipment, in the same manner as described in the operating expenses section above. All GST (or HST) paid is recoverable and is not part of the cost of the asset. The PST, however, is part of the cost of the asset being purchased as it is not recoverable.

Property, Plant, and Equipment with PST

The following is the entry for the purchase of office furniture on May 20 from Staples, on account, for $1,000 plus applicable sales taxes in Manitoba, where PST is 7% and GST is 5%.

May 20	Furniture ($1,000 + $70* PST)	1,070	
	GST Recoverable ($1,000 × 5%)	50	
	Accounts Payable		1,120
	To record purchase of office furniture.		

*$1,000 × 7% = $70

A	=	L	+	OE
+1,070		+1,120		
+50				

Cash flows: no effect

Because the PST is not recoverable, the cost of the furniture is $1,070, inclusive of the PST.

Compare this entry made by the buyer to record the purchase with the entry made by the seller (Staples) to record the sale, shown earlier in this appendix. Both companies record accounts payable and accounts receivable in the same amount, $1,120. However, the seller records both GST and PST payable while the buyer records only GST recoverable. The PST paid by the buyer is not recoverable, so it becomes part of the cost of the office furniture, $1,070.

In Saskatchewan, where PST is 5% and GST is 5%, the same entry would be recorded as follows:

May 20	Furniture ($1,000 + $50* PST)	1,050	
	GST Recoverable ($1,000 × 5%)	50	
	Accounts Payable		1,100
	To record purchase of office furniture.		

*$1,000 × 5% = $50

A	=	L	+	OE
+1,050		+1,100		
+50				

Cash flows: no effect

Property, Plant, and Equipment with HST

In Ontario, where HST is 13%, the entry would be recorded as follows:

A = L + OE
+1,000 +1,130
+130

Cash flows: no effect

May 20	Furniture	1,000	
	HST Recoverable ($1,000 × 13%)	130	
	Accounts Payable		1,130
	To record purchase of office furniture.		

As we have noted before, the type and amount of sales taxes paid change the amount recorded as the cost of the office furniture in each province: $1,070 in Manitoba, $1,050 in Saskatchewan, and $1,000 in Ontario.

Remittance of Sales Taxes

>> **STUDY OBJECTIVE 4**

Record the remittance of sales taxes.

As mentioned in the introduction, businesses act as agents of the federal and provincial governments in charging and later remitting taxes charged on sales and services. For example, Staples, the seller of office furniture shown earlier in the appendix, must remit GST or HST to the Receiver General for Canada and PST to the Minister of Finance, where applicable. Notice that even if Staples has not received payment from a customer buying on account before the due date for the remittance, the tax must still be paid to the government authorities. As a registrant, however, Staples will also benefit from claiming input tax credits and recording a reduction in amounts payable from applying GST/HST on sales.

GST (OR HST)

When remitting the amount owed to the federal government at the end of a reporting period for GST (or HST), the amount of GST/HST payable is reduced by any amount in the GST (or HST) Recoverable account. Any difference is remitted, as shown in the following journal entry, using assumed payable and recoverable amounts:

A = L + OE
−2,500 −6,250
−3,750

↓ Cash flows: −3,750

June 30	GST (or HST) Payable	6,250	
	GST (or HST) Recoverable		2,500
	Cash		3,750
	To record remittance of GST (or HST).		

The electronic filing of GST/HST returns requires the registrant to report at specified dates, depending on the business's volume of sales. The amount of the sales and other revenue as well as the amount of GST/HST charged on these sales, whether collected or not, is reported on the return. The amount of the input tax credits claimed is also entered to reduce the amount owing to the Receiver General. If the GST/HST recoverable exceeds the GST/HST payable, the return should be filed as soon as possible in order to ask for a refund. The entry to record the cash receipt from a GST/HST refund will be similar to the entry shown above, except that there will be a debit to Cash, instead of a credit.

The above discussion of the remittance of GST/HST explains why all registrants need two general ledger accounts—a payable account and a recoverable account. The GST (or HST) Payable account is used to keep track of all GST or HST charged on sales and revenues. The second account, GST (or HST) Recoverable, is used to keep track of the GST/HST input tax credits that have been paid on all of the business's purchases. Both amounts must be reported on the return. Failure by a business to capture the proper amounts of input tax credits has a significant impact on income and on cash flows.

PST

The remittance of PST to the Minister of Finance of the applicable province is similar to that of GST/HST except that, since no credit can be claimed, the amount paid at the end of each reporting period is the amount of the balance in the PST Payable account.

Consequently, the entry to record a remittance of PST, using an assumed amount payable, would appear as follows:

June 30	PST Payable	7,400	
	Cash		7,400
	To record remittance of PST.		

A	=	L	+	OE
−7,400		−7,400		

↓ Cash flows: −7,400

Conclusion

Be careful when you record the amounts of taxes charged or claimed in the business accounts. Numbers must be rounded carefully. If the amount of the tax calculated on a credit sale is less than half a cent, the amount should be rounded down. If the amount of the tax as calculated comes to more than half a cent, the amount should be rounded up. For example, applying 13% HST on an amount of $49.20 would give you $6.396. The tax amount to be recorded must be rounded up to $6.40. On the other hand, if the sale is a cash sale, due to the abolition of the one-cent coin (the penny), the amount of the sale, including all taxes, must be rounded to the nearest five cents. Rounding might seem insignificant, but when a business has many transactions, the amounts can add up and the registrant is responsible to the government authorities for any shortfall created in error.

Sales tax law is intricate. It has added a lot of complexity to the accounting for most transactions flowing through today's businesses. Fortunately, computers that are programmed to automatically determine and record the correct sales tax rate for each good or service provided have simplified matters somewhat. Before recording sales tax transactions, however, it is important to understand all of the relevant sales tax regulations. Check the federal and provincial laws in your jurisdiction.

▶ Brief Exercises

BEB–1 List the various sales taxes in Canada and explain the main differences between the types. In what way are they alike to the consumer?

Explain the different types of sales taxes. (SO 1) AP

BEB–2 Record the sale on account, for $1,600, of merchandise costing $900 in the province of Quebec. Assume the company uses a perpetual inventory system. The QST is 9.975%.

Record sales—perpetual inventory system—Quebec. (SO 2) AP

BEB–3 Half of the shipment described in BEB–2 is returned as the incorrect sizes have been shipped. Record the return of merchandise on the seller's books.

Record sales return—perpetual inventory system—Quebec. (SO 2) AP

BEB–4 Record the sale in BEB–2 and the sales return in BEB–3 assuming the business uses a periodic inventory system.

Record sales and sales return—periodic inventory system—Quebec. (SO 2) AP

BEB–5 Record the billing for $450 of services by D. R. Wong, dentist, in the province of British Columbia. Dental services are exempt from GST and PST.

Record exempt services—British Columbia. (SO 2) AP

BEB–6 Record the billing of accounting services of $700 for the preparation of personal income tax returns in the territory of Nunavut. GST is applicable on this service. Nunavut does not charge PST.

Record fees—Nunavut. (SO 2) AP

BEB–7 Record the purchase on account of $4,100 of merchandise for resale in the province of Manitoba, where the PST is 7%. The company uses a perpetual inventory system and the purchase is PST exempt.

Record inventory purchase—perpetual inventory system—Manitoba. (SO 3) AP

BEB–8 Record the return of $500 of the merchandise purchased in BEB–7.

Record purchase return—perpetual inventory system—Manitoba. (SO 3) AP

Record inventory purchase—perpetual inventory system—New Brunswick. (SO 3) AP

BEB–9   Record the purchase on account of $4,100 of merchandise for resale in the province of New Brunswick, where HST is 13%. The company uses a perpetual inventory system.

Record purchase return—perpetual inventory system—New Brunswick. (SO 3) AP

BEB–10   Record the return of $500 of the merchandise purchased in BEB–9.

Record purchase of supplies—Saskatchewan. (SO 3) AP

BEB–11   Record the cash purchase of $600 of office supplies in the province of Saskatchewan, where PST is 5%.

Record purchase of supplies—Nova Scotia. (SO 3) AP

BEB–12   Record the cash purchase of $600 of office supplies in the province of Nova Scotia, where HST is 15%.

Record purchase of vehicle—Prince Edward Island. (SO 3) AP

BEB–13   Record the purchase on account of a $32,000 delivery truck in the province of Prince Edward Island, where HST is 14%.

Record purchase of vehicle—British Columbia. (SO 3) AP

BEB–14   Record the purchase on account of a $32,000 delivery truck in the province of British Columbia, where the PST is 7%.

Record purchase of supplies and inventory—perpetual inventory system—Manitoba. (SO 3) AP

BEB–15   Record the purchase on account of $300 of office supplies and $5,000 of merchandise for resale in the province of Manitoba. The company uses a perpetual inventory system and the purchase of merchandise is PST exempt. The PST rate is 7%.

Record remittance of GST and PST—British Columbia. (SO 4) AP

BEB–16   Record two payments: one cheque to the Receiver General for GST and one to the Minister of Finance of British Columbia for PST. The balances in the accounts are as follows: GST Payable $6,120, GST Recoverable $940, and PST Payable $8,570.

Record HST refund. (SO 4) AP

BEB–17   Record the deposit of a cheque from the Receiver General for a refund of $690 following the filing of an HST return. The balances in the accounts are as follows: HST Payable $3,920 and HST Recoverable $4,610.

▶ Exercises

Record purchase and sales transactions—perpetual inventory system—Manitoba. (SO 2, 3) AP

EB–1   Wu Limited is a merchant operating in the province of Manitoba, where the PST rate is 7%. Wu uses a perpetual inventory system. Transactions for the business are shown below:

May   1   Paid May rent to the landlord for the rental of a warehouse. The lease calls for monthly payments of $7,300 plus 5% GST.

        3   Sold merchandise on account and shipped merchandise to Marvin Ltd. for $25,000, plus applicable sales taxes, terms n/30, FOB shipping point. This merchandise cost Wu $18,600.

        5   Granted Marvin Ltd. a sales allowance of $800 for defective merchandise purchased on May 3. No merchandise was returned.

        7   Purchased on account from Macphee Ltd. merchandise for resale for $11,000, plus applicable tax.

     12   Made a cash purchase at Home Depot of a desk for the shipping clerk. The price of the desk was $600 before applicable taxes.

     31   Paid the quarterly remittance of GST to the Receiver General. The balances in the accounts were as follows: GST Payable $7,480 and GST Recoverable $1,917.

Instructions

Prepare the journal entries to record these transactions on the books of Wu Limited.

Record purchase and sales transactions—perpetual inventory system—Alberta. (SO 2, 3) AP

EB–2   Refer to Wu Limited in EB–1. Assume instead that the company operates in the province of Alberta, where PST is not applicable.

Instructions

Prepare the journal entries to record these transactions on the books of Wu.

Record purchase and sales transactions—perpetual inventory system—Ontario. (SO 2, 3) AP

EB–3   Refer to Wu Limited in EB–1. Assume instead that the company operates in the province of Ontario, where HST is 13%.

Instructions

Prepare the journal entries to record these transactions on the books of Wu. Assume that the GST balances on May 31 are the balances in the HST accounts.

EB–4 Using the information for the transactions of Wu Limited in EB–1, assume now that Wu uses a periodic inventory system and operates in the province of Manitoba.

Instructions

Prepare the journal entries to record these transactions on the books of Wu Limited.

Record purchase and sales transactions—periodic inventory system—Manitoba. (SO 2, 3) AP

EB–5 Using the information for the transactions of Wu Limited in EB–1, assume now that Wu uses a periodic inventory system and operates in the province of Alberta, where PST is not applicable.

Instructions

Prepare the journal entries to record these transactions on the books of Wu.

Record purchase and sales transactions—periodic inventory system—Alberta. (SO 2, 3) AP

EB–6 Using the information for the transactions of Wu Limited in EB–1, assume now that Wu uses a periodic inventory system and operates in the province of Ontario, where HST is 13%.

Instructions

Prepare the journal entries to record these transactions on the books of Wu. Assume that the GST balances on May 31 provided in EB–1 are the balances in the HST accounts.

Record purchase and sales transactions—periodic inventory system—Ontario. (SO 2, 3) AP

EB–7 Leon Cheng is a sole proprietor providing accounting services in the province of British Columbia, where PST is charged at the rate of 7% and GST is at the rate of 5%. Transactions for the business are shown below:

Record transactions for services, equipment, and supplies—British Columbia. (SO 2, 3, 4) AP

June 1 Paid cash to a local courier for the delivery of documents to several clients. The invoice was for $200 plus GST and PST.

5 Paid $800 cash plus GST and PST to have the office painted. Use Repairs Expense.

10 Purchased photocopy paper for $250 from a local stationery store, on account. The store added the appropriate sales taxes to the purchase price.

13 Billed a client for accounting services provided. The fee charged was $4,700 and the appropriate sales taxes were added to the fee billed.

15 Collected $896 on account. This included accounting services of $800, GST of $40, and PST of $56.

22 Paid $720 cash plus applicable taxes to Air Canada for an airline ticket to Ottawa to meet with a client. Airfare is subject to both PST and GST.

30 Received invoice from BC Tel. for telephone service for the month of June. The invoice is for $150 plus GST and PST.

30 Paid the quarterly remittance of GST to the Receiver General. The balances in the accounts were as follows: GST Payable $1,890.50 and GST Recoverable $741.60.

30 Paid the quarterly remittance of PST to the Minister of Revenue for the province of British Columbia. The balance in the PST Payable account was $2,640.00.

Instructions

Prepare the journal entries to record these transactions on the books of Leon Cheng's accounting business.

EB–8 Ruby Gordon L.L.B. is a sole proprietor providing legal services in the province of Newfoundland and Labrador, where the HST rate is 13%. Transactions for the business are shown below:

Record transactions for services, equipment, and supplies—Newfoundland and Labrador. (SO 2, 3, 4) AP

June 8 Purchased equipment for scanning and printing on account at a cost of $1,500. The appropriate taxes were added to this purchase price.

10 Purchased toner for the equipment for $100 cash from a local stationery store. The store added the appropriate taxes to the purchase price.

12 Billed Lee Ltd. for legal services provided. The fee charged was $1,250 plus appropriate taxes.

18 Paid cash of $220 plus applicable taxes to have a boardroom table repaired.

22 Collected from Lee Ltd. account billed on June 12.

30 Paid the quarterly remittance of HST to the Receiver General. The balances in the accounts were as follows: HST Payable $2,520.60 and HST Recoverable $820.45.

Instructions

Prepare the journal entries to record these transactions on the books of Ruby Gordon's legal practice.

EB–9 Refer to the data for Ruby Gordon, L.L.B. in EB–8. Assume instead that Ruby is operating her legal practice in Alberta and that on June 30 she paid a quarterly remittance of GST, as opposed to HST, to the Receiver General. Assume the balances were as follows: GST Payable $970.50 and GST Recoverable $315.55.

Instructions

Prepare the journal entries to record these transactions on the books of Ruby Gordon's legal practice.

Record transactions for services, equipment, and supplies—Alberta. (SO 2, 3, 4) AP

▶ Problems

Record purchase and sales transactions—perpetual inventory system—Ontario. (SO 2, 3) AP

PB–1 Mark's Music is a store that buys and sells musical instruments in Ontario, where the HST rate is 13%. Mark's Music uses a perpetual inventory system. Transactions for the business are shown below:

Nov. 2 Purchased three electric guitars from Fender Supply Limited, on account, at a cost of $900 each.

4 Made a cash sale of two keyboards for a total invoice price of $2,600, plus applicable taxes. The cost of each keyboard was $675.

5 Received a credit memorandum from Western Acoustic Inc. for the return of an acoustic guitar that was defective. The original invoice price before taxes was $700 and the guitar had been purchased on account. Mark's Music intends to return the defective guitar to the original supplier.

7 One of the keyboards from the cash sale of November 4 was returned to the store for a full cash refund because the customer was not satisfied with the instrument. The keyboard was returned to inventory.

8 Purchased supplies from a stationery store. The price of the supplies is $200 before all applicable taxes.

10 Sold one Omega trumpet to Regional Band, on account, for an invoice price of $5,100 before applicable taxes. The trumpet had cost Mark's Music $2,850.

13 Purchased two saxophones from Yamaha Canada Inc. on account. The invoice price was $1,900 for each saxophone, excluding applicable taxes.

14 Collected $4,150 on account. The payment included all applicable taxes.

16 Returned to Yamaha Canada Inc. one of the saxophones purchased on November 13, as it was the wrong model. Received a credit memorandum from Yamaha for the full purchase price.

20 Made a payment on account for the amount owing to Fender Supply Limited for the purchase of November 2.

Instructions

Prepare the journal entries to record the Mark's Music transactions.

Record purchase and sales transactions—perpetual inventory system—British Columbia. (SO 2, 3) AP

PB–2 Transaction data for Mark's Music are available in PB–1. Assume instead that the company operates in the province of British Columbia, where the PST rate is 7% and the GST rate is 5%.

Instructions

Prepare the journal entries to record these transactions on the books of Mark's Music.

Record purchase and sales transactions—periodic inventory system—Ontario. (SO 2, 3) AP

PB–3 Transaction data for Mark's Music are available in PB–1. Assume that the company uses a periodic inventory system instead of a perpetual inventory system and operates in the province of Ontario, where the HST rate is 13%.

Instructions

Prepare the journal entries to record the Mark's Music transactions.

Record purchase and sales transactions—periodic inventory system—British Columbia. (SO 2, 3) AP

PB–4 Transaction data for Mark's Music are available in PB–1. Assume that the company uses a periodic inventory system instead of a perpetual inventory system and operates in the province of British Columbia, where the PST rate is 7% and the GST rate is 5%.

Instructions

Prepare the journal entries to record these transactions on the books of Mark's Music.

Record service transactions—Alberta. (SO 2, 3, 4) AP

PB–5 Manny Lee, L.L.B., is a lawyer operating as a sole proprietor in the province of Alberta. Alberta does not charge provincial sales taxes and the GST rate is 5%. Transactions for the business are shown below:

May 1 Signed a two-year lease for the office space and immediately paid the first and last months' rent. The lease calls for monthly rent of $1,650 plus applicable taxes.

4 Purchased furniture, on account, from George's Furniture at a cost of $4,100. The appropriate sales taxes were added to this purchase price.

5 Returned one chair to George's due to a defect. The cost of the chair before taxes was $800.

6 Billed a client for the preparation of a contract. The client was very pleased with the document and immediately paid Manny's invoice for fees of $2,500 plus taxes.

10 Purchased paper for the photocopier for $300 cash from a local stationery store. The store added the appropriate sales taxes to the purchase price.

13 Billed Manson Ltd. for legal services rendered connected with the purchase of land. The fee charged is $1,100 plus applicable taxes.

18   Paid George's for the furniture purchase of May 4, net of returned items.

19   Paid $22 cash to a local grocery store for coffee for the office coffee machine. Groceries are GST and HST exempt. Use Office Expense.

21   In accordance with the lease agreement with the landlord, Manny must pay for water supplied by the municipality. The water invoice was received and the services amounted to $150. No GST is charged for municipal water.

25   Collected a full payment from Manson Ltd. for the May 13 bill.

27   Completed the preparation of a purchase and sale agreement for Pedneault Inc. and billed fees of $600.

Instructions

(a) Prepare the journal entries to record these transactions on the books of Manny Lee's law practice.

(b) Determine the balances in the GST Payable and GST Recoverable accounts. Determine if the company must make a payment to the Receiver General or if it will apply for a refund. Record the appropriate journal entry.

PB–6   Refer to Manny Lee in PB–5. Assume instead that Mr. Lee operates in the province of Ontario, where the HST rate is 13%.

Record service transactions— Ontario. (SO 2, 3, 4) AP

Instructions

(a) Prepare the journal entries to record these transactions on the books of Manny Lee's law practice.

(b) Determine the balances in the HST Payable and HST Recoverable accounts. Determine if the business must make a payment to the Receiver General or if it will apply for a refund. Record the appropriate journal entry.

In the textbook, we learned how to record accounting transactions in a general journal. Each journal entry was then individually posted to its respective general ledger account. However, such a practice is only useful in a company where the volume of transactions is low. In most companies, it is necessary to use additional journals (called special journals) and ledgers (called subsidiary ledgers) to record transaction data.

We will look at subsidiary ledgers and special journals in the next sections. Both subsidiary ledgers and special journals can be used in either a manual accounting system or a computerized accounting system.

The illustrations provided in this appendix are taken from a manual accounting system. Computerized accounting systems vary in the way in which the accounting information is captured, processed, and reported. The software nevertheless is programmed to provide the same basic information that is maintained in a manual accounting system. If you can understand how a manual system works, you will be able to follow how a computerized system is capturing, recording, and reporting transactions for a business of any size or type.

Subsidiary Ledgers

Imagine a business that has several thousand customers who purchase merchandise from it on account. It records the transactions with these customers in only one general ledger account—Accounts Receivable. It would be virtually impossible to determine the balance owed by an individual customer at any specific time. Similarly, the amount payable to one creditor would be difficult to locate quickly from a single accounts payable account in the general ledger.

>> **STUDY OBJECTIVE 1**

Describe the purposes and advantages of maintaining subsidiary ledgers.

Instead, companies use subsidiary ledgers to keep track of individual balances. A subsidiary ledger is a group of accounts that share a common characteristic (for example, all accounts receivable). The subsidiary ledger frees the general ledger from the details of individual balances. A subsidiary ledger is an addition to, and an expansion of, the general ledger.

Two common subsidiary ledgers are:

1. The accounts receivable (or customers') ledger, which collects transaction data for individual customers
2. The accounts payable (or creditors') ledger, which collects transaction data for individual creditors

Another subsidiary ledger, as described in Chapter 5, is the inventory ledger, which collects transaction data for each inventory item purchased and sold. The inventory ledger may also include information used by the purchasing department, such as the terms negotiated with suppliers. Computerized systems can be programmed to automatically produce purchase orders when the inventory is low to avoid shortages. Some companies also use a payroll ledger, detailing individual employee pay records. Other companies use a long-lived asset ledger to keep track of each item of property, plant, and equipment. In each of these subsidiary ledgers, individual accounts are arranged in alphabetical, numerical, or alphanumerical order.

The detailed data from a subsidiary ledger are summarized in a general ledger account. For example, the detailed data from the accounts receivable subsidiary ledger are summarized in Accounts Receivable in the general ledger. The general ledger account that summarizes subsidiary ledger data is called a control account.

Each general ledger control account balance must equal the total balance of the individual accounts in the related subsidiary ledger. This is an important internal control function.

EXAMPLE

An example of an accounts receivable control account and subsidiary ledger is shown in Illustration C-1 for Mercier Enterprises.

ILLUSTRATION C-1
Accounts receivable general ledger control account and subsidiary ledger

GENERAL LEDGER

Accounts Receivable No. 112

Date	Explanation	Ref.	Debit	Credit	Balance
2014					
Jan. 31			12,000		12,000
31				8,000	4,000

ACCOUNTS RECEIVABLE SUBSIDIARY LEDGER

Aaron Co. No. 112-172

Date	Explanation	Ref.	Debit	Credit	Balance
2014					
Jan. 11	Invoice 336		6,000		6,000
19	Payment			4,000	2,000

Branden Inc. No. 112-173

Date	Explanation	Ref.	Debit	Credit	Balance
2014					
Jan. 12	Invoice 337		3,000		3,000
21	Payment			3,000	0

Caron Co. No. 112-174

Date	Explanation	Ref.	Debit	Credit	Balance
2014					
Jan. 20	Invoice 339		3,000		3,000
29	Payment			1,000	2,000

The example is based on the following transactions:

Credit Sales			Collections on Account		
Jan. 11	Aaron Co.	$ 6,000	Jan. 19	Aaron Co.	$4,000
12	Branden Inc.	3,000	21	Branden Inc.	3,000
20	Caron Co.	3,000	29	Caron Co.	1,000
		$12,000			$8,000

The total debits ($12,000) and credits ($8,000) in Accounts Receivable in the general ledger match the detailed debits and credits in the subsidiary accounts. The balance of $4,000 in the control account agrees with the total of the balances in the individual accounts receivable accounts (Aaron $2,000 + Branden $0 + Caron $2,000) in the subsidiary ledger.

Rather than relying on customer or creditor names in a subsidiary ledger, a computer system expands the account number of the control account. For example, if the general ledger control account Accounts Receivable was numbered 112, the first customer account in the accounts receivable subsidiary ledger might be numbered 112-001, the second 112-002, and so on. Data entry in a computerized system is much faster if account numbers, rather than customer names, are used. Most systems allow inquiries about specific customer accounts in the subsidiary ledger (by account number) or about the control account.

As shown, postings are made monthly to the control account in the general ledger. We will learn, in the next section, how special journals facilitate monthly postings. We will also learn how to fill in the posting references (in the Ref. column) in both the general ledger and subsidiary ledger accounts. Postings to the individual accounts in the subsidiary ledger are made daily. The rationale for posting daily is to ensure that account information is current. This enables Mercier Enterprises to monitor credit limits, send statements to customers, and answer inquiries from customers about their account balances. In a computerized accounting system, transactions are simultaneously recorded in journals and posted to both the general and subsidiary ledgers.

ADVANTAGES OF SUBSIDIARY LEDGERS

Subsidiary ledgers have several advantages:

1. They show transactions that affect one customer or one creditor in a single account. They provide up-to-date information on specific account balances.
2. They free the general ledger from excessive details. A trial balance of the general ledger does not contain vast numbers of individual customer account balances.
3. They make a division of labour possible in posting. One employee can post to the general ledger while different employees post to the subsidiary ledgers. This strengthens internal control, since one employee verifies the work of the other.
4. They help locate errors in individual accounts. The potential for errors is minimized by reducing the number of accounts in one ledger and by using control accounts.

In a computerized accounting system, the internal control achieved by the double-checking of work performed by one employee by another employee, as described in item 3 above, doesn't happen as often. The accounting software is programmed to perform mathematical functions without error and to post entries to the subsidiary and general ledgers simultaneously. Consequently, computerized accounting systems do not make errors such as calculation errors and posting errors. Other errors, such as entry errors, can and do still occur. Internal control must be done using different means in computerized systems since account transactions are posted automatically.

Special Journals

As mentioned earlier, journalizing transactions in a two-column (debit and credit) general journal is satisfactory only when there are few transactions. To help with the journalizing and posting of multiple transactions, most companies use special journals in addition to the general journal.

If a company has large numbers of similar transactions, it is useful to create a special journal for only those transactions. Examples of similar transactions that occur frequently include all sales of merchandise on account, or all cash receipts. The types of special journals a company will use depend largely on the types of transactions that occur frequently for that company.

While the form, type, and number of special journals used will vary among organizations, many merchandising companies use the journals shown in Illustration C-2 to record daily transactions. The letters that appear in parentheses following the journal name represent the posting reference used for each journal.

>> **STUDY OBJECTIVE 2**

Record transactions in special journals and post to subsidiary and general ledgers.

Sales Journal (S)	Cash Receipts Journal (CR)	Purchases Journal (P)	Cash Payments Journal (CP)	General Journal (J)
All sales of merchandise on account	All cash received (including cash sales)	All purchases on account	All cash paid (including cash purchases of merchandise)	Transactions that cannot be entered in a special journal, including correcting, adjusting, and closing entries

▶ **ILLUSTRATION** C-2
Use of special journals and the general journal

If a transaction cannot be recorded in a special journal, it is recorded in the general journal. For example, if you have four special journals, as listed in Illustration C-2, sales and purchase returns and allowances are recorded in the general journal. Similarly, correcting, adjusting, and closing entries are recorded in the general journal. Other types of special journals may sometimes be used in certain situations. For example, if sales returns and allowances are frequent, an additional special journal may be used to record these transactions. A payroll journal is another example of a special journal. It organizes and summarizes payroll details for companies with many employees.

The use of special journals reduces the time needed for the recording and posting process. In addition, special journals permit a greater division of labour. For example, one employee may journalize all cash receipts. Another may journalize credit sales. The division of responsibilities ensures that one person does not have control over related aspects of a transaction. In this instance, recording the sale and account receivable has been separated from recording the collection of cash from that receivable. This may reduce the opportunity for intentional fraud or unintentional error, and is one aspect of good internal control.

For a merchandising company, the same special journals are used whether a company uses the periodic or perpetual system to account for its inventory. The only distinction is the number of, and title for, the columns each journal uses. We will use Karns Wholesale Supply to show the use of special journals in the following sections. Karns uses a perpetual inventory system. The variations between the periodic and perpetual inventory systems are highlighted in helpful hints for your information. In addition, special journals under a periodic inventory system are shown more fully at the end of this appendix.

SALES JOURNAL

The sales journal is used to record sales of merchandise on account. Cash sales of merchandise are entered in the cash receipts journal. Credit sales of assets other than merchandise are entered in the general journal.

Journalizing Credit Sales

Under the perpetual inventory system, each entry in the sales journal results in one entry at selling price and another entry at cost. The entry at selling price is a debit to Accounts Receivable (a control account supported by a subsidiary ledger) and a credit of an equal amount to Sales. The entry at cost is a debit to Cost of Goods Sold and a credit of an equal amount to Merchandise Inventory. Some companies also set up Merchandise Inventory as a control account supported by a subsidiary ledger.

A sales journal with two amount columns can show a sales transaction recognized at both selling price and cost on only one line. The two-column sales journal of Karns Wholesale Supply is shown in Illustration C-3, using assumed credit sales transactions.

▶ **ILLUSTRATION** C-3
Sales journal—
perpetual inventory system

			KARNS WHOLESALE SUPPLY			
			Sales Journal			**S1**
Date	**Account Debited**	**Invoice No.**	**Ref.**	**Accts. Receivable Dr. Sales Cr.**	**Cost of Goods Sold Dr. Merchandise Inventory Cr.**	
2014						
May 3	Abbot Sisters	101		10,600	6,360	
7	Babson Co.	102		11,350	7,370	
14	Carson Bros.	103		7,800	5,070	
19	Deli Co.	104		9,300	6,510	
21	Abbot Sisters	105		15,400	10,780	
24	Deli Co.	106		21,210	15,900	
27	Babson Co.	107		14,570	10,200	
				90,230	62,190	

Helpful hint In a periodic inventory system, the sales journal would have only one column to record the sale at selling price (Accounts Receivable Dr., Sales Cr.). The cost of goods sold is not recorded. It is calculated at the end of the period.

The reference (Ref.) column is not used in journalizing. It is used in posting the sales journal, as explained in the next section. Also, note that, unlike in the general journal, an explanation is not required for each entry in a special journal. Finally, note that each invoice is prenumbered to ensure that all invoices are journalized.

If management wishes to record its sales by department, additional columns may be provided in the sales journal. For example, a department store may have columns for home furnishings, sporting goods, shoes, etc. In addition, the federal government and practically all provinces require that sales taxes be charged on items sold. If sales taxes are collected, it is necessary to add more credit columns to the sales journal for GST Payable and PST Payable (or HST Payable).

Posting the Sales Journal

Postings from the sales journal are made daily to the individual accounts receivable accounts in the subsidiary ledger. Posting the total sales for the month to the general ledger is done monthly. Illustration C-4 shows both the daily postings to the accounts receivable subsidiary ledger and the monthly postings to the general ledger accounts. We have assumed that Karns Wholesale Supply does not maintain an inventory subsidiary ledger. However, if it did, the procedure is similar to that illustrated for the accounts receivable subsidiary ledger.

▶ ILLUSTRATION C-4
Sales journal—
perpetual inventory system

KARNS WHOLESALE SUPPLY
Sales Journal   S1

Date	Account Debited	Invoice No.	Ref.	Accts. Receivable Dr. Sales Cr.	Cost of Goods Sold Dr. Merchandise Inventory Cr.
2014					
May 3	Abbot Sisters	101	√	10,600	6,360
7	Babson Co.	102	√	11,350	7,370
14	Carson Bros.	103	√	7,800	5,070
19	Deli Co.	104	√	9,300	6,510
21	Abbot Sisters	105	√	15,400	10,780
24	Deli Co.	106	√	21,210	15,900
27	Babson Co.	107	√	14,570	10,200
				90,230	62,190
				(112)/(401)	(505)/(120)

Individual amounts are posted daily to the subsidiary ledger.

Totals are posted at the end of the accounting period to the general ledger.

ACCOUNTS RECEIVABLE SUBSIDIARY LEDGER

Abbot Sisters

Date	Ref.	Debit	Credit	Balance
2014				
May 3	S1	10,600		10,600
21	S1	15,400		26,000

Babson Co.

Date	Ref.	Debit	Credit	Balance
2014				
May 7	S1	11,350		11,350
27	S1	14,570		25,920

Carson Bros.

Date	Ref.	Debit	Credit	Balance
2014				
May 14	S1	7,800		7,800

Deli Co.

Date	Ref.	Debit	Credit	Balance
2014				
May 19	S1	9,300		9,300
24	S1	21,210		30,510

GENERAL LEDGER

Accounts Receivable   No. 112

Date	Ref.	Debit	Credit	Balance
2014				
May 31	S1	90,230		90,230

Merchandise Inventory   No. 120

Date	Ref.	Debit	Credit	Balance
2014				
May 31	S1		62,190	62,190cr[1]

Sales   No. 401

Date	Ref.	Debit	Credit	Balance
2014				
May 31	S1		90,230	90,230

Cost of Goods Sold   No. 505

Date	Ref.	Debit	Credit	Balance
2014				
May 31	S1	62,190		62,190

Accounts Receivable is a control account.

The subsidiary ledger is separate from the general ledger.

[1]The normal balance for Merchandise Inventory is a debit. But because of the sequence in which we have posted the special journals, with the sales journal first, the credits to Merchandise Inventory are posted before the debits. This posting sequence causes the temporary credit balance in Merchandise Inventory, which exists only until the other journals are posted.

A check mark (√) is inserted in the reference posting column to indicate that the daily posting to the customer's account has been made. A check mark is used when the subsidiary ledger accounts are not individually numbered. If the subsidiary ledger accounts are numbered, the account number is used instead of the check mark in the reference posting column. At the end of the month, the column totals of the sales journal are posted to the general ledger. Here, the column totals are posted as a debit of $90,230 to Accounts Receivable (account no. 112), a credit of $90,230 to Sales (account no. 401), a debit of $62,190 to Cost of Goods Sold (account no. 505), and a credit of $62,190 to Merchandise Inventory (account no. 120). Inserting the account numbers below the column totals indicates that the postings have been made. In both the general ledger and subsidiary ledger accounts, the reference S1 indicates that the posting came from page 1 of the sales journal.

Proving the Ledgers

The next step is to "prove" the ledgers. To do so, we must ensure two things:

1. The sum of the subsidiary ledger balances must equal the balance in the control account.
2. The total of the general ledger debit balances must equal the total of the general ledger credit balances.

The proof of the postings from the sales journal to the general and subsidiary ledgers follows:

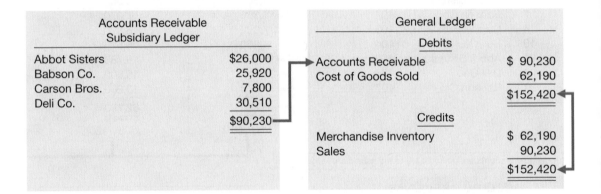

Advantages of the Sales Journal

The use of a special journal to record sales on account has a number of advantages. First, the one-line–two-column entry for each sales transaction saves time. In the sales journal, it is not necessary to write out the four account titles for the two transactions. Second, only totals, rather than individual entries, are posted to the general ledger. This saves posting time and reduces the possibility of errors in posting. Third, the prenumbering of sales invoices helps to ensure that all sales are recorded and that no sale is recorded more than once. Finally, there is a division of labour if the individual responsible for the sales journal is not given responsibility for other journals, such as cash receipts. These last two advantages help internal control.

CASH RECEIPTS JOURNAL

All receipts of cash are recorded in the cash receipts journal. The most common types of cash receipts are cash sales of merchandise and collections of accounts receivable. Many other possibilities exist, such as a receipt of money from a bank loan and cash proceeds from disposals of equipment. A one- or two-column cash receipts journal would not have enough space for all possible cash receipt transactions. A multiple-column cash receipts journal is therefore used.

Generally, a cash receipts journal includes the following columns: a debit column for cash, and credit columns for accounts receivable, sales, and other accounts. The Other Accounts column is used when the cash receipt does not involve a cash sale or a collection of accounts receivable. Under a perpetual inventory system, each sales entry is accompanied by another entry that debits Cost of Goods Sold and credits Merchandise Inventory. A separate column is added for this purpose. A five-column cash receipts journal is shown in Illustration C-5.

KARNS WHOLESALE SUPPLY
Cash Receipts Journal

CR1

Date	Account Credited	Ref.	Cash Dr.	Accounts Receivable Cr.	Sales Cr.	Cost of Goods Sold Dr. Mdse. Inv. Cr.	Other Accounts Cr.
2014							
May 1	D. Karns, Capital	301	5,000				5,000
7			1,900		1,900	1,240	
10	Abbot Sisters	√	10,600	10,600			
12			2,600		2,600	1,690	
17	Babson Co.	√	11,350	11,350			
22	Notes Payable	200	6,000				6,000
23	Carson Bros.	√	7,800	7,800			
28	Deli Co.	√	9,300	9,300			
			54,550	39,050	4,500	2,930	11,000
			(101)	(112)	(401)	(505)/(120)	(X)

Individual amounts are posted daily to the subsidiary ledger.

Totals are posted at the end of the accounting period to the general ledger.

ACCOUNTS RECEIVABLE SUBSIDIARY LEDGER

Abbot Sisters

Date	Ref.	Debit	Credit	Balance
2014				
May 3	S1	10,600		10,600
10	CR1		10,600	0
21	S1	15,400		15,400

Babson Co.

Date	Ref.	Debit	Credit	Balance
2014				
May 7	S1	11,350		11,350
17	CR1		11,350	0
27	S1	14,570		14,570

Carson Bros.

Date	Ref.	Debit	Credit	Balance
2014				
May 14	S1	7,800		7,800
23	CR1		7,800	0

Deli Co.

Date	Ref.	Debit	Credit	Balance
2014				
May 19	S1	9,300		9,300
24	S1	21,210		30,510
28	CR1		9,300	21,210

The subsidiary ledger is separate from the general ledger.

Accounts Receivable is a control account.

GENERAL LEDGER

Cash   No. 101

Date	Ref.	Debit	Credit	Balance
2014				
May 31	CR1	54,550		54,550

Accounts Receivable   No. 112

Date	Ref.	Debit	Credit	Balance
2014				
May 31	S1	90,230		90,230
31	CR1		39,050	51,180

Merchandise Inventory   No. 120

Date	Ref.	Debit	Credit	Balance
2014				
May 31	S1		62,190	62,190Cr.
31	CR1		2,930	65,120Cr.

Notes Payable   No. 200

Date	Ref.	Debit	Credit	Balance
2014				
May 22	CR1		6,000	6,000

D. Karns, Capital   No. 301

Date	Ref.	Debit	Credit	Balance
2014				
May 1	CR1		5,000	5,000

Sales   No. 401

Date	Ref.	Debit	Credit	Balance
2014				
May 31	S1		90,230	90,230
31	CR1		4,500	94,730

Cost of Goods Sold   No. 505

Date	Ref.	Debit	Credit	Balance
2014				
May 31	S1	62,190		62,190
31	CR1	2,930		65,120

▶ ILLUSTRATION C-5
Cash receipts journal—perpetual inventory system

Helpful hint In a periodic inventory system, the Cash Receipts journal would have one column fewer. The Cost of Goods Sold Dr. and Merchandise Inventory Cr. would not be recorded.

Additional credit columns may be used if they significantly reduce postings to a specific account. For example, cash receipts from cash sales normally include the collection of sales taxes, which are later remitted to the government. Most cash receipts journals have a separate credit column for sales tax collections. Other examples include the cash receipts of a loan company, such as Household Financial Centre, which cover thousands of collections from customers. These collections are credited to Loans Receivable and Interest Revenue. A significant saving in posting time would result from using separate credit columns for Loans Receivable and Interest Revenue, rather than using the Other Accounts credit column. In contrast, a retailer that has only one interest collection a month would not find it useful to have a separate column for Interest Revenue.

Journalizing Cash Receipts Transactions

To illustrate the journalizing of cash receipts transactions, we will continue with the May transactions of Karns Wholesale Supply. Collections from customers are for the entries recorded in the sales journal in Illustration C-3. The entries in the cash receipts journal are based on the following cash receipts:

May	1	D. Karns makes an investment of $5,000 in the business.
	7	Cash receipts for merchandise sales total $1,900. The cost of goods sold is $1,240.
	10	A cheque for $10,600 is received from Abbot Sisters in full payment of invoice No. 101.
	12	Cash receipts for merchandise sales total $2,600. The cost of goods sold is $1,690.
	17	A cheque for $11,350 is received from Babson Co. in full payment of invoice No. 102.
	22	Cash is received by signing a 4% note for $6,000, payable September 22 to the National Bank.
	23	A cheque for $7,800 is received from Carson Bros. in full payment of invoice No. 103.
	28	A cheque for $9,300 is received from Deli Co. in full payment of invoice No. 104.

Further information about the columns in the cash receipts journal follows:

Debit Columns:

1. Cash. The amount of cash actually received in each transaction is entered in this column. The column total indicates the total cash receipts for the month. The total of this column is posted to the cash account in the general ledger.
2. Cost of Goods Sold. The Cost of Goods Sold Dr./Merchandise Inventory Cr. column is used to record the cost of the merchandise sold. (The sales column records the selling price of the merchandise.) The cost of goods sold column is similar to the one found in the sales journal. The amount debited to Cost of Goods Sold is the same amount credited to Merchandise Inventory. One column total is posted to both accounts at the end of the month.

Credit Columns:

3. Accounts Receivable. The Accounts Receivable column is used to record cash collections on account. The amount entered here is the amount to be credited to the individual customer's account in the accounts receivable ledger.
4. Sales. The Sales column is used to record all cash sales of merchandise. Cash sales of other assets (property, plant, and equipment, for example) are not reported in this column. The total of this column is posted to the account Sales.
5. Merchandise Inventory. As noted above, the Cost of Goods Sold Dr./Merchandise Inventory Cr. column is used to record the reduction in the merchandise available for future sale. The amount credited to Merchandise Inventory is the same amount debited to Cost of Goods Sold. One column total is posted to both accounts at the end of the month.
6. Other Accounts. The Other Accounts column is used whenever the credit is not to Accounts Receivable, Sales, or Merchandise Inventory. For example, in the first entry, $5,000 is entered as a credit to D. Karns, Capital. This column is often referred to as the sundry accounts column.

In a multi-column journal, only one line is generally needed for each entry. In some cases, it is useful to add explanatory information, such as the details of the note payable, or to reference supporting documentation, such as invoice numbers if cash sales are invoiced. Note also that the Account Credited column is used to identify both general ledger and subsidiary ledger account titles. The former is shown in the May 1 entry for Karns' investment. The latter is shown in the May 10 entry for the collection from Abbot Sisters.

Debit and credit amounts for each line must be equal. Some accountants use the expression "the journal cross-adds" to describe this feature. When the journalizing has been completed, the amount columns are totalled. The totals are then compared to prove the equality of debits and credits in the cash receipts journal. Don't forget that the Cost of Goods Sold Dr./Merchandise Inventory Cr. column total represents both a debit and a credit amount. Totalling the columns of a journal and proving the equality of the totals is called footing (adding down) and cross-footing (adding across) a journal.

The proof of the equality of Karns' cash receipts journal is as follows:

Debit		Credits	
Cash	$54,550	Accounts Receivable	$39,050
Cost of Goods Sold	2,930	Merchandise Inventory	2,930
	$57,480	Sales	4,500
		Other Accounts	11,000
			$57,480

Posting the Cash Receipts Journal

Posting a multi-column journal involves the following steps:

1. All column totals, except for the Other Accounts total, are posted once at the end of the month to the account title specified in the column heading, such as Cash, Accounts Receivable, Sales, Cost of Goods Sold, and Merchandise Inventory. Account numbers are entered below the column totals to show that the amounts have been posted to the general ledger.
2. The total of the Other Accounts column is not posted. Individual amounts that make up the Other Accounts total are posted separately to the general ledger accounts specified in the Account Credited column. See, for example, the credit posting to D. Karns, Capital. The symbol X is inserted below the total for the Other Accounts column to indicate that the amount has not been posted.
3. The individual amounts in a column (Accounts Receivable, in this case) are posted daily to the subsidiary ledger account name specified in the Account Credited column. See, for example, the credit posting of $10,600 to Abbot Sisters.

The abbreviation CR is used in both the subsidiary and general ledgers to identify postings from the cash receipts journal.

Proving the Ledgers

After the posting of the cash receipts journal is completed, it is necessary to prove the ledgers. As shown below, the sum of the subsidiary ledger account balances equals the control account balance. The general ledger totals of the accounts that have been affected by the entries are also in agreement.

Accounts Receivable Subsidiary Ledger	
Abbot Sisters	$15,400
Babson Co.	14,570
Deli Co.	21,210
	$51,180

General Ledger	
Debits	
Cash	$ 54,550
Accounts Receivable	51,180
Cost of Goods Sold	65,120
	$170,850
Credits	
Merchandise Inventory	$ 65,120
Notes Payable	6,000
D. Karns, Capital	5,000
Sales	94,730
	$170,850

PURCHASES JOURNAL

All purchases on account are recorded in the purchases journal. The most common types of purchases on account are inventory and supplies but there are a variety of other items purchased, or expenses incurred, on account. Each entry in this journal results in a credit to Accounts Payable and a debit to either Inventory, Supplies or other accounts as appropriate. Each business designs its purchases journal based on the types of transactions that occur frequently that involve a credit to Accounts Payable.

The purchases journal for Karns Wholesale Supply includes separate columns for purchases of inventory and for supplies because these are the most common types of transactions on account for Karns. All other purchases on account are recorded in the Other Accounts columns. Karns' purchases journal for May is shown in Illustration C-6, with assumed credit purchases.

▶ ILLUSTRATION C-6
Purchases journal—
perpetual inventory system

KARNS WHOLESALE SUPPLY
Purchases Journal
P1

Date	Account Credited	Terms	Ref.	Accounts Payable Cr.	Merchandise Inventory Dr.	Supplies Dr.	Other Accounts Account Debited	Ref.	Amount
2014									
May 6	Jasper Manufacturing Inc.	n/20	√	21,000	21,000				
10	Eaton and Howe, Inc.	n/20	√	7,200			Equipment	151	7,200
14	Fabor and Son	n/20	√	6,900	5,000	1,900			
19	Jasper Manufacturing Inc.	n/20	√	17,500	17,500				
26	Fabor and Son	n/20	√	8,700	7,800	900			
28	Eaton and Howe, Inc.	n/20	√	12,600	12,600				
				73,900	63,900	2,800			7,200
				(201)	(120)	(129)			(X)

Individual amounts are posted daily to the subsidiary ledger.

Totals are posted at the end of the accounting period to the general ledger.

Helpful hint When a periodic inventory system is used, the debit to the Merchandise Inventory account is replaced by a debit to the Purchases account.

ACCOUNTS PAYABLE SUBSIDIARY LEDGER

Eaton & Howe, Inc.

Date	Ref.	Debit	Credit	Balance
2014				
May 10	P1		7,200	7,200
28	P1		12,600	19,800

Fabor and Son

Date	Ref.	Debit	Credit	Balance
2014				
May 14	P1		6,900	6,900
26	P1		8,700	15,600

Jasper Manufacturing Inc.

Date	Ref.	Debit	Credit	Balance
2014				
May 6	P1		21,000	21,000
19	P1		17,500	38,500

The subsidiary ledger is separate from the general ledger.

GENERAL LEDGER

Merchandise Inventory No. 120

Date	Ref.	Debit	Credit	Balance
2014				
May 31	S1		62,190	62,190 Cr.
31	CR1		2,930	65,120 Cr.
31	P1	63,900		1,220 Cr.

Supplies No. 129

Date	Ref.	Debit	Credit	Balance
2014				
May 31	P1	2,800		2,800

Equipment No. 151

Date	Ref.	Debit	Credit	Balance
2014				
May 31	P1	7,200		7,200

Accounts Payable No. 201

Date	Ref.	Debit	Credit	Balance
2014				
May 31	P1		73,900	73,900

Accounts Payable is a control account.

Journalizing Credit Purchases

Entries in the purchases journal are made from purchase invoices. The journalizing procedure for the purchases journal is similar to that for the cash receipts journal. In contrast to the cash receipts journal, there is a column indicating the terms of the purchase to ensure that a purchase discount is not missed.

Posting the Purchases Journal

The procedures for posting the purchases journal are similar to those for the cash receipts journal. In this case, postings are made daily to the accounts payable subsidiary ledger accounts and monthly to the accounts in the general ledger. In both ledgers, P1 is used in the reference column to show that the postings are from page 1 of the purchases journal.

Proof of the equality of the postings from the purchases journal to both ledgers is shown by the following:

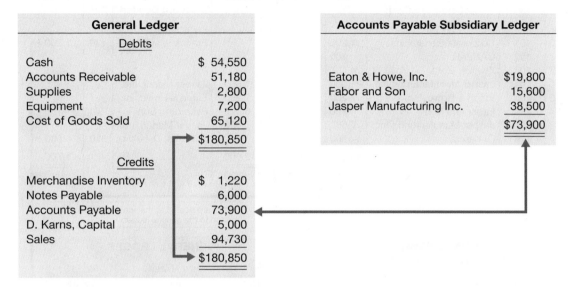

General Ledger	
Debits	
Cash	$ 54,550
Accounts Receivable	51,180
Supplies	2,800
Equipment	7,200
Cost of Goods Sold	65,120
	$180,850
Credits	
Merchandise Inventory	$ 1,220
Notes Payable	6,000
Accounts Payable	73,900
D. Karns, Capital	5,000
Sales	94,730
	$180,850

Accounts Payable Subsidiary Ledger	
Eaton & Howe, Inc.	$19,800
Fabor and Son	15,600
Jasper Manufacturing Inc.	38,500
	$73,900

Note that not all the general ledger accounts listed above have been included in Illustration C-6. You will have to refer to Illustration C-5 to determine the balances for the accounts Cash, Accounts Receivable, Cost of Goods Sold, Notes Payable, D. Karns, Capital, and Sales.

CASH PAYMENTS JOURNAL

All payments of cash are entered in a cash payments journal. Entries are made from prenumbered cheques. Because cash payments are made for various purposes, the cash payments journal has multiple columns. A four-column journal is shown in Illustration C-7.

Alternative terminology The cash payments journal is also called the *cash disbursements journal.*

Journalizing Cash Payments Transactions

The procedures for journalizing transactions in this journal are similar to those described earlier for the cash receipts journal. Each transaction is entered on one line, and for each line there must be equal debit and credit amounts. It is common practice in the cash payments journal to record the name of the company or individual receiving the cheque (the payee), so that later reference to the cheque is possible by name in addition to cheque number. The entries in the cash payments journal shown in Illustration C-7 are based on the following transactions for Karns Wholesale Supply:

May 3 Cheque No. 101 for $1,200 issued for the annual premium on a fire insurance policy from Corporate General Insurance.
3 Cheque No. 102 for $100 issued to CANPAR in payment of freight charges on goods purchased.
7 Cheque No. 103 for $4,400 issued for the cash purchase of merchandise from Zwicker Corp.
10 Cheque No. 104 for $21,000 sent to Jasper Manufacturing Inc. in full payment of the May 6 invoice.
19 Cheque No. 105 for $7,200 mailed to Eaton & Howe, Inc., in full payment of the May 10 invoice.
24 Cheque No. 106 for $6,900 sent to Fabor and Son in full payment of the May 14 invoice.
28 Cheque No. 107 for $7,500 sent to Jasper Manufacturing Inc. in partial payment of the May 19 invoice.
31 Cheque No. 108 for $500 issued to D. Karns as a cash withdrawal for personal use.

▶ILLUSTRATION C-7

Cash payments journal—perpetual inventory system

KARNS WHOLESALE SUPPLY
Cash Payments Journal   CP1

Date	Cheque No.	Account Credited	Cash Cr.	Mdse. Inventory Dr.	Accounts Payable Dr.	Account Debited	Ref.	Other Accounts Dr.
2014								
May 3	101	Corporate General Ins.	1,200			Prepaid insurance	130	1,200
3	102	CANPAR	100	100				
7	103	Zwicker Corp.	4,400	4,400				
10	104	Jasper Manufacturing Inc.	21,000		21,000	Jasper Manuf. Inc.	√	
19	105	Eaton & Howe, Inc.	7,200		7,200	Eaton & Howe, Inc.	√	
24	106	Fabor and Son	6,900		6,900	Fabor and Son	√	
28	107	Jasper Manufacturing Inc.	7,500		7,500	Jasper Manuf. Inc.	√	
31	108	D. Karns	500			D. Karns, Drawings	310	500
			48,800	4,500	42,600			1,700
			(101)	(120)	(201)			(X)

Individual amounts are posted daily to the subsidiary ledger.

Totals are posted at the end of the accounting period to the general ledger.

ACCOUNTS PAYABLE SUBSIDIARY LEDGER

Eaton & Howe, Inc.

Date	Ref.	Debit	Credit	Balance
2014				
May 10	P1		7,200	7,200
19	CP1	7,200		0
28	P1		12,600	12,600

Fabor and Son

Date	Ref.	Debit	Credit	Balance
2014				
May 14	P1		6,900	6,900
24	CP1	6,900		0
26	P1		8,700	8,700

Jasper Manufacturing Inc.

Date	Ref.	Debit	Credit	Balance
2014				
May 6	P1		21,000	21,000
10	CP1	21,000		0
19	P1		17,500	17,500
28	CP1	7,500		10,000

The subsidiary ledger is separate from the general ledger.

Accounts Payable is a control account.

GENERAL LEDGER

Cash   No. 101

Date	Ref.	Debit	Credit	Balance
2014				
May 31	CR1	54,550		54,550
31	CP1		48,800	5,750

Merchandise Inventory   No. 120

Date	Ref.	Debit	Credit	Balance
2014				
May 31	S1		62,190	62,190cr.
31	CR1		2,930	65,120cr.
31	P1	63,900		1,220cr.
31	CP1	4,500		3,280

Prepaid Insurance   No. 130

Date	Ref.	Debit	Credit	Balance
2014				
May 31	P1	1,200		1,200

Accounts Payable   No. 201

Date	Ref.	Debit	Credit	Balance
2014				
May 31	C1		73,900	73,900
31	CP1	42,600		31,300

D. Karns, Drawings   No. 310

Date	Ref.	Debit	Credit	Balance
2014				
May 31	CP1	500		500

Helpful hint In a periodic inventory system, the debits to Merchandise Inventory would be recorded to the accounts Purchases and Freight In.

Note that, whenever an amount is entered in the Other Accounts column, a specific general ledger account must be identified in the Account Debited column. The entries for cheque numbers 101 and 108 show this situation. Similarly, a subsidiary account must be identified in the Account Debited column whenever an amount is entered in the Accounts Payable column (as, for example, the entry for cheque no. 104).

After the cash payments journal has been journalized, the columns are totalled. The totals are then balanced to prove the equality of debits and credits. Debits ($4,500 + $42,600 + $1,700 = $48,800) do equal credits ($48,800) in this case.

Posting the Cash Payments Journal

The procedures for posting the cash payments journal are similar to those for the cash receipts journal:

1. Cash and Merchandise Inventory are posted only as a total at the end of the month.
2. The amounts recorded in the Accounts Payable column are posted individually to the subsidiary ledger and in total to the general ledger control account.
3. Transactions in the Other Accounts column are posted individually to the appropriate account(s) noted in the Account Debited column. No totals are posted for the Other Accounts column.

Helpful hint If a company has a subsidiary ledger for merchandise inventory, amounts in the merchandise inventory column would be posted daily in the cash payments journal, as well as in the sales, cash receipts, and purchases journals.

The posting of the cash payments journal is shown in Illustration C-7. Note that the abbreviation CP is used as the posting reference. After postings are completed, the equality of the debit and credit balances in the general ledger should be determined. The control account balance should also agree with the subsidiary ledger total balance. The agreement of these balances is shown below. Note that not all the general ledger accounts have been included in Illustration C-7. You will also have to refer to Illustration C-5 to determine the balances for the Accounts Receivable, Cost of Goods Sold, Notes Payable, Capital, and Sales accounts.

General Ledger		Accounts Payable Subsidiary Ledger	
Debits			
Cash	$ 5,750	Eaton & Howe, Inc.	$12,600
Accounts Receivable	51,180	Fabor and Son	8,700
Merchandise Inventory	3,280	Jasper Manufacturing Inc.	10,000
Supplies	2,800		$31,300
Prepaid Insurance	1,200		
Equipment	7,200		
D. Karns, Drawings	500		
Cost of Goods Sold	65,120		
	$137,030		
Credits			
Accounts Payable	$ 31,300		
Notes Payable	6,000		
D. Karns, Capital	5,000		
Sales	94,730		
	$137,030		

EFFECTS OF SPECIAL JOURNALS ON THE GENERAL JOURNAL

Special journals for sales, purchases, and cash greatly reduce the number of entries that are made in the general journal. Only transactions that cannot be entered in a special journal are recorded in the general journal. For example, the general journal may be used to record a transaction granting credit to a customer for a sales return or allowance. It may also be used to record the receipt of a credit from a supplier for purchase returns or allowances, the acceptance of a note receivable from a customer, and the purchase of equipment by issuing a note payable. Correcting, adjusting, and closing entries are also made in the general journal.

When control and subsidiary accounts are not used, the procedures for journalizing and posting transactions in the general journal are the same as those described in earlier chapters. When control and subsidiary accounts are used, two modifications of earlier procedures are required:

1. In journalizing, both the control and the subsidiary account must be identified.
2. In posting, there must be a dual posting: once to the control account and once to the subsidiary account.

To illustrate, assume that on May 31, Karns Wholesale Supply returns $500 of merchandise for credit to Fabor and Son. The entry in the general journal and the posting of the entry are shown in Illustration C-8. Note that if cash had been received instead of the credit granted on this return, then the transaction would have been recorded in the cash receipts journal.

▶ILLUSTRATION **C-8**
General journal

Helpful hint In a periodic inventory system, the credit would be to the Purchase Returns and Allowances account rather than to Merchandise Inventory.

KARNS WHOLESALE SUPPLY
General Journal   **J1**

Date	Account Title and Explanation	Ref.	Debit	Credit
2014				
May 31	Accounts Payable—Fabor and Son	201/ √	500	
	Merchandise Inventory	120		500
	Received credit for returned goods.			

ACCOUNTS PAYABLE SUBSIDIARY LEDGER
Fabor and Son

Date	Ref.	Debit	Credit	Balance
2014				
May 14	P1		6,900	6,900
21	CP1	6,900		0
26	P1		8,700	8,700
31	J1	500		8,200

GENERAL LEDGER

Merchandise Inventory   No. 120

Date	Ref.	Debit	Credit	Balance
2014				
May 31	S1		62,190	62,190Cr.
31	CR1		2,930	65,120Cr.
31	P1	63,900		1,220Cr.
31	CP1	4,500		3,280
31	J1		500	2,780

Accounts Payable   No. 201

Date	Ref.	Debit	Credit	Balance
2014				
May 31	C1		73,900	73,900
31	CP1	42,600		31,300
31	J1	500		30,800

Notice that in the general journal, two accounts are indicated for the debit (the Accounts Payable control account and the Fabor and Son subsidiary account). Two postings (201/√) are indicated in the reference column. One amount is posted to the control account in the general ledger (no. 201) and the other to the creditor's account in the subsidiary ledger (Fabor and Son).

SPECIAL JOURNALS IN A PERIODIC INVENTORY SYSTEM

Recording and posting transactions in special journals is essentially the same whether a perpetual or a periodic inventory system is used. But there are two differences. The first difference relates to the accounts Merchandise Inventory and Cost of Goods Sold in a perpetual inventory system. In this system, an additional column is required to record the cost of each sale in the sales and cash receipts journals, something that is not required in a periodic inventory system.

The second difference concerns the account titles used. In a perpetual inventory system, Merchandise Inventory and Cost of Goods Sold are used to record purchases and the cost of the merchandise sold. In a periodic inventory system, the accounts Purchases and Freight In accumulate the cost of the merchandise purchased until the end of the period. No cost of goods sold is recorded during the period. Cost of goods sold is calculated at the end of the period in a periodic inventory system.

Each of the special journals illustrated in this appendix is shown again here in Illustrations C-9 to C-12. Using the same transactions, we assume that Karns Wholesale Supply uses a periodic inventory system instead of a perpetual inventory system.

▶ILLUSTRATION C-9
Sales journal—
periodic inventory system

KARNS WHOLESALE SUPPLY
Sales Journal   S1

Date	Account Debited	Invoice No.	Ref.	Accts Receivable Dr. Sales Cr.
2014				
May 3	Abbot Sisters	101	√	10,600
7	Babson Co.	102	√	11,350
14	Carson Bros.	103	√	7,800
19	Deli Co.	104	√	9,300
21	Abbot Sisters	105	√	15,400
24	Deli Co.	106	√	21,210
27	Babson Co.	107	√	14,570
				90,230

Helpful hint Compare this sales journal with the one presented in Illustration C-4.

▶ILLUSTRATION C-10
Cash receipts journal—
periodic inventory system

KARNS WHOLESALE SUPPLY
Cash Receipts Journal   CR1

Date	Account Credited	Ref.	Cash Dr.	Account Receivable Cr.	Sales Cr.	Other Accounts Cr.
2014						
May 1	D. Karns, Capital	301	5,000			5,000
7			1,900		1,900	
10	Abbot Sisters	√	10,600	10,600		
12			2,600		2,600	
17	Babson Co.	√	11,350	11,350		
22	Notes Payable	200	6,000			6,000
23	Carson Bros.	√	7,800	7,800		
28	Deli Co.	√	9,300	9,300		
			54,550	39,050	4,500	11,000

Helpful hint Compare this cash receipts journal with the one presented in Illustration C-5.

Helpful hint Compare this purchases journal with the one presented in Illustration C-6.

▶ILLUSTRATION C-11
Purchases journal—
periodic inventory system

KARNS WHOLESALE SUPPLY
Purchases Journal   P1

Date	Account Credited	Terms	Ref.	Accounts Payable Cr.	Purchases Dr.	Supplies Dr.	Other Accounts Account Debited	Ref.	Amount
2014									
May 6	Jasper Manufacturing Inc.	n/20	√	21,000	21,000				
10	Eaton and Howe, Inc.	n/20	√	7,200			Equipment	151	7,200
14	Fabor and Son	n/20	√	6,900	5,000	1,900			
19	Jasper Manufacturing Inc.	n/20	√	17,500	17,500				
26	Fabor and Son	n/20	√	8,700	7,800	900			
28	Eaton and Howe, Inc.	n/20	√	12,600	12,600				
				73,900	63,900	2,800			7,200

▶ILLUSTRATION C-12
Cash payments journal—periodic inventory system

Helpful hint Compare this cash payments journal with the one presented in Illustration C-7.

KARNS WHOLESALE SUPPLY
Cash Payments Journal — CP1

Date	Cheque No.	Payee	Cash Cr.	Accounts Payable Dr.	Account Debited	Ref.	Other Accounts Dr.
2014							
May 3	101	Corporate General Ins.	1,200		Prepaid Insurance	130	1,200
3	102	CANPAR	100		Freight In	516	100
7	103	Zwicker Corp.	4,400		Purchases	510	4,400
10	104	Jasper Manufacturing Inc.	21,000	21,000	Jasper Manuf. Inc.	√	
19	105	Eaton & Howe, Inc.	7,200	7,200	Eaton & Howe, Inc.	√	
24	106	Fabor and Son	6,900	6,900	Fabor and Son	√	
28	107	Jasper Manufacturing Inc.	7,500	7,500	Jasper Manuf. Inc.	√	
31	108	D. Karns	500		D. Karns, Drawings	310	500
			48,800	42,600			6,200

▶ Brief Exercises

Calculate subsidiary ledger and control account balances. (SO 1) AP

BEC–1 Information related to Bryan Company is presented below for its first month of operations. Calculate (a) the balances that appear in the accounts receivable subsidiary ledger for each customer, and (b) the accounts receivable balance that appears in the general ledger at the end of January.

Credit Sales			Cash Collections		
Jan. 7	Chiu Co.	$1,800	Jan. 17	Chiu Co.	$ 700
15	Elbaz Inc.	6,000	24	Elbaz Inc.	2,000
23	Lewis Co.	3,700	29	Lewis Co.	3,700

Identify general and subsidiary ledger accounts. (SO 1) K

BEC–2 Identify in which ledger (general or subsidiary) each of the following accounts is shown:

1. Rent Expense
2. Accounts Receivable—Chen
3. Bank Loan Payable
4. Service Revenue
5. Salaries Payable
6. Accounts Payable—Dhankar
7. Merchandise Inventory
8. Sales

Identify special journals. (SO 2) K

BEC–3 Chisholm Co. uses special journals and a general journal. Identify the journal in which each of the following transactions is recorded:

1. Sold merchandise on account.
2. Granted a cash refund for a sales return.
3. Received a credit on account for a purchase return.
4. Sold merchandise for cash.
5. Purchased merchandise for cash.
6. Received a collection on account.
7. Recorded depreciation on vehicles.
8. Purchased equipment on account.
9. Purchased merchandise on credit.
10. Paid utility expense in cash.

Identify special journals—perpetual inventory system. (SO 2) K

BEC–4 Swirsky Company uses the cash receipts and cash payments journals illustrated in this appendix for a perpetual inventory system. In October, the following selected cash transactions occurred:

1. Made a refund to a customer for the return of damaged goods that had been purchased on credit.
2. Received payment from a customer.
3. Purchased merchandise for cash.
4. Paid a creditor.
5. Paid freight on merchandise purchased.
6. Paid cash for equipment.
7. Received a cash refund from a supplier for merchandise returned.
8. Withdrew cash for personal use of owner.
9. Made cash sales.

Indicate (a) the journal and (b) the columns in the journal that should be used in recording each transaction.

BEC–5 Identify the journal and the specific column title(s) in which each of the following transactions is recorded. Assume the company uses a periodic inventory system.

Identify special journals—periodic inventory system. (SO 2) K

1. Cash sale
2. Credit sale
3. Sales return on account
4. Return of merchandise purchased for cash refund
5. Payment of freight on merchandise delivered to a customer
6. Cash purchase of merchandise
7. Credit purchase of supplies
8. Payment of freight on merchandise purchased from a supplier

BEC–6 Willis Company has the following year-end account balances on April 30, 2014: Service Revenue $53,800; Rent Revenue $12,000; Salaries Expense $19,400; Depreciation Expense $8,000; Supplies Expense $3,500; B. Willis, Capital $97,000; and B. Willis, Drawings $18,000.
  Prepare the closing entries for Willis Company.

Use general journal for closing entries. (SO 2) AP

BEC–7 As part of the year-end procedures, depreciation for furniture was recorded in the amount of $6,800 for Leelantna Company. Prepare the adjusting entry dated November 30, 2014, using the appropriate journal.

Use general journal for adjusting entry. (SO 2) AP

BEC–8 Following the preparation of the bank reconciliation for Lolitta Services, a correcting journal entry was needed. A cheque issued for the correct amount of $960 for a payment on account was recorded in the amount of $690. Prepare the correcting entry dated February 28, 2014, using the appropriate journal.

Use general journal for correcting errors. (SO 2) AP

▶ Exercises

EC–1 Below are some transactions for Dartmouth Company:

Identify special journals. (SO 2) K

1. Credit received for merchandise returned to a supplier
2. Payment of employee salaries
3. Sale of land for cash
4. Depreciation on equipment
5. Purchase of supplies on account
6. Purchase of merchandise on account
7. Purchase of land for cash
8. Payment on account
9. Return of merchandise sold for credit
10. Collection on account from customers
11. Revenues and expenses closed to income summary
12. Sale of merchandise on account
13. Sale of merchandise for cash

Instructions

For each transaction, indicate whether it would normally be recorded in a cash receipts journal, cash payments journal, sales journal, purchases journal, or general journal.

EC–2 Wong Company, a sole proprietorship owned by V. Wong, uses special journals and a general journal. The company uses a perpetual inventory system and had the following transactions:

Record transactions in sales and purchases journals— perpetual inventory system. (SO 2) AP

Sept.	2	Sold merchandise on account to T. Lu, $2,720, invoice #321, terms n/30. The cost of the merchandise sold was $1,960.
	3	Purchased supplies on account from Berko Co., $175.
	10	Purchased merchandise on account from Leonard Co., $800, FOB shipping point, terms n/30.
	11	Paid freight of $90 to A&F Shippers.
	11	Returned unsatisfactory merchandise to Leonard Co., $200, for credit on account.
	12	Purchased equipment on account from Wells Co., $7,700.
	16	Sold merchandise for cash to L. Maille, for $860. The cost of the merchandise sold was $490.
	18	Purchased merchandise for cash from Leonard Co., $450, FOB destination.
	20	Accepted returned merchandise from customer L. Maille, $860 (see Sept. 16 transaction). Gave full cash refund. Restored the merchandise to inventory.
	24	Paid the correct amount owing for the merchandise purchased from Leonard earlier in the month.
	25	Received payment from T. Lu for Sept. 2 sale.

26   Sold merchandise on account to M. Gafney, $890, invoice #322, terms n/30, FOB destination. The cost of the merchandise was $570. The appropriate party paid $75 to Freight Co. for shipping charges.

30   Paid September salaries, $2,360.

30   Withdrew cash for owner's personal use, $1,250.

30   Paid for supplies purchased on September 3.

Instructions

(a) Draw a sales journal and a purchases journal (see Illustrations C-3 and C-6). Use page 1 for each journal.

(b) Record the transaction(s) for September that should be recorded in the sales journal.

(c) Record the transaction(s) for September that should be recorded in the purchases journal.

Record transactions in cash receipts, cash payments, and general journals—perpetual inventory system. (SO 2) AP

EC–3   Refer to the information provided for Wong Company in EC–2.

Instructions

(a) Draw cash receipts and cash payments journals (see Illustrations C-5 and C-7) and a general journal. Use page 1 for each journal.

(b) Record the transaction(s) provided in EC–2 that should be recorded in the cash receipts journal.

(c) Record the transaction(s) provided in EC–2 that should be recorded in the cash payments journal.

(d) Record the transaction(s) provided in EC–2 that should be recorded in the general journal.

Record transactions in sales and purchases journals—periodic inventory system. (SO 2) AP

EC–4   Refer to the information provided for Wong Company in EC–2.

Instructions

(a) Draw a sales journal and a purchases journal (see Illustrations C-9 and C-11). Use page 1 for each journal.

(b) Record the transaction(s) for September that should be recorded in the sales journal.

(c) Record the transaction(s) for September that should be recorded in the purchases journal.

Record transactions in cash receipts, cash payments, and general journals—periodic inventory system. (SO 2) AP

EC–5   Refer to the information provided for Wong Company in EC–2.

Instructions

(a) Draw cash receipts and cash payments journals (see Illustrations C-10 and C-12) and a general journal. Use page 1 for each journal.

(b) Record the transaction(s) provided in EC–2 that should be recorded in the cash receipts journal.

(c) Record the transaction(s) provided in EC–2 that should be recorded in the cash payments journal.

(d) Record the transaction(s) provided in EC–2 that should be recorded in the general journal.

Record transactions in general journal and explain posting. (SO 1, 2) AP

EC–6   Lee Ltd. has the following selected transactions during October:

Oct.   2   Purchased equipment on account costing $13,200 from Lifelong Inc.

        5   Received credit memorandum for $720 from Lyden Company for merchandise returned that had been damaged in shipment to Lee.

        7   Issued a credit memorandum for $600 to M. Presti for merchandise the customer returned. The returned merchandise has a cost of $375 and was restored to inventory.

Lee Ltd. uses a purchases journal, a sales journal, two cash journals (receipts and payments), and a general journal. Lee also uses a perpetual inventory system.

Instructions

(a) Record the appropriate transactions in the general journal. If a transaction should be recorded in one of the special journals indicate the name of that journal.

(b) Assume now that Lee Ltd. uses a periodic inventory system. Record the appropriate transactions in the general journal.

(c) In a brief memo to the president of Lee Ltd., explain the postings to the control and subsidiary accounts.

Determine control account balances and explain posting. (SO 1, 2) AP

EC–7   Sven Co. uses both special journals and a general journal. On June 30, after all monthly postings had been completed, the Accounts Receivable control account in the general ledger had a debit balance of $137,800, and the Accounts Payable control account had a credit balance of $144,200.

The July transactions recorded in the special journals are summarized below. Sven Co. maintains a perpetual inventory system. No entries that affected accounts receivable and accounts payable were recorded in the general journal for July.

Sales journal: total sales, $98,670; cost of goods sold, $56,440

Purchases journal: total purchases, $39,700

Cash receipts journal: accounts receivable column total, $79,680

Cash payments journal: accounts payable column total, $42,300

Instructions

(a) What is the balance of the Accounts Receivable control account after the monthly postings on July 31?
(b) What is the balance of the Accounts Payable control account after the monthly postings on July 31?
(c) To what accounts are the column totals for total sales of $98,670 and cost of goods sold of $56,440 in the sales journal posted?
(d) To what account(s) is the accounts receivable column total of $79,680 in the cash receipts journal posted?

EC–8 On September 1, the balance of the Accounts Receivable control account in the general ledger of Mac Company was $10,960. The customers' subsidiary ledger contained account balances as follows: Jana, $2,440; London, $2,640; Cavanaugh, $2,060; and Zhang, $3,820. At the end of September, the various journals contained the following information:

> Sales journal: Sales to Zhang, $800; to Jana, $1,260; to Iman, $1,030; and to Cavanaugh, $1,100. The cost of each sale, respectively, was $480, $810, $620, and $660.
> Cash receipts journal: Cash received from Cavanaugh, $1,310; from Zhang, $2,300; from Iman, $380; from London, $1,800; and from Jana, $1,240.
> General journal: A $190 sales allowance is granted to Zhang on September 30.

Post journals to control and subsidiary accounts. (SO 1, 2) AP

Instructions

(a) Set up control and subsidiary accounts, and enter the beginning balances.
(b) Post the various journals to the control and subsidiary accounts. Post the items as individual items or as totals, whichever would be the appropriate procedure. Use page 1 for each journal.
(c) Prepare a list of customers and prove the agreement of the control account with the subsidiary ledger at September 30.

▶ Problems

PC–1 Selected accounts from the chart of accounts of Jinnah Ltd. are shown below:

Record transactions in special and general journals— perpetual inventory system. (SO 2) AP

101	Cash	201	Accounts payable
112	Accounts receivable	401	Sales
120	Merchandise inventory	412	Sales returns and allowances
126	Supplies	505	Cost of goods sold
157	Equipment	729	Salaries expense

The company uses a perpetual inventory system. The cost of all merchandise sold is 60% of the sales price. During January, Jinnah completed the following transactions:

Jan.	3	Purchased merchandise on account from Sun Distributors, $7,800.
	4	Purchased supplies on account from Moon Inc., $480.
	4	Sold merchandise on account to R. Wong, $6,500, invoice no. 371.
	5	Returned $1,450 of damaged goods to Sun Distributors.
	6	Made cash sales for the week totalling $2,650.
	8	Purchased merchandise on account from Irvine Co., $5,400.
	9	Sold merchandise on account to Tops Corp., $2,600, invoice no. 372.
	11	Purchased merchandise on account from Lewis Co., $4,300.
	13	Paid Sun Distributors account in full.
	13	Made cash sales for the week totalling $5,290.
	15	Received payment from Tops Corp. for invoice no. 372.
	15	Paid semi-monthly salaries of $11,300 to employees.
	17	Received payment from R. Wong for invoice no. 371.
	17	Sold merchandise on account to NFQ Co., $7,500, invoice no. 373.
	19	Purchased equipment on account from Mark Corp., $6,600.
	20	Cash sales for the week totalled $1,400.
	20	Paid Irvine Co. account in full.
	23	Purchased merchandise on account from Sun Distributors, $4,800.
	24	Purchased merchandise on account from Levine Corp., $4,690.
	27	Made cash sales for the week totalling $4,370.
	30	Received payment from NFQ Co. for invoice no. 373.
	31	Paid semi-monthly salaries of $11,000 to employees.
	31	Sold merchandise on account to R. Wong, $7,380, invoice no. 374.

Jinnah Ltd. uses a sales journal, a purchases journal, a cash receipts journal, a cash payments journal, and a general journal.

Instructions

(a) Record the January transactions in the appropriate journals.

(b) Foot and cross-foot all special journals.

(c) Show how postings would be made by placing ledger account numbers and check marks as needed in the journals. (Actual posting to ledger accounts is not required.)

Record transactions in special and general journals—perpetual inventory system. (SO 2) AP

PC–2 Selected accounts from the chart of accounts of Zu Company are shown below:

101	Cash
112	Accounts receivable
120	Merchandise inventory
126	Supplies
140	Land
145	Buildings
201	Accounts payable
401	Sales
505	Cost of goods sold
610	Advertising expense

The company uses a perpetual inventory system. The cost of all merchandise sold was 65% of the sales price. During October, Zu Company completed the following transactions:

Oct.	2	Purchased merchandise on account from Madison Co., $5,800.
	4	Sold merchandise on account to Petro Corp., $8,600, invoice no. 204.
	5	Purchased supplies on account from Frey Co., $315.
	7	Made cash sales for the week that totalled $9,610.
	9	Paid the Madison Co. account in full.
	10	Purchased merchandise on account from Chen Corp., $4,900.
	12	Received payment from Petro Corp. for invoice no. 204.
	13	Issued a debit memorandum to Chen Corp. and returned $260 of damaged goods.
	14	Made cash sales for the week that totalled $8,810.
	16	Sold a parcel of land for $45,000 cash, the land's book value.
	17	Sold merchandise on account to Trudeau Co., $5,530, invoice no. 205.
	18	Purchased merchandise for cash, $2,215.
	21	Made cash sales for the week that totalled $8,640.
	23	Paid in full the Chen Corp. account for the goods kept.
	25	Purchased supplies on account from Frey Co., $260.
	25	Sold merchandise on account to Golden Corp., $5,520, invoice no. 206.
	25	Received payment from Trudeau Co. for invoice no. 205.
	26	Purchased for cash a small parcel of land and a building on the land to use as a storage facility. Of the total cost of $45,000, $26,000 was allocated to the land and $19,000 to the building.
	27	Purchased merchandise on account from Schmid Co., $9,000.
	28	Made cash sales for the week that totalled $9,320.
	30	Purchased merchandise on account from Madison Co., $16,200.
	30	Paid advertising bill for the month from The Gazette, $600.
	30	Sold merchandise on account to Trudeau Co., $5,200, invoice no. 207.

Zu Company uses a sales journal, purchases journal, cash receipts journal, cash payments journal, and general journal.

Instructions

(a) Record the October transactions in the appropriate journals.

(b) Foot and cross-foot all special journals.

(c) Show how postings would be made by placing ledger account numbers and check marks as needed in the journals. (Actual posting to ledger accounts is not required.)

PC–3 The post-closing trial balance for Perrault Music Co. follows:

Record transactions in special and general journals— perpetual inventory system. (SO 1, 2) AP

PERRAULT MUSIC CO.
Post-Closing Trial Balance
December 31, 2013

		Debit	Credit
101	Cash	$ 17,900	
112	Accounts receivable	38,000	
115	Notes receivable	45,000	
120	Merchandise inventory	22,600	
140	Land	25,000	
145	Building	75,000	
146	Accumulated depreciation—building		$ 38,800
157	Equipment	6,450	
158	Accumulated depreciation—equipment		1,950
200	Notes payable		–
201	Accounts payable		34,200
275	Mortgage payable		67,400
301	M. Perrault, capital		87,600
310	M. Perrault, drawings	–	
401	Sales	–	
410	Sales returns and allowances	–	
505	Cost of goods sold	–	
725	Salaries expense	–	
		$229,950	$229,950

The subsidiary ledgers contain the following information:

1. Accounts Receivable—S. Armstrong, $6,500; R. Goge, $30,000; B. Lu, $1,500
2. Accounts Payable—Denomme Corp., $4,000; Harms Distributors, $16,000; Watson & Co., $14,200

Perrault Music Co. uses a perpetual inventory system. The transactions for January 2014 are as follows:

Jan.	3	Sold merchandise to B. Rohl, $3,000. The cost of goods sold was $1,250.
	5	Purchased merchandise from Warren Parts, $2,900.
	7	Received a cheque from S. Armstrong, $4,000, in partial payment of its account.
	11	Paid Lindon Co. freight on merchandise purchased, $350.
	13	Received payment of account in full from B. Rohl.
	14	Issued a credit memo to R. Goge for $6,000 as a sales allowance for a previous sale on account.
	15	Sent Harms Distributors a cheque in full payment of account.
	17	Purchased merchandise from Voyer Co., $4,900.
	18	Paid salaries of $3,900.
	20	Gave Watson & Co. a 60-day note for $14,000 as a partial payment of account payable.
	23	Total cash sales amounted to $7,700. The cost of goods sold was $4,840.
	24	Sold merchandise on account to B. Lu, $7,800. The cost of goods sold was $3,300.
	27	Sent Warren Parts a cheque for $1,150 in partial payment of the account.
	29	Received payment on a note receivable of $35,000 from S. Lava.
	30	Returned merchandise costing $400 to Voyer Co. for credit.
	31	Withdrew $1,300 cash for personal use.

Instructions

(a) Open general and subsidiary ledger accounts and record December 31, 2013, balances.
(b) Record the January transactions in a sales journal, a purchases journal, a cash receipts journal, a cash payments journal, and a general journal, as illustrated in this appendix.
(c) Post the appropriate amounts to the subsidiary and general ledger accounts.
(d) Prepare a trial balance at January 31, 2014.
(e) Determine whether the subsidiary ledgers agree with control accounts in the general ledger.

Record transactions in special and general journals, post, and prepare trial balance— perpetual inventory system. (SO 1, 2) AP

PC–4 The post-closing trial balance for Lee Co. follows. The subsidiary ledgers contain the following information:

```
                              LEE CO.
                      Post-Closing Trial Balance
                          April 30, 2014
```

		Debit	Credit
101	Cash	$ 36,700	
112	Accounts receivable	15,400	
115	Notes receivable—Cole Company	48,000	
120	Merchandise inventory	22,000	
157	Equipment	8,200	
158	Accumulated depreciation—equipment		$ 1,800
200	Notes payable	–	
201	Accounts payable		43,400
301	C. Lee, capital		85,100
310	C. Lee, drawings	–	
401	Sales		–
410	Sales returns and allowances	–	
505	Cost of goods sold	–	
725	Salaries expense	–	
730	Rent expense	–	
		$130,300	$130,300

The subsidiary ledgers contain the following information:

1. Accounts Receivable—W. Karasch, $3,250; L. Cellars, $7,400; G. Parrish, $4,750
2. Accounts Payable—Summers Corp., $10,500; Cobalt Sports, $15,500; Buttercup Distributors, $17,400

Lee uses a perpetual inventory system. The transactions for May 2014 are as follows:

May	3	Sold merchandise on account to B. Simone, $2,400. The cost of the goods sold was $1,050.
	5	Purchased merchandise from WN Shaw, $2,600, on account.
	7	Received a cheque from G. Parrish, $2,800, in partial payment of account.
	11	Paid freight on merchandise purchased, $318.
	12	Paid rent of $1,500 for May.
	13	Received payment in full from B. Simone.
	14	Issued a credit memo to acknowledge $750 of merchandise returned by W. Karasch. The merchandise (original cost, $325) was restored to inventory.
	15	Sent Buttercup Distributors a cheque in full payment of account.
	17	Purchased merchandise from Lancio Co., $2,100, on account.
	18	Paid salaries of $4,700.
	20	Gave Cobalt Sports a two-month, 10% note for $15,500 in full payment of account payable.
	20	Returned merchandise costing $510 to Lancio for credit.
	23	Total cash sales amounted to $9,500. The cost of goods sold was $4,450.
	27	Sent WN Shaw a cheque for $1,000, in partial payment of account.
	29	Received payment on a note of $40,000 from Cole Company.
	30	Purchased equipment on account from Summers Corp., $4,000.
	31	C. Lee withdrew $1,000 cash for personal use.

Instructions

(a) Open general and subsidiary ledger accounts and record April 30, 2014, balances.
(b) Record the May transactions in a sales journal, a purchases journal, a cash receipts journal, a cash payments journal, and a general journal, as illustrated in this chapter.
(c) Post the appropriate amounts to the subsidiary and general ledger accounts.
(d) Prepare a trial balance at May 31, 2014.
(e) Determine whether the subsidiary ledgers agree with the control accounts in the general ledger.

Record transactions in special and general journals—periodic inventory system. (SO 2) AP

PC-5 Selected accounts from the chart of accounts of Martin Ltd. are shown below:

101	Cash	401	Sales
112	Accounts receivable	412	Sales returns and allowances
126	Supplies	510	Purchases
157	Equipment	512	Purchase returns and allowances
201	Accounts payable	729	Salaries expense

During February, Martin completed the following transactions:

Feb.	3	Purchased merchandise on account from Zears Co., $4,200.
	4	Purchased supplies on account from Green Deer Inc., $290.
	4	Sold merchandise on account to Gilles Co., $5,220, invoice no. 371.
	5	Issued a debit memorandum to Zears Co. and returned $450 worth of goods.
	6	Made cash sales for the week totalling $1,950.
	8	Purchased merchandise on account from Fell Electronics, $7,200.
	9	Sold merchandise on account to Earlton Corp., $2,050, invoice no. 372.
	11	Purchased merchandise on account from Thomas Co., $9,100.
	13	Paid Zears Co. account in full.
	13	Made cash sales for the week totalling $3,850.
	15	Received payment from Earlton Corp. for invoice no. 372.
	15	Paid semi-monthly salaries of $14,100 to employees.
	17	Received payment from Gilles Co. for invoice no. 371.
	17	Sold merchandise on account to Lumber Co., $1,800, invoice no. 373.
	19	Purchased equipment on account from Brown Corp., $16,400.
	20	Cash sales for the week totalled $4,900.
	20	Paid Fell Electronics account in full.
	23	Purchased merchandise on account from Zears Co., $4,800.
	24	Purchased merchandise on account from Lewis Co., $5,130.
	27	Made cash sales for the week totalling $4,560.
	28	Received payment from Lumber Co. for invoice no. 373.
	28	Paid semi-monthly salaries of $14,900 to employees.
	28	Sold merchandise on account to Gilles Co., $9,810, invoice no. 374.

Martin Ltd. uses a sales journal, purchases journal, cash receipts journal, cash payments journal, and general journal. Martin uses a periodic inventory system.

Instructions

(a) Record the February transactions in the appropriate journal.
(b) Foot and cross-foot all special journals.
(c) Show how postings would be made by placing ledger account numbers and check marks as needed in the journals. (Actual posting to ledger accounts is not required.)

Cumulative Coverage—Chapters 2 to 6 and Appendix C

Review the opening account balances in Winter Company's general and subsidiary ledgers on January 1, 2014. All accounts have normal debit and credit balances. Winters uses a perpetual inventory system. The cost of all merchandise sold was 40% of the sales price.

GENERAL LEDGER

Account No.	Account Title	January 1, 2014 Opening Balance
101	Cash	$ 35,050
112	Accounts receivable	14,000
115	Notes receivable	39,000
120	Merchandise inventory	20,000
125	Supplies	1,000
130	Prepaid insurance	2,000
140	Land	50,000
145	Building	100,000
146	Accumulated depreciation—building	25,000
157	Equipment	6,450
158	Accumulated depreciation—equipment	1,500
201	Accounts payable	36,000
275	Mortgage payable	125,000
301	A. Winters, capital	80,000

	Accounts Receivable Subsidiary Ledger		Accounts Payable Subsidiary Ledger	
Customer	January 1, 2014 Opening Balance	Creditor	January 1, 2014 Opening Balance	
R. Draves	$1,500	Liazuk Co. ·	$10,000	
B. Jacovetti	7,500	Mikush Bros.	15,000	
S. Tang	5,000	Nguyen & Son	11,000	

Winters' January transactions follow:

Jan. 3 Sold merchandise on credit to B. Sota $3,100, invoice no. 510, and J. Ebel $1,800, invoice no. 511.
   5 Purchased merchandise on account from Welz Wares for $3,000 and Laux Supplies for $2,700.
   7 Received cheques for $5,000 from S. Tang and $2,000 from B. Jacovetti on accounts.
   8 Paid freight on merchandise purchased, $180.
   9 Sent cheques to Liazuk Co. for $10,000 and Nguyen & Son for $11,000 in full payment of accounts.
   9 Issued credit memo for $400 to J. Ebel for merchandise returned. The merchandise was restored to inventory.
   10 Summary cash sales totalled $16,500.
   11 Sold merchandise on credit to R. Draves for $1,900, invoice no. 512, and to S. Tang for $900, invoice no. 513.
   15 Withdrew $2,000 cash for Winters's personal use.
   16 Purchased merchandise on account from Nguyen & Son for $15,000, from Liazuk Co. for $13,900, and from Welz Wares for $1,500.
   17 Purchased supplies on account from Laux Supplies, $400.
   18 Returned $500 of merchandise to Liazuk and received credit.
   20 Summary cash sales totalled $17,500.
   21 Issued $15,000 note to Mikush Bros. in payment of balance due. The note bears an interest rate of 10% and is due in three months.
   21 Received payment in full from S. Tang.
   22 Sold merchandise on credit to B. Soto for $1,700, invoice no. 514, and to R. Draves for $800, invoice no. 515.
   23 Sent cheques to Nguyen & Son and Liazuk Co. in full payment of accounts.
   25 Sold merchandise on credit to B. Jacovetti for $3,500, invoice no. 516, and to J. Ebel for $6,100, invoice no. 517.
   27 Purchased merchandise on account from Nguyen & Son for $14,500, from Laux Supplies for $1,200, and from Welz Wares for $2,800.
   28 Purchased supplies on account from Laux Supplies, $800.
   31 Summary cash sales totalled $19,920.
   31 Paid salaries of $6,900.
   31 Received payment in full from B. Soto and J. Ebel on account.

   In addition to the accounts identified in the trial balance, the chart of accounts shows the following: No. 200 Notes Payable, No. 230 Interest Payable, No. 300 Income Summary, No. 310 A. Winters, Drawings, No. 401 Sales, No. 410 Sales Returns and Allowances, No. 505 Cost of Goods Sold, No. 711 Depreciation Expense, No. 718 Interest Expense, No. 722 Insurance Expense, No. 725 Salaries Expense, and No. 728 Supplies Expense.

Instructions

(a) Record the January transactions in the appropriate journal—sales, purchases, cash receipts, cash payments, and general.
(b) Enter the opening balances in general and subsidiary ledger accounts. Post the journals to the general and subsidiary ledgers. New accounts should be added and numbered in an orderly fashion as needed.
(c) Prepare an unadjusted trial balance at January 31, 2014. Determine whether the subsidiary ledgers agree with the control accounts in the general ledger.
(d) Prepare and post adjusting journal entries. Prepare an adjusted trial balance, using the following information: (1) Supplies at January 31 total $700 (2) Insurance coverage expires on September 30, 2014 (3) Annual depreciation on the building is $6,000 and on the equipment is $1,500 (4) Interest of $45 has accrued on the note payable (5) A physical count of merchandise inventory has found $44,850 of goods on hand.
(e) Prepare a multiple-step income statement and a statement of owner's equity for January, and a classified balance sheet at the end of January.
(f) Prepare and post the closing entries.
(g) Prepare a post-closing trial balance.

Company Index

Subject Index